Hoodlums

HOODLUMS

Black Villains and Social Bandits in American Life

William L. Van Deburg

THE UNIVERSITY OF CHICAGO PRESS CHICAGO AND LONDON

William L. Van Deburg is the Evjue-Bascom Professor of
Afro-American Studies at the University of Wisconsin–
Madison. He is the author of five books, including
*New Day in Babylon: The Black Power Movement and
American Culture, 1965–1975,* and *Black Camelot:
African-American Culture Heroes in Their Times,
1960–1980.*

The University of Chicago Press, Chicago 60637
The University of Chicago Press, Ltd., London
© 2004 by The University of Chicago Press
All rights reserved. Published 2004
Printed in the United States of America

13 12 11 10 09 08 07 06 05 04   1 2 3 4 5
ISBN: 0-226-84719-5

Library of Congress Cataloging-in-Publication Data

Van Deburg, William L.
   Hoodlums : Black villains and social bandits in
American life / William L. Van Deburg.
        p. cm.
   Includes bibliographical references and index.
   ISBN 0-226-84719-5 (alk. paper)
   1. African American criminals—History.   2. Crime
and race—United States—History.   3. African
Americans—Social conditions.   4. African Americans
in popular culture.   5. Villains in popular culture.
6. United States—Race relations.   I. Title.
   HV6791.V36 2004
   305.896′073—dc22

                                        2004003549

To Ethan Lloyd Hunt   *As Sweetback said, "He's our future, Br'er."*

Now, the papers gon call us thugs and hoodlums. A lot of people ain't gon know what's happening. But the brothers on the block, who the man's been calling thugs and hoodlums for four hundred years, gon say, "Them some out of sight thugs and hoodlums up there!" The brothers on the block gon say, "Who is these THUGS and HOODLUMS? . . . Well, they've been calling us niggers, thugs, and hoodlums for four hundred years, that ain't gon hurt me, I'm going to check out what these brothers is doing!"

Bobby Seale, chairman, Black Panther Party, 1968

I've lived on this street for the past thirty-four years. I just don't know what happened. The people have changed, the city, the kids . . . everything has changed. . . . Use to see kids playing basketball, baseball or skipping rope . . . not anymore. They all look old, mean and serious. The dope and the hoodlums done made everybody stay in their houses.

retired Detroit postal worker, 1986

Contents

Introduction

Heroes and villains are the yin and yang of American cultural expression, providing creative artists with a varied palette of moral shadings for their observations on the human condition. Real-world heroes and villains greet us daily, insinuating themselves into our lives via the news media and through random personal encounters. Our national history is a veritable treasure trove of heroes and villains—many of whom become mythologized over time. All told, it is likely that a rough equality exists between the two opposed but complementary forms. Nevertheless, with all due respect to the many contributions that real, imagined, and historically enhanced heroic beings have made to American life, the chief concern of this book is with the yin, the dark force, the villain. Indeed, its central characters are villains who possess both spiritual and physical darkness. But why villainy? Why black villains?

As revealed daily via our major avenues of popular cultural expression, heroes have an uncanny ability to beat the odds, secure the victory, hog the spotlight, and live to fight another day. Villains, on the other hand, receive few celebratory proclamations or municipal parades. More often they are subjected to whispered slurs and bad press. Their public, if one can call it that, is encouraged by the mainstream to eschew emulation and to keep both professed interest and personal loyalty a closely guarded secret. Since most Americans are socialized into hero worship rather than villain worship, the latter group seldom has been studied with any comparable degree of seriousness. One result of this academic oversight is that most of us fail to make connections between heroes and villains that transcend the obvious. Fixating on their ability to shock and/or entertain, we frequently underestimate the villain's contribution both to the development of heroic models and to a more complete understanding of humanity's dark side. As if cowering from purposeful scrutiny, villains have yet to experience their day in the sun.

The same can be said for black people and their history. Despite more than seventy-five years of Black History Month celebrations and a post-1960s proliferation of black studies programs, overall societal understanding of the African American historical experience, its uniqueness and its challenges, remains problematic. Lamentably, many otherwise well-schooled individuals—including numerous black Americans—still do not have enough accurate information about the nation's racial past to make historically informed decisions on present-day issues. In part, this problem can be traced to three closely related, culture-based tendencies: (1) whites' long-term stereotyping of blacks as crude, cursed, and criminal; (2) blacks' spirited refusal to accept or validate these negative images; and (3) African Americans' equally determined efforts to balance the bad with the good through the celebration of race heroes.

Understandably, the black response to unwarranted vilification often has been shaped by a highly selective historical amnesia. In this slander-induced mental state, there is a marked tendency to treat all but the most sympathetic African American villains as aberrations—or as heroically inclined helpmeets known as social bandits. Those in serious denial are tight-lipped when presented with evidence to the contrary. They see white conspirators everywhere and manage to find "extenuating circumstances" for all manner of black-on-black crime. Some seem to equate racial loyalty with uncritical acceptance of aberrant behavior. Others obsess over group solidarity but are quick to vilify those within the black public sphere who dispute their orthodoxies. None of these defensive postures are grounded in a clear-eyed understanding of hoodlums and their ever-changing roles in the multicultural mix. It is hoped that this study of both real and imagined villains and social bandits will contribute to the formulation of a more accurate, less self-conscious African American history even as it sheds new light on the darkness of mind revealed in racist stereotypes.

To accomplish these goals, *Hoodlums* draws on a variety of data sets. Traditional historical sources such as autobiographical narratives, personal correspondence, period newspapers, and travel accounts are utilized. But so are Hollywood films, music lyrics, folklore studies, and ghetto gothic novels. Here, it is believed preferable to negotiate the twists and turns of history and myth with assistance from as many disciplinary perspectives and modes of inquiry as possible; to tease out fresh insights from often-studied events— and from the detritus of our popular culture. The final product is wide ranging and resists narrow definitions of "hero" and "villain." Although analytical and interpretive, it is not meant to be "definitive." Hopefully, *Hoodlums* will encourage open and thoughtful discussion of its subject.

Chapter 1 examines the history and diversity of villains in Western society, their defining characteristics and modus operandi. The villains' numerous social roles are outlined and their motivations probed for insight into timeless questions: whether or not some individuals are "born bad"; the root cause and purpose of evil in human society. A major concern is the cultural connection that European Americans have made between moral evil and the color black. The syllogistic notion that since villainy is closely related to blackness, then dark-skinned peoples are in some way villainous is traced from Greco-Roman days through the Middle Ages to the era of the Atlantic slave trade. By the time English popular culture was transshipped to the North American colonies, numerous "bloodie" blackamoors and sinful sons of Ham were available for public scrutiny—and condemnation. Inherited images of black Africans as a race of villains provided ego enhancement for whites, helping shape white supremacist beliefs.

In chapter 2, this national "morality play" that racialized villainy for several generations of Americans is dissected and evaluated. Slave-era literary and theatrical entertainments, state legal codes and plantation rules, as well as a variety of proslavery and pseudoscientific writings are probed for clues as to why antebellum whites felt it necessary to conceptualize blacks as members of an inferior and dangerous race.

Chapter 3 details the key tenets of an oppositional worldview that black Americans forwarded in the hope of combating their fellow countrymen's denigration of all things African. Unafraid to engage influential whites in a debate over group portraiture and skin-color symbolism, self-directed writers, "race men," and brothers on the block identified with the victims of history. To tell their story, defenders of minority-group virtue developed new literary tropes and offered revised interpretations of racial history. In black-authored accounts, slave subversives were transformed into noble social bandits. Plantation patriarchs were deemed "white devils." African Americans who lost their moral bearings, betrayed kinsmen, or strayed too far from their roots were considered "bad blacks," that is, race traitors. Variants of each reimagined character type could be seen throughout the postbellum era in poetry and political broadsides; in Afrocentric history texts and orally transmitted folklore; in antilynching plays and blaxploitation films. All had prominent roles in the sociodrama of black villainy.

Chapter 4 brings the story up-to-date with discussions of late twentieth-century urban unrest, the black underclass, and changes in the nature and perception of black-on-black crime. Separate subsections examine specific groups that have been linked in the public mind to villainous lifestyles: black mob and youth gang members, prison inmates, and gangsta rappers. Both real-world examples and popular cultural representations of each cohort are considered. Hopefully, their ghettocentric stories can provide insight into the prospect of reforming today's hoodlums—or of altering our culture-bound attitudes toward them. In the spirit of social bandits throughout history, the study concludes by challenging both European Americans and African Americans to rethink received wisdom on the nature and prevalence of black villainy.

1 *Villainy in Black and White*

Villains, by definition, are bad people. They are flawed beings whose negative moral attributes overshadow the positive. Lacking a well-developed social conscience, villains are prone to base behaviors and criminal acts. Typically opportunistic and exploitative, they are habituated to greed, treachery, and the ignoble desire to expand their power over others by any means necessary. Whether termed a rogue or scoundrel, knave or blackguard, the villain is a mean-spirited individual who, to varying degrees, lacks the average mortal's requisite quotient of honesty, empathy, and compassion. Fully aware that evil lurks in every human heart, villains cherish this thought and seek to corner the market on immoral conduct.

From time to time, nonvillains exhibit certain of these same characteristics. We all have bad days. Each of us has said or done things that have diverged from group norms so tellingly that we have hurt others and embarrassed ourselves. Dyed-in-the-wool villains, however, feel no shame when they cause pain. Their bad habits are carried to excess and reinforced through constant repetition. Finding virtue in socially unacceptable acts, they do not view themselves as victims of circumstance nor do they spend a great deal of time in concocting alibis or in feeling remorseful. A true villain enjoys the work and has made evildoing a lifestyle choice. In an existential sense, villains do not become real until they are causing someone, somewhere, considerable trouble.

If the world's first villain was the serpent who cajoled Adam and Eve into breaking God's freshly minted moral code, inheritors of this Edenic tradition have been no less reptilian in character. Early on, Abel's murderous sibling, Cain, proved that not all of us aspire to be our brother's keeper. Other archetypal hard cases such as Judas Iscariot, Caligula, Attila the Hun, Lucrezia Borgia, the Marquis de Sade, Benedict Arnold, Rasputin, Adolf Hitler, Tokyo Rose, Idi Amin, and Charles Manson drive home the point and show that no nation, age, or ethnic group has yet managed to gain a monopoly on in-your-face immorality.

Most villains do not behave badly twenty-four hours a day, 365 days per year. Nor do they appear the incarnation of evil to every observer. Often, neither their most unsavory attributes nor their ultimate intentions are apparent. This is due, in part, to the fact that villains are masters of artifice and disguise. Indeed, throughout history they have adopted a maddening variety of physical forms. Particularly noticeable in the case of fictional, folkloric, and theatrical villains, each successive incarnation reveals some hitherto unexamined nuance of nastiness. As a result, the villain's family album serves as a useful field guide for those who would seek to learn more about the attractive force of these chameleonic beings.

The villains who inhabit our popular culture frequently can be identified either by their given names or via familiar visual clues such as a shaved head, a curled mustache, or an eye patch. Because of their creator's careful attention to nuanced nomenclature, it is difficult to conceptualize *Sleeping Beauty*'s foul fairy godmother Maleficent, Flash Gordon nemesis Ming the Merciless, or Sir Mordred, the wily traitor of Arthurian legend, as anything other than an evildoer.[1] The same goes for puppy-stealing fur fetishist Cruella De Vil in *101 Dalmatians*; Pinocchio's fast-talking con artist, J. Worthington Foulfellow; and Vultura, a World War II–era serial film baddie played in prototypically arch fashion by Lorna Gray.[2]

Such characters often possess physical traits as thoroughly villain-specific as the blood-spattered butcher's smock and flayed human-skin mask worn by Leatherface, the psychopathic butcher/cannibal of cult filmdom's legendary *Texas Chain Saw Massacre*.[3] For example, in *Oliver Twist*, Charles Dickens described a hateful London ruffian named Bill Sikes as

> a stoutly-built fellow of about five-and-thirty, in a black velveteen coat, very soiled drab breeches, lace-up half-boots, and grey cotton stockings, which enclosed a very bulky pair of legs, with large swelling calves;—the kind of legs, that in such costume, always look in an unfinished and incomplete state without a set of fetters to garnish them.[4]

Similarly, in Harriet Beecher Stowe's antislavery classic, *Uncle Tom's Cabin*, the flawed moral character of Louisiana planter Simon Legree could be assayed in a single glance. Undoubtedly, it was hoped that virtuous readers would join gentle, upright Uncle Tom in feeling "an immediate and revolting horror" when confronted with the nightmare vision of Legree's "round, bullet head" topped by "stiff, wiry, sunburned hair," his "large, coarse mouth . . . distended with tobacco," and his pair of "large, hairy, sunburned, freckled, and very dirty" hands.[5] Stowe and Dickens were describing neither choirboys nor handsome maiden-rescuing heroes, and they wanted to be sure that their readers could distinguish between vice and virtue before proceeding further.

Of course, not all pop culture villains have been drawn as unkempt, ill-formed individuals who, like Ian Fleming's Auric Goldfinger, look as if they "had been put together with bits of other people's bodies."[6] Some are real charmers. In this group one would find Alain Charnier, aka "the Frog," a suave heroin smuggler played by Fernando Rey in the 1970s *French Connection* films; "the Jackal," novelist Frederick Forsyth's debonair but deadly six-foot-two blond assassin; *Ben-Hur*'s Messala (Stephen Boyd), poster boy for Rome's iron-fisted rule of occupied Judea; and countless silicone-enhanced she-creatures of late-night cinema.[7]

Other villains possess brilliant intellects but place their considerable gray matter in the service of evil. The cunning Dr. Fu Manchu (a mental giant said to possess the brainpower of any three men of genius) matches this rarified profile. So, too, does James Bond's eggheaded adversaries Ernst Stavro Blofeld (a famous allergist plotting to destroy the world's food supply), Hugo Drax (*Moonraker*'s orchid-loving, genocidal mad scientist), and Dr. No (a criminal genius who heads SPECTRE—Special Executive for Counterintelligence, Terrorism, Revenge, and Extortion).[8]

Still other villains are neither terribly good-looking nor Phi Beta Kappas, but nevertheless occupy positions of trust that demand a variety of specialized skills. Here, one can identify villainous law enforcement officers (Robin Hood's nemesis, the Sheriff of Nottingham; foxlike Citizen Chauvelin, head of the French Republic's Secret Service, in *The Scarlet Pimpernel* novels), health care professionals (Big Nurse Ratched in *One Flew Over the Cuckoo's Nest;* the manipulative, mentally unstable asylum director in *The Cabinet of Dr. Caligari*), and businessmen (Sweeney Todd, the "demon barber of Fleet Street"; industrialist Stanford Marshall, aka Lamont Cranston's slouch-hatted foe "the Black Tiger," in the 1940 film *The Shadow*). These deceptive disguises make it more difficult to determine exactly what sort of evil lurks in the hearts of such characters.[9]

Some villains are solitary sorts who prefer to work their wiles in relative isolation, unaided by co-conspirators (Dracula, *The Silence of the Lambs*' Hannibal Lecter, and burly badman Bluto in the *Popeye* cartoons).[10] Conversely, a fair number are team players and can be identified by the corrupt company they keep (the tobacco-chewing, hippie-hating bullies in *Billy Jack;* the muttering, inbred mountain men of *Deliverance;* and the various combinations of super-baddies who constantly plot against Batman and Robin).[11] Loyal assistants or apprentices in evil are common, too. Oddjob and Jaws of the James Bond films, Dr. Frankenstein's Igor, and the squadron of Oz-based flying monkeys controlled by the Wicked Witch of the West add dimension to the portrayal of each head villain even as they warn of evil's many seductions.[12]

For better or for worse, consumers of American popular culture tend to ignore these warnings. Transfixing us with their lustful leers, the many variants of both real-world and fanciful villains fascinate endlessly. As noted by veteran Hollywood "hissable" Claude Rains in 1941, "Good men, while slated to inherit the earth and the kingdom of Heaven, too, are rarely as captivating to the eye as a polished blackguard. Or to the mind, for that matter. People can't help saying, 'My, my. If only the rascal had turned his talents in the proper channels—what a power for good he would have become!'"[13] Why is this true? Does their hypnotic appeal more accurately reflect the villains' strength or our susceptibility to salacious suggestion? Beyond sending cold chills down our spines, what social purposes are served by these malevolent beings?

Villains specialize in providing upright individuals with a variety of vicarious experiences. Brash, thrill-seeking masters of the guilty pleasure, they understand that vice excites far more than virtue. Like an antisocial alter ego, they offer the law abiding an opportunity to participate in audacious acts without fear of punishment. Here, the villain becomes a societal safety valve, purging us of repressed tendencies and unwanted feelings. It is the villain who hates and lusts, is arrogant, uncaring, and at times quite mad, we say nobly, happy to declare our comparative rectitude. Both fascinated and repulsed by these characters, people love to hate villains because by doing so they can claim to have their own wicked impulses under control.

By functioning as a cultural yardstick with which to measure an individual's adherence to group mores, villains simplify moral choices and help shape the ritual drama of American social life. They teach us how not to behave, make clear the possible consequences of engaging in foul play, and greatly enhance the typological vocabulary (brute, fiend, hoodlum, ogre, outlaw, renegade, reprobate, roughneck, traitor, troublemaker, tyrant) through which we attribute relative degrees of good and evil. Moreover, just as the crude folkways of medieval peasants (villeins) served to define the civility of the court and bourgeoisie, villainy gives definition to heroism. While not exactly the relationship established by Robert Louis Stevenson's Dr. Jekyll and Mr. Hyde, heroes and villains maintain a complex interdependence.

Through their bad behavior, villains create a variety of crisis situations to which the hero must respond. When faced with the choice of death or dishonor, a champion of the established order typically springs into action, saves the day, and thereby promotes a greater good. But without the villain's challenge to the status quo, there would be far fewer occasions for heroic endeavor and a corresponding decline in socially beneficial resultants. No stranger to paradox and irony, villains often unwittingly strengthen accepted community standards by deviating from them.[14]

A somewhat different moral universe is established when a villain defeats a hero. Even if only temporary, the hero's eclipse may prove to be more than a dramatic way of galvanizing the communal spirit in response to a threat posed by villainous outsiders. Such a precipitous event may signal a splintering of the group consensus—a sign that the natives are restless and have selected a new champion to represent them in presenting their grievances to the world. Telling evidence that one person's hero can be someone else's villain, this disruptive turning of the tables often is the work of a disaffected societal subgroup questing for freedom. Here, establishment pariahs become rebel heroes and reflect anti-institutional tendencies present within the oppressed population.

Perhaps better placed within the folk heroic tradition of social banditry, such individuals are the proper villain's first cousins. But they also display attributes—strength, courage, loyalty to cause—normally associated with fully accredited heroes. Social bandits like Robin Hood, for example, are highly selective in their villainy. Their cruelty is legitimized as vengeance. "Feared by the bad, loved by the good," as the theme song of the 1950s CBS TV show would have it, Robin and his Merry Men were hunted as outlaws by representatives of a usurpatious political elite. But to poor peasants long consigned to the lower depths of the social order, this troublesome band of scofflaws seemed an army of liberation—selfless agents of justice whose moral compass pointed in the same direction as their own. In such cases, the social bandit/villain provides a useful counterpoint to skewed, imposed, or outmoded conceptualizations of morality and heroism. Both fictional and real-world representatives of this wrong-righting guild can be of considerable use in helping us distinguish just from unjust societal relationships.[15]

Villains, then, entice, excite, and entertain. In doing so, they help assuage our natural desire to feel good about the values we hold dear. Remarkably malleable in a cultural sense, part of their attractive power can be traced to a willingness to be placed just about anywhere on anyone's personalized moral continuum. They are capable both of enabling and of dethroning reigning nobility. While terms such as "evenhanded," "fair-minded," and "incorruptible" are best reserved for use in describing the essential nature of traditionally conceptualized heroes, it often is the case that major differences between specific villains, heroes, and social bandits are difficult to ascertain. This is especially true in regard to methodology as opposed to motivation. At such times, we are forced to stop and ask hard questions of these enigmatic figures. Certainly, it would be useful to know the villains' views on the root causes of their morally challenged condition; whether they believe themselves to have been made malicious by nature or nurture; and how wicked folk explain the presence of evil in the world. Straightforward responses to such queries would enable us to address a number of existential concerns that have vexed moral philosophers for centuries. But given what we know about villains, how could we trust them to tell the truth? And even if they did, whose favorite outlaw, cheat, or bully would we choose to believe? In light of such problems, it might for the moment be best to conduct an independent investigation of these issues.

It is well known that villains tend to reject the values that heroes operating in the same sociocultural setting promote. Also obvious is the fact that they take considerable pleasure in posing either a physical or moral threat to the hero's core constituency. Less well understood is *why* a villain does these things. Certainly, heroes are more easily fathomed. Exemplary personifications of predominating ideals and culturally sanctioned achievement, heroes are highly esteemed because they stimulate common people to do better, to reach their potential, to innovate. After being elevated to the status of group champion, they gird their followers for battle against formidable foes. They offer consolation when unpleasant realities block the realization of dreams. Heroes aspire, inspire, and offer support because people need them to do so. They serve as loyal allies in the ongoing struggle with the challenges of everyday life.[16] But beyond providing a useful foil for heroes, is there a comparable need for villains that certain individuals attempt to meet through their wickedness? If so, are their acts of selfishness, perversity, and criminality largely volitional or shaped by biological inheritance? Are the determinants of villainy and heroism to be found in a genetic or a moral code?

Humanists tend to believe that villains are so essential to art that writers would have to invent them if they didn't already exist. Social scientists, however, are far less concerned about crafting compelling story lines and personifying societal evils. Instead of worrying about when, where, and how the wolf confronts Little Red Riding Hood, they fret about the possibility that some people are "born bad." Finding little utility in the creation of human misery, specialists in criminal behavior seek to fathom—and then to clini-cally treat—the criminal mind by tracing antisocial tendencies to their source. In support of this effort, sociologists and psychotherapists have for-warded a bewildering array of inconclusive conclusions about the relation-ship between individual responsibility, social conditioning, and a purported biogenetic predisposition to wrongdoing.

Some likely would agree with the scheming Edmund of Shakespeare's *King Lear* that few among us are "villains on necessity; fools by heavenly com-pulsion; knaves, thieves, and treachers by spherical predominance; drunk-ards, liars, and adulterers by an enforced obedience of planetary influ-ence."[17] Privileging free will over any sort of astrological determinism or biological imprinting, "classical" criminologists of the eighteenth and early nineteenth centuries held that antisocial acts were the result of an individ-ual's conscious decision to violate group mores. It was assumed that law-breakers weighed potential gain and loss. Then, after concluding that the net rewards of crime were greater than the burden posed by community-instituted disincentives, they willfully trampled on the rights of others in search of self-gratification.[18] Later researchers added environmental and psychological determinants to the mix, tracing villainous behavior to alien-ation, anomie, oedipal guilt, parental rejection, relative deprivation, and ad-verse social conditions. In such studies, violent acts were treated as socially constructed phenomena or learned responses to frustrating situations. Here, again, heredity was deemed less a contributing factor than was a poverty-induced "tangle of pathology."[19]

Other researchers have raised the even more disturbing possibility that criminality is less a matter of personal choice or societal estrangement than it is the working out of one's biological destiny. Echoing Verdi's Iago in the be-lief that social outcasts are "born into vileness," these writers maintain that some are predisposed to villainy through genetic inheritance.[20] During the late nineteenth and early twentieth centuries, proponents of this notion at-tempted to link body type with temperament. The result was a series of re-markable revelations about hereditary disingenuousness. Criminals, it was said, were biologic anomalies—throwbacks to primitive times who exhibited an "irresistible craving for evil for its own sake." Doomed even before birth to a villainous lifestyle, the extent of their atavism was apparent to all who had occasion to observe a murderer's receding forehead and sloping shoulders; the rapist's "fleshy, swollen and protruding lips"; or the long, thin fingers of swindlers, thieves, and pickpockets.[21] In more recent times, presumed anatomical correlates to criminality have become somewhat less vivid. Social scientists no longer consider the lawbreaker to be "a relic of a vanished race" but continue to posit a biogenetic substrate for villainy.[22] Frequently, chemical imbalances and metabolic and chromosomal disorders are blamed. Thus, aggressive, antisocial behaviors may be the product of (1) malfunctioning endocrine glands; (2) low blood sugar; (3) damage in the limbic regions of the brain; or (4) elevated levels of plasma testosterone and the presence of an extra Y chromosome in men. Somewhat more visible indicators of villainous tendencies are said to include (1) a mesomorphic physique; (2) high andromorphy; and (3) a lack of facial attractiveness.[23]

Unfortunately, the key to finding the precise mix of hereditary and environmental factors that shape human intellect and character eludes us. Given the difficulty of treating either the soma or the psyche in isolation, the question of whether or not some humans are "born bad" may never be definitively determined. Nevertheless, whether more correctly conceptualized as creatures of impulse, inheritance, or purposeful action, villains—and the threat they pose to society—remain a compelling subject for scholarly investigation. This is true both because of the evildoers' inscrutability and our own frustrating inability to explain precisely what, if anything, makes them so different from normal people.

The root causes of villainy also continue to generate interest because the problem of societal evil is equally a moral problem. It has religious and theological implications that cannot be addressed by the available data on either genetic abnormalities or dysfunctional families. If secular-minded folk experience a certain amount of discomfort when presented with the notion of linking wrongdoing to biblical concepts such as sin and iniquity, hellfire and damnation, others diligently search the Scriptures for answers to age-old questions: If there is an omnipotent God who is wholly good, why does evil exist? Why have all human societies been plagued by individuals who reject the good in order to create human misery through acts of senseless violence? As one would expect, responses to these ancient puzzles vary with each respondent's conceptualization of the moral universe.

Moral evil, of course, need not be given a specific humanoid form. Indeed, some are prone to describe it as an abstract, intuited concept. Others perceive human nature as morally bivalent—a composite of good and bad potentialities—or split hairs endlessly over the distinction between an egregious evil and a simple wrong. Often, faceless forces like fate, destiny, expediency, and circumstance are blamed for our antisocial actions. But such approaches take much of the mystery and all of the fun out of the attempt to fathom villainy. Like Ronald Reagan describing the Soviet Union as an "evil empire," any abstract moral wrong becomes more tangible when personified. The pedagogical value of this technique is enhanced even further when the evil entity is given a virtuous adversary.

As noted by psychologist Carl Gustav Jung, it is illogical to "assume that one can state a quality without its opposite."[24] For example, height is difficult to conceptualize if there is no depth. For its magnitude to be perceived correctly, great good must be viewed in the context of immense—not merely second-rate—evil. Accordingly, in the traditional Judeo-Christian morality play, Adam and Eve make convincing transgressors but terrible villains. Seduced into facilitating the entrance of evil into human society by what Augustine termed "the misuse of free will," they are sinners but not sin incarnate.[25] The creator God, it seems, could neither be blamed for intending evil nor for deigning to spar with midgets. Thus, humankind's Fall necessarily was accompanied by the rise of the Devil (aka Belial, Beelzebub, the Evil One, Lucifer, Old Nick, and Satan), a mighty fallen angel whose rebellion against God has caused trouble for Adam's descendants ever since they left the Garden of Eden.

Only a few world religious traditions (the Christian, ancient Hebrew, Islamic, and Zoroastrian) include the concept of a single demonic personification of radical evil. Christianity's "devil" is indirectly derived from the Hebrew *satan* (meaning obstructor or adversary of humankind) and (as *diabolos*) first was applied to the Evil One when the Old Testament was translated into Greek in the third century. At the same time, the Greek word *satanas* was used in the New Testament to denote an enemy of God, himself. English translations of these texts, culminating in the standard King James Version of 1611, conflated and permanently consolidated these meanings and terms.[26] The Devil, then, is the ultimate enemy of both God and man. A liar and sinner (John 8:44, I John 3:8); tempter (Matthew 4:1–11); and foe of all who, like Christ, seek to facilitate a reconciliation between divinity and humanity (I Thessalonians 2:18, John 13:2), Satan is a worthy adversary—and a tireless recruiter—in the ongoing battle over moral standards and mortal souls.

Remarkably, this prideful deceiver makes relatively few appearances in Scripture. Only sporadically identifiable as an objectified being, the Devil has made it hard for humans to agree on a standardized physical portrayal. As noted by nineteenth-century French poet Charles Baudelaire, perhaps this is due to the fact that "the finest ruse of the devil is to persuade you that he does not exist."[27] That the demonic trickster is a virtuoso shape-shifter also contributes to our confusion. In any case, the Devil that we see in artists' renderings comes in a variety of guises.

Almost universally depicted as male, Satan is fearful to behold. Looking for all the world like prototypes of some of Hollywood's most imaginative nightmare fantasies, folkloric representations reveal him to be a monstrous, deformed being of mingled parts. Neither man nor beast, his tail and horns, cloven hooves or talons, large and enveloping batlike wings, oversize nose and phallus, coarse body hair, and backward-facing knees (occasioned by the precipitous fall from heaven) provide graphic physical evidence of gross spiritual defect.[28]

Equally symbolic is the unambiguous color coding of traditional European American devil lore. Only one of Satan's Old and New Testament incarnations is given explicit color. This was the "great red dragon" of Revelation 12. But before the end of the sixth century—and likely earlier—Christians were adding new mysteries to the sacred canon. In their writings, they described a devil-like being: "black, sharp-faced, with long beard, hair to the feet, fiery eyes, breathing flame, spiky wings like a hedgehog, bound with fiery chains."[29] Already, it seems, the die was cast. Estranged from goodness and light, the Evil One most often has been presented to us as having black skin or wearing dark-colored clothing. He rides a black horse, practices the black arts, commands the armies of darkness, and presides over the gloomy pit of hell. Black cats and goats, shaggy black dogs, ravens, and bats are favored disguises.

One noteworthy consequence of our making the Devil black is that a disproportionate number of his helpers have become inextricably associated with darkness of one sort or another. Like Dracula (Romanian for "devil"), prince of Transylvanian vampires, noteworthy evildoers favor black clothing and accessories. Certainly, no self-respecting, stereotypical Wild West outlaw or wicked witch would want to be seen doing dastardly deeds without a black chapeau. Frequently, as was the case with novelist George du Maurier's mesmeric music master, Svengali, this attire is complemented by the villain's "thick, heavy, languid, lustreless black hair," "bold, brilliant black eyes," and "beard of burnt-up black." Pirates like Blackbeard and *Peter Pan*'s "cadaverous and blackavised" Captain Hook even prowl the seven seas under the skull and crossed bones of the Jolly Roger—the black flag of all seafaring predators who are on a first-name basis with Satan (Old Roger). Termed a "child of the devil" and an "enemy of all righteousness" in Acts 13:10, such individuals are said to be "full of all subtilty and all mischief."[30]

Is there cultural significance in our blackening of prominent villains and in the manner in which they have been linked to the Great Deceiver, fount of natural evil? To be sure, not all "black-hearted" souls have become feared enemies. With some, we tend to be charitable and overlook major flaws. How else does one account for the hoards of partygoers who descend upon Tampa each February to attend the gala festival that memorializes a murderous, rapine-prone buccaneer named Gasparilla?[31] Nevertheless, many who have been tarred with the dark pigment seem destined to remain in permanent moral exile. Decent people hold them at arm's length, hoping thereby to protect the virtue of their beloved community. If in Western society, black is somehow related to evil, one necessarily puzzles over whether this long-term relationship is more a product of the villain's flawed character or of the "upright" citizen's aversion to blackness.

Like all other pigmentational shadings found in nature, the color black is capable of eliciting emotions and setting moods. It can be used symbolically and interpreted as variously as any controversial news event. Cambridge University's John Harvey, a close observer of the emblematic and allegorical aspects of material culture, terms black a "paradox-colour." Others categorize it as a noncolor. According to the first chapter of Genesis, black is the most ancient of colors and was "upon the face of the deep" at the time of Earth's creation. On the other hand, black also is the color of dirt, decay, and putrefaction. As an observed phenomenon, it is most like the dark of night even though it can be seen clearly in the light of day. But when completely surrounded by it—as in a pitch-black cave—we say, "I can't see a thing!" At such times, black becomes invisible, a void of coloration.[32]

Throughout history, Westerners have donned black clothing in order to reflect both formality and simplicity; professionalism and social position; asceticism, austerity, gravity, and penitence. The color has been a favorite of both ruling elites and countercultural naysayers. Bad guys wear black, but so do clerics and many other good people. It is slimming on a size 3X frame but carries the weight of authority when seen on a Supreme Court justice.

Despite this impressive sartorial adaptability, the color black also has come to be associated with several of the most troubling aspects of the human experience. Mourners wear black and were doing so in ancient Greece and Rome. During the Middle Ages, lepers often were required to dress in black, as were knights who had disgraced their order. But even earlier, people feared the darkness. Frightened by forest creatures that go "bump" in the night—as well as by those "ghoulies and ghosties and long-leggety beasties" that none had encountered but all suspected were lurking in the shadows—

they linked evil with the absence of light. In such cases, paradoxical meanings are easily overwhelmed by negative connotations. Somber hues are equated with contamination, death, and censure for wrongdoing. Through constant repetition of negative references, black devolves into a sinister color and is made an accessory to crime.[33]

Whether drawn from primal instinct or learned response to real or imagined predators, this unfortunate relationship was confirmed by philosophers, theologians, and other writers who employed the color black in moral allegories about spiritual defect and societal decay. Here, black was a signifier for sin and served as a negative reference point for acceptable ethical behavior. It was the antithesis of white, symbol of purity, chastity, virtue, and innocence. Since God was spirit and light, the gloom associated with the color black could represent only those forces opposed to or alienated from God. If, as taught by both Plato and Augustine, physical light reflected "the pure fire within us," it was unlikely that "black sheep" would be allowed to enter the brightly lit heavenly homeland of the church triumphant. "Black," wrote Shakespeare, "is the badge of hell, the hue of dungeons, and the school of night."[34]

Thus, over time, villains, great moral evil, and the color black have been joined in unholy union. The resulting ebony-toned and evil entity is a most useful cultural creation. The fear elicited by villains of this type has done much to steer us away from the pit. Their very presence makes virtue attractive. Without them, our stories would have fewer morals to teach. Filmed entertainments would be all too dull. But the physical and spiritual darkness associated with such figures creates numerous problems as well. These affect real people, not just the stock characters of stage, screen, and fiction. Among the most grievous are the unique burdens that the ancestors of modern-day African Americans were forced to bear even before there was an America. In effect, the villains' many evils have been imputed to people of color irrespective of their individual character, deeds, or moral worth. This ongoing human tragedy is the result of thousands of interpretive acts over several centuries of European American history. The syllogistic notion that since villainy is closely related to blackness then those who are black by heredity are in some way villainous is both illogical and, seemingly, inescapable. Although seldom articulated clearly, it informs and provides a historical subtext for the working out of all contemporary racial relationships.

The Greeks and Romans knew a great deal about Africa and Africans. Experts on the ancients tell us that they put these understandings to good use and, more often than one might expect, gave their dark-skinned brothers and sisters across the Mediterranean credit whenever credit was due. Zeus and his fellow Olympians were said to have taken great pleasure in feasting with the Ethiopians, whose piety and reverence for justice became the stuff of legend. Celebrated by both the gods and their earthly subjects, Ethiopian kings such as Hydaspes and Sabacos won acclaim for implementing a nonexpansionist foreign policy and for refusing to employ take-no-prisoners tactics on the battlefield. This generosity of spirit was thought to be so pervasive that these highly principled black people who lived "at the world's end . . . where the Fountains of the Sun gush and the River Aithiops flows," had need for neither locks nor doors on their dwellings. Given these early favorable impressions of Africans, it is not at all surprising that the bold and resourceful Odysseus considered a "dusky, woolly-headed" chap named Eurybates to be the most valuable of his men-at-arms. As noted by Homer, the black herald had "a shrewd head, like the captain's own."[35]

Greco-Roman egalitarianism was rooted in both the ancients' philosophical proclivities and in the nature of Mediterranean slavery. For many, including the Athenean comic playwright Menander, nobility was determined by "natural bent." External appearances were of little consequence. In practical terms, this meant that heartfelt tribute could be paid to fallen black heroes like the skilled arena champion Olympius ("O wonderful, O bold, O swift, O spirited, O always ready!"). Poets were free to offer unblushing praise of Didyme, Andromeda, and other femmes fatales whose dark beauty was compared to that of rosebuds, violets, and hyacinths.[36] The fact that the slavery of antiquity was largely independent of race and that the vast majority of bond laborers in this part of the world were white, not black, assured that no single group would be singled out as being slavish by accident of birth.[37]

Nevertheless, one must not overstate the case for the evenhandedness of the ancients. Even confirmed racists sometimes praise "exceptional" specimens of a population thought, on average, to be inferior. Focusing too intently on racial slavery as opposed to racial prejudice can mislead. Certainly, subsequent chapters of the European American historical record provide numerous examples of the latter thriving long after the demise of the former. The fact that all manner of non-Hellenes were considered barbarous and unworthy of full citizenship rights did not prevent some culturally chauvinistic observers from sowing the seeds of a more race-specific animus. That Rome established no comprehensive color bar or test for racial purity is no guarantee that its people did not evidence color consciousness in ways that would seem familiar to residents of the segregation-era American South.

Because these early European cultures associated the color white with goodness and the color black with bad character, death, and the Underworld, some considered a dark complexion to be ominous. The most imaginative recounted tales of ill-starred individuals who crossed paths with an Ethiopian just before experiencing great misfortune. Others employed color symbolism in a potentially harmful fashion when they used Latin and Greek words like *melas* and *niger* as metaphors for "wicked," "malignant," or "sinister." If the development of negative color coding was a slow and often unconscious process, it nevertheless proved to be an ill omen for all *Aethiopes*. The lyric poet and satirist Horace provided a succinct but accurate forecast of future race relations when he warned: "This is the blackened soul: men of Rome, beware!"[38]

By the end of the Middle Ages, an even more direct connection had been made between Africans and evil. Elaborations on the Old Testament account of Noah's stormy relationship with his son Ham transformed a simple tale sanctioning the enslavement of the Hebrews' Canaanite enemies into a confused but widely adopted apologia for the trans-Saharan slave trade. In the bare-bones Genesis 9 narrative, an unclothed and inebriated Noah curses grandson Canaan, saying that he was to be a "servant of servants . . . unto his brethren." But, at least to modern sensibilities, the fact that Canaan's father, Ham, had briefly glimpsed Noah's naked form hardly seems justification for such a cruel edict. Was there more to the story than meets the eye? And what wisdom is one to take from it? Unfortunately, the text provides no further insight into (1) the nature and magnitude of the offense that occasioned "Ham's curse"; (2) the length of Canaan's servitude; or (3) whether these matters were in any way linked to culturally based concerns about race or ethnicity. If, today, it seems reasonable to believe that the Genesis account was meant to be applied to an eastern Mediterranean people who were conquered and treated as slaves by kings David and Solomon, most early interpreters appeared to be searching for decidedly more colorful explanations.[39]

Because the Old Testament is a common source of Jewish, Christian, and Muslim traditions, the vilifying and Africanizing of Ham/Canaan has been a cooperative venture. Sixth-century rabbinic retellings of the Genesis 9 story suggested that Ham's crime actually was most heinous. Instead of being enslaved for failing to avert his gaze or to cover Noah's nakedness, Ham and his lineage were disciplined—justly and in perpetuity—for gross sexual transgressions. In this scenario, the wayward son either sinned by having intercourse with his wife while in the ark or emasculated his father.[40] Later, Muslim writers opined that deeds of this nature necessarily resulted in harsh punishments. Noah's curse was said to have transformed Ham's descendants into a people with dark complexions and "distorted" features.[41] Appearing to be in complete agreement with the Koranic notion that hellfire blackens the skin, Christian commentators added a final, suitably moralistic component to the equation: Ham, the "wicked brother," first "merited the name of slave" because "slaves came from sin." Thus, long before the average European had an opportunity even to *see* an African, this informal ecumenical alliance of racial theorists had pieced together an odd but compelling portrait of a morally corrupt, sexually deviant, and divinely accursed Hamitic race. As noted in one sixteenth-century English account, the Devil's prompting of Ham to commit great evil resulted in a "posteritie . . . so blacke and lothsome, that it might remaine a spectacle of disobedience to all the worlde. And of this . . . came all these blacke Moores which are in Africa."[42]

Less idle speculation than a mechanism developed to rationalize and justify slave trading, the Africanization of Canaan via emendations to Genesis 9 coincided with a noticeable "darkening" of Near Eastern slavery after the sixth century. Unfortunately, cross-cultural transmission of the belief that human bondage should be a race-based institution grounded in the human resources of sub-Saharan Africa cannot be traced with absolute precision. We do not have a definitive date for the awful moment in human history when a significant mass of nonblacks first equated "Negro" with "slave." But, if—as seems likely—slavery in Muslim lands had become a decidedly black institution by 1000 AD, one can assume that contemporary Europeans were making mental notes and charting their options. As nationalism blossomed and maritime technology advanced during the later Middle Ages, slave-mongers headquartered north of the Mediterranean came to imitate their Islamic counterparts. By the time the first Iberian slavers dropped anchor off the Upper Guinea Coast in the 1440s, supply and demand, cultural chauvinism, and scriptural subterfuge had conspired to make those who bore the stain of Noah's curse seem the perfect God-given solution to the labor problems of "civilized" societies.[43]

Although fundamentally an economic endeavor, the Atlantic slave trade was grounded in a culture-based habit of mind that latter-day scholars have termed "racial objectification"—the attempt to turn a person into a thing on the basis of observable racial differences. Here, the all-but-universal desire to distinguish "us" from "them" leads one group to define itself as the embodiment of all that is "human." Competing, typically smaller or weaker, groups fall short of the mark and are consigned to a category of "indeterminate otherness." Neither men nor monsters, these unfortunate "objects" are seen as grotesques. Their essential humanness is questioned but not altogether denied. Often perceived as a mixture of the humorous and the horrible, they are too normal to be treated as subhuman and too strange to be considered "civilized." Thus, in the era of the transatlantic trade, nonwhites did not become nonpeople. They became slaves and were made to occupy the socially constructed space between personhood and property.[44]

This troubling practice of conflating "he/she" and "it" can be traced to medieval ancestors who willfully populated uncharted seas and unexplored landforms with a fantastic array of ethnological and zoological oddities. Making their crude homes just beyond the frontiers of European discovery, some fifty different "monstrous" varieties of humankind were thought to exist in Africa, Asia, and the Far North and East. Most often seen peering out from the borders of illuminated manuscripts and world maps, imaginative renderings of these exotic folk show them to be a curious compound of human and animal creation. They had owl eyes, dog heads, horse hooves instead of feet, and massive ears or lips that doubled as sunshades and blankets. Some walked on all fours. Others breathed flames. In such a marvelously colorful bestiary, bearded women and hirsute, club-wielding men with backward-turned feet seemed almost "normal."[45]

Medieval inexactitude in describing these strange beings did little to discourage their objectification. In fact, the confused melding of Indian and Ethiopian, Pygmy, dwarf, and wild man actually solidified the view that dark-skinned peoples were to be set apart and treated as the Europeans' far-distant, often venal and villainous cousins. Linked to spiritual darkness and savagery via the mountainous wilderness landscape with which they were associated, "monstrous" Africans inspired both fear and distaste in the "civilized" mind. And for good reason. Their indeterminate otherness was quite striking. The Blemmyae, for example, were held to lack both necks and heads, making do with faces implanted on their chests. Curly shoulder-to-toe hair and boar's tusks accentuated their bestial nature. Other "Ethiopians," including speechless, cave-dwelling troglodytes and diminutive dark-skinned Pygmies, were similarly grotesque. Their abnormalities generated speculation as to whether such beings might not have been created by God on a day separate from the rest of humankind. If so, perhaps what was described as their "terrifying appearance" was meant to denote a congenital habituation to immoral behavior. As one mid-fifteenth-century work of natural history concluded, black Africans were "full of great cruelty" and exhibited "customs and conditions strange to the human race."[46]

Although markedly different from the ancient Greeks' vision of pious, principled Ethiopians, this unsympathetic portrayal failed to deter Europeans from venturing into the wilds of Africa. They quested for the mythical Christian kingdom of Prester John; for a safe passageway to the treasures of the Indies; and for Guinea Coast gold and slaves.[47] Inevitably, these journeyings brought white folk cheek by jowl with real, as opposed to fancifully constructed, Africans. But the intellectual task of separating truth from fiction, monstrous from normative humanity, was a daunting one. Cultural parochialism and the love of a ripping yarn too often were stronger than an adventurer's devotion to facts faithfully ascertained. As a result, sixteenth- and seventeenth-century travel narratives were spiced with snippets of disinformation gleaned from a variety of legendary tales. The resulting mélange of fact and falsehood made for a hearty literary stew resonant with pejorative images of Africans.

European geographers and explorers filled their accounts of sub-Saharan lands with faint praise and heavy censure. For every favorable comment ("although the people were blacke and naked, yet they were civill"), there were a half-dozen nasty gibes about the Africans' skin color (a "blot of infection"), physique ("almost beasts in human form"), and moral character ("very lecherous, and theevish, and much addicted to uncleanenesse").[48] In what can only be interpreted as a case of the pot calling the kettle black, English slaver John Hawkins complained that he "seldome or never found truth" among his black trading partners. Richard Eden, chronicler of John Lok's 1554–55 voyage to Guinea, scored its inhabitants for their supposed lack of "a God, lawe, religion, or common wealth." Privateer turned Portuguese prisoner of war Andrew Battell told of cannibalism, infanticide, human sacrifice, and "men in women's apparel" whom the Angolans kept "among their wives." Numerous others spread unsavory rumors about the Africans' biological links to the anthropoid apes and spoke openly of frequent acts of "beastly copulation or conjuncture" between the two groups.[49]

Awkwardly juxtaposing fact and fantasy, such tales were made believable by preexisting notions of skin-color symbolism and the deleterious effects of Noah's curse on Hamitic peoples. Just as chimpanzees and baboons were said to approximate the behavior of "Devils whom they resemble," black Africans, too, came to be seen as being biologically wedded to the powers of darkness. "Burnt, and dreadful to look upon," they were in both color and condition "little other than Devils incarnate." Ignorant of "true godliness" and incapable of distinguishing between "good and bad, honesty and dishonesty," these practitioners of animistic religions were "much given to sorcery, and divinations," "prodigious Idolatry," and "adoration of falce godes, and the Devill." To many a European of this great age of discovery, they seemed

"Men [come] out of Hell." There was little doubt in the proto-colonialist mind that such moral and physical grotesques were "born and bred Villains."[50]

Eventually, these harsh evaluations of Africans and their customs were incorporated into theatrical entertainments. During the years in which the Atlantic trade in slaves was regularized, white Europeans seemed intent on making black Africans their intellectual as well as their chattel property. As in the accounts penned by explorers and traders, this property was treated as damaged goods and condemned. English dramatists were particularly active on this front—both validating, manipulating, and commodifying cultural stereotypes found in travel books, journals, geographies, and encyclopedias. Through repeated use, negative portrayals became conventional and therefore increasingly difficult to contradict. This theatrical objectification of blackness conditioned the perceptions of many theatergoers, providing them with a ready reference guide that could be used in interpreting both the playwrights' intent and the nature of contemporary geopolitical and racial relationships.

The theatrical tradition associating blackness with estrangement from God and polite society can be traced to the miracle and morality plays of late medieval times. Here, in accordance with already-established iconographic practices, fallen angels, demons, and damned souls were represented by actors costumed in black. "Alas, alas, and wele-wo! / lucifer, whi fell thou so?" these tormented beings wailed as they were punished for sinning by being made "blak as any coyll, / And vgly, tatyrd as a foyll."[51] Emblematic of great evil, a dark-painted face was treated allegorically and provided audiences with advance warning of a character's spiritual disposition.

By the middle of the sixteenth century, these cultural understandings were being reflected in English court masques. In these grand entertainments, courtiers wearing black gloves, stockings, and masks approximated the appearance of North African Moors. Surviving texts show "Nigritae" as exotic Others whose close association with distant lands and unfamiliar cultures added considerable "local color" to such events. They also provided a quick ego boost for white celebrants. Ben Jonson's *The Masque of Blackness*, for example, traded on the notion that a pale complexion—especially in women—is a highly coveted mark of distinction. Africans were shown longing to "blanch" themselves white, so that they, too, could be considered beautiful.[52]

Late sixteenth-century English plays were less allegorical, more mimetic, and increasingly concerned with secular history and the naturalistic portrayal of people and events. Black-faced personifications of vice evolved into rigidly typecast villains with remarkable ease as dramatists' more literal style enhanced the fiction that such figures had real-world analogues. Stereotypically malevolent foreigners were, of course, familiar to most theatergoers because of Christian Europe's ill-starred Crusades against the forces of Middle Eastern Islam. Whether white, black, or tawny, Moors—like fellow-Muslim Turks and Saracens—had earned a reputation for being fierce warriors and brazen, unrepentant sinners. In addition to being treated as religious and political outcasts, the "blackamoors" of northwestern Africa were obliged to shoulder an additional burden: the already weighty onus of their racial past. When they took the stage, characters representing this tradition were expected to play the villain. As forecast in the twelfth-century epic poem *The Song of Roland*, blacks could not escape being depicted as a "race of infidels."[53]

Chief among these Elizabethan evildoers were members of the blackamoor elite: Muly Mahamet, the "tyrant king" in George Peele's historical drama *The Battle of Alcazar;* Aaron, nemesis and moral counterpoint to Shakespeare's tragic hero in *Titus Andronicus;* and the equally troublesome Eleazar in Thomas Dekker's tale of palace intrigue, *Lust's Dominion*. Collectively, they represented the best and brightest of their racial kinsmen. To the English playwrights, this meant that lechery and avarice dominated the Moors' personalities and their ambition knew no bounds.

Boastful and duplicitous, yet plagued by a streak of cowardice, Muly Mahamet is depicted as being "Blacke in his looke, and bloudie in his deeds." He is a "foule, ambitious Moore"—a shameless manipulator who targets family members for death in order to advance Machiavellian schemes. Unlike his uncle Abdelmelec—a "white" Moor whose historical counterpart stood somewhat higher in the estimation of English historians—Mahamet lacks both dignity and piety. His barbarism and irreligion are mirrored in the rants that he delivers in the names of classical underworld gods. Indeed, the lower realms seem a most appropriate final resting place for the soul of one whose attendants appear as "devils coted in the shapes of men." Like many a latter-day villain, he displays no noteworthy redeeming qualities and dies swearing vengeance upon his enemies by telling them "we [will] meete in hell."[54]

Shakespeare's Aaron is in all ways Mahamet's equal as a vengeful schemer. But he seems to derive considerably more sadistic pleasure from his work. "O, how this villainy / Doth fat me with the very thoughts of it. / Let fools do good and fair men call for grace, / Aaron will have his soul black like his face," he coos after committing one of many violent, disgusting deeds. Here, evildoing is portrayed as a consciously conscienceless act. Fully aware of his ability to "beget / A very excellent piece of villainy," this smartly cynical political opportunist takes pride in outwitting less clever Roman foes. "Now," he chuckles to himself at one point, "what a thing it is to be an ass." Described by one of Titus Andronicus's sons as "an incarnate devil" with a "fiend-like face," Aaron's appetite for wrongdoing is insatiable. As he notes in the play's concluding scene, "If one good deed in all my life I did / I do repent it from my very soul." One can almost smell the essence of brimstone wafting across the stage.[55]

Similarly, in *Lust's Dominion*, the play's chief villain is referred to as "that damned Moor, that Devil, that Lucifer." A power-hungry plotter with designs on the throne of Spain, Eleazar does little to discourage the association of blackness with evil. On one occasion, he even urges fellow Moors to seek out the dark side by committing murder, noting: "Your cheeks are black, let not your souls look white." Possessing a variety of insatiable appetites, Eleazar is single-minded in his manipulation of people and events and an expert at using sex as a weapon of political intrigue. Totally self-aggrandizing, he is shown to lack even a smattering of compassion for his many victims. Little wonder that upon meeting Eleazar for the first time, a friar named Cole is moved to remark, "Truth to tell; / Seeing your face, we thought of hell."[56]

Without question, each of these Moorish characters was meant to be eminently hissable. They were made so by their arch demeanor. Nevertheless, a blackamoor's reputation for villainy also rested on Elizabethan-era understandings of Hamitic Africans, the Devil, and the color black. As imaginative composites of all three, Eleazar, Aaron, and Muly Mahamet radiated an essence of evil that was palpable to seventeenth-century English audiences. These fearful visions both reflected and strengthened prevailing biases, encouraging belief in the facile notion that complex cultural differences could be encapsulated and expressed in simplistic dichotomies of black and white.

As one would expect, later dramatists attempted to tap into this compelling fount of theatrical wickedness. William Rowley's *All's Lost by Lust*, Aphra Behn's *Abdelazer*, and Edward Ravenscroft's adaptation of *Titus Andronicus* all contain Moorish bad guys whose lawlessness and lust matched— and occasionally surpassed—that of first-generation stage villains.[57] Misguided strivers with regal aspirations and reprehensible morals, each helped fix pejorative stereotypes of blacks in the public mind. So vivid were these images that not even the appearance of more sympathetic characters, such as Shakespeare's Othello, could drive negative portrayals from the stage.

When English popular culture was transshipped to the infant North American colonies, the black villains were included as part of the Old World cultural baggage. As conservators of established values, British dramatists provided ample warning of the Moorish miscreants' imminent arrival. Barbarism, notes one of Rowley's characters, was "naturall" to a "base African" because their "inside's blacker than [their] sooty skin."[58] Primed in this fashion, whites went about the business of staging the epic morality play known as American history. Quite immodestly but with serviceable sincerity and a complex rationale rooted in their own racial past, English immigrants selected themselves to represent the Forces of Goodness and Light. The black newcomers were cast as Princes of Darkness. To be sure, this was an unsavory role, but one well suited to a race of supposed villains.

The colonization of British North America provided English settlers with a New World of social possibilities. For a time, it was all a bit overwhelming. The frontier environment, its unfamiliar flora and fauna, and the strange ways of its native inhabitants seemed to induce a sensory overload in the English mind. As a result, expatriate Elizabethans couldn't reach a consensus as to whether they had entered an earthly paradise or were about to become lost in a howling wilderness. For some, the vast continent so overflowed with "plentie" that it was likened to a "delicate garden" of unequaled abundance.[1] Here, certainly, spiritual refuge and temporal prosperity were all but assured. To others, however, the new garden more closely resembled the original Eden in decline—a once-unspoiled land that had become tainted by evil. According to this formulation, savages and slaves, not Satan and the serpent, were the chief malefactors. Given the settlers' cultural heritage, it was understandable that a dark skin tone came to be considered a key indicator of both moral worth and criminal intent.

White settlers' problems with the Indians of America are well known and easily fathomed. After permanent settlement replaced exploration and small-scale trade as the predominant English preoccupation, Native Americans became a terrible burden. In geopolitical terms, the Indian nations stood square in the path of an advancing European civilization and had to be removed by any means necessary. When placed in the context of seventeenth-century metaphysics, their resistance to British expansion was seen as an allegory for Satan's opposition to the divinely approved plans of the righteous. Thus, it was with considerable conviction that early settlers justified their own inhumanity by dehumanizing nonwhite enemies. Claims that Indians were "atheistical, proud, wild, cruel, barbarous, brutish (in one word) diabolicall creatures" fed the expansionist fervor and enabled whites to conceptualize themselves as virtuous victims engaged in a heroic struggle for God and country.[2] Revisited time and again in histories, romances, and Indian captivity narratives, such unabashed scapegoating irrevocably poisoned race relations on the American frontier.

Less concerned about the Indians' noticeable difference in skin color than about their preexisting claims to the land and supposed predilection to unprovoked savagery, the English nevertheless succeeded in "blackening" the reputation of their foes. It was said that native tribes not only lived "under a dark Night in things relating to Religion," but that their "Habitations of Cruelty" were located in "the Dark places of New-England."[3] Since only the most optimistic, charitable whites escaped the pernicious influence of this negative imagery, few pale faces doubted that darkness was the preferred cloak of all who were "captivated . . . to Satans tyranny in foolish pieties, mad impieties, wicked idlenesse, busie and bloudy wickednesse."[4] Even those who were so bold as to forward the notion that "very bright Talents may be lodg'd under a very dark Skin" held that it would take "great industry" to bring "civility" to such "rude, barbarous" people.[5]

This English habituation to the use of blackness to connote and contextualize evil more often was revealed in colonial-era commentaries on slave imports from West Africa. If they possessed no viable claims to wilderness acreage, enslaved blacks constituted a clear threat to Anglo-American standards of religious faith and societal order. Moreover, they were socially defined as members of a "black," not a "tawny," "swarthy," "copper colored," "tanned," or "browne-skinned" race. Oddly, this latter fact has been downplayed by many modern-day historians—including those engaged in the academic "chicken-or-egg" debate over which appeared first, slavery or racism.[6]

Admittedly, prioritization of causal factors is the scholar's prerogative and stock in trade. But by de-emphasizing the centrality of color coding to the shaping of American commercial and social relationships, such writers risk giving undue weight to the roles that economics, availability, and international precedent have played in the development of plantation agriculture and in the genesis of the nation's intractable racial inegalitarianism. Without question, slavery could not have existed without economic and social need— that is, chronic shortages of agricultural workers and the perceived unsuitability of European indentured servants and Native Americans for long-term service as bond laborers. Certainly, as latecomers to New World plantation agriculture, the British learned much about the mechanics of enslavement— including cost effectiveness and the relative vulnerability of exploitable populations—from their Dutch, French, Spanish, and Portuguese counterparts. However fragmented, surviving legislative and court records *do* seem to indicate that white settlers only gradually—in the fifty years after 1619—came to the conclusion that hereditary enslavement was the optimal legal status for African peoples in the Americas. Even so, it is neither an act of despair nor of political incorrectness to consider the possibility that the United States was "born racist"; that cultural inheritance predisposed the English settlers to vilify black-skinned peoples; and that the Africans' enslavement was, to a degree, designed to calm racial fears present in the collective white psyche. White racism both facilitated and provided many compelling rationalizations for the economic exploitation of "unfamiliar" and "dangerous" black people.

CULTURAL AFFAIRS

Like their English cousins, white Americans of the slave era produced and consumed literary and theatrical entertainments that helped shape these contemporary understandings about race. As in any other pioneering venture, America's first novelists, poets, short-story writers, and dramatists faced competing demands on time and talent. Laboring in an intellectual atmosphere that owed much to British precedent, they were obliged to adapt Old World conventions to what the eighteenth-century playwright John Murdock termed "the circumstances of a republican people."[7] Well aware of the popular dictum that held that "between the Bible and novels there is a gulf fixed which few novel readers are willing to pass," they had to remain true to their muse while appearing staunch champions of prevailing moral standards.[8] Having entered into the task of creating and then catering to the whims of a new and unsophisticated public, some faced the additional challenge of choosing between pro- and antislavery viewpoints or of celebrating the Revolution even as they sounded a cautionary warning against further societal dislocation. Others debated whether to craft true-to-life history-based tales or to risk trafficking in works of romance and fancy—the sort of literary expression that somber critics said fostered "a bloated imagination, sickly judgment, and disgust towards all the real business of life."[9] Certainly, numerous hazards loomed large amidst an abundance of interpretive choices. Understandably, depictions of slaves varied, frequently appearing vague, incomplete, or internally contradictory.

Given the topsy-turvy state of early cultural affairs, contemporaries could be forgiven for puzzling over whether the writers' collective musings on slavery-related issues would reveal their adopted land to be a paradise or a wilderness; a moral beacon or a quagmire of spiritual decay. The perspective provided by two additional centuries of American history permits a less confused picture to emerge. While appearing to reflect a diversity of opinion in regard to race-based hierarchies, several of the major African American character types created by members of this white literary vanguard helped popularize the notion that blacks were a primitive, sometimes savage people whose very presence threatened the white settlers' nation-building experiment. In one way or another, all were linked to racially determined villainy by the indelible stain of "otherness." Among the most noteworthy of these white inventions of the pre–Civil War years are the following:

Noble Savages. Employed extensively by British and American reformers in their campaign against the Atlantic slave trade, this late eighteenth-century construction remained in the antislavery arsenal for decades. An exotic, weak-willed being whose fragile constitution contrasted greatly with the bold and decisive—if sometimes cruel and conscienceless—Anglo-American, noble savages were by no means prone to purposeful villainy. They did, however, exhibit certain precipitous behaviors that served to link them with earlier portrayals of the ill-fated sons of Ham.

In the 1793 story "The Desperate Negroe," one such bondsman was faced with the prospect of being punished for a supposed violation of plantation etiquette. Fearful and feeling unjustly accused, Quashi hid in the quarters but soon was discovered. A terrible fight ensued. Said to be a stout fellow, the slave quickly gained the upper hand, wrestled his master to the ground, and drew out a knife. As the helpless white man lay "in dreadful expectation" of imminent death, the noble savage delivered a heart-rending soliloquy:

> Master, I was bred up with you from a child; I was your playmate when a boy; I have loved you as myself; your interest has been my study; I am innocent of the cause of your suspicion; had I been guilty, my attachment to you might have pleaded for me. Yet, you have condemned me to a punishment, of which I must ever have borne the disgraceful marks; thus only can I avoid them.[10]

Then, instead of punishing his accuser, Quashi drew the sharp blade across his own throat, groaned, and fell dead. Although bathed in the noble savage's blood, the slaveholder lived to tell the tale.

Foreshadowing many future antislavery storylines, this fictional account of a tormented bondsman's stormy, sentimentalized death taught readers a good deal about the nature of African peoples. As noted by Harriet Beecher Stowe, best-known nineteenth-century legatee of this literary tradition, slaves were assumed to be members of an "exotic race."[11] To be sure, Stowe and her reform-minded contemporaries meant to highlight the nobility of these unfree immigrants to America. Nevertheless, in recounting the tragic consequences of removing blacks from their natal paradise, well-meaning white writers conveyed a most unsettling notion: any race cursed with "black blood" forever was destined to remain a hothouse transplant in Western society. If ennobled by adversities that limited their ability to engage in villainous behavior, the Africans' attachment to the "Dark Continent" and its legendary wild men caused them to respond to personal crises in a violent, panic-stricken manner. According to white-authored reformist literature, this unfortunate racial trait often contributed to their premature demise.

Grotesques. The exaggeration of physical differences between Europeans and Africans was central to the development of a sociocultural rationale that could legitimize the "peculiar institution." Early white writers contributed importantly to this intellectual process by popularizing the notion that black slaves were grotesque in speech, manners, and physiognomy. Just as the African captives' aberrant acts of self-inflicted violence served as a negative reference point for white acculturation, the outlandish appearance of these awkward, comical characters provided nonslave contemporaries with an extensive list of reasons for maintaining racial separatism as a way of life.

Early dramatists found African American dialect to be one of the elements of characterization most useful for depicting the slaves' assumed nature. Unfortunately, few eighteenth- or early nineteenth-century playwrights recorded black dialect with any degree of accuracy or consistency. Even within a single play, spelling often was capricious and syntax varied widely. Black English, as interpreted by whites, made the slaves' striving for respectability seem ludicrous. For example, in *The Candidates,* some southern whites conversed in a rustic, rural patois, but playwright Robert Munford reserved the most humorous mispronunciations of the English language for a loyal body servant named Ralpho. In an exclamation of gratitude for a hand-me-down suit of clothes given to him by master Wou'dbe, the slave exhibited both his unmerited pomposity and his inability to use multisyllabic words correctly:

> God bless your honour! What a good master! Who would not do every thing to give such a one pleasure? But, e'gad, it's time to think of my new clothes: I'll go and try them on. Gadso! This figure of mine is not reconsiderable in its delurements, and when I'm dressed out like a gentleman, the girls, I'm a thinking, will find me desistible.[12]

Other stage slaves melded Ralpho's poor sense of diction with a bewildering array of dialect-based foibles. In A. B. Lindsley's *Love and Friendship,* a

South Carolina house servant named Harry was shown to be critical of master Dick Dashaway's habitual drunkenness. Nevertheless, he sought partial relief from homesickness in Dashaway's liquor cabinet. Eventually, he resigned himself to separation from Africa in an awkwardly delivered soliloquy:

> But why me do no happy? he bees be happy I can, now I here poor slave and no can git backa my country gin. So, now massa Dicky de gone drunk to bed and leava de wine here, I set up chair and sot myself down happy like he, and drink my glass like gemman.[13]

A curious mixture of stage Indian, Norwegian, and Italian, Harry's English was embarrassing, but it elicited howls of laughter from early nineteenth-century theatergoers.

Such comedic bowdlerizations of Black English led to even more bizarre approximations of black dialect in the skits of white "Ethiopian Delineators" who performed for the audiences of traveling circuses, medicine shows, and menageries during the 1820s and 1830s. When the first full-fledged minstrel shows appeared in the early 1840s, white culture consumers were suitably primed for a theater of jokes and music that would make the African American's mispronunciations and malformations the stuff of legend. Fantastically popular in the years before the Civil War, minstrelsy more often reinforced than challenged prevailing social attitudes regarding racial identity. For many, formulaic presentations were welcomed because they enhanced feelings of well-being and security. Habituation to formula also limited the minstrel show's repertoire of characters to no more than a handful of standardized types.

Ranking high among these burnt-cork personalities was an odd-looking slave named Jim Crow. Typically, this somewhat obtuse character appeared in ill-fitting clothes with patches on his trousers and gaping holes in his shoes. The broad-brimmed hat perched atop the minstrel's head could not shade a wide grin, which illuminated his expressive face. Addicted to gin, watermelons, and midnight raids on chicken coops, Jim Crow pranced, joked, and sang before backdrops of cotton patches, slave cabins, and levees piled high with cotton bales. These thematic elements became so familiar to antebellum audiences that many were convinced they saw more reality than fiction in his exaggerated mannerisms and cornball humor.

With "beef stake lips" and eyes "so bery big, / Dey both run into one," a blackface character like Jim was tailor-made for songs and sight gags that ridiculed black physiognomy.[14] Carrying depictions seen in earlier novels and stage productions to the grossest of extremes, antebellum skits exaggerated racially distinctive features to the point where the bondsmen of minstrelsy were reduced to burlesques of real people. Especially favored by white audiences were songs describing slave romances in which the lovers appeared awkward, ill smelling, and physically grotesque. Indeed, who would be so stupid as to court a woman who "look'd jis like a charcoal rose, / Her face so dark she scar'd de crows"?[15] What kind of man would seek to win the hand of Dinah from Carolina, whose "mouth stretch'd from ear to ear"—or of Lubly Fan, whose lips were "like de oyster plant"?[16] Oddly, all were attractive—according to minstrel standards. Whether she had "de biggest foot, / In all de country round" or was born with hair "curl'd so bery tight, / She couldn't shut her mouth," the black female slave was an ideal mate for male suitors whose taste in women was supposed to be the biggest joke of all.[17]

Brutes. Unaccepting of New World bondage but emotionally fragile, the noble savage posed little threat to white hegemony. A typical slave grotesque was no more worrisome. Nevertheless, these two major variants of pre–Civil War slave portraiture were fictive kin to a far more foreboding character type: the black brute. In truth, all can be seen as blood brothers because each was viewed by mainstream Americans as aberrant and inferior—cursed by heredity and, therefore, estranged from a common bond with whites.

It was well known that black servants enjoyed testing their owner's patience. They seemed to think plantation rules were made to be broken. Some, like Harriet Beecher Stowe's mischievous Topsy, freely admitted that they were "mighty wicked," but "can't help it, no how."[18] However, not all "bad" slaves were brutes. Even if referred to as one of "Old Nick's own brood," a misbehaving bondsman could be relatively harmless.[19] To compensate for their sassiness, sloppiness, and malingering, these sly stage slaves provided white dramatists with a proven vehicle for generating laughter. Brute slaves, on the other hand, were capable only of generating fear.

Appearing most frequently in novels and short fiction, black brutes were rude, rebellious, and totally lacking in humor. Both sides of the debate over slavery were in agreement on these basics. Differences in perspective stemmed largely from divergent views on precisely how such slaves became vicious. When attempting to explain this phenomenon, northern and antislavery writers tended to privilege nurture over nature. More often than not, southern and proslavery authors reversed the order. In neither case was blackness wholly irrelevant to the interpretive outcome.

To antislavery champions, hereditary servitude was "unparalleled / In hate of man and blasphemy of God." It far exceeded "all other tyrannies of earth combined." A product of "proud Satan's triumph over lost mankind" at the time of Adam and Eve's fall from grace, slavery was held to be the seedbed of all wickedness and the cause of an untold number of "direful tragedies." Frequently color coding this fount of evil, impassioned writers termed the institution a "dark, accursed blot . . . [a] damning spot" on the nation's social fabric. As such, it stood in stark contrast to the "bright orb of Liberty" that white reformist authors believed would appear at "Freedom's dawning." Logically, many versified entreaties to activism were set in rice swamps "dank and lone" where only a few "sickly sunbeams" managed to penetrate slavery's moral murk.[20]

Antislavery authors agreed that the chief perpetrators of plantation villainy were the members of a white southern agricultural elite. To emphasize this point, planters and their minions were provided with a negative moral shading. Of such men it was said, "If you an't the devil, . . . you's his twin brother"—and the reprobate in question would thank their accuser for the compliment.[21] Over time, all manner of "dark deeds" would be attributed to this cadre of "black-hearted" cutthroats.

Tragically, victims of the white-run system also were estranged from goodness and light. Some, said the reformers, were so hardened by the cruelties of slave life that they became incorrigible. Overlooking the possibility that even a community of sufferers was capable of providing a modicum of shelter from physical and psychological oppression, white writers assumed that the planters served as the blacks' chief (negative) role models and their full-time instructors in "Idleness, Treachery, Theft, and the like."[22] As noted by eighteenth-century poet Timothy Dwight, the African was "form'd a man" but "condition'd as a brute." Thought to be "generally sprightly and ingenious" as youngsters, black children eventually were subjected to a fullblown assault by "the voice of power, the eye of scorn." Before reaching their teenage years, many were said to "sink into stupidity, or give themselves up to vice."[23] Born with a potential for nobility but educated in savagery, the troublesome blacks of antislavery literature provided both moral/ethical as well as coldly practical reasons for abolishing the system. "We are breaking all humanizing ties, and making them brute beasts," warned one particularly prescient slaveholder of antebellum fiction, "and, if they get the upper hand, such we shall find them."[24]

Proslavery writers discounted neither the slaves' brutishness nor the danger that millions of unassimilated bond laborers posed to an advancing southern civilization. They did, however, take umbrage at claims that slaves were being schooled in savagery. In truth, they said, the die had been cast long before Africans were brought to the western hemisphere. Disabilities rooted in racial distinctives prevented many from taking full advantage of the opportunities available to them. Indeed, blacks were fortunate to have been rescued from the "moral blight" of "barbarous Guinea." Working with extremely raw material under difficult frontier conditions, southern whites were doing the best job possible to transform a race of brutes into an efficient labor force.[25] It was hoped that claims like these would discredit the antislavery argument by making the antebellum plantation seem less a den of iniquity than an institution of acculturation and uplift.

Success stories of savages made noble via enslavement filled the pages of southern literature, but proslavery writers were quick to admit that the civilizing of backward Africans was, at best, a work in progress. "Negroes schooled by Slavery" might plausibly "embrace / The highest portion of the Negro race," but dropouts were an ongoing problem. Northern reformers' crusade to win an early graduation for unprepared student/laborers brought additional worries. To highlight these dangers, concerned authors issued a dire warning. If released from restraint by the machinations of misguided philanthropists or through individual acts of self-theft, the average slave was likely to devolve into "a drone or knave . . . the mere barbarian he begun." Close supervision had to be maintained at all times lest the bondsman's "natural tiger-like disposition get the upper hand" and bring "*death* to the planter."[26]

Remarkably, then, pro- and antislavery authors found common ground on at least one key point. Despite serious disagreement over the question of whether or not black slavery was an unmitigated evil, both groups held that evil blacks were a menace to white society. Whether the roots of their supposed barbaric tendencies were located in deepest, darkest Africa or in the environs of the American South was a question that would be debated endlessly. Determined early on was the "fact" of black brutishness and the immediate, decidedly visceral threat this condition posed to white people.

Fictionalized accounts of slave revolts provided an appropriately dramatic setting for black brutes. Here, they could display their most aberrant behaviors *and* make what white authors hoped would become definitive statements on abolishing/expanding America's system of racial slavery. Predictably, northern and antislavery writers claimed the bondsmen were driven to rebellion by privation and abuse. Placing these violent acts in historical context, some cited "Christian precedent" for the slaves' use of "sword, and fire . . . to break their galling yokes."[27] Southern and proslavery voices countered with testimonials to the planters' success in modifying their servants' "heedless and irresponsible temperament." Insurgent slaves were rare, they noted—typically the product of lax discipline. But the few exceptions were used to reiterate an important plantation rule of thumb: Even a seemingly docile servant could revert to Old World ways and become "the most irreclaimable of culprits."[28] Both ideological camps portrayed black rebels as savage beings whose conscienceless acts of retribution made them appear demonic.

Whether sparked by the whipping of a loved one or the reading of an abolitionist tract, rebellious behavior in slaves often was said to be accompanied by manifestations of brutishness. Overcome by passions normally held in check by the "artificial constraint" of white law, slave rebels became "altered" men. Such was the case with Thomas, a character in Richard Hildreth's antislavery novel, *The White Slave*. After his wife died as the result of an overseer's abuse, it was noted that the grieving bondsman's "countenance grew convulsed; his bosom heaved; and he only found relief in half-uttered threats and muttered execrations." Before long, the formerly upright, obedient slave took to strong drink and began to neglect his appearance. Periods of sullenness alternated with wildly incoherent ramblings. "Blood for blood," he raged, promising vengeance on the cruel white man. Eventually, even coconspirators voiced the fear that Thomas was suffering from "fits of partial insanity."[29]

Unkempt and savage in appearance, slave insurrectionists who resembled "the ourang outang mixed with the devil" often frequented desolate, densely forested locales.[30] Like Harriet Beecher Stowe's swamp-dwelling fugitive, Dred, they may have compared themselves to "John the Baptist in the wilderness, girding himself with camel's hair, and eating locusts and wild honey," but acquaintances had grave doubts about the nature of the black militant's religious walk. "Chile," warned one fellow bondsman, "you take care! Keep clear on him! He's in de wilderness of Sinai; he is with de blackness, and darkness, and tempest. He han't come to de heavenly Jerusalem." Dressing oddly and speaking a "wild jargon of hebraistic phrases, names, and allusions," rebels such as Dred were suspected of mixing Christian belief with ancient superstition. They saw visions, charmed snakes, and claimed to be gifted with second sight. Overt displays of these "peculiar magical powers" encouraged some in the belief that the professed prophet actually was possessed by an evil spirit.[31]

Because actions tend to speak louder than words, there was ample support for this claim. Imagining themselves to be "an instrument of doom in a mightier hand," rebels struck out at white oppressors with an almost super-natural vengeance.[32] Wholly lacking in restraint, such assaults were said to be driven by "blind malice." Even whites who were "guiltless of wrong, and . . . deserving of affection and gratitude" were shown no mercy. Pikes, bludgeons, butcher knives, scythes, and sickles cut a broad and bloody swath through the southern gentry. As in *Sheppard Lee* by physician-playwright Robert Montgomery Bird, wives and teenaged daughters of slaveholders might be spared, but only because they were to be apportioned as spoils of battle. "I'll be de great man, and I shall hab my choice ob de women," the leader of Bird's rebels boasted to a subordinate. "You shall hab Massa Maja's wife, and you shall cut his head off fust. As faw de oder niggas he-ah, what faw use ob quar'lin? We shall have wifes enough when we kills white massas; gorry! we shall hab pick!" Fearing above all else a black man's "impure touch," some of the women opted to "escape by death a fate otherwise in-evitable." Unfortunately, antebellum readers of these nightmare tales were even less able to escape being confirmed in the belief that a discontented slave was "a devil incarnate . . . bold, cunning, and eager for blood."[33]

Both anti- and proslavery writers attempted to allay white anxiety. Some counseled bondsmen to "bear meekly—as ye've borne—your cruel woes" until reformers succeeded in transforming southern institutions.[34] Others chose to focus on penitent rebels or on the severe punishments meted out in the aftermath of failed uprisings.[35] But none of these approaches could allay the primal fears generated by black brutes. Even when not engaged in active rebellion, they elicited feelings of dread. As shown in fictional works by William Gilmore Simms and Mary Langdon, ties of ethnic kinship were no guarantee of protection against a slave whose lack of human compassion "made cruelty itself draw back appalled." Enemies of all ethnic backgrounds were well advised to steer clear of the bondsman who was so fond of inflicting pain as to declare: "I don't like ter have folks *die,*—dat's too good, de a'n't no pain in *dat,* I likes ter have 'em live, . . . so I can do it again."[36] Worst of all was the lingering suspicion that *all* slaves felt this way and were capable of such deeds.

Akin to whistling in the dark to sustain courage, denial of the brute's om-nipresence was the ultimate in antebellum era wishful thinking. Although the fact was disguised by white authors' fixation on less threatening character types, black brutes were always lurking in the shadows of the Big House. Like most villains, these fictional evildoers were inscrutable and deceptive. As was said of Dred, whites found it extremely "difficult to fathom the dark recesses of a mind so powerful and active . . . , placed under a pressure of ignorance and social disability so tremendous."[37] Moreover, brutish slaves typically possessed the ability to move from servility to sadism at will, easily misleading the unwary as to their true nature. "Dey's all like me," cackled one such mean-spirited bondsman who appeared in Langdon's *Ida May*, "ony dey keeps it in, . . . and dey *purtends—dey purtends.* . . ."[38] Posing an obvious threat to the societal equilibrium, brute slaves *had* to be seen as aberrations by white America. Their widespread existence was a prospect too terrible to contemplate. Whenever it was—even in a literary or theatrical context—the white community's psychic panic button flashed red.

No pre–Civil War author was more effective in revealing the psychological roots of this fear than Edgar Allan Poe. In *The Narrative of Arthur Gordon Pym*, the master poet and storyteller created a Manichaean fantasy world where seemingly harmless noble savages on an uncharted South Seas island were revealed to be murderous fiends. Tsalal (Hebrew for "shadow") was a land of darkness situated close by the geo-mass of polar whiteness known as Antarctica. Here, both the native flora and fauna were black. In fact, no light-colored substance of any kind could be seen. Upon entering this extraordinary world, a group of white explorers found the inhabitants primitive but unexpectedly friendly. Prone to childlike fits of thigh-slapping laughter, Chief Too-wit and his cave-dwelling subjects were inquisitive and ever so accommodating. Efforts to establish a barter system went smoothly. The blacks "fully delighted in the exchange," frequently offered their goods "without price," and "never, in any instance, pilfer[ed] a single article."[39] It seemed too good to be true.

As the voyagers prepared to leave Tsalal, it became apparent that the natives' expressions of kindness were part of a carefully calculated plan designed to bring about the whites' destruction. Fearing—and therefore hating—anyone and anything not of their own dark color, Too-wit's warriors gave no quarter on the field of battle. Surging forward in quest of plunder, the black warriors howled "like wild beasts" and never stopped to attend to their own wounded. Those in the white party who managed to avoid being "overwhelmed, trodden under foot, and absolutely torn to pieces" by the rampaging Tsalalians concluded that their relentless adversaries were, without a doubt, "the most wicked, hypocritical, vindictive, bloodthirsty, and altogether fiendish race of men upon the face of the globe."[40]

First published in 1838, Poe's novel was more than a simple adventure tale about polar exploration. It was an allegorical observation on the most critical black-white polarities of the day. In *Gordon Pym*, Poe identified and probed the chief racial fears of white Americans. Its dark waters offering a stark contrast to the continual daylight of the Antarctic region, Tsalal was the slaveholders' hell. Populated by noble savages and grotesques gone totally brutish, the exotic land was part of a mystical "region of novelty and wonder"—but also of death. Indeed, interlopers unable to recognize that black-skinned peoples frequently camouflaged their true nature were shown to have paid a high price for naïveté. Unceasing vigilance not only was encouraged; it was mandated.[41]

Like the Old World masques and plays that color-coded group distinctives, Poe's racial parable was strikingly direct. It never mentioned cotton plantations or rebellious slaves, but its message cut through the tedious rhetoric of the antebellum nature/nurture debate and superseded all manner of convoluted political arguments about the viability of black slavery. Here, the essential wisdom was as follows: literary and theatrical attempts to comfort the public with less troubling visions were deceptive and dangerous. In the end, it was the brute black—more precisely, the brutishness and villainy of blacks—that would have to be faced.

SLAVE CODES

To ascertain how white America sought to meet this challenge, one need look no further than the various state legal codes of the pre–Civil War years. But due caution is recommended. Legal statutes of any kind and from any age can mislead. They often misrepresent actual behavior—thereby calling into question the abolitionists' claim that southerners rarely, if ever, gave "public license to evil practices not prevalent among them, and which they do not intend to practise and sustain."[42] Frequently, laws reflect the desires of a single economic class or politically influential interest group. In such cases, the view that southern slave codes constituted "a faithful exposition of the sentiments of the people" should be treated with considerable skepticism.[43] Some laws outlive their usefulness but remain "on the books" for years. Others are passed with great ceremony and then only sporadically enforced. Little wonder, then, that historians of the American South have been known to puzzle over whether a specific piece of legislation established a precedent or was merely a belated response to already existing social practices. And how can one ever hope to be absolutely certain whether an ameliorative law was a sign of moral enlightenment or of the planters' desire to quell open discontent, thereby increasing profits?

Fortunately, to recognize these problems is the first step toward surmounting them. When used with care, the slave codes reveal a great deal about white Americans' perceptions of blacks and about how white-controlled institutions faced (or evaded) the contradictions created when a society chooses to classify people as chattel property. In such laws, disruptive race-influenced behavior was revealed to be more than a theatrical convention. It was considered a serious problem with the potential to subvert established political, economic, and social relationships. If contemporary lawmakers frequently exaggerated the danger that slaves posed to the security of white settlements, their passionate deliberations and the statutes they crafted have provided researchers with a detailed psychological portrait of majoritarian fears. Premised on the notion that any bondsman was capable of committing the grossest of misdeeds at any time, expansive, decidedly draconian slave laws sought to bring reassurance that no racial cataclysm was in the offing.

The influence of early American slave codes extended well beyond the courtroom. Slave law sanctioned group mores and behaviors. Although typically crafted by elites, the statutes educated the general public in the belief that, as chattels, blacks were to be seen as "things." This was neither the law of nature or of nature's God, but of white opinion shapers who viewed the African American as "naturally mendacious, and . . . thievish."[44] As Chief Justice Roger B. Taney would write in the *Dred Scott* decision of 1857, blacks were considered "beings of an inferior order, and altogether unfit to associate with the white race, either in social or political relations; and so far inferior, that they had no rights which the white man was bound to respect."[45] Cut off from any claim to customary human rights, black slaves were labeled and treated as villains by several generations of American lawmakers. With eradication of the villains' threat high on every slaveholding community's civic agenda, the control of black "crime" became inextricably linked to the preservation of the Old South labor system and to the solidification of white hegemony.

Lawmakers addressed the problems created by misbehaving slaves in several ways. First, they defined the parameters of villainy by legislating against the pernicious behaviors to which black villains were said to be prone. Then, they attempted to isolate presumed malefactors from potential allies. Finally, detailed legal procedures and systems of punishment were established that served to (1) put the fear of God and the gallows pole into bondsmen and (2) rationalize both the keeping of slaves and the corollary ideology of white supremacy.

During the seventeenth and eighteenth centuries, lawmakers operated on the assumption that slaves were masters of deception. A supposed habituation to illegal acts made it imperative that black badmen be accomplished skulkers and expert liars. To counteract these disruptive tendencies, legislation was enacted that limited slaves' rights to assembly and established nighttime curfews. Access to strong drink—even cider, in some places—was restricted. Possession of dangerous weapons—including large sticks and walking canes—was forbidden. Preparation or administration of medicine and the building of bonfires by slaves were made illegal in order to guard against poisonings and arson. In many cases, the white citizenry was obliged to supplement surveillance efforts of local police by conducting periodic cabin searches. Some governmental units were quite specific about what measures the public needed to take in order to defend against the villains' wiles. A 1770 Georgia act, for example, required all white males to be armed with "a gun, or a pair of pistols . . . with at least six charges of gunpowder and ball."[46] If such vigilance resulted in the capture of black perpetrators, it was assumed that the slaves' "base and corrupt natures" prevented them from providing reliable court testimony.[47] Thus, in 1737, when the clerk of a York County, Virginia, court recorded the name of a bondsman accused of stealing an ax as "Toney alias Dick alias Jack," he was simply reiterating the commonplace understanding that such defendants were practiced deceivers who could be trusted only to be untrustworthy.[48]

Government officials also understood the military principle of divide and conquer. Like fingers on a hand prevented from forming a fist, deceptive blacks were to be kept from joining in a common cause. The resulting, artfully crafted statutes prevented slaves from congregating in large groups (i.e., more than three in some instances), visiting neighboring plantations for more than a few hours at a time, and traveling on little-used roads or during the nighttime hours. A South Carolina law of 1722 prevented bondsmen from keeping and breeding horses that could be used to "convey intelligences from one part of the country to another, and carry on their secret plots and contrivances for insurrections and rebellions."[49] Motivated by similar concerns, Georgia lawmakers forbade slaves to possess drums, horns, and other "loud Instruments" because they could be used to "give Sign or Notice to one another of their wicked Designs."[50] Potential nonblack allies were discouraged from joining in these conspiratorial activities by legislation that mandated stiff penalties for persuading servants to leave their owners or for engaging in any sort of unauthorized trade with slaves. In some locales, the principle of guilt by association was written into statute law, and it became illegal for a white person to be found drinking with an assumed black villain.

The punishments meted out to villainous blacks were designed to stimulate deep slave-quarter contemplation of sin's wages. Virginia, alone, sent 983 slaves into exile between 1801 and 1865, condemned at least 555 to death between 1706 and 1784, and executed 628 in the eighty years after 1785.[51] Here, as elsewhere, whipping was a favored penalty for all manner of infractions but could be joined with even more extreme measures such as branding or ordering a misbehaving slave's ears to be nailed to the pillory and then lopped off. Some districts made corporal punishment of slaves "progressive"—in a wholly negative sense. For example, in early eighteenth-century South Carolina, first-time fugitives from plantation justice could expect to receive up to forty lashes for remaining at large more than twenty days. A second escape would cause the fugitive to be branded on the cheek with the letter "R." A third resulted in the loss of an ear. Further recidivism was discouraged by the threat (to males) of castration or additional branding and ear cropping (of females). Slaves who chose to disregard this stern warning—and who managed to survive yet another mutilation—would have their Achilles tendon severed after a sixth attempt at flight.[52] Codes such as the South Carolina act of 1712 resulted in governmentally sanctioned modes of slave "correction" that were scarcely less harsh than those to which colonial-era witches and traitors were subjected. Moreover, in their employment of emasculative surgery, white lawmakers seemed to be borrowing from early animal husbandry manuals that recommended gelding for particularly unruly bulls and stallions. To many lawmakers of the day, such comparisons seemed appropriate. Habitually insubordinate slaves were viewed as traitorous, animalistic, and possessed by evil spirits—the consummate villains. Surely individuals as dangerous as these would have to be kept under close supervision until such time as slaveholder wardens felt they were fit for parole.

Strictly enforced codes were meant to deter "crime" in incompletely acculturated black populations, thereby protecting the peculiar institution against subversion from within. They also served as encouragements to white supremacist beliefs. By establishing substantially different procedures for dealing with slave and nonslave criminals, American lawmakers privileged whiteness in a manner that could have only the most negative consequences for the nation's racial future. In North Carolina, a law of 1715 directed the state's special slave courts to try bondsmen "guilty of any crime or Offense." This volte-face effectively inverted the traditional assumption that a defendant was innocent until proven guilty beyond a reasonable doubt. A later statute sentenced whites convicted of maliciously murdering a slave to a year's imprisonment. They would have to be convicted of a second slave murder before receiving the death penalty. Such incidents weren't even considered capital crimes if the slave perished "in the Act of Resistance to his lawful Owner" or died "under Moderate Correction."[53] South Carolina's 1740 code made all crimes for which whites could be arraigned criminal when committed by a slave, but slaves could be prosecuted for many additional offenses as well. "Blacks-only" capital crimes included poisoning, attempted poisoning, wounding or striking (third offense) a white person, and burning crops. Under the code, slave testimony was severely restricted. Bondsmen could testify in trials of other blacks but were prohibited from contradicting any statement of a white witness or prosecutor.[54] In 1765 Virginia's legislature allowed slaves convicted of manslaughter to plead for benefit of clergy—a one-time reprieve from execution—but only when the victim was another slave. It was not until 1792 that bondsmen could plead self-defense when "wantonly assaulted" by a white person. By the time of the Civil War, there were more than sixty offenses for which Virginia slaves could be condemned to death that would result in a lesser punishment if committed by a nonslave.[55]

Differential treatment before the law was a fact of African American life in all slaveholding districts. Each slave state's legal code was peppered with such legislation. If punishments were made less severe over time, white law continued to delimit and degrade black humanity. By placing a far higher value on white lives than on black, America's governing elite institutionalized the belief that "good" and "bad" were color-coded values. As a result, a white person accused of committing an offense against a slave was given the benefit of the doubt by fellow whites. Too black—and, therefore, too villainous to benefit from skin-color privilege—slaves accused of similar crimes found the scales of justice weighted against them. African Americans were treated as dangerous criminals so frequently that it was difficult for many whites to conceptualize them as innocent victims of the nation's greatest crime.

PATRIARCHAL MANAGEMENT

The various state legal codes set behavioral standards and influenced public sentiment, but they were not the slaveholder's only guide to successful plantation management. Because the long arm of the law sometimes failed to reach isolated frontier regions with any degree of regularity, swift and sure punishment often had to be meted out by the planters themselves. More than willing to don Solomon's robes, it was the resident patriarch, not some far-distant legislator or judge, who most frequently determined what constituted justice. In the process of doing so, these agricultural elites also revealed the importance of black villainy for white self-definition.

As modern-day scholars such as Bertram Wyatt-Brown and Kenneth Greenberg have shown, wealthy slaveholders viewed themselves as fair-minded and honorable men.[56] Convinced that inner virtue was reflected in public actions, southern gentlemen professed to reject all that was lowly, alien, and shamed. A slave, they said, was a person without honor and there-fore prone to dishonorable deeds. If planters were to be true to their assigned station in life, they had to police their own moral sphere. But, in addition, a righteous representative of the patriarchal order had to create functioning be-havioral codes for members of their slave-quarter community. Ideally, such guides would establish a well-defined chain of command, list unacceptable workforce practices (as well as penalties for engaging in them), and encour-age the laborers in moral uplift. From the patriarch's perspective, such rules were at least as important as any handed down by more formally constituted legislative bodies.

Throughout the Old South, a large, smoothly running agricultural opera-tion was viewed as proof of its director's wisdom, skill, and patience. Status-conscious peers identified with such individuals, deeming them worthy of respect and emulation. To fall short of the goal—to allow one's estate to be overrun by dissembling slaves—was considered far more than a personal failure. It was viewed as a disservice to family, region, class, and race. On the other hand, each unauthorized, underhanded deed committed by a roguish slave served to differentiate honorable masters from dishonorable servants. In effect, the planters couldn't live with and couldn't live without black vil-lains. White elites may have defined black villainy in both cultural and legal terms, but black villains were equally capable of giving definition to white honor. Even as ill-behaving slaves tested the established mechanisms for maintaining plantation discipline, they enhanced whites' view of themselves as virtuous and benevolent.

If generally unacknowledged, this love-hate relationship is evidenced in the advice white southerners gave one another on the subject of slave man-agement. A frequent topic of discussion in southern agricultural journals, African Americans' lack of honor was considered an unfortunate fact of na-ture. "Negroes are troublesome customers any way you can fix them," con-cluded Georgia physician John Stainback Wilson. Even "the little 'niggers'" of the plantation South were "prone to commence . . . depredations" on the possessions and property of unwary whites.[57] Other seasoned observers agreed wholeheartedly—as if this mantra of unanimity, by itself, would alleviate the problem. Commiserating with fellow sufferers, they spoke often of blacks' "tyrannical . . . dispositions" and the way slave husbands abused their wives and mothers mistreated their children. They warned of the "natural fickleness . . . always dominant in inferior animal natures" that caused the men of the slave community to "violate their marriage obligations" by engaging in "roving licentiousness."[58] Above all, they recommended self-discipline and patience to every white person forced to deal daily with the ignorance, improvidence, and deceptions of black slaves.

The vexing flaws observed in the slaveholders' rough-hewn workers were to be lamented but could not be allowed to impede American economic and commercial growth. Planters were honor-bound to address this problem by adopting managerial practices capable of counteracting the negative race-based traits of slaves. Believing that a bondsman's character was "like the plastic clay, which may be moulded into agreeable or disagreeable figures, according to the skill of the moulder," they were hopeful that observable changes in slave behavior would result from sound techniques, sanely applied.[59] All seemed eager to display their mastery of the patriarchal arts by sharing a favored remedy for slave dissembling:

> Marriage at home, should be encouraged among them. The practice of taking wives abroad, should as much as possible be prevented. It engenders a habit of rambling, which is injurious to the constitution of the negro, besides removing him frequently, and at important times from the influence of the domestic police, which should be always strict. "Give the negro an inch, and he will as surely take an ell."[60]

> There should be a rule, and suitable provision and arrangement for the washing, and . . . this should constitute a part of the established plantation regulation. I am very much inclined to the opinion that cleanliness is not only promotive of health, but he who carries a dirty skin and wears a dirty shirt, will be very apt to do dirty deeds.[61]

> If there be a church in the vicinity of the planter's residence, he should oblige all of his negroes to attend it. . . . This has an excellent effect. Most negroes take Sunday as their day of visiting; and it not unfrequently happens, that they do more mischief on that day . . . than on any other. Now, the attendance upon church permits them to meet their relatives and friends there, and, at the same time, keeps them out of all mischief.[62]

It was assumed that the adoption of practices such as these would promote acceptable slave behavior, thereby enhancing a planter's reputation as a
wise and skillful steward of human and material resources. Conversely, improper plantation management was perceived as dishonorable and dangerous. As noted in numerous articles in antebellum agricultural papers, lax
governance of one's estate was considered tantamount to relinquishing control to a band of black brigands. "Many a negro who would never have committed a theft in the course of a long life, with a careful overseer or master,
has not been able to resist the temptation, when a careless overseer or master
has left keys lying about," wrote a Virginia planter in 1834. "And when once
the ice is broken and they lose character, they soon become hardened in villainy."[63] Here, the wrongheaded acts of whites were seen as having disadvan-
tageous effects on blacks. Agricultural elites who would admit to this degree
of culpability were forced to grapple with the unsettling possibility that in-
cautious slaveholders were creating legions of potentially disruptive slaves.

Fearing societal upheaval and financial ruin, veteran planters encouraged
employment of managerial practices designed to forestall the bondsmen's
devolution into abject villainy. In addition to removing obvious temptations
like quarters' card playing, access to grog shops, and attendance at political
rallies where "the sayings and doings of abolitionists are freely proclaimed,"
planters were to carefully monitor their own behavior whenever in a slave's
presence. Some advised against overfamiliarity and "loose and irregular" systems of discipline where slaves were, in effect, "as free as the master."[64] But a
significant number went on record as favoring a more personalized, decidedly more humane approach. Understanding that it was easier to catch flies
with honey than with vinegar, they warned that persistent scolding rendered
some slaves "stupid and foolish." Others were transformed into "hardened,
perverse, stubborn scoundrels" or "hopeless vagabonds, and confirmed runaways" by a planter's fulminations. By proceeding even further on this perilous course, a harsh disciplinarian risked breaking the slave's spirit through
excessive physical punishment. This, too, was considered counterproductive
because gross mistreatment or deprivation caused field hands to become
"unprofitable, unmanageable; a vexation and a curse." Thus, all who aspired
to having successful dealings with slaves were advised to heed this common-
sense wisdom: "He who fights most, and blusters most, and threatens most,
is not the man who has the most work done." When treated fairly, bondsmen
would have every reason to be obedient and none to play the villain. Slave behavior could be altered without recourse to dishonorable techniques. As one

plainspoken Virginia sage recommended, "The very best remedy for hog stealing is to give the rogues a plenty of pork to eat."[65]

Obviously, these notions of the ideal in plantation management were an imperfect guide to actual practices. How often slaveholders heeded their own advice could be determined with any degree of certainty only by individuals whose testimony had little or no standing in American law. Even so, this flawed database can be used to gain a better understanding of the psychology of slaveholding and of southern whites' connection to black villainy. In truth, plantation elites gave just the sort of advice one would expect to receive from honorable men with reputations to protect. Even as they were ennobled by efforts to reform black humanity, the constant frustrations of slave management provided ample opportunity to contrast African American and European American behavioral traits. Sympathetic white contemporaries couldn't help but view them as generous, self-sacrificing individuals whose campaign to eradicate the stain of black villainy was essential to societal stability. But the purported difficulty of the task also permitted slaveholders to call for continued vigilance against as-yet-unreconstructed slave villains— and to do so without sounding like cowards or hypocrites.

PROSLAVERY THOUGHT

During the antebellum era, all manner of white Americans struggled to perfect social, cultural, and legal mechanisms that would distinguish white from black, bond from free, honor from dishonor, and vice from virtue. Throughout these years, white people needed black villains to authenticate their freedom, establish the fact of their honor, and facilitate the transformation of their vices into virtues.

Assisting in this process was a determined cohort of proslavery ideologues. Resident in both northern and southern states, they were drawn from a broad cross-section of those white Americans who possessed both a modicum of literary/oratorical ability and the courage of their convictions. Although more easily recognized after the abolitionist movement caught fire during the 1830s, individuals promoting racially inegalitarian belief systems had been present from the earliest years of the Republic. Over time and in response to the abolitionist critique of southern institutions, proslavery adherents crafted an influential series of arguments in support of state's rights, King Cotton, and perpetual servitude for blacks. By the end of the antebellum period, their views on slavery and race could be seen in novels and plays, in history texts, and throughout the periodical press. These skewed but con-

vincingly presented beliefs provided a subtext for virtually all proslavery legislation and helped many planters deal with a troubled conscience.

As they worked to defend Old South institutions, proslavery theorists
elaborated on favored themes. Slavery, they said, was a divinely approved
plan to bring civilization to primitive Africans and, while engaged in this
lengthy process, to protect them against self-destructive tendencies. It also
was a time-tested social mechanism for elevating the character of the master
class—making the prototypical slaveholder "lofty and independent in his
sentiments, generous, affectionate, brave and eloquent." Any significant disturbance of this system would disrupt the educational and moral advancement of "the happiest three millions of human beings on whom the sun
shines." In addition, the future of white society would be imperiled. Without
the beneficent influence of slavery to ameliorate the most barbarous aspects
of their nature, blacks would again be free to act the savage—a condition
from which even those who benefited most from whites' "fostering care"
were never far removed.[66]

According to proslavery writers, to reject this worldview was to place oneself on the wrong side of a great moral chasm—and thereby don the guise of
Satan. Indeed, all who posed threats to the continued growth and prosperity
of the southern labor system were vilified in one way or another. White northern reformers—especially those calling for immediate emancipation—were
likened to Jacobins and accused of instigating insurrectionary plots. Proponents of gradual emancipation fared only slightly better. Their piecemeal approach to black freedom was said to foster discontent, therefore endangering
the status quo. Free blacks, even if unaffiliated with organized reform, also
were considered "moral conductor[s] . . . of mischief." Stereotyped as racial
bad examples, these "*drones* and *pests*" of southern society stood accused of
encouraging still-enslaved African Americans to conceive of liberty as "idleness and sloth with the enjoyment of plenty." If allowed unsupervised access
to the plantations, they would corrupt their black brothers and sisters—
prompting slaves to scheme, steal, and dissemble. In effect, slaveholders
viewed the activities of all meddlesome outsiders as encouragements to
temptation. And, as pointed out by Virginia educator and essayist Thomas R.
Dew in 1832, every white southerner with experience in slave management
knew only too well that "strong temptation makes the villain."[67]

Ranging far and wide, across the learned disciplines, and back into history, proslavery writers searched for data that would support their beliefs. The
most diligent discovered a wealth of useful information in the interrelated
literatures of moral philosophy and pre–Civil War science. These findings

seemed to offer conclusive proof that black villainy—unlike that to which white abolitionists were prone—was part of the natural order. It was hoped that this new evidence could be used to supplement Bible-based theories of black inferiority—and to do so in a manner acceptable to the leading lights of both contemporary science and religion. If skillfully crafted, arguments incorporating these perspectives had the potential to convince all open-minded individuals of the continued need for black supervision under slavery.

At the center of this expansive body of proslavery thought lay a most controversial premise: the European and African branches of humankind differed so greatly that they may have been separate creations. During the latter half of the eighteenth century, American and European intellectuals were attracted to this notion but feared that they would be considered heretics for amending the Genesis account of a single Eden. As a result, they were forced to go through all manner of mental gymnastics to explain the origin of racial differences. Some, like Scottish philosopher Lord Kames, refused any longer to countenance the Old Testament commentaries related to Canaan's Africanization and began to search the Scriptures in the hope of discovering new interpretive models. Kames found his alternative Creation story in the eleventh chapter of Genesis: after being "scattered everywhere" by the linguistic "confusion" at the Tower of Babel, each group of pilgrims was forced to adapt to new regions and climates. Those who made their way to sub-Saharan Africa were isolated from the mainstream of civilization and became progenitors of a dark-skinned savage race.[68] Other equally inventive theorists placed all living things in rank order via a hierarchical construction known as the Great Chain of Being. Inevitably, the black race was situated last among the various gradations of humankind—just above the great apes and far removed from God and the angels.[69] Still other commentators courted controversy by melding scientific and proslavery thought. For example, in his *Notes on the State of Virginia*, first published in 1787, Thomas Jefferson voiced the suspicion that "whether originally a distinct race, or made distinct by time and circumstances," blacks were inferior to whites in "the endowments both of body and mind." While disavowing any mean-spirited attempt to "degrade" the African race, he nevertheless noted that nature's distinctions were proving an insurmountable obstacle to the emancipation of America's slaves.[70] Full-blown polygenism would make it permissible to maintain that slavery was a social institution well suited to the limited abilities of a separately created black race.

By the time of the Civil War, proslavery ethnologists Josiah Nott and George Gliddon had it all sorted out. Each race had "an especial destiny."

Some were born to rule; others to be ruled. In all ages, they said, the Caucasian race had been "teeming with gigantic intellects" and therefore was "destined eventually to conquer and hold every foot of the globe where climate does not interpose an impenetrable barrier." Africa, on the other hand, was the homeland of "a succession of human beings with intellects as dark as their skins." This unfortunate congenital condition rendered any expectation of radical improvement a "Utopian dream, philanthropical, but somewhat senile." History, then, affirmed that neither formal education nor "any influence of civilization" was capable of producing marked changes in either the physical or moral character of a race handicapped by "inferior organization."[71] If not as widely accepted as the ancient curse of Ham, this mid-nineteenth-century polygenist vision consigned the darkest-skinned variant of humankind to a similarly bleak future.

Belief in a biologically ordered system of explaining racial hierarchies provided whites with a pseudoscientific security blanket. Not only were European Americans flattered by the many superlatives that graced descriptions of their ancestors in virtually all contemporary ethnological studies, but they no longer had to fret over the possibility that noncomplexional distinctions would generate political factionalism and class conflict. When compared to the vast hereditary chasm that separated African from Caucasian, the "petty distinctions of human pride, vanity, and accident" seemed somehow insignificant.[72] Nevertheless, there was no sating an avid researcher's appetite for documenting black inferiority. As the abolitionist crusade advanced, scholars of the polygenist persuasion published numerous works delineating race-based differences. In this manner, American and English academicians produced the first quantifiable measurements of African American villains.

In order to test the proposition that blacks composed an intermediate species that bridged the gap between European American and ape, contemporary scientists employed what were considered the most advanced, objective methodologies available. After skull capacities and facial angles were measured, hair textures examined, and cadavers probed, they concluded that the anatomical dissimilarity between black and white was "greater than the difference in the skeletons of the Wolf, Dog and Hyena, which are allowed to be distinct species."[73] This remarkable discovery of "deep, radical and enduring differences" between the races was based on the following, equally astounding, findings:

A negro's head was covered with a type of dark-colored "pile" that differed only from sheep's wool in its degree of "felting power." By way of contrast, the hair of Caucasians was far more complex in its construction and, therefore, could be considered "more perfect" hair.[74]

"The negro is not only a negro on the skin, but under the skin." Muscle and tendon, blood, bile, and sweat—even the central nervous system, brain, and other internal organs of blacks were "tinctured with a shade of the pervading darkness."[75]

On average, the capacity of a Negro's skull was nine cubic inches less than a white person's. Particularly defective in "the anterior or intellectual lobes," blacks' "imperfect" brain was comparable to that of "a 7 month's infant in the womb of the White."[76]

All members of the black race emitted a "strong odor." When "warmed by exercise" or "intoxicated with pleasure"—as would be the case during plantation dances—the musk of the black male was so overwhelming that their partners often were thrown into "paroxysms of unconsciousness."[77]

Findings such as these enabled polygenist popularizers and their proslavery supporters to conclude that (1) the Garden of Eden was a Caucasians-only homeland and but one of several "primordial centres of the human family"; (2) a black skin provided prima facie evidence of gross anatomical imperfection and mental incapacity; and (3) the Negro was "a slave by nature, and can never be happy, industrious, moral, or religious, in any other condition than the one he was intended to fill."[78]

Antebellum revelations suggesting that members of the African race constituted a separate, decidedly inferior species made it easy for self-congratulatory whites to attribute a multitude of villainous traits to black slaves. Not to be overlooked, however, is the fact that even those thinkers who remained committed to a belief in the unity of the human race frequently depicted dark-skinned peoples as brutish. In such cases, it made little difference whether one accepted or rejected the notion that Africans were but lamp-blackened white men. Monogenetic portrayals of blacks as second-class citizens of the genus *Homo* were remarkably similar and, in some cases, virtually indistinguishable from those of the polygenists.

Guided by a belief in the proposition that the various races were varieties of a single human species made diverse through the effects of geography and climate, monogenists became firm friends of early antislavery activists. Their ostensibly nonhierarchical system of racial classification meshed well with both biblical revelation and the late eighteenth-century assumption that education and an improved social environment were the keys to universal human progress. As the general population became more secular and slavery was declared a positive good by southerners, Enlightenment tenets and environmentalist orientations declined in popularity within the scientific community. Stalwarts holding to the view that "all the tribes of men are of one family" continued to do battle with polygenists throughout the pre-Darwinian era but could not remain isolated from intellectual trends coursing through the larger society.[79] Despite professions of uncommon objectivity, these early scientists evidenced a commoner's susceptibility to the most bizarre tenets of racist mythology.

For many years, there was widespread disagreement over the number of human races. Estimates ran as high as sixty-three discrete groups.[80] Rarely were the systems developed to describe and classify these diverse populations free of bias. If not overtly racist, they were culturally chauvinistic. When constructed by a researcher of European heritage, one could be certain that white ancestors more often would be praised than pilloried. One of the earliest taxonomic works, the *Systema naturae* of eighteenth-century Swedish botanist Carolus Linnaeus, set the standard for later models. In dividing humankind into four major varieties, Linnaeus inexplicably mixed brief but vivid evaluations of racial temperament with anatomical descriptions. Men of the flaxen-haired, blue-eyed *Homo Europaeus* variety were described as "active" and "ingenious." They favored tailored clothing and were "governed by customs." The dark-skinned, "kinky"-haired *Homo Afer,* however, were considered "phlegmatic" and "indulgent." Governed by "whim," they were said to be crafty, lazy, and negligent.[81] Southern African Hottentots had considerable difficulty clearing the racial bar. Linnaeus considered but rejected the possibility that they actually were apes. Instead, he placed them in a catchall category, *Monstrosus,* alongside troglodytes and "large, indolent" Patagonians.[82] While not a strictly hierarchical ranking, the Linnaean system of imposing binomial order on the known biological universe clearly imputed racial rank and station.

This predisposition to denigrate dark-skinned varieties of the species was evidenced in later years by European and American researchers attached to the monogenist school. While noting that skin color, hair texture, and cranial shape were useful adaptations to life in the racial homelands that had been established after early humans moved from the site of Creation, many monogenists looked to such traits for evidence of divergence from Adamic norms. Over time, it was believed, each human variety had strayed from Eden's perfection. Because they had the good sense to make their homes in temperate climes, Europeans were said to have suffered the least pronounced decline, Africans the most severe. The long-term effects of climate, diet, and "force of custom" caused blacks to become the rudest sort of men—"hunters and savage inhabitants of forests" who had abandoned both hard labor and the "restraints and subordinations of civil society."[83] As English physician, linguist, and race theoretician James Cowles Prichard asserted in 1813, people residing in such inhospitable regions were forced to place considerable reliance on the senses of hearing, smell, and taste for their day-to-day survival. Consequently, they were far less able than Europeans to develop "a more capacious form of the skull . . . on which an increase of intellectual power is probably dependant." Thus, instead of advancing the frontiers of knowledge, the "African savage" lived naked amidst filth and depended upon the "spontaneous productions of the climate" to fill their larder. Even in modern times, noted Prichard, whenever an anthropological researcher came across a population of "barbarians running wild in the woods," their subjects were likely to be "Negroes, or very similar to Negroes."[84]

Some monogenists—most notably South Carolina minister and naturalist John Bachman and University of Virginia professor James Lawrence Cabell—believed that, over many generations, the various racial groups had become permanent varieties. Here, supposed proponents of human unity strayed perilously close to the biological racism of proslavery polygenists.[85] Others, like moral philosophy professor and ethnologist Samuel Stanhope Smith, maintained a firm faith in the transforming power of the environment. This emphasis on the "pliant nature of man" found favor with pre–Civil War reformers, buoying the hope that "progress in the arts of civilization" would lead to a corresponding improvement in the character of the American people.[86]

Typically, neither group of monogenists seemed capable of transcending Linnaeus's flawed relativism. Invariably, visions of brute blacks emerged whenever one of their number was asked to evaluate how well *Homo Afer* stacked up against the white competition. According to German craniologist Johann Friedrich Blumenbach, Caucasians had "that kind of appearance which, according to our opinion of symmetry, we consider most handsome." "Rosy" cheeks, a "full and rounded" chin, and an "oval, straight" face made these fortunate sons of Adam "the most beautiful race of men." Representative specimens of the "bandy-legged" Ethiopian variety fared less well in this anthropological beauty contest. Resting awkwardly beneath the African's "knotty, uneven" forehead was a thick, indistinct nose, a set of "very puffy" lips, and a "retreating" chin.[87] Similarly, uncomplimentary references to blacks' "uncouth peculiarities" could be found throughout the scientific literature of the day. "Discoloured" skin, distended lips, and the "prognathous form of the head" were said to "display themselves in proportion to the moral and physical degradation of the race."[88] And, one might add, in proportion to the Eurocentrism of the white observers.

Whether conducted by poly- or monogenist (or incorporated into pro- or antislavery arguments), early scientific research on racial origins endowed whiteness with a near-mythic status. Certainly, Blumenbach spoke for many of his colleagues when he asserted that white must have been "the primitive colour of mankind" because it was "very easy for that to degenerate into brown, but very much more difficult for dark to become white."[89] It was equally difficult for blacks to escape the fate of being seen as crude and barbaric when placed in the umbral shadow of this European American crown of creation. Dazzled by their own brilliance, whites easily confused essentialism with empiricism as they placed science in the service of racial subordination.

DAY-TO-DAY RESISTANCE

By midcentury, then, influential constituencies within the church, the state, and the scientific and the arts community had certified black slaves as members of an inferior and villainous race. Some profited directly from their exploitation of slave labor; others less tangibly from an assortment of skin-color privileges. Without exception, all feared the slave unchained and the turmoil that would result from any unrestrained expression of natural villainy. In both the public and private spheres, white anxiety over slave subversion peaked during times of open revolt. But these concerns often proved impossible to repress even after societal order had been restored. The slaves' day-to-day resistance kept whites on constant alert. Indeed, none knew the day or hour when a field hand's individual display of pique would spark a deadly conflagration. Many, however, understood plantation power relationships well enough to believe that such an event likely would occur without warning—instigated by a cohort of black villains. Frequent sightings of suspected subversives on the lam or in the process of purloining livestock spurred rumors of revolt, making insurrectionary activity seem imminent and, at times, omnipresent. As a result, slaves engaged in a variety of illegal activities were perceived as rebels in training and linked with societal upheaval.

If one assumes that it was in the slaveholder's best interest to be somewhat discreet in the reporting of plantation "crimes," it is reasonable to believe that modern-day historians are able to document only a small portion of the total number of day-to-day acts of resistance. Firsthand accounts produced by former bondsmen add detail to the picture, but these are limited in number; their focal areas dictated by the perceived needs of intended audiences. Even so, what we *do* know about the slaves' proto-insurrectionary activity confirms the antebellum belief that thievish rogues were everywhere.

Slaves stole both for immediate gratification and to obtain goods suitable for barter with unscrupulous millers, merchants, peddlers, and grog shop operators. They made nocturnal visits to chicken coops, hog pens, and smokehouses; refreshed themselves with libations found in unsecured liquor cabinets; and engaged in the unauthorized unloading of railroad cars. In lowland regions, they secreted baskets of rice from their owners' fields and hid the booty in the swamps—returning later to process the grain in mortars fashioned from hollowed-out tree stumps. In urban factories, they eroded profit margins by smuggling contraband in the folds of their clothing. Even mine operators complained about the continual draining of resources— which in some cases was occasioned by the black laborers' practice of concealing gold dust in their hair. Given the number and variety of complaints, it is not surprising to find that white southern churches more often disciplined their slave communicants for theft than for any other offense.[90] As one frustrated manager of slave iron workers wrote early in 1861, "I had a notion of Comeing down tomorrow evening, . . . but I am afraid if I leave here they will steal the place. They come very near it while I am here."[91]

Slaves also disrupted the pace of agricultural work. This revolt against white exploitation was characterized by purposeful malingering and the feigning of a variety of disabilities. Among the most egregious offenders were slave women whose recurring and little understood female complaints made them "nearly valueless" for work. Suspected of "play[ing] the lady," they capitalized on what one northern visitor described as the "liability of women . . . to disorders and irregularities which cannot be detected by exterior symptoms."[92] Other troublemakers included field hands who misplaced tools, maimed livestock, or falsified weights in order to meet daily quotas. Even planters who held that this "disinclination to labour" was a race-based trait were perturbed by the slaves' carelessness, their apparent indifference to the Protestant work ethic, and the disingenuous manner in which they attempted to disguise shortcomings.[93]

While whites considered duplicity to be "one of the most prominent traits" in the African American character, slaves rejected the notion that their petty thefts and job-related shirking constituted true villainy.[94] Careful to distinguish between stealing (from poor blacks) and taking (from wealthy whites), they attempted to justify the latter with claims that a slave could "never take nothin' but what been belong to him."[95] All such illicit appropriations were to be considered nothing more than belated compensation for services rendered. Here, the white South's decision to classify black bondsmen as "chattels personal" backfired. "If one piece of property took off another," wrote former slave Henry Bibb, "there could be no law violated in the act; no more sin committed in this than if one jackass had rode off another." According to black abolitionist Frederick Douglass, slave theft was to be conceptualized as more a "question of removal" than of dishonesty: "taking . . . meat out of one tub and putting it in another."[96] By adopting what historian Alex Lichtenstein has termed a "coherent counter-morality," the black plantation underclass was able to rationalize lawbreaking.[97] The most accomplished deceivers utilized it to contest dominant ideologies and economic relationships. Over time, the slaves' refusal to consider themselves criminals enabled them to shape their own definitions of good and evil; to define heroism and villainy in ways that were relevant to members of an oppressed caste. In such matters, the perceptual gap between master and slave proved as difficult to bridge as the racial gap. Neither was resolved by the events of the Civil War era.

RUNAWAYS

Convinced that slaves were improvident, unprincipled, and skilled in the art of "shamming illness" to avoid work, southern whites had little trouble believing that all would flee the plantations if given an opportunity.[98] Although greatly enhanced by rumor and myth, such concerns were valid. While the Underground Railroad seldom was overbooked, runaways were a persistent problem. Throughout the nineteenth century, perhaps as few as a thousand fugitives per year found sanctuary in the free states or Canada. But many others started freedom's journey only to be caught and remanded to their master's custody. Modern estimates suggest that by 1860 more than fifty thousand bondsmen were absconding annually.[99] In attempting to "steal" themselves, the discontented laborers caused their owners considerable inconvenience. Whether undertaken individually or in groups, acts of self-theft jeopardized public safety and threatened to sully the reputations of supposedly benevolent patriarchs.

Even if no harm was done to white people or their property, any slave temporarily free from institutional control was in revolt against duly constituted sources of authority. And this caused many whites to be in a state of denial. Refusing to admit that enslavement was, by itself, sufficient provocation, slaveholders frequently claimed that blacks fled without just cause and for reasons unknown. Instead of faulting the system, they blamed the victim— scapegoating runaways as base individuals motivated by criminal intent. As revealed in an advertisement seeking the return of a fugitive named Charles, such slaves were considered "extremely artful, and ready at inventing specious Pretences to conceal villainous Actions or Designs."[100] Capable of putting the fear of God—or, more correctly, of the Devil—in entire communities, a single black runaway cast a remarkably long shadow. White apprehensions magnified the actual threat posed by such slaves, influencing the way mainstream society viewed *all* African Americans.

In the ritual drama of plantation life, fugitive slaves were relegated to the role of "heavy." As if responding to a long-awaited call from central casting, these Old South hard cases seemed eager to prove themselves capable of making children cry, womenfolk swoon, and cats arch their backs. To angry, aggrieved slave owners, "artful" runaways like Charles were among the most loathsome of blackguards. Confirming white fears and reinforcing prevailing stereotypes, advertisements placed in local papers made such slaves appear every bit the bogeyman.[101]

They were ugly. Distinguishing characteristics included missing or rotted teeth, "pock-pitted" skin, and twisted limbs. Small, "hollow," reddish eyes and stooped shoulders gave some a "down cast sly Look." Others were made grotesque by the physical evidence of previous indiscretions: partially severed iron chains, shackles, and padlocks; cropped ears; and the letter "R" branded on forehead, cheek, or breast. Often, the backs of repeat offenders were "scarred with severe whipping, for running away."[102]

They were alien and barbaric. Ads seeking the return of "salt-water" Negroes described African-born fugitives as being thick-tongued and capable of speaking only "very indifferent English." Marks of ritual scarification, filed teeth, and African-style jewelry (or holes for brass rings and silver bobbins in the ears) differentiated them from more acculturated compatriots. Commonly referred to as "outlandish," that is, without skills or training in Western ways, they were thought to be more "depraved" than "country-born" chattels. "Coromantees" from the Gold Coast were deemed hardy and unafraid of danger, but ferocious when angered—unwilling to forgive any wrong done to them. Those shipped from ports in the Niger Delta were considered superstitious and suicidal. Angolans were born runaways. West Indian "refuse" slaves were incorrigible troublemakers. All could be transformed into caricatures of tragicomic jungle brutes by angry slaveholders. "A stately *Baboon* hath lately slipp'd his Collar and run away," noted one early eighteenth-century advertisement. "He is big-bon'd, full in Flesh, and has learn'd to walk very erect on his two Hind-Legs, he grins and chatters much, but will not bite, he plays Tricks impudently well, and is mightily given to clambering, whereby he often shews his A__."[103]

They were diseased. In addition to the ailments that have plagued humankind from time immemorial, black slaves were said to be susceptible to at least two serious, racially linked ailments. As described by Louisiana physician and future assistant surgeon general of the Confederacy, Samuel Cartwright, *Dysaesthesia Aethiopica* dulled its victim's intellectual faculties. Inadequate "decarbonization" of the bloodstream caused sufferers to wander about as if in "a half nodding sleep." Those most seriously afflicted were plagued by skin lesions and exhibited a variety of bizarre, destructive behaviors. They abused farm animals, broke tools, engaged in petty theft, and slighted fieldwork. Overseers labeled their condition "rascality." When punished for this unpremeditated mischief-making, the *bipedum nequissimus* ("arrant rascal") felt neither pain nor resentment but likely would continue to display a "stupid sulkiness" until receiving adequate treatment—that is, until they were put to "some hard kind of work in the open air and sunshine." In like manner, *Drapetomania,* a mental illness said to spur runaway attempts, was to be treated without recourse to pharmaceutics. It was believed that an absconding slave's alienation from their divinely assigned role as a "submissive knee-bender" could be alleviated by reestablishing "order and good discipline" on the plantation. A master who had gained a reputation for being both firm and fair was better able to exact "awe and reverence" from his servants and, thereby, prevent a reoccurrence of the troublesome disease.[104]

They were vice-ridden and deceitful. Slaveholders often voiced their frustration over the loss of bondsmen who fled in order to avoid punishment or sale. In such cases, self-theft was but the most recently reported incident in what could be a lengthy history of disruptive behavior. "He is greatly addicted to drink, and when drunk is insolent and disorderly," wrote Thomas Jefferson of a "corpulent" fugitive shoemaker named Sandy. "In his conversation he swears much, and his behavior is artful and knavish."[105] Owners of particularly roguish slaves were prompt to warn neighbors that one or more devilishly clever ruses likely would be employed to facilitate escape. Some even suggested that Old Nick was serving as a technical adviser in these deceptions.[106] Ads for fugitives told of slaves masquerading as free blacks, Indians,

Spaniards, or "Portugueze"; of women dressing as men and men attired in clothing "beyond their condition to purchase." Disguising intentions and identities beneath what Jefferson termed "that eternal monotony, . . . that immoveable veil of black which covers all [their] emotions," runaways feigned piety and humility, deafness and simplemindedness. With "bewitching and deceitful tongue[s]," they capitalized on their gift of glibness to bluff shamelessly and effectively. If questioned by suspicious whites, some runaways produced counterfeit passes, indentures, baptismal certificates, or freedom papers. Others employed aliases ("James, sometimes known by name Vulcan, but commonly answers to Buck"). One clever fugitive from an eighteenth-century Pennsylvania estate was said to be capable of "alter[ing] his voice on each extreme." All claimed to be "about . . . masters business."[107]

They were a financial drain. Slaves who absented themselves from their labors for even a short period of time caused whites to incur a variety of unbudgeted expenses. To the eventual cost of replacing appropriated food, clothing, currency, and items such as knives, swords, guns, and the occasional horse or canoe, planters were obliged to add service fees levied in connection with apprehending their valuable human property. Expenditures for newspaper ads, postage, informant's and captor's rewards, and workhouse charges could be burdensome. Jailers had to be paid for food, travel expenses, and any whipping, branding, or ear cropping ordered as punishment; storekeepers and neighboring slaveholders reimbursed for damage or theft. If runaways were frequent, a planter might try to trim expenses by placing a joint advertisement in a local paper—listing rewards and noting that "many of the Negroes . . . are constantly running away."[108] Far more difficult to reduce was the psychic cost of living with the knowledge that a fugitive's expression of personal autonomy likely would encourage others to test their master's authority, thereby lowering both comfort levels and profit margins even further.

Above all, they were not alone. It was only to be expected that the prototypical single male fugitive would seek refuge among potential allies. Here, in backcountry lairs, they would league together with one or more groups of certified social outcasts to wreak havoc on the plantations. The following topped the slaveholders' short list of usual suspects:

Maroons. A constant temptation to well-behaved black servants, independent communities of runaways were neither as populous nor as powerful as the *cimmarones, palenques,* and *quilombos* of Caribbean and Latin American slave societies. Nevertheless, North American *marronage* was a serious inconvenience to whites living near centers of maroon activity. Whether located in the Dismal Swamp along the Virginia–North Carolina border, in the Blue Ridge Mountains, or in the wilds of Florida or Louisiana, "outlying" slaves of "bad and daring character"—"monsters in human shape"—were accused of "decoying" field hands into their ranks and turning them into marauders. It was believed that every vexatious "nest of miscreants" had the potential to become the nucleus of a death-dealing guerrilla army.[109]

Indians. Troublesome in their own right, various Indian nations harbored runaways and formed alliances of opportunity with maroon communities. Although beset by numerous difficulties, such relationships likely had been in existence since North America's first black fugitives escaped from their Spanish captors and fled into the swamps of South Carolina in 1526. In later years, Anglo-American settlers feared that the two nonwhite groups would combine forces. To prevent the unthinkable, colonial officials included recovery clauses in treaties with Native American tribes, offered bounties for the slaves' recapture, and operated patrols in frontier areas. This policy of divide and rule was only sporadically successful in poisoning relations between Native Americans and African Americans. Black-Indian military collaborations peaked during the Seminole Wars of the early nineteenth century, confirming whites' worst nightmares.[110]

Foreign Foes. At one time or another, French settlers in Canada, Spanish officials in St. Augustine, and Loyalist supporters of the English crown were all accused of conspiring to convert fleet-of-foot runaways into dangerous security risks. During the mid-eighteenth century, the British bore the brunt of such charges. Outspoken American patriots such as Thomas Paine labeled George III "the Royal Brute" and took king and Parliament to task for (1) foisting African slaves on unwilling colonial subjects and (2) using their "barbarous and hellish power" to "[stir] up the Indians and Negroes." Wartime freedom declarations by British officials spurred slaves to flight, filling the ranks of former Virginia governor Lord Dunmore's "Ethiopian Regiment" with a bountiful contingent of foragers, guides, pilots, and support troops. Contemporaries estimated that the South lost more than fifty thousand bondsmen—many of whom evacuated with the English or were emancipated at war's end. In their wake, sightings of black banditti and rumors of their plots and plundering spread unchecked. The fact that most such reports were unfounded did little to calm patriot fears of a black/redcoat alliance. As was noted during the early days of the Revolution, massacres and insurrections were "Words in the mouth of every Child."[111]

Poor Whites/Free Blacks. Like the war, the revolutionary actions of free blacks and unpropertied white laborers had the potential to weaken stratified systems of class and to disrupt race relations. During slavery's first century, whites held to indenture contracts risked severe penalties if they opted to flee their master's estate before completion of agreed-upon terms of service. Often viewed as "the very scumm and refuse of mankind" by privileged elites, bound white laborers were vilified whenever they had the temerity to run off in the company of a valuable black chattel. In such cases, distraught owners assumed that the deceitful duo would travel as master and slave so as not to arouse suspicion. After being provisioned en route by base but hospitable persons of color or representatives of the "lower order of white people," it was anticipated that the fugitives would seek shelter amidst the bustle and anonymity of a major city. Here, removed from a master's control, bondsmen would be "encouraged to gamble, steal and practice every species of vice." Their teachers: degenerate whites well versed in the ways of urban crime and free blacks whose disproportionate representation in municipal jails served as a negative character reference for the race.[112]

Abolitionists. Slaveholders and radical abolitionists related to one another about as well as oil and water. Issues associated with fugitive slaves were a constant source of conflict between the two groups. Especially noisome to planters were those who sheltered runaways, served on vigilance committees, or helped liberate recaptured bondsmen from northern jails. If infrequent, confrontations between proslavery whites and free black activists determined to protest enforcement of the 1850 Fugitive Slave Act were guaranteed to be incendiary. Such was the case in the autumn of 1851 when a party of Maryland slave catchers surrounded the Lancaster County, Pennsylvania, home of a black mutual protection organization leader named William Parker and demanded the surrender of two runaways who were being sheltered inside. After a tense standoff in which the disputants traded epic boasts ("Before I give up, you will see my ashes scattered on the earth"; "My property I will have, or I'll breakfast in hell"), a riot engulfed the tranquil farming community of Christiana. Summoned by Parker's wife, Eliza—herself a Maryland fugitive—between 75 and 150 blacks armed with pistols, hunting rifles, corn cutters, and scythes attacked the small federal marshal's posse. The runaway's owner, Edward Gorsuch, was knocked to the ground, shot repeatedly, and robbed. According to local whites, his corpse then was hacked to a bloody pulp by "blood-thirsty, howling demons . . . whooping and yelling with savage glee." Three other members of the slave-catching contingent were wounded. Eventually, a company of marines was summoned from the Philadelphia navy yard to restore order. Numerous arrests were made, but no convictions resulted. As noted with great satisfaction by Underground Railroad operative William Still, the Christiana riot proved to be a signal victory for the friends of freedom. Slaveholders had been taught a "wholesome lesson": the Fugitive Slave Act was "no guarantee against 'red hot shot.'" In 1859 John Brown and his black co-conspirators would reinforce this teaching—moving many southern whites to believe that only a successful secessionist movement could shield them from such unspeakable acts of villainy.[113]

REVOLTS

Recognizing that the difference between a riot and a revolt sometimes was more a matter of extent than intent, slaveholders grew uneasy upon learning that one or more groups enshrined in their rogues' gallery of antislavery villains had been tampering with the racial status quo. But to what degree were such concerns justified? Was this vision of a social system turned topsy-turvy by black brutes and their allies a rational response to recurring events or part of an elaborate, guilt-driven fantasy world? A careful evaluation of the historical record reveals that whites had good reason to fear black revolts. But such fears often were exaggerated and, at times, quite irrational.

In comparative terms, the British North American experience with servile uprisings was minimal. Latin American and Caribbean plantation societies bore the brunt of New World insurrectionary activity.[114] But, however limited, the United States' experience with rebellious slaves was sufficiently traumatic to strike terror. Like all subsequent views of blacks as villains, the perception that slaves were dangerous subversives was grounded in both social reality and racial myth. In a very real sense, any instance of large-scale slave unrest had the potential to become a defining moment in the psychological history of the nation. The reputed actions of real-world rebels confirmed Bible- and science-based beliefs about the moral character of African peoples, breathed life into unnerving literary and theatrical portrayals, and served to justify draconian legislation designed to protect an embattled white citizenry. All of these were peculiarly, perhaps uniquely American responses to the threat posed by bondsmen in revolt. As the Civil War approached, the prospect of a black-over-white cataclysm loomed large in the minds of those most responsible for the maintenance of societal equilibrium.

To many, revolts and insurrection scares seemed the fulfillment of dire prophesies made in the formative years of America's dalliance with slave-mongering. Early antislavery voices had warned both of the trade's inherent dangers and of the corrosive influence that large-scale importation of foreign-born bondsmen would have on American institutions. To import chattel slaves was to hasten moral decay and multiply mortal enemies. Every shipload of African laborers, they said, "is to our nation what the Grecian's wooden horse was to Troy."[115] As noted by English visitor Charles William Janson in 1807, this corrupt maritime commerce had so increased the number of "lurking assassins" that they "swarm[ed] wherever the planter turns his eyes."[116] Understandably, each rumor of revolt rekindled fears that all were about to be punished for their forefathers' errors in judgment.

Even whites skilled in the art of distinguishing slave carelessness from maliciousness experienced considerable difficulty in ridding themselves of nagging fears. They slept with pistols under bedcovers, built pens in the woods to shelter their families, and participated in rites of fasting and humiliation in the hope of obtaining divine protection from "risings." If, on occasion, local blacks were suspected of circulating rumors of impending insurrectionary activity just to see the white folks run about in panic, self-preservation demanded that even the most bizarre stories be investigated thoroughly. Until they were discredited, such troubling tales rubbed nerves raw—setting slaveholding communities on edge and breeding fatalism. "I have not slept without anxiety in three months," wrote a dispirited Virginian caught in the midst of that state's insurrection scare of 1831–32. "Our nights are sometimes spent in listening to noises. A corn song, or a hog call, has often been a subject of nervous terror, and a cat, in the dining room, will banish sleep for the night. . . . I am beginning to lose my courage about the melioration of the South. . . . There is no principle of life. *Death is autocrat of slave regions*."[117] At such times, both the emotional toll of maintaining constant vigilance and the black villain's ability to wage effective psychological warfare were everywhere apparent.

If locally incited upheaval failed to materialize, there was always the threat of imported revolution to furrow one's brow. Pornographically vivid accounts of Caribbean and South American slaves indiscriminately murdering "in a most cruel manner . . . all the white people they could come at" circulated widely. Fed by fear of foreign intrigue and African fetishism, stateside slave subversion was linked to Haiti's bloody 1791 revolution, to the reported excesses of the island's black leaders, and to Vodun-practicing Haitian émigrés in the American South. Black insolence, insubordination, and an increase in instances of "people of colour" engaging in dangerous "conversations" were viewed as the inevitable fallout from the thirteen-year struggle to overthrow white rule in Saint Domingue. By the time of the United States' own civil war, "the example in the West Indies" and of ruthless arch-villain Jean-Jacques Dessalines were said to have contributed to the hatching of plots in Virginia,

South Carolina, and Louisiana.[118] Events in Haiti informed the apocalyptic *Appeal* of free black militant David Walker, inspired the leaders of the Gabriel conspiracy in Richmond during the spring and summer of 1800, and figured prominently in the development of Denmark Vesey's plan for an African American takeover of Charleston, South Carolina. Although governed by its own internal dynamic, Nat Turner's legendary Southampton County, Virginia, insurrection began, quite ominously, in the early morning hours of August 22, 1831—the fortieth anniversary of the uprising that launched the island revolution. Little wonder, then, that white southerners felt themselves to be under perpetual siege. Nervously, they awaited the day and hour when seditious ideas spread by "French Negroes" would raise up yet another black Spartacus. As one beleaguered South Carolinian told fellow sufferers in 1825, the history of New World plantation societies taught a most "melancholy truth": "One educated slave, or coloured freeman, with an insinuating address, is capable of infusing the poison of insubordination into the whole body of the black population."[119] When black villains stalked the land, the earth trembled and the heavens wept.

Some anxious whites sought security in the comforting cocoon of skin-color privilege; others through military preparation and a well-organized patrol system. Often "an over-ruling Providence" was relied upon to "confound [the] Councils" of those conspiring to foment "Intrigues" and "bloody Tragedy."[120] But not even an early warning system grounded in religious faith seemed capable of safeguarding against black villainy. Incidents involving rebellious servants kept slaveholders ever vigilant, but confused and at a loss for answers. Could it be that their foes were being assisted by powerful allies from the dark side? Indeed, what were the white faithful to make of Mark, an eighteenth-century Charlestown, Massachusetts, conspirator whose New World religious education had succeeded only in convincing him that it was scripturally sound to kill one's master if the murderous deed could be accomplished without bloodshed? Or of Candy, a Salem slave charged with "wickedly, malliciously and felloniously" casting witches' spells on her mistress during the summer of 1692? Or of Sharper, accused by his Stafford County, Virginia, owner in 1773 of seeking out a local black conjurer "to procure Poison . . . to destroy White People"? Rumors of bondsmen uniting in "secret and wide-spread organization[s] of a Masonic character, having its grip, pass-word, and oath," increased tensions further—causing planters to wonder whether their slaves were becoming tools of northern abolitionists or of the Devil. Undoubtedly, some wondered whether these dark-skinned deceivers were guided by a moral compass of *any* kind.[121]

Among potential victims, fear of physical harm was almost palpable, but matters of the spirit also were of great concern. Inextricably connected with Africa, irreligion, and age-old symbolism attached to the color black, African American slave rebels were perceived as uniquely sinister. When they schemed and plotted "in their country language," rejected "true religion" for "fanaticism," and vowed in blood oaths to sweep all the "damnd white people" from the land, slave insurgents conjured up horrific images of moral darkness. If captivated by the insurrectionary impulse, even the most faithful servant could be transformed into a black imp fresh from the sulfurous pit and hell-bent on doing Satan's dirty work.[122]

Typically unrecognized or devalued by scholars of our more overtly secular age, concerns of this nature expressed during the pre–Civil War years revealed a deep-seated fear of blackness. Due to the stark color coding of the participants, armed struggles between masters and slaves threatened to overturn what whites considered to be universal standards of right and wrong, truth, beauty, justice, and order. The awful prospect of exchanging European American civilization for West African savagery—of being a party to the Africanization of the Americas—transformed what in some cases were little more than servile squabbles into morally charged contests pitting absolute virtue against wholesale vice. To the ultimate victor would go supernal spoils—trusteeship of a rising world power guided either by God's grace or the Devil's wiles. Each revolt was white America's Judgment Day; every insurrection, the slaveholders' Armageddon.

Although staged infrequently, major American slave revolts and insurrection scares provided more than enough high drama for anyone's taste.[123] Rich in racial symbolism, these widely reported incidents were as allegorical as any English morality play or court masque. Here, "outlandish" Africans stood in for scheming, lecherous "blackamoors." Superstitious black brutes—body doubles of those found throughout plantation fiction—were cast as fallen angels. As in days of yore, godly, long-suffering white people continued to play themselves.

Religiously unacculturated protagonists were believed to have accepted key roles in early servile sociodramas. During the spring of 1712, Coromantee and Pawpaw conspirators not long from the West African homeland set fire to a building on New York City's East Side and then ambushed panic-stricken whites who rushed to douse the blaze. Nine were killed and seven wounded before the sword-, stave-, and ax-wielding rebels retreated to the woods of Harlem. Subsequent investigation into the backgrounds of the more than two dozen conspirators revealed that recruits had been bound to secrecy "by

Sucking ye blood of each Others hand" and had been given a special powder said to make them invulnerable to harm.[124]

In the early hours of September 9, 1739, at Stono Bridge in the Carolina low country southwest of Charles Town, an Angolan named Jemmy launched a rebellion that left twenty-one whites dead and the rich rice-growing region "full of Flames." Two of the victims—storekeepers—were robbed of guns and powder and then decapitated. Their severed heads were left on the front steps of their shops—a gruesome ritual display rooted in the martial culture of West Africa. Other unfortunates were said to have perished in a "most cruel and barbarous Manner." After routing the main rebel contingent, members of the local militia company reported that their slave adversaries had acted like Bakongo warriors of old—singing, beating drums, and marching in formation under banners that were thought to have protective powers. In order to guard against future uprisings, officials sought to restrict the number of new slaves arriving from Africa and the West Indies while actively promoting, via subsidies, the immigration of "poor Protestants" from Europe. In addition, two "Country born young Negroes" were permitted to be trained as teachers and placed in special schools where they would offer black and Indian youngsters instruction "in the chief Principles of the Christian Religion." Perhaps recognizing that they were engaged in both physical and spiritual warfare with osnaburg-clad demons, four Charles Town slave dealers were among the initial sixteen contributors to one such school's building fund.[125]

That religious-based behavior modification was but imperfectly realized became evident during the Vesey scare of 1822. At his sentencing, convicted conspirator Gullah Jack was condemned for having employed "all the powers of darkness, . . . the most disgusting mummery and superstition," in his attempts to recruit rebel troops from among "the ignorant and credulous" of greater Charleston. Once under the conjurer's spell, they were to have formed one of several military companies organized according to African ethnic background (i.e., Congo-Angolan, Ibo, Mandingo). Some, it was said, 'were to be responsible for putting poison "into as many pumps as [they] could about town." One of several native-born Africans filling key leadership roles among the plotters, Jack also had instructed his fellows to eat nothing but parched corn and groundnuts on the day of the assault and to hold "cullahs" (crab claws) in their mouths as protection against being wounded in battle. If all went according to plan, it was anticipated that armies from Saint Domingue and Africa would "come over and [help] cut up the white people." Understandably, those who believed that mysterious forces prevented the bewhiskered necromancer from being "killed, shot, or taken" were afraid to testify at Jack's trial. They feared that supernatural retribution would be meted out to informers.[126]

Equally eager to escape the insurrectionists' score settling, whites were dismayed that not even the more fully acculturated element of the black population could be trusted to uphold the social order. Living proof that "a little learning is a dangerous thing," free black conspirator Denmark Vesey was said to have used religion—and class meetings held at the local African Church—as a "perfidious cover" for his "devilish plan." Likened to a haughty "Eastern Bashaw" whose "[w]rong conception of the Bible" caused him to preach the heresy that slavery was contrary to God's laws, Vesey was deemed a bad influence on African American Christians. In truth, said his accusers, subversive messages equating southern black bondage with that experienced by the ancient Israelites under Egyptian rule most likely were crafted by the Dark Prince himself. How else could a right-thinking religionist explain the apparent ease with which Old Testament passages such as Zechariah 14:1–2 ("Behold, the day of the Lord cometh . . . and the city shall be taken, and the houses rifled, and the women ravished") were torn from their historical context and used to sanction "crimes of the blackest hue"? Surely, wrote one greatly relieved white Charlestonian following Vesey's execution, nothing but the "merciful interposition of our God" had saved the city from the villain's "diabolical scheme."[127]

Church gatherings also were used for recruitment purposes by Henrico County, Virginia, bondsmen involved in an ill-fated plot to capture the state capitol, take Governor James Monroe hostage, and spread revolution throughout the Mid-Atlantic region. During the summer of 1800, rebel emissaries visited meetinghouses and outdoor "preachment[s], Fish feasts and Barbecues" in the hope of convincing blacks to join in what was referred to as "the War." "There was this expression in the Bible that delays breed danger," potential recruits were told. "Five of you shall conquer an hundred & a hundred a thousand of our enemies." Ultimately, incendiary messages spread by the aptly named Gabriel and his minions may have been heard by slaves in as many as ten counties. If what whites later described as a "providential" rainstorm hadn't swelled area streams—washing out roads and bridges, disrupting lines of communication, and sapping momentum and morale—all of southern history may have been altered by this rebellious blacksmith who chose to fashion swords from scythes rather than transform them into plowshares and pruning hooks as recommended in the book of Isaiah.[128]

While visions of armed apostates were still fresh in their minds, northern reformers encouraged Virginians to

remember ere too late,
The tale of St. Domingo's fate.
Tho' *Gabriel* dies, a host remain
Oppress'd with slavery's galling chain.[129]

But slaveholders, cloaked in self-righteousness, were unrepentant. They seemed to have learned precious little from numerous narrow escapes. As punishment, some were subjected to the horrors of servile war unleashed by the militant mystic Nat Turner. In 1831 this slave preacher's vengeance-seeking band of sixty or more killed at least fifty-seven whites—more than half of them women and children—before being dispersed. Believed to have been "concerted and concocted under the cloak of religion," the bloody rampage spurred calls for a silencing of "negro preachers . . . who, full of ignorance, are incapable of inculcating any thing but notions of the wildest superstition."[130]

To many, "Nat the Contriver" seemed a classic villain—a dark-skinned, black-hearted bogeyman for the ages. Thomas Gray, the Southampton County lawyer who interviewed the chained rebel just before his execution, considered Turner a "great Bandit," a "gloomy fanatic" possessed of a "bewildered, and overwrought mind." That the convicted insurrectionist and murderer claimed to be a seeker of "true holiness" who had been instructed by the spirit of God (as manifested in vividly symbolic visions and heavenly voices) to "fight against the Serpent" seemed proof both of his impiety and evidence of mental instability. Certainly, one who had heard such claims firsthand while seeking behavioral clues in the slave's "fiend-like face" must have understood what it was like to be in the presence of great spiritual evil. "I looked on him," Gray wrote in the widely circulated *Confessions of Nat Turner*, "and my blood curdled in my veins."[131]

If "Nathaniel" meant "the gift of God" in Hebrew, after August 1831 it meant "spawn of Satan" throughout the American South. Greatly embellished by rumor and exaggeration, remembrances both too vivid and too hazy, Turner subsequently was enshrined as the profane prophet of southern thralldom. Some said that his devilish deceits had attracted as many as twelve hundred followers—the boldest of whom conducted their military drills openly and in uniform.[132] Others employed whispered tones whenever discussing Nat's religious writings—inscrutable documents filled with "hieroglyphical characters . . . traced with blood," numerological calculations, and drawings of the crucifix.[133] Still others claimed that the tree limb from which the black insurgent was hanged became cursed and died; that the physicians who dissected Turner's body found his skull to be misshapen and unusually thick; that a dark letter "W" for "War" was clearly visible on the soles of his feet.[134] Thus, even in death, a slave villain who had claimed extraordinary powers over disease, the weather, and the seasons proved a formidable threat to white psychological security. Gray seemed to partake of the departed prophet's powers of divination when he predicted that the events of 1831 would "be long remembered in the annals of our country" and that "many a mother as she presses her infant darling to her bosom, will shudder at the recollection of Nat Turner, and his band of ferocious miscreants."[135]

LOYAL RETAINERS

Regularly reiterated by politicians, poets, and polemicists, the image of blacks as slave subversives became indelibly imprinted on the white racial consciousness. Over time, mainstream Americans grew accustomed to employing this terrifying vision as a negative signifier for white civilization. Many became expert in using pejorative black portraiture to formulate a comprehensive index of repudiation that could be applied to any aspect of African American life—particularly those areas deemed to be falling short of the purportedly Olympian standards set by whites. In this manner, European Americans of the pre–Civil War years adapted their English heritage to frontier conditions. They contextualized the value-laden concept of blackness—imbuing it with special meaning for a pioneering people hell-bent on creating an Eden in the wilds of North America. Blacks, they concluded, were natural-born villains whose enslavement was both their divinely authorized punishment and their only hope of salvation. Until such time as the moral contagion that they represented was contained, a most exacting vigilance would have to be maintained. White survival required that all avenues of cultural expression, every institution and belief system, be utilized to warn of the black villains' wiles.

But it is one thing to defend against evil in the abstract. As could be seen during times of servile unrest in the plantation South, it is quite another matter to look a black villain square in the face, turn, and walk away confident in the life-affirming (and preserving) powers of skin-color privilege. Certainly, living with the knowledge that one's courage might be tested at any moment was traumatic, but bravado could become a requisite for survival. What were beleaguered whites to do when cowardice was not an option—when to shudder in the villain's presence would be interpreted as a sign of racial weakness or seen as an invitation to commit even more hideous depredations?

In their attempt to solve this conundrum and thereby enable their fellows to stand the storm of black villainy, captains of the European American social order attempted to mitigate the fright factor that had come into play whenever whites were forced into a confrontation with blackness. In their novels and plays, songs, sermons, speeches, and scientific papers, they strove to bolster majoritarian resolve through ego enhancement and the deification of exemplary race champions. At the same time, a concerted effort was made to soften the image of African Americans as evildoers—to vary racial portraiture and thereby de-emphasize the universality of black devilishness. Some would say that this amounted to self-deception. Perhaps so. But it was not their intention to discount the dangers of unchecked villainy. They sought only to guard against a widespread paralysis of fear.

Struggling mightily not to fixate on the threat posed by black brutes, white opinion makers and culture shapers recounted their experiences with servants who acted the fool, worshipped their white overlords, and worked overtime to cultivate an ever-more joyous subservience. Instead of skulking, plotting, and engaging in pagan rituals, these slaves ran from ghosts, repeatedly refused offers of freedom, and comforted white people with heartfelt statements such as "Oh! master, I wish I may find everybody as well off as I am"; and "The great Shepherd above is you' fodder, and you' old black mammy is your friend."[136] Said to be staunch members of an interracial fellowship of faith, they fretted over whether worldly whites would "get converted to de Lord" so that the entire plantation family could "meet . . . in de sweet Heaven," garbed in "de white robes of de Lamb." Some, like Harriet Beecher Stowe's beatific Uncle Tom, were so self-sacrificial that they offered to give "every drop of blood in this poor old body . . . as the Lord gave his for me" if it would bring about a master's salvation.[137]

In grateful response, white patriarchs sang the praises of loyal retainers who somehow had managed to overcome the most noisome of inherited disabilities. Such individuals were put on display whenever a liberal-minded slaveholder sought to convince skeptics that there was no reason "why a body may not like a negro as well as a white man." Often poetic tributes were offered when one of these "honest simple old creature[s]" exchanged their mortal coil for a pair of angel's wings.[138] As revealed in Big House eulogies and churchyard epitaphs, loyalty definitely had its rewards. It might even mean casting off the curse of blackness for all eternity:

> HERE lies the best of slaves,
>   Now turning into dust;
> Caesar the Ethiopian craves
>   A place among the just:
> His faithful soul is fled,
>   To realms of heavenly light,
> And by the blood that Jesus shed
>   Is chang'd from BLACK to WHITE.[139]

Sometimes grotesque, but neither noble nor savage, these most domesticated of bondsmen were so revered that their smiling servility became an integral part of southern lore.

This romanticized black portraiture had special meaning for a slaveholding people forced to grapple with the contemporary wisdom that held that "Negroes only cease to be children when they degenerate into savages."[140] As historian Ronald Takaki has shown, antebellum whites desperately needed to smooth over the contradictions inherent in their jerry-rigged, ahistorical constructions of race.[141] They also stood in need of a serviceable set of psychological defense mechanisms to shield them from an uncomfortable plantation reality: most slaves found to be acting like children *were* acting—and only members of the slave community knew how long the play would run or what the final act would reveal. By emphasizing the supposedly docile, dependent nature of African Americans, anxious planters hoped both to alleviate concerns about the morality of slaveholding and to lessen the mental burden of living in a world plagued by subversive activity. In effect, ancient apprehensions did more than cause European Americans to tremble and turn ashen upon realizing that black barbarians had found their way into white homes, business establishments, and houses of worship. Subliminal fears also moved whites to transform a considerable number of these raging brutes into ostensibly harmless children who responded to enslavement by radiating the spirit of Christian charity.

To be sure, such rationalizations tell us a good deal more about white phobias than they do about black personality types or the nature of the African American freedom struggle. But they also confirm the fact that race—and the negative symbolism attached to dark skin tones—was central to the shaping of the American Republic. As historian Winthrop Jordan has suggested, the West Africans' color and cultural background greatly influenced the decision-making process that put blacks in the holds and whites on the decks of slave ships.[142] Subsequently, skin-color coding enabled nonblacks of all occupations and statuses to conceptualize and to treat African slaves as a race of primitive, eternally cursed beings fresh from the pit. To quote one colonial-era judge grown weary of the slave subversives' "treachery, blood-thirstiness, and ingratitude," such bondsmen were prone to "the most horrid and detestable pieces of villainy, that ever satan instilled into the heart of human creatures."[143] Certainly, long-winded soliloquies about faithful serving men and devoted Mammies never completely dissipated the lingering essence of brimstone.

Indeed, throughout the nation's history, white racial presumption and display have belied the fear within. Unnaturally loud laughter generated by the appearance of clownish black grotesques has masked many a nervous smile. Tears shed upon the death of stereotypically noble, self-sacrificing servants have mingled with sweat in an untold number of pale palms. Like the timorous ancients who kept to their homes lest they be devoured by creatures of the night, countless Americans of more modern times have refused to make unescorted forays into black communal lairs. In dreaded anticipation of a cataclysmic "rising" from the depths, European Americans have attempted to appropriate the moral high ground for themselves—continually denigrating black behavioral standards and defining the African Americans' history as a catalog of dark deeds. That these artful maneuverings are well understood by those whose very survival depends on locating chinks in the armor of white supremacy continues to make the black "subversive" a formidable foe of complexional hierarchies.

Blacks and Social Banditry

ANTEBELLUM

Long before the Civil War, African American scholars, storytellers, and "race men" challenged majoritarian claims to racial supremacy. In folklore and fiction, poems, plays, and history texts, they sought to discredit received wisdom on the color coding of virtue and vice. Some held that blacks were a beautiful people, uniquely gifted and endowed by their Creator with both high moral character and a revolutionary spirit. Others assumed the role of intragroup watchdogs—ever alert to the threat posed by dark-skinned race traitors. Most recognized that what whites considered to be villainy more accurately could be conceptualized as social banditry—the act of being bad for a good reason. Whether real or imagined, black social bandits typically were depicted as tough, self-reliant subversives steeped in the warrior tradition and grounded in communal mores. As agents of change, they might kill or maim, but they would do so in order to improve the lives of beleaguered kinsmen. By way of contrast, the evils perpetrated by white Americans were seen as unjustifiable, ultimately inexcusable crimes against humanity. To clear their own good name, pioneering black authors engaged influential whites in a highly charged debate over group portraiture, skin-color symbolism, and the imputation of race-based villainy.

Early black writers understood that they were part of an activist vanguard. Lashing out against false piety, misguided paternalism, and pejorative notions about racial inheritance, these prickly social critics sought to change the course of history. As outspoken physician/newspaper editor Martin Delany asserted in 1852, whites long had presumed to "*think* for, dictate to, and *know* better what suited colored people, than they knew for themselves." One result of this intellectual usurpation was that African American perspectives on key issues often were neither properly nor fairly presented. To remedy this situation—and thereby win freedom from what he described as "moral and mental" slavery—Delany championed independence of thought and expression. Blacks, he said, had to believe themselves capable of becoming the "originators of their own designs, the projector of their own schemes, and creators of the events that lead to their destiny."[1]

To these ends, African American authors promoted a positive group self-image. Hoping to "inflame the latent embers of self-respect" that the cruelties of slavery had "nearly extinguished," they began the arduous process of re-envisioning blackness. As both a color and as an indicator of moral worth, black was said to signify "beauty . . . most rare." When used to describe racial distinctives, the term connoted talent, ambition, and possession of a "noble, manly spirit." That dark-skinned Americans remained woefully underrepresented in the professions was attributed to discrimination, not to a heritable disability. As was noted by a character in Frank J. Webb's *The Garies and Their Friends* (1857), when the majority of blacks were removed from the "blighting influences" of bondage and caste, it would become obvious to all that "a man can be a gentleman even though he has African blood in his veins." Within the antebellum free black community, increased race pride was seen as an antidote to the self-hatred that was fostered by white Americans' denigration of all things African.[2]

In addition to outlining the rise and progress of institutions such as the black church and commenting on both contemporary politics and northern racism, black authors spoke out against the assumption that their natal homeland was uncivilized. In his *Treatise on the Intellectual Character, and Civil and Political Condition of the Colored People of the United States* (1837), Boston minister Hosea Easton listed the contributions that the West had made to the arts and sciences, but questioned "whether they are any where near its standard, as they once existed in Africa." Said to have been founded in 2188 BC by a son of Ham, the kingdom of Egypt was deemed the showpiece of African achievement. Its people noble, generous, and possessed of "true greatness," this black land had done more to "cultivate such improvements as comports to the happiness of mankind, than all the descendants of Japhet[h] put together." According to Easton, Africa's many gifts to world culture would be far more evident had not Europeans destroyed "every vestige of history" that fell into their hands during their exploitative raids of the continent.[3]

Other revisionist accounts of black history focused on individuals who had led distinguished lives while slaves and on those ex-slaves who exhibited sound judgment and a selfless concern for others. It was hoped that their "unremitting industry and economy"—as well as their faith in the power of God, family, and black humanity—would serve to discredit claims that manumission invariably led to idleness, drunkenness, and thievery.[4] Especially noteworthy in this regard were those freedom-loving patriots of color whose Revolutionary-era military exploits helped secure American independence. According to antebellum reformer William Wells Brown, an admirable record of "valor and . . . invincibility" proved that these "sable sons" could pass any national "test of loyalty."[5] Unfortunately, their claim to equal citizenship rights had been denied repeatedly. Thus, while bold strivers such as Crispus Attucks and Peter Salem bore little resemblance to villainous stereotypes, their example of principled sacrifice highlighted mainstream hypocrisy.

In like manner, portraits of runaway slaves penned by African American authors stood in quarrelsome contrast to those imagined by white contemporaries. Giving voice to the unarticulated sentiments of slave-quarter residents who protected plantation runaways, free black writers sympathized with the fugitives' struggles and admired their open defiance of unjust laws. No less liberty loving than the boldest patriot minuteman, runaway slaves were said to have risked their lives in order to reclaim the "heaven born right" of personal freedom. With hearts beating "firm and true," they struggled mightily to escape the clutches of "mean and craven foes." If successful in reaching free soil, they invariably dropped to their knees and thanked God for deliverance. Overall, there was little ambiguity in such tales. Blacks were conceptualized as long-suffering "Children of Heaven"; white tormentors as "False Teachers."[6]

Sympathetic case studies of Old South insurrectionists solidified black America's belief that most white characterizations of the master/slave relationship wronged the race by reversing the roles of hero and villain. Antebellum black writers often defined the strength of a Nat Turner or Joseph Cinque as principled rebelliousness; their native intelligence as the ability to understand the oppressor without revealing one's true intentions.[7] White authority figures experienced considerable difficulty keeping these clever moral giants in chains. In one such fictionalized account of events aboard the slave ship *Creole* in 1841, a "tall, symmetrical" bondsman named Madison Washington masterminded a successful mutiny. Described by abolitionist author Frederick Douglass as "one to be sought as a friend, but to be dreaded as an enemy," Washington possessed both "Herculean strength" and a "mesmeric power which is the invariable accompaniment of genius." After gaining his victory via a surprise attack from the ship's hold, the black "general-in-chief" refused to execute captive crew members. Though fellow rebels sought retribution, he demanded only that the slaves be granted their "rightful freedom." This noble restraint earned him the begrudging respect of the whites. As one sailor recalled, "I forgot his blackness in the dignity of his manner, and the eloquence of his speech. It seemed as if the souls of both the great dead (whose names he bore) had entered him." In the end—after courageously piloting the ship through a fierce squall—Washington docked the brig at a Nassau wharf amidst the cheers of sympathizers. Douglass's protagonist had shown that he was in no respect inferior to the most highly honored white heroes.[8]

While black-authored portrayals contradicted mainstream depictions of slave rebels as superstitious savages, white characters drawn by African American playwrights, poets, and novelists more than made up for any shortfall in the nation's supply of evildoers. Exhibiting abhorrent personal and behavioral defects that belied their pretensions to civility, slaveholders brutalized the field hands by feeding them roach-infested food, clothing them in coarse, tattered garments, and whipping them until "the flesh turn[ed] open in gashes streaming down with gore." Perceived as "white devils" by their tormented victims, plantation patriarchs presided over a cotton-culture version of Dante's hell in which laws crafted by "Lucifer . . . below" had replaced traditional moral codes.[9]

In many cases, these vivid depictions of white villainy were modeled on actual events. Finding only the most egregious hypocrisy in slave-code prohibitions that spoke of physical cruelty as being "highly unbecoming" and "odious" to all who had "any Sense of Virtue or Humanity," escaped bondsmen stoked the fires of abolitionism with heartrending accounts of white inhumanity.[10] Whenever the opportunity arose, former victims provided a detailed inventory of the slaveholders' tools of torment. Their published narratives were filled with descriptions of whips, weights, shackles, and iron collars; of being locked in the stocks, imprisoned in cramped "nigger boxes," or forced to run the gauntlet. Far less concerned about scholarly objectivity than those latter-day historians who have described how barbaric misuse of valuable human property declined during the nineteenth century, these on-the-spot observers recounted incidents of branding, ear cropping, and sexual mutilation; of pregnant slave women being beaten with paddles or whipped while made to lie over a shallow pit dug in the ground; and of slaves who were punished by having an angry cat "hauled" down their backs. Despite the planters' admonitions that supervisors of slave labor should strive to avoid "violence of demeanor," the catalog of atrocities grew ever thicker as the Civil War approached.[11]

Those who adhered to the African American worldview identified with the victims of history. Vowing never to forget the worst abuses, they refused to believe proslavery assertions that the cruelest masters were "the emigrant Scotch and English" or "northern gentlemen who marry southern heiresses."[12] As kidnapped northerner Solomon Northup noted after his release from twelve years of bondage in the Red River region of Louisiana, "They are deceived who flatter themselves that the ignorant and debased slave has no conception of the magnitude of his wrongs."[13] There simply were too many eyewitness accounts of slaveholding villainy.

Numerous stories circulated in reform circles that recounted the plight of those who, like Northup, had been forced to drink from the peculiar institution's "bitter cup."[14] Tales of black torture victims being held over burning coals, torn limb from limb, raped, or buried alive became even more unpalatable when the arbitrary nature of white "justice" was factored into the equation. In many instances, sheer caprice seemed to dictate the nature and extent of punishment. Bondsmen resented being whipped for poor cooking or for allowing livestock to escape; for "being out of place" or "not remembering the courtesy due a white man, both in word and deed." Unable to fathom the rationale behind judicial sentences that mandated fifteen lashes for "impudence," twenty for being "saucy," and twenty-five for using "insolent language," they assumed that white society's strange notions about moral behavior actually were rooted in white immorality.[15] To many, harsh sentences meted out for minor infractions should have been reserved for villainous whites who had rigged the scales of justice to serve their own selfish interests.

Black liberationist stirrings seemed to bring out the worst in even the best of these slaveholding bullies. Both rumored and fully actualized insurrectionary activity caused white elites to charge the servile black masses with sinister intent. Then, after helping to whip the subservient white masses into a state of near apoplexy, they proceeded to behave as if possessed by demons. Colonial-era insurrection scares invariably concluded in orgies of judicially sanctioned sadism. For example, in 1712 participants in the failed New York City "Conspiracy to murder the Christians" were subjected to punishments that Governor Robert Hunter described as "most exemplary." Of the nineteen slaves executed, fourteen were hanged and two burned at the stake. A bondsman named Tom was roasted over "a slow fire in torment for eight or ten hours." Others were racked and broken on the wheel or gibbeted in chains until they starved to death. Given the harshness of the sentences, it is likely that an informed understanding of the white "Christians'" wrathful nature explains why a half-dozen conspirators chose suicide over capture.[16]

In the nineteenth century, suspected slave rebels were treated to a somewhat different but no less gruesome range of punishments. When black "barbarians" appeared at the gates, the guardians of white civilization seemed, themselves, to devolve into savagery. As one Mississippi slaveholder admitted after a 1835 insurrection scare led to a series of lynchings, the whites' vengeful response promised to become "a greater evil than that it was intended to correct." The regulators, he said, "need regulating."[17] During such times of societal upheaval, hurriedly organized posses combed the countryside with little regard for slave life or for the civil rights of free blacks. Suspected conspirators were hunted down and subjected to summary trials in which anonymous witnesses presented hearsay evidence before a closed-minded court. As was the case in Charleston, following the Denmark Vesey scare of 1822, informers sometimes received substantial rewards from governmental coffers while the bodies of those convicted and executed were put on public display, interred in hastily dug graves, or "delivered to the surgeons for dissection." Eventually, all blacks in the region were likely to suffer in some fashion for their assumed complicity in the real, imagined, or greatly exaggerated conspiracy. Insurrectionary activity was a major encouragement to the introduction of draconian legislation designed to restrict the legal, economic, educational, and social rights of a racial group deemed "the *Jacobins* of the country . . . the *common enemy of civilized society.*" Within affected black communities, this professed white civility seemed a cruel misnomer, but there was little doubt that a common pale-skinned enemy was making their lives a living hell.[18]

From a black perspective, the fruits of white villainy were nowhere more apparent than in Southampton County, Virginia, in the aftermath of Nat Turner's revolt. The "great Bandit's" bloody rampage sparked a series of reprisals in which indiscriminate retribution by vigilantes and militiamen took a heavy toll. Perhaps 120 or more suspected conspirators perished before the fever subsided. Moved by what the editor of the *Richmond Whig* described as "vindictive ferocity," search parties stormed through the backwoods brutalizing innocent blacks. Some unfortunates were bound to trees and "hacked at" by sword-wielding whites. The severed heads of other victims were placed on poles as a warning to all who would countenance revolutionary schemes. Elsewhere, the homes of free blacks were ransacked and robbed. According to observers in the community, town patrols behaved "like a troop of demons, terrifying and tormenting the helpless." Hoping to "make 'em lie against one another," men, women, and children were flogged "till the blood stood in puddles at their feet." On occasion, the whites even stooped so low as to plant incriminating evidence. In light of these events, few blacks throughout the region could have been totally surprised when a most unpleasant rumor began to circulate about the disposition of Nat Turner's corpse. Following his trial and hanging, it was said that souvenir purses were made of Turner's skin.[19]

African American men and women of letters viewed the white response to these freedom struggles as evidence of their own moral superiority. This rarified folk sensibility often distinguished their fictional protagonists from white characters and was an essential component of the developing black worldview. As historian Mia Bay has recognized, antebellum black intellectuals devoted considerably less time and effort to theorizing about the causes of white behavior than their mainstream counterparts spent trying to explain black inferiority and to justify black subordination. Nothing about white people *as a race* struck them as forcibly as the European Americans' collective abuses of family, friends, and forebears. On those relatively few occasions when they had the power to impose stereotypical images on whites, the oppressor's skin color did not become a major preoccupation. Rarely was it the singular element used to define their oppressors.[20] Nevertheless, some black commentators found considerable satisfaction in discrediting white claims to creation's moral crown. To such individuals, even the best-behaved whites were capable of heinous crimes. They were far more dangerous than the vast majority of those who were considered hereditary criminals because of Noah's curse.

Like their West African ancestors who suspected that European slave traders practiced cannibalism, the boldest of these writers suggested that whites were "natural enemies." Compared to the "humane and merciful" people of the Black Diaspora, European Americans seemed a loathsome lot.[21] When African civilization was "filling the world with amazement," said pioneering black nationalist Henry Highland Garnet, the Anglo-Saxon "abode in caves under ground, either naked or covered with the skins of wild beasts." Progenitors of the most debased civilization imaginable, they made the nighttime "hideous" with savage shouts and darkened Old World skies with the smoke from their altars of human sacrifice. Centuries later the heirs to this ignoble tradition would cross the Atlantic, steal land from the Indians, and force Africans into perpetual servitude. Condemned by their lineage and history, these European expatriates retained in principle—frequently in manner—"all the characteristics of their barbarous and avaricious ancestors." As William Wells Brown concluded in 1863, "Ancestry is something which the white American should not speak of, unless with his lips to the dust."[22]

Black writers were especially fond of skewering white southerners whose professions of piety failed to disguise a flawed moral character. Their novels and plays contained many unflattering character studies of white Christians who allowed inegalitarian social practices to shape theological views. Far from being the good shepherds of southern ecclesiastical lore, malevolent ministers used their catechisms to teach black subservience, permitted slave auctions to be held in church sanctuaries, and traded in slaves to pay "travellin' expenses." Antebellum reform literature characterized these spiritual leaders as the basest of hypocrites. For most, a saintly appearance could not mask a heart hardened by racism. In William Wells Brown's theatrical satire *The Escape,* a cleric named Reverend Pinchen even maintained that the southern caste system extended into the afterlife. After overhearing his rapturous description of heaven as revealed in a dream, a house servant named Hannah asked if the white minister had seen her "ole man Ben" there. "No, Hannah," he replied tersely, "I didn't go amongst the niggers."[23]

Activist authors condemned slaveholding theologians and encouraged bondsmen to abandon the white gospel because it was "false preaching" from "the stony hearts of . . . pretended Christians." Advocating black religion as a liberating alternative to traditional "servants obey in all things your masters" preachments, they claimed that a black-oriented faith would give slaves "a hope this side of the vale of tears" and "something on this earth as well as a promise of things in another world." The choice for black believers was clear. Instead of serving their masters' interests, bondsmen could choose to live by their own interpretation of the gospel and take another step toward freedom.[24]

The black rebels who appeared in these fictional works believed that religion and revolution were compatible concepts. It was the juxtaposition of Christianity and slavery that jarred the moral universe. In Martin Delany's serialized novel *Blake; or, The Huts of America* (1859), a Mississippi slave named Henry Holland was transformed into a fiery militant after being forcibly separated from his wife. Thereafter, he traveled throughout the South "sowing the seeds of future devastation and ruin to the master and redemption to the slave." Scornful of servitude, Holland continued to "trust the Lord as much as ever" but no longer would maintain a Job-like patience with the slow progress of black liberation. "Now is the accepted time, today is the day of salvation," he told one of his fellows. "This is very different to standing still." Opening his clandestine organizational meetings with prayer, he made sure that the rebels understood the need for making black religion support group goals. Just as God had instructed the Hebrew slaves to "borrow from their neighbors all their jewels" before fleeing Egypt, Holland encouraged the Mississippi bondsmen to loot their masters' homes and strike out for freedom in the North. According to Delany, such behavior was evidence of a higher faith, not of a lapse into savagery. This "determined and courageous, but always mild, gentle and courteous" protagonist may have seemed a "destroying angel" to the planters, but he appeared as a "messenger of light" to black captives whose minds had been "darkened" by white oppression.[25]

Fond of confounding conventional notions of good and evil, "handsome, manly and intelligent" social bandits such as Henry Holland transmitted essential wisdom about imputed black villainy.[26] As the curious, questioning Frederick Douglass had discovered at an early age, white teachings on race were compromised by self-interest and fear. It was "not *color,* but *crime,* not *God,* but *man*" who had shaped the origins of black bondage.[27] Once stripped of religious sanctions, customary beliefs could be altered dramatically. In the antebellum African American worldview, white often was employed as a negative signifier. Black was neither "dirty' nor "foul." There was no inherent conflict between revolutionary behavior and religiosity. For those who subscribed to tenets such as these, there was nothing more certain than that the South's "bottom rail" one day would be on top. Informed and energized by the social bandits' refusal to accept mainstream connotations of blackness, subsequent generations made this self-defining aesthetic a foundational component of an African American culture of opposition.

But not all antebellum blacks were considered paragons of virtue. Within African American communities, a distinction was made between authentic social bandits and those slaves and free blacks whose refusal to support group initiatives caused them to be viewed as social pariahs. The former can be likened to those noble robbers, resistance fighters, and avengers of the European folk tradition who were lionized for the manner in which they broke rank and risked all to rid their homeland of corrupt leaders. Because their acts of violence were directed against common enemies, such figures could count on enthusiastic support from fellow sufferers. Although such boldness sometimes shaded into excess, they could be regarded as actual criminals only by those who feared a just social order.[28] Truly bad blacks, on the other hand, would never be confused with Robin Hood. Unconcerned about the frequency with which they violated communal mores, they preyed upon the weak as well as the strong. Conniving, ruthless, and immoral, they possessed few redeeming qualities and could not be trusted. With no social agenda beyond that of self-aggrandizement, a bad black served as a negative reference point for lessons in principled behavior. In this respect, they seemed a lot like white people.

Black slaveholders were the worst of the race traitors. Numbering over 3,600 in 1830, they composed 2 percent of the South's free black population and held title to more than 12,300 slaves.[29] If some purchased bondsmen to protect kin or to reunite families, many others held slaves for less altruistic reasons. Like Louisiana sugar planter Andrew Durnford, such individuals operated on the belief that southern society was composed of "two distinct parts"—"wolves and foxes, and . . . lambs and chickens." Owning slaves required that free blacks cast their lot with "wolves," but spared them from becoming prey. By demonstrating that their ultimate loyalties were to class, not race, African American slaveholders sought to obtain white patronage and protection. If they worked hard to amass wealth, gained a reputation for respectability, and proved themselves "safe" on controversial issues, it was hoped that their own freedom would be made that much more secure. To distance oneself from those whom Durnford labeled "rotten people" or "rascally Negroes" was viewed both as a pragmatic accommodation to the rules governing antebellum capitalism and as a highly visible way of showcasing one's own fitness for self-government.[30]

Non-slaveholding African Americans resented the aid and encouragement black masters gave to the Old South regime. Corrupted by "the teachings of their Negro-fearing master-fathers," the lightest-skinned of this villainous cohort were said to "go sneaking about with the countenance of a criminal, of one conscious of having done wrong to his fellows."[31] Fond of flaunting symbols of acculturation, the "colored aristocracy" furnished comfortable homes with marble-top dressers, grandfather clocks, and four-poster beds; bred racehorses; and hired private tutors to instruct the young. Judging anyone who would mingle with servants and lower-class free blacks at a "Darkey Ball" to be a "pure pure Negro at Heart," these most color-conscious of black slaveholders rode in elegant carriages, dressed in the latest fashions, and sought to have their children marry well within their own social circle.[32] Aggressively acquisitive, they allied themselves with whites as business associates while seeking to ascend to the leadership ranks of their caste through contacts made in exclusive associations such as Charleston's Friendly Moralist and Brown Fellowship societies.

Even more troubling than their pretensions to upper-class gentility was the manner in which African American elites governed chattel property. Both fair-skinned and dark-complected masters were said to be capable of immense cruelty. For every story that circulated about the servants of benevolent black masters attending night classes to acquire the tools of literacy, entering into equitable self-purchase agreements, or living in quasi-freedom, a dozen others related incidents of abusive treatment. Black slaveholders fathered children by slave mistresses, separated families at auction, hired slave catchers to pursue runaways, and utilized all of the disciplinary machinery at their disposal to maintain order in their fields and workshops. Like Alabama master George Wright, some reportedly sold their slave offspring "ter de highes' bidder . . . for cash."[33] Others, such as South Carolina rice planters John and Samuel Holman, were successful slave traders.[34] Still others followed the course of action taken by the family of cotton planter/gin wright William Ellison and became model Confederates during the Civil War.[35] Berating those who permitted their laborers "to be idle" while noting "how much good it does some people to get whip[p]ed," certain black masters seemed determined to cultivate a reputation for harshness—perhaps to prove themselves worthy of whites' trust.[36] As a result, African American elites who made little apparent effort to distinguish their stewardship of slaves from that of white contemporaries risked being read out of the race. "Dey was a big dif'ence make 'tween slave niggers and owner niggers," recalled the freeborn nephew of an aloof black slaveholder from Louisiana. "Dey so much dif'ence as 'tween white folks and cullud folks."[37]

Slaves who vowed that they "wouldn't be sold to a coloured master for anyting" found the prospect of laboring under the supervision of an abusive black driver equally unpalatable.[38] Part of an unfree agricultural elite that also included artisans and house servants, drivers led the hands to the field, assigned tasks, and set the pace of the day's work. They monitored the condition of farm implements and supervised the midday feeding of workers and draft animals. Some drivers also kept basic accounts, distributed weekly rations, and served as their master's agent in dealings with merchants and tradesmen. After turning in a nightly report of activities and accomplishments, they were responsible for policing the quarters. Whenever necessary, they mediated disputes and meted out punishments. Typical perquisites accruing to capable drivers included superior housing, extra allotments of food and clothing, and bonuses of tobacco, whiskey, or cash. In some cases, this combination of power and privilege enhanced an elite slave's standing with fellow blacks. Skilled, resourceful individuals who attempted to represent the interests of fellow laborers were respected and remained close to their communal roots.[39] On the other hand, black labor supervisors who relied on brute force as a motivational tool or whose conspicuously consumed bounty spurred resentment were vilified and kept at arm's length.

Because of antebellum whites' tendency to enhance their own reputation for benevolence by demonizing black "whipping bosses," tyrannical drivers may be more numerous in legend than in fact. Nevertheless, their presence was far too frequently noted—and their cruel deeds too vividly detailed—for such portrayals to be considered wholesale fabrications. Aptly conceptualized as "men in the middle" by historians of the American South, drivers occupied a tenuous position within the managerial hierarchy of plantation agriculture.[40] Like modern-day factory foremen, they were torn between enforcing the dictates of their superiors and maintaining the active cooperation of less privileged laborers. Encouraged to feel superior to "common" field hands, the weaker-willed among them were swayed by the planters' special indulgences and material inducements. Some came to identify with the master class and thereby compromised their mediational role. Deeply hated within the quarters for the alacrity with which they did the whites' bidding, such individuals seemed to have forgotten that they, too, were "human property" living under constant threat of punishment or sale.

Like black slaveholders, abusive drivers often acted as if they had tested and then rejected the Golden Rule. Indeed, it was difficult to dispel the impression that they took a certain degree of sadistic pleasure in their work. Neither the concept of racial loyalty nor commonplace notions of human brotherhood appeared to mitigate their insensitivity to suffering. While far less likely than white contemporaries to stereotype all African American males as being "by nature tyrannical in their dispositions," long-suffering bondsmen echoed the views of those planters who characterized the worst of the lot as "merciless task-masters."[41] Ex-slaves recalled drivers who abused children, forced themselves on slave women, and gave such "awful beatin's" that their victims went mad or suffered miscarriages.[42] Initiated whenever the black supervisor "done took de notion" and sometimes lasting "half a day" or more, these punishments were described as being both excessive and unjustified. Any hand who "look[ed] tired" or was "caught prayin'" risked being lashed "'twell de blood run from him lack he was a hog." A Kentucky driver was even said to have whipped his own wife to death for stealing a pig.[43] As noted by former South Carolina bondsman Gus Feaster, to treat fellow members of the slave-quarter community in this manner caused one to be viewed as a "sorry nigger"—one "dat never had no quality in him a'tall."[44]

While some African American observers described the performance-related demands placed on black supervisors or posited the notion that a cruel driver simply mirrored "de bad part of Massa," others preferred to view black villainy as a personal moral failing.[45] In this view, when planters selected the "hardest-hearted and most unprincipled" type of slave for the post, they were dealing with a known quantity. If, on occasion, privileged bondsmen needed to be reminded that any deviation from strict disciplinary standards would cause the lash to fall on their own backsides, little additional encouragement to brutality was required. Already "bad as he could be," the prototypical abusive driver found great satisfaction in "strut[ting] 'round wid a leather strap on his shoulder," issuing threats. He enjoyed "exceeding the authority given by the master" and used his whip to settle personal scores. Unlike supervisory elites who faked whippings, sheltered runaways, or shared stolen supplies with the field hands, villainous drivers squandered their allotment of free will. As a result, those who were most cruelly treated considered their black tormentor to be "de meanest debil dat eber libbed on de Lawd's green yearth." To some, he was "de meanest man, white or black" they would ever meet.[46]

As revealed in their sacred songs, aggrieved bondsmen were eager to be "done wid massa's hollerin', / done wid missus' scoldin', / done wid driber's dribin'."[47] To speed the process along, slaves sometimes retaliated against black field supervisors who "got too smart" for their own good or "did too much whippin'." Most probably felt little remorse over the demise of brutal drivers who were poisoned with powdered glass, "horribly cut to pieces," or murdered because of overzealous use of the cow skin. Viewed as foes, not kin, such men became targets of communally sanctioned black-on-black violence when they lost their moral bearings, embraced villainy, and began to wage war against their oppressed brothers and sisters.[48]

In like manner, the hands shed few tears when members of a third cohort of bad blacks—thieves and informants—received punishments appropriate to their crimes. Arrogant and amoral, these unsavory characters neither owned human property nor served as the whites' disciplinary agents, but their devil-take-the-hindmost approach to life generated considerable friction within the quarters. In some cases, this unapologetic attraction to antisocial acts made them seem "just as mean as white folks."[49]

Black thieves were masters of self-aggrandizement. They felt no guilt over feathering their own nest at the expense of the flock. If less frequently reported than similar acts affecting whites, these transgressions against communal mores were an ongoing problem that threatened group unity and re-inforced the slaves' feelings of victimization. Certainly, theft was burdensome to a population possessing little material wealth. Concerned African American preachers exhorted members of their congregations not to steal from one another while slaveholding whites wrote to agricultural journals with tips on how to reduce instances of thievery. Unfortunately, this interracial instruction in ethics and morality often did little to improve matters. As one ex–South Carolina slave lamented, "You'll find a whole passle of bad niggers when you gits a thousand of them in one flock."[50] Long-fingered bondsmen caused slave-quarter residents to keep valuables in locked closets and moved planters to institute communal kitchens as a way to keep the hands from stealing each other's food. In some places, fugitives and "outlying" maroons preyed on black- and white-owned property indiscriminately. In others, black-on-black crime sparked violence as victimized slaves defended their belongings and their honor against intruders.[51] Although criminal acts such as these may have been encouraged by the privations of antebellum African American life, bondsmen were careful to distinguish between slaves who pilfered from the poor and those who stole only from whites. As noted in Jacob Stroyer's account of plantation life in South Carolina, instead of being honored as local folk heroes, traitorous thieves were ferreted out with the help of a truth serum made from "graveyard dust." Repeated threats of being sent to hell and "burned in fire and brimstone" served as additional encouragements to approved behavior. If unrepentant, the malefactor could be deemed incorrigible and ostracized by his peers.[52]

Black informants didn't lose much sleep over the possibility of separation from communal life. Villains of this sort were convinced that currying favor with white elites was preferable to sharing scraps with African American commoners. Some undoubtedly came to this conclusion after being called to task for one or more antisocial outrages against their fellows. Others did so as secretively as possible, hoping to forestall both exposure to hell's flames and physical punishment from aggrieved members of the slave-quarter community. Over time, black turncoats, slave and free, compiled an extensive catalog of duplicitous dealings with the enemy. Those bold (or foolish) enough to risk censure helped slave traders recapture runaways, tattled on hands who attended unauthorized frolics, and broke ranks to reveal insurrectionary plots. In one bizarre case, a free black man from Kentucky teamed with a white partner to entice slaves to flee. The pair then caught and returned the fugitives, pocketing the posted rewards. In another, a black Washington, D.C., hack driver foiled the escape of a group of more than seventy slaves because he was upset over the small tip he received after transporting various members of the party to the shipyards.[53]

Informants whose "acts of perfidy" harmed innocents or compromised the plans of African American insurgents may have garnered whites' gratitude or a small stipend and a new suit of clothes, but these rewards came at considerable cost. Guided by the biblical precept "He that is not with me is against me" (Luke 11:23), the black community made life difficult for collaborationists. Even if they managed to escape physical assault and the deleterious effects of spells cast by local conjurers, black traitors were shunned, shamed, and refused shelter. Labeled "despicable tale-bearers and mischief-makers" by racial loyalists, such individuals were said to possess "little or no honor, no high sense of duty." They were "lazy and mean"—content to "grovel in the mire of degradation."[54] As noted in Solomon Northup's account of an 1840 Louisiana uprising that was short-circuited by betrayal, any black person who "sacrifice[d] all his companions" for personal gain was certain to be "despised and execrated by all his race." Well aware of the enormity of their sins, African American informants sometimes were forced to beg white protectors to keep their identities secret. If already unmasked, they could hope to be rewarded with freedom and assistance in relocating to more congenial environs. If these requests were denied, the outcast literally had nowhere to turn. Their Faustian bargain with white villains had backfired and, like a fallen angel separated from all that is holy, they were cast adrift—rootless and estranged from righteousness and honor.[55]

Ultimately, it was this separation from the roots of African American community life that most tellingly distinguished black villains from social bandits. Those who adopted European American elites as role models, did their dirty work with alacrity, or violated customary ethical standards in order to acquire material symbols of success were labeled "rale wite folk's nigga[s]" and shunned by former friends.[56] Like the "bad seed" of any social group, they also were considered extremely dangerous. Lacking the social bandit's disinclination to risk permanent alienation from the folk culture, bad blacks were both unpredictable and indiscriminate in their mischief making. Answerable to no one, they became a terror to all.

In the antebellum African American worldview, it was difficult for a white person to be considered wholly trustworthy or for one of African ancestry to be viewed as irredeemable. Without question, the perpetrators of black-on-black crime tested the limits of racial brotherhood. But they also provided a useful corrective to mainstream beliefs about the relationship between blacks and evil. Like ex-slave Lucretia Alexander, most black Americans understood that certain people "would catch you and kill you for the white folks and then there was some that wouldn't."[57] Here, within the subculture, the meaning of villainy came to be determined more by word and deed than by ancient curses or complexion-based distinctions. The term denoted a personality type, not a stereotype; a dishonorable individual rather than a dishonored race. Bad blacks were at all times and everywhere present, but they were not normative. In most cases, they were neither revered nor welcomed. If this focus on instances of communal disharmony does damage to certain widely held assumptions about the unity of purpose one can expect to find within an oppressed social group, it nevertheless reveals that the majority of antebellum African Americans were determined to define themselves as upright and "good." The fact that most whites were unable to distinguish bad blacks from social bandits greatly hindered this effort. Ultimately, a victory in the battle for racial self-definition proved even more difficult to achieve than emancipation from slavery. In 1865, when the latter was effected, black social bandits—real and imagined—were still locked in a death struggle with race traitors and their villainous white allies.

POSTBELLUM

Freedom for America's 4 million enslaved blacks both recontextualized familiar fears and facilitated a mind-expanding array of new sociocultural possibilities. Among the former was the apocalyptic prospect of agricultural laborers settling scores with ex-Confederate masters. At the same time, events of the 1860s and early 1870s increased the likelihood that the African American perspective on villainy would be permitted to circulate freely among a less intractable public. With improved access to the tools of literacy, black opinion makers soon began to craft revised racial narratives that were as innovative as any of the Radical Republicans' intended political reforms. To their dismay, such notions often faced the same fate as the Reconstruction era's most unpopular legislative initiatives. White intellectual intransigence would be a long-term national problem. Nevertheless, the freedmen were determined to have their opinions matter. Believing that these cultural visions more closely approximated reality than those championed by whites, former bondsmen sought to distance the race from negative stereotypes; to warn of potential enemies; and to establish the fact of black humanity by promoting a value system conducive to the flowering of racial nobility. Indeed, the tenacity with which subsequent generations of black Americans have continued to forward such iconoclastic views in the face of widespread disbelief is a compelling story that speaks of heroism, not villainy.

African American writers of the late nineteenth century recognized that there were important continuities between the Old South and the New. Numerous contemporary social sins were said to be rooted in the antebellum master/slave relationship. As historian and Union army veteran George Washington Williams explained in 1883, black bondage had "touched the brightest features of social life, and they faded under the contact of its poisonous breath." Under the influence of slavery, whites became licentious, profligate, cruel, and selfish—unfavorable character traits that were extremely difficult to eradicate within a single generation.[58] Later black writers affirmed this belief in the unchanging nature of racial oppression. They wrote of "new pictures set in old frames, new wine poured into old bottles"; of a "cancer eating into the nation's heart" that had yet to be fully eradicated; and, eventually, of rat-infested urban ghettoes as "asphalt plantation[s]."[59]

White America's reckless disregard for black life and the human rights of others was among the most recognizable links between past and present. Within the late nineteenth-century oppositional culture, the lingering social death of slavery had been replaced by fear of a more immediate physical death at the hands of a lynch mob. Slave Power conspiracies to wrest control of the federal government were superseded by Democratic schemes to delimit minority-group progress. In such conceptualizations, pale-skinned evildoers remained a troublesome constant but served a useful interpretive and symbolic purpose.

As one would expect, white America's initial response to black freedom helped shape both the content and character of this postbellum worldview. The unwavering opposition of former Confederates convinced even the most optimistic African Americans that freedom would, indeed, be a constant struggle. Smarting from a devastating military defeat and unable to conceptualize ex-slaves as their equals, southern whites employed an array of ingenious—if ignoble—schemes to maintain racial hegemony. Emboldened by for-blacks-only legal codes that imposed burdensome penalties for possessing firearms, making "seditious" speeches, violating curfews, or being absent without leave from work-related tasks, landholders disregarded labor contracts and failed to pay stipulated wages. As a result, sharecroppers became enmeshed in perpetual debt and bound to the land. Offering their strong-armed support to this New South system of serfdom, Jayhawkers, Regulators, Red Shirts, and members of rifle clubs and secret societies such as the Ku Klux Klan and the Knights of the White Camelia targeted the freedmen for retributive justice, keeping them away from the polls and in constant fear of brutalization or death. At the same time, legislative allies sought to effect a permanent counterrevolution by enacting a series of discriminatory suffrage requirements, intermarriage bans, and exclusionary acts designed to discourage "promiscuous" social intermingling. Before the turn of the century, poll taxes and gerrymandering, the "white primary" and "grandfather clause" had greatly attenuated black voting power. Segregation was the law of the land. Unfortunately, the patent inequality of the era's "separate but equal" ideology seemed lost on white Americans of both sections. By any fairminded measure, this national acquiescence in enforced inequality reflected poorly on majoritarian institutions and constituted a major retreat from commitments made to the freedmen by the party of Lincoln during the earliest days of Reconstruction.[60]

It was for good reason, then, that whites remained prime candidates for villainization in minority-group cultural expression. Because the unity of each feuding constituency was strengthened by conflict with the other, white villainy actually assisted African Americans in setting parameters of acceptable behavior for members of their own group. By committing cruel, lawless acts that no self-respecting black person would tolerate, whites helped oppressed communities distinguish "race traitors" from social bandits and thereby to defend against subversion from within. To understand the distinction many within modern-day black America make between being bad for a good reason and acting immorally, that is, "acting white," one must look carefully at the white villains who populated this postbellum world, their darkskinned partners in crime, and several generations of heroic social bandits who valorized blackness while defending their fellows from what was perceived as a vast genocidal conspiracy.

White Villains: The Lynch Mob

Lynching is almost synonymous with villainy and has come to symbolize black oppression in what has been described as "that part of the United States lying below the Smith and Wesson line."[61] A form of extralegal collective violence that affirms caste boundaries and enforces conformity to prevailing racial roles, the postbellum lynching bee was denounced vigorously by activists of the day and continues to generate a deep emotional response within black America. The ritualized violence of "spectacle" lynching has been depicted in numerous period photographs and paintings, decried in protest verse and popular song, and dramatized in a variety of theatrical productions. Requiring little embellishment, fictionalized portrayals of the gruesome lynching scenario have been used to jog the communal memory, to unmask racist and gendered assumptions of white male supremacy, and to reinforce resolve while exorcising fear.[62] For many blacks, lynching was symptomatic of what National Association for the Advancement of Colored People (NAACP) executive secretary Walter White termed the pervasive "moral, spiritual, and intellectual sterility and blindness" of white America. Through active participation, tacit encouragement, and silent acquiescence in these terroristic acts, whites' conspiratorial tendencies were unmasked; their perversities fully revealed. As noted by activist and author James Weldon Johnson in 1933, not even the "fiends in hell" could surpass the "inhuman savagery" of a lynch mob. Thus, for every African American sacrificed, a European American perpetrator was damned. In the black worldview, the New South blood sport was intimately connected to matters of political economy and group psychology, but at its core was believed to be a problem of "saving . . . black America's body and white America's soul."[63]

The sheer number of incidents that constituted what former abolitionist Frederick Douglass termed "a perfect epidemic of mob law and persecution" seemed to confirm the pervasiveness of white villainy; the excruciatingly slow progress made in redirecting white anger into less deadly avenues of expression, its intractability.[64] In the five decades between the end of Radical Reconstruction and the start of the Great Depression, more than 3,200 black men, women, and children were executed by southern mobs. Few of the perpetrators were brought to justice, fewer still punished for their crimes. Evidencing a marked June-to-August seasonality and heavily concentrated in the "Black Belt" running through Georgia, Alabama, Mississippi, and Louisiana, this plague of lynching fever peaked during the 1890s, went into remission during World War I, reappeared in the early 1920s, and experienced a final decline during the 1930s. Despite the best efforts of the reform press, the black pulpit, and groups such as the Commission on Interracial Cooperation and the NAACP, vigilante "justice" was meted out to a black victim nearly once a week, every week between 1882 and 1930.[65] Lynching, said those who survived to campaign against it, had become an "integral part of our national folkways"—an "exciting form of sport" in a "nation of murderers."[66]

In condemning these deadly deeds, African American reformers defended the moral character of lynching victims and attempted to discredit stereotypes that defamed the entire race. Refusing to remain silent in the face of libelous charges that had been "presented with abundant repetition, with startling emphasis, and with every advantage to [white southerners'] side of the question," they disputed the widely accepted notion that lynching was a rational response to black criminality. Negroes were not beasts, they said, and the assertion that black men were "particularly given to assault" on white women constituted "a falsehood of the deepest dye." Sensationalistic press accounts of lynchings obscured the fact that mobocratic violence was part of a racist agenda to limit black political and economic independence and thereby keep societal power securely in the hands of white males. These acts of savagery were viewed as doing little to protect southern womanhood against imagined predators. Instead, lynching was held to pollute the minds of white youth, to promote political demagoguery in southern politics, and to place the peace, security, and international reputation of the entire nation in considerable peril. By calling into question the white southerners' litany of rationalizations and providing alternative explanations for the phenomenon of lynching, African American activists made clear their conviction that it was white, not black, "civilization" that was on trial. Like antilynching crusader Ida B. Wells, they stood firm in the belief that "the Afro-American race is more sinned against than sinning."[67]

For as long as the lynching fever raged, black novelists, poets, and playwrights sought to recast the received narrative—to set the literary record straight by distancing victim from villain. Their wrenching exposés placed the most dramatic elements of the lynching phenomenon in a true-to-life setting, imputed motivation, and suggested appropriate responses. As noted by black literature/folklore researcher Trudier Harris, such treatments were simultaneously artistic creations and cultural documents. By adding both human faces and dramatic storylines to bare-bones press accounts, each helped to perpetuate a folk tradition of resistance to terrorism.[68] Over time, three interconnected themes emerged from this literature. Taken together, they reveal a great deal about how and why the mutilated body of a black man hanging from a tree limb became the synecdochic image of the late nineteenth-century black condition; the lynch mob's animalistic ferocity, a litmus test for modern-day villainy.

Theme #1: Verisimilitude

Like the circumspect reformers who assisted in shaping the slave narratives for use in the abolition crusade, African American writers of the post-Reconstruction years understood that imaginative reconstructions of controversial events would be scrutinized closely. Anticipating charges of antiwhite bias, many made a conscious effort to avoid any imputation of exaggeration or invention. In the tradition of activist forebears, they employed verisimilitude as a rhetorical weapon—touting the authenticity of their accounts while denying that the material had been doctored to enhance commercial appeal. Distancing themselves from mobocrats who were said to treat lynching bees as "a lark, . . . a diversion that furnished amusement as well as satiated their lust for blood," black authors claimed to be concerned citizens who were actuated by humanitarian motives. Far from being "overdrawn and luridly colored," their storylines were "simply reproduced . . . from actual occurrences" and could be verified by reliable eyewitnesses. They offered only one caveat: in particularly disturbing cases, authors sometimes found it advisable to "soften . . . the abhorrence of the reality" for "decency's sake."[69]

Lynching, however, was a preternaturally indecent phenomenon and the black writers' commitment to social justice was never compromised by undue concern for the tender sensibilities of their public. Graphic depictions of unimaginable events forced all who entered this fictive New South chamber of horrors into a series of close encounters with villainy. It was hoped that the explicit nature of this material would spur the unenlightened to take immediate ameliorative action.

In the novels and plays of lynching, night-stalking lunatic mobs scoured the rural countryside for prey, falling on unsuspecting blacks with "that terror-instilling sound known as the 'rebel yell'" and cries of "Burn him!" "Lynch 'em!" "Kill the bastards!" If not shot immediately or butchered on the spot, the targeted individual might be tortured—battered by clubs; flesh torn by knives and corkscrews; eyes gouged out; fingers cut off one by one. Some mobs castrated their victims or dragged them behind a speeding jalopy until all semblance of the human form was erased. Following these grotesque preliminaries, the scene shifted to a jerry-built gallows or crude kerosene-fueled pyre. There, the crowd grew rapidly in size, its numbers augmented by curious, spectacle-starved thrill seekers. Southern belles "munching bon-bons and saying silly nothings to their attendant cavaliers" rubbed delicate shoulders with entrepreneurs peddling ice cream as well-appointed squires hurled epithets at the writhing figure before them. Soon, all inhibitions would be cast aside. Celebratory songs about hanging "ever nigger t a sour apple tree" rose heavenward, mingling with bluish smoke that reeked of charred flesh. Not-so-random gunshots from dozens of revolvers riddled the sagging corpse, "putting the struggling soul beyond the reach of misery." And, then, an undignified scramble for "souvenir" body parts commenced. The mob's behavior would have shamed a community of cannibals. Finally, when the bloodlust of all had been sated, the crowd dispersed, proud of their trophies and secure in the knowledge that they had "upheld white civilization."[70]

In the hands of a skilled black wordsmith, fictional treatments of events such as these became so immediate, so palpable, that one could almost feel the bonfire's heat. Most African Americans found such stories far superior to journalistic accounts of lynchings penned by whites. So socially realistic that they were difficult to stomach, the black-authored tales never made excuses for the pathological behaviors of white people, never denied or sugarcoated the nature of their villainy.

Theme #2: Virtuous Victims

In *Cane,* Jean Toomer's lyrical meditation on racial identity and changing regional folkways circa 1920, a black Georgia sharecropper named Layman introduced a northern visitor to both the intricacies and perils of the color line. "Nigger's a nigger down this away," he warned. "An only two dividins: good an bad. An even they aint permanent categories. They sometimes mixes um up when it comes t lynchin." By apprising the naive Ralph Kabnis of the fact that his status as a Negro "gentleman" might prove to be insufficient protection against angry "white folks," Layman conveyed wisdom that was central to black survival and to an understanding of the African American worldview: When apportioning racial virtue and vice, whites almost always got the relationships wrong.[71] Far too often they sought to enhance their own self-image by misapplying or inverting the terms, confusing their meanings. Saints were taken for sinners and then persecuted according to the tenets of European American devil lore masquerading as southern justice.

Vehemently denying that there was an intimate connection between Africans and evil, black writers infused their campaign for accuracy in the reporting of contemporary events with a timeless moral fervor. As representatives of an oppositional culture burdened by imputations of inferiority, they sought to revise the white-authored historical record by transforming anti-lynching tracts into allegory-rich morality plays. Maintaining that their people more closely resembled dark princes than princes of darkness, African American poets, novelists, and playwrights employed a variety of biblical allusions to tell their side of the story.

In this literature, lynching victims stood on the side of the angels. They were described as "martyred Christian[s]"—unoffending innocents subjected to the justice of hell. With souls "untouched by baser metals," these moral giants responded to the mob's abuse in a calm and dignified manner. As curses and spittle rained down, some offered thanks for past blessings and "in childlike simplicity" asked God to provide for their families. Others expressed the hope that their blood sacrifice would help turn public opinion against all such "fell customs," thereby sparing the black community further misery and removing sin's burden from the entire nation. Seeking to be remembered as role models for the oppressed," these "big-bodied—big-souled" individuals met death without reproach—"wild 'n' proud" with heads held high. As their spirit ascended heavenward with the smoke, the lynching victim was assured that a just God would not allow a saint's "crucifixion" to go unpunished.[72]

Since they felt no compulsion to blame fellow blacks for what W. E. B. Du Bois termed "the guilt of the untouched guilty," creators of fictional lynching scenarios explained the outbreaks of mob activity by using dramatic examples that seemed familiar to early twentieth-century antilynching activists. Innocent African Americans were targeted for abuse for reasons that had little to do with commonplace notions of villainy. They were set upon and manhandled as a result of (1) acquiring property and competing with established businesses; (2) fixing up their homes, purchasing automobiles, and "livin' like white folks"; (3) organizing sharecroppers; (4) denouncing mob violence; and (5) being "saucy" or otherwise contravening established norms of racial etiquette. Cursed not by God, but by white avarice, spite, and unwarranted fear, blacks were martyred for teaching "Northern equality notions" and for speaking to or accidentally bumping up against (i.e., "insulting") white women; for defending a loved one from harm and for neglecting to "look down at the groun' . . . when a white man is talkin'."[73]

As in real life, certain of the white characters drawn by black writers deemed these unauthorized behaviors to be the first fruits of an "enforced equality" that foreshadowed both sectional and racial degeneration. According to a prototypically reactionary political demagogue who appeared in Charles Chesnutt's *The Colonel's Dream,* the "decay" introduced by the Fourteenth Amendment's equal rights section was spreading rapidly and had to be kept in check. "Equality anywhere, means ultimately, equality everywhere," he thundered. "Equality at the polls means social equality; social equality means intermarriage and corruption of blood. . . . What gentleman here would want his daughter to marry a blubber-lipped, cocoanut-headed, kidney-footed, etc., etc., nigger?"[74] Antilynching novels and plays spoke directly to the stupefying illogic of such beliefs by exhibiting southern blacks' lack of hostile intent. The boldest writers then proceeded to trace the outlines of an insidious postbellum plot to keep the race terrorized and intimidated. As a fictional conspirator created by Chesnutt's contemporary, the prolific black novelist Sutton Griggs, revealed in an unguarded moment: "We lynch niggers down here for anything. We lynch them for being sassy and sometimes lynch them on general principles. The truth of the matter is the [crime] that paves the way for a lynching whenever we have the notion, is the crime of being black."[75] Because few actual mobocrats were willing to be as candid, African American authors considered it their duty to highlight the Christlike walk of racial kinsmen and to inform truth seekers of all backgrounds that racist schemers were attempting to manipulate public opinion by transforming their own vices into virtues.

Theme #3: Imputing Villainy

During an era of sectional reconciliation in which longtime political adversaries were cozying up and exchanging Cheshire cat smiles, African Americans had good reason to wonder whether former "friends of freedom" had abandoned their "sable brethren" in the quest for national unity. In earlier times, only about a quarter of southern whites had held title to other human beings while many northerners either were deeply troubled by the "peculiar institution" or actively engaged in orchestrating its demise. By the turn of the century, however, mainstream Americans had returned to the business of business as usual. International expansionist initiatives overshadowed internal reform, and key opinion shapers showed neither shame nor apparent remorse in turning a cold shoulder to the struggling southern peasantry. More than ever before—or at least more than a reasonable person would expect to find after reading glowing accounts of the nation's multiple "missions" and "burdens"—sympathetic whites seemed the exception to the rule. As a result, when contrasting the saintly behavior of lynching victims with the perversities of their pursuers, African American writers evidenced an increased receptivity to the notion that white people were uniquely estranged from "the good." More than a misguided response to a specific incidence of Negro "misbehavior," the meanness (and cowardice) displayed whenever a lynch mob vented its fury was thought to be rooted in the European American past. Because the prospect of immediate change seemed chimerical, activist authors sought to warn their public of danger by providing detailed descriptions of white villains. Given the seriousness of the situation, they felt compelled to take the controversial position that the nation's greatest problem was "not what men will do with the negro," but what can be done to control the savage behavior of "the reckless, lawless white men who murder, lynch, and burn their fellow-citizens."[76]

In crafting literary and theatrical exposes of lynching's "red record," African American writers utilized several symbolic and metaphorical representations that served to separate white people from both a common humanity and modern-day standards of civilized behavior:

Barbarians. When mobs ripped a fetus from a pregnant woman's belly and "stuck it t a tree" or stormed a segregated hospital ward in search of prey because they considered it "a damn shame to let 'at nigger die in a nice white bed," the oppressed had ample reason to fear that whites were "retrograding toward barbarism." Some, it seems, already had descended to the level of brute creation. Their "baser passions" easily aroused by the presence of an upright, aspiring black citizenry, this "savage element" in American society took great pleasure in committing depraved acts and then gloating over their victims. As noted by the narrator of James Weldon Johnson's *The Autobiography of an Ex-Colored Man* (1912), such a people were out of touch with "humanitarianized thought" and in no way could be considered enlightened. Both their horrific crimes and "many of their general ideas" harkened back "to a former century, some of them to the Dark Ages."[77]

Beasts. The cold, cruel gaze of a lynch mob participant in pursuit of a black sacrifice lacked any connection to normal human sensibilities. In the torch-lit darkness, animalistic passions reigned supreme. Acting like wild beasts in search of prey, the mob was compared to a pride of prowling lions; individual members to "the chattering ape and the surly bear, . . . the ghoulish hyena and the skulking panther, . . . the deadly cobra and the cowardly jackal." Every blood-soaked triumph was marked by an unearthly howling that echoed across the southern countryside like "the hungry voice of some great-throated wild thing." To the hunted, their pursuers appeared "monstrous and prodigious." Like the storied Gorgon or Hydra, they were "abominable in shape and to sight."[78]

Demons. By all accounts, the lynch mob was Old Nick's chosen instrument for creating a little bit of hell on earth. Unmindful of the pain they caused and unafraid to violate the sanctity of houses of worship even on the Sabbath, satanic mobocrats expressed a "fiendish glee" when their victim was cornered, beaten into submission, and brought to the sacrificial altar. There, as the bonfire crackled, "devils with white skins" cavorted about the pyre like imps awaiting the dispensation of Satan's justice. Reflecting the paganism of caste that had overspread white America, the mob's "Christless prejudices" were displayed in such a graphic manner that even a devout churchgoer could be led to question the efficacy of prayer. In extreme cases, black believers might even begin to doubt God and to call upon the demons of hell to imbue them with the "bitterness, gall and hatred" needed to exact vengeance. Such were the spiritually polluting fruits of the evil deeds committed by Satan's minions.[79]

If a picture is worth a thousand words, these word portraits of white villains in the throes of passion speak volumes about how the most pernicious elements in southern society were perceived within black America. But what about the "better sort" of white people—those to whom the black writers appealed for redress? Were they really all that different? Given suitable motivation and opportunity, could a "race liberal" become demonic? If these questions rarely were posed in a manner capable of eliciting a definitive response, black-authored depictions of the South's "best people" suggest that both overt terrorist acts as well as the far more common "sins of omission" were deeply resented by people of color. Each set of behaviors helped to define racial character; to distinguish African American from European American.

Even when they refused to join the canaille in debauchery, "solid" citizens treated blacks shamefully. Unduly influenced by social Darwinist notions of "strong" and "weak" races, they refused either to coddle or delude blacks by giving them false hopes of equality. Instead, pieties were offered. The world, they lamented, "is not ready for it yet." Cowed by public opinion and fearful that support of black interests would bring social ostracism and economic retaliation, such individuals literally ran from controversy. Whenever racist deviltry was afoot, they seemed to vanish into thin air—reappearing only after the horrific deed was done to offer pity, excuses, and further evasions of difficult questions. Like the misguided Levite of Luke 10:32 who refused to assist an injured man on the road to Jericho, white Americans "passed by on the other side." This proven inability to "reason in a Negro's favor" or to evidence compassion by sharing the "cream" of life's abundance with those forced by circumstance of birth to "pay a sweet price for skimmed milk" made "the best people" seem little more that an abstraction. From the perspective of American society's bottom rung, apologists or co-conspirators seemed more appropriate designations. Sister Johnson, a bitter, aggrieved character who appeared in Langston Hughes' *Not without Laughter* (1930), wasn't shy about offering just such a critique: "Don't tell me 'bout white folks bein' good," she lectured a friend, "'cause I knows 'em. . . . White folks is white folks, an' dey's mean!"[80]

While by no means abandoning hope of forging alliances across racial lines, many early twentieth-century African Americans shared this pessimistic view of white people. Like well-known "race man" W. E. B. Du Bois, they were attracted to the subversive notion of "carving God in night / painting hell in white" and sought to reformulate received wisdom by disputing truisms about southern chivalry and African primitivism.[81] The broad strokes that were used to draw unfavorable portraits of light-complected villains while beatifying persecuted dark-skinned Everymen speak of a race-conscious sensibility that continues to percolate through African American social thought. Deeply felt group loyalties forged in slavery and tempered during the heyday of Judge Lynch have encouraged intellectuals and common folk alike to view blackness as life affirming; whiteness as death dealing. Drawn from the actual historical experiences of the southern peasantry, not from the fantasy lives of southern hate-mongers, these oppositional cultural beliefs have enabled several generations of black strivers to conceptualize themselves as members of a martyred and misunderstood, but morally upright race. Given the amount of black blood staining the altar of white villainy, it is understandable that those born into this oppressed community might find it difficult to imagine that any racial kinsman would commit so immense a crime.

White Villains: The Conspirators

According to many modern-day history texts, the chief legacy of lynching was fear. According to the black worldview, it was suspicion. While subtle, the differences between these perspectives are significant. The first conjures up visions of a panic-stricken black peasantry in urgent need of the powerful and compassionate white liberal's help. Most critically, assistance is required to police the more unruly elements of the Caucasian population and to teach these ruffians some lessons in civility. The latter posits the existence of a self-directed African American community capable of calmly and accurately processing information essential to survival. After evaluating their situation vis-à-vis the white world, its members respond to contemporary events by implementing protective strategies. When appropriate, mutual assistance pacts may be made with liberal whites, but unconditional faith in an outsider's declaration of goodwill is rare. More commonly, blacks maintain that actions speak louder than words and refrain from putting too much stock in the liberals' claims of being different from "the worst sort." In the postbellum black worldview, it is considered necessary to entertain the suspicion that all whites are potential conspirators against minority-group interests. Like the sage Uncle Daniel, a character in Frances E. W. Harper's 1892 novel, *Iola Leroy*, vigilant, historically aware African Americans recognize that "white man's so unsartin, black man's nebber safe."[82]

Within early twentieth-century intellectual circles, speculation on the origin of whites' conspiratorial nature was encouraged by a widely held belief that each racial group possessed a unique set of attributes or "gifts." W. E. B. Du Bois's reading and interpretation of this patently racialist concept was among the most distinctive. According to the Harvard-educated activist's nuanced depiction, blacks were a race of artists, endowed with a unique sense of beauty—of sound, color, and "spiritual joyousness." A "tropical" love of life not only enabled the peoples of the African Diaspora to benefit from the therapeutic properties inherent in laughter, song, and dance, but also led them to place a premium on the development of personal qualities such as honesty, humility, faith, and compassion. Strong, resilient, yet "deliciously human," African Americans were not hardened by centuries of struggle against man and nature. As a result, their contribution to Western civilization was more aesthetic and spiritual than technological or military. But it was an element essential to its vitality and survival. The black community provided an "oasis of simple faith and reverence" in an artificial and hypocritical land.[83]

Contrasting dramatically with this idealized ancestral race, the United States' branch of the European American family tree was believed to be horribly diseased. Its contamination of American culture was in an advanced critical stage. Indeed, to Du Bois, the terms "Anglo-Saxon" and "Teuton" stood for all that was wrong with contemporary society. Crass, self-indulgent, and boastful, white people were practiced deceivers. They had a taste for "the tawdry and flamboyant" but were incapable of camouflaging their essential meanness of spirit. Having deified self and adopted "kill or be killed" as a behavioral watchword, this joyless, emotionally stunted race was said to be governed by the "cool logic of the Club"—might transformed into sacred right at the expense of human brotherhood. Lacking the leavening, humanizing component of blackness, their history was nothing less than a study in "moral obtuseness and refined brutality"—of "murder, theft, rape, deception, and degradation."[84]

On at least one occasion, Du Bois gave public thanks that to the best of his knowledge no Anglo-Saxon blood flowed through his veins. Nevertheless, deeply felt racial loyalties did not prevent him from urging fellow blacks to share their racial gifts with the mainstream. He considered proud, race-conscious African Americans to be "the spiritual hope of this land"—the "harbinger of that black to-morrow which is yet destined to soften the whiteness of the Teutonic to-day." By providing a complement and corrective to the whites' brash and bloody mind-set, it was hoped that they would win long-overdue recognition as coworkers in the kingdom of culture.[85] But could the moral power of the oppressed actually redeem their tormentors and thereby salvage the American dream? How long should this gentle, loving, and just people continue to reject the notion of answering hate with hate? Here, even Du Bois seemed to waiver. In the 1928 novel *Dark Princess,* he described an insidious Ku Klux Klan–sponsored campaign to "pit the dark peoples against each other—Japanese against Chinese; Indians against Negroes; Negroes against Arabs; Mulattoes against Blacks."[86] Given the nation's racial history, it seemed only logical to conclude that the Anglo-Saxons' hunger for power was insatiable; their conspiratorial bent, intractable.

During the Depression years of the 1930s, many who had come to doubt the ability of black redemptive society to provide the sort of tropical leaven capable of transforming Nordic cruelty into compassion were attracted to the separatist message of the Nation of Islam. Determined to redeem the dark-skinned tribe of Shabazz from centuries of white rule, patriarch Elijah Muhammad urged his followers to escape "mental poisoning" by relocating to a "state or territory of their own—either on this continent or elsewhere." If frequently couched in eschatological language or hidden in cryptic references to "the earth that originally belonged to us," the black Muslim position on territorial nationalism was clear. Only by (re-)establishing a vibrant Islamic culture "beyond the white world" could the North American branch of a once-powerful "Asian Black Nation" find relative safety from white conspirators.[87]

In the Nation of Islam's decidedly nonorthodox theology, African Americans were considered divine by nature—"the first and last, maker and owner of the universe." Nevertheless, a black creator God had seen fit to test their mettle. A race of inherently evil spawns of science was allowed to dominate and mislead the "so-called Negroes." For centuries both mental and physical chains had kept blacks ignorant of the fact that they were a chosen people, sacred to Allah and destined for greatness. Fortunately, the time of judgment for these "blue-eyed devils" was fast approaching. Hell was "kindling up" and soon would be densely populated by cadres of colorless Caucasians. After Armageddon, America was to burn in a great lake of fire for 390 years but eventually would become the Original People's brave new world—a black Muslim promised land with neither sickness nor sorrow; worry or white people.[88]

According to the faithful, both this fantastic futurescape and Elijah Muhammad's interim program of territorial nationalism had the devils in a perpetual state of panic. As a result, whites continually schemed and plotted in order to maintain their hegemony over the smarter, more physically attractive black race. Major conspiratorial schemes included: (1) the enslavement of Allah's chosen ones in the wilderness of North America; (2) all subsequent cultural dislocations wrought by a force-feeding of Western Christianity; (3) the devastating moral pollution of black "Sacred Vessels" by strong drink, filthy songs, suggestive dancing, and the "sexual worship of the same sex"; and (4) deceptively packaged "smooth lies" such as integration, interracial marriage, and government-sponsored birth control programs. Secretive in intent but bold in their display of evil and indecency, "cowardly enemy devils" understood that their days were numbered and sought to implicate as many blacks as possible in their crimes. As Muhammad asserted in a cautionary message to his followers, "Since hell is their appointed place, they are trying to get us to go to hell with them on false promises."[89]

The separation of the races that would allow blacks to avoid both moral contamination and Allah's coming wrath even extended to dietary matters. When leaders of the Nation urged believers to heed the wisdom of Revelation 18:4 and "come out of her, my people, that ye be not partakers of her sins, and that ye receive not of her plagues," they might as well have added "and savor not her cuisine."[90] Convinced that all human illness—"from social disease to cancer"—could be traced to white evildoers, Elijah Muhammad viewed mainstream foodways as part of a corrupt scheme to shorten the life span of the righteous. Because it was their nature "to do the opposite of right," the Nation's enemies ate the wrong foods and ate them far too often. They sought to weaken the black race by encouraging the consumption of spicy, greasy, hastily prepared dishes. "Filthy hog meat," catfish—"the pig of the water"—"half-cooked breads," and overly sweet or starchy items were particularly harmful. Indeed, a modern fast-food diet was said to be "enough to wear out the intestines of a brass monkey." A single serving of walnuts or "that concrete-like peanut butter" could shorten one's life by five years. According to black Muslim lore, "eating as beasts eat" during their centuries-long exposure to the white world's dietary practices had multiplied illness and decreased life expectancy dramatically. Due to a healthful regimen of infrequent vegetarian meals and monthly fasting, the African Americans' earliest ancestors were believed to have lived to the extremely ripe old age of one thousand.[91]

Accustomed to far less healthy fare "in the hills and caves of Europe, where he ate all his food raw," the Caucasian came to be more ghoul than gourmand. In addition to serving as negative role models for personal hygiene and a sensible diet, New World whites conspired to make food an instrument of destruction. Apparently, the slow death brought about by eating corn bread, pork, and "scavenger fish" wasn't alleviating the problem of troublesome blacks quickly enough. To hasten their demise, scientists were said to have developed a variety of toxins that, when introduced into the food chain and water supply, shortened black lives. According to the Nation, this deliberate adulteration of foodstuffs was done so that white physicians and undertakers could "make more money." Certainly, this was just the sort of behavior one expected from a race of swine-eating schemers. To thwart their ghoulish conspiracy, it was deemed essential that black folk shun the blue-eyed devils, stay away from their tainted food, and "eat to live."[92]

For the remainder of the century, black America's response to rumors concerning white conspiracies ran the gamut from healthy skepticism to debilitating paranoia. As the least likely segment of the community to envision an integrated future for people of color, nationalist-oriented African Americans came to be especially adept at crafting worst-case scenarios. Equal parts organizational raison d'être, ancient history lesson, and self-promotional tool, their chilling theories focused on identifying enemies and attributing motivation; less so on mapping viable survival strategies. Here, individualistic, exploitative "Ice People" replaced Du Bois's warlike Anglo-Saxons and Muhammad's blue-eyed devils as the chief threat to communalistic, spiritually gifted "Sun People." Separated from their Nile Valley roots by a prehistoric migration to Ice Age Europe, the Neanderthal-Caucasoids' subsequent evolution in an unforgiving glacial environment was believed to have had telling consequences for future generations. Aggressive, territorial tendencies and the deep-seated need to acquire material possessions were useful survival tools, well adapted to rugged environs. Unfortunately, as the climate of this European cradle of civilization became more temperate, the Caucasians continued to react to outmoded environmental stimuli. Increasingly out of touch with the times, they were unable to cope with change in a rational manner. Recognizing that the beneficial adaptive properties of light-colored skin no longer were critical to group survival, but finding it impossible to permanently darken the Caucasian complexion, this melanin-deficient race became painfully aware of its abnormality. As a result, white people's frustrations and insecurities came to be vented in pathological, antiblack behaviors. In short, black nationalist conspiracy theories were rooted in the belief that caveman ways die hard—that "you can take the Savage out of Europe, but you can't take the savage out of the European."[93]

Caucasoid psychobiology determined whites' obsessive-compulsive need to dominate groups that are more proficient in producing the hormone melatonin, but jealousy was a key motivating factor in the hatching of conspiratorial plots. Updating Du Boisian terminology, late-century nationalist writers claimed that it was marvelous to be a "hueman." Certainly, melanin-rich peoples were gifted with far more than natural sunscreen. They were credited with encompassing the totality of the human condition in ways that made their chalky-faced cousins positively green with envy. As "perhaps the most fantastic stuff on the planet," the pigment melanin was said to confer paranormal powers and to enhance athletic ability. It enabled blacks to experience higher levels of spiritual awareness and was responsible for both the ecstatic nature of African American religious expression and the rhythmic, emotionally charged character of secular music and dance. Considered the "neurochemical basis of what we call 'soul,'" melanin purportedly allowed Sun People to "decode the energy emanations from plants" and "negotiate the vibrations of the universe." Understandably, powers such as these generated feelings of envy in Caucasoid circles. Unable to jettison the burden of genetically recessive white skin, European Americans sought to forestall their own racial annihilation by plotting against the black nation.[94]

Rooted in what City College of New York black studies professor Leonard Jeffries has termed "anti-Kemetism," or "the inability to deal with the blackness of the Nile," this struggle for white genetic survival was seen as an ongoing conflict orchestrated by various conspiratorial groupings of Ice People.[95] Some modern-day conspiracy theorists claimed to have identified a "cabal of elitists and money lords . . . beyond just the powerful and rich" that had successfully infiltrated traditional Establishment circles and was using its influence to "enslave the people."[96] Others were more specific, holding "rich Jews" responsible for all manner of antiblack deceptions—in effect, making them honorary Ice People so that their ancestors could be blamed for financing the international slave trade.[97] Still others announced that the U.S. Joint Chiefs of Staff was planning a war against urban youth "under the pretext of national security" and that survivalist militias were "polishing up their rifles in anticipation of a violent showdown." At the very least, a "white media conspiracy" was seeking to discredit nationalist prophets like themselves.[98] Whatever the specific leadership cohort, any threat to Caucasian self-preservation was believed capable of mobilizing the white masses in support of acts that were both desperate and deadly.

During a volatile nuclear age in which governments periodically experimented with ethnic cleansing as a geopolitical solution to the problems of state, white genetic survival came to be seen as the ultimate skin-color privilege; genocidal plots against nonwhites, the penultimate conspiratorial act. Seeming plausible even to marginalized individuals who had ridiculed and rejected every other programmatic aspect of contemporary black nationalism, the concept of a "black genocide" was widely discussed by intellectuals and common folk alike. Indeed, the nationalists' notion of "cannibalistic" whites emerging en masse from their "carnivorous condo caves" in order to purge the most melanin-rich element of the population from the "hue-man chain" was so repugnantly bizarre that both debate and elaboration were virtually guaranteed. Ultimately, the catchphrase "black genocide" was used to describe a wide variety of rumored conspiracies. Perceived by many to be the "logical conclusion of racism," it served as a clarion call summoning activists to organize their communities for survival.[99]

In 1951 the black Left had led the way, condemning Congress for its failure to exercise world moral leadership by ratifying the United Nations Convention on the Prevention and Punishment of the Crime of Genocide. Dismissing cold war–era claims that the compact would infringe upon American sovereignty and dupe African Americans into becoming "catspaws for the Soviet Fifth Column," advocates appealed to the world body for assistance in counteracting "a massive conspiracy . . . often concealed by euphemisms, but always directed to oppressing the Negro people." Carried out via "psychological terror" and "race murders," "police killings" and the "incitements to genocide" contained in segregationist speeches, this mass intimidation and slaughter of innocent African Americans was said to be "gilded with the trappings of respectability" by government bureaucrats. The threat to both black survival and international peace was clear. White America's "Hitler-like" racial beliefs and its rapidly mounting tally of human rights violations were believed capable of spawning "the larger genocide that is predatory war."[100]

The failure of a succession of U.S. presidential administrations to win congressional approval for the Genocide Convention gave credence to these allegations. As a result, conspiracy theorists of the 1960s and '70s were kept busy identifying new plots and posting periodic warnings. Escalating police brutality suggested that whites were capable of having "the gas ovens built before you realize that they're already hot." Many found little in the military's conduct in Vietnam to alleviate the fear that it *could* happen here—that the Nazis' reign of terror soon might be "replayed on American soil with a new cast of characters." By the time right-wing opposition was overcome and the Genocide Convention ratified in 1986, a host of African American activists had joined the discussion. Claiming that their people existed in "a pre-genocidal state" characterized by frequent physical and psychological abuse, they called for increased vigilance, group unity, and the promotion of self-defensive behaviors. Recognizing that mass murder "always remains a live option when those in power hold contempt for those who are powerless in their midst," the boldest among them spoke of fomenting a preemptive Black Power revolution.[101]

For the revolutionary nationalist supporters of the Black Panther Party, there was little to debate. Both the Johnson administration's aggressively interventionist foreign policy and the "Nixon clique's" domestic strategy of "repression and containment" signaled the existence of a "Fascist Genocidal Conspiracy" against people of color. Once they had napalmed the Vietcong into submission, the nation's leaders were sure to give blacks their undivided attention. Already, "gestapo police" were on the warpath in the urban ghetto—rousting outspoken militants and filling gulag-like penitentiaries with members of a socioeconomic caste made expendable by advances in technology. Those escaping incarceration or elimination were sent on a forced march through the power elite's maze of poverty programs. Here, a sinister corps of social workers recruited from the silent majority practiced bait-and-switch tactics—luring entire communities into welfare dependency only to cut funding so that they could watch the poor fight to the death over the remaining crumbs.[102]

In response to these cruel white initiatives, the West Coast Panther vanguard declared themselves a consciousness-raising cadre of "revolutionary executioners." Party members worked to educate the "sleeping masses" in effective liberation strategies. They instituted an impressive number of community-based "survival programs" and petitioned the United Nations for redress and reparations. Most effectively of all, they put the white Establishment on notice that blacks were willing to risk death in order to forestall a racial holocaust. "We're not going to play Jews," Panther minister of information Eldridge Cleaver told an interviewer in 1968. "We see our struggle as inextricably bound up with the struggle of all oppressed peoples, and there is no telling what sacrifices we in this country may have to make before that struggle is won." Before they would accept genocide, Panther loyalists were prepared to launch a "War of Salvation" capable of inflicting "Total Destruction upon Babylon."[103]

Meanwhile, at the other end of the Black Power movement's ideological spectrum, cultural nationalists and fellow-traveling dramatists, poets, and fiction writers enhanced the revolutionary narrative with a variety of cautionary tales. Recognizing that distinguishing an actual conspiracy from an imaginary one was, at best, a subjective process, African American authors let their imaginations run wild. Melding partially documented evidence with inference and rumor masquerading as fact, their stories gave voice to recurring fears that Washington was primed to implement a program of black population control. Incapable of generating compassion for others, the "rhythmless hearts" of the white leaders were said to harbor only thoughts of death and destruction. There was no middle ground. High-status public officials, military officers, and government scientists wanted black people enslaved or buried.[104]

In Floyd McKissick's short story "Diary of a Black Man," the tip-off that the black pogroms were about to begin came with congressional passage of strict gun-control legislation. After police and national guardsmen had disarmed the African American population, a National Registration Act ordered all blacks to carry special identification cards. Then, in a television address, the president urged implementation of a National Heritage Act that would declare subversive all overt expression of "alien" cultures. At about the same time, development of a new "pill bomb" was announced. No larger than an aspirin tablet, it could destroy limited areas without danger of widespread fallout. After testing in Bedford-Stuyvesant, black bodies were to be cleared away and the bombed-out district redeveloped by major corporations.[105]

Other fictionalized depictions of the evil white empire's response to "nigger unrest; nigger demands; nigger population; niggers period" were somewhat more subtle but no less insidious. In Ben Caldwell's play *Top Secret, or A Few Million after B.C.*, "Operation Pre-Kill" was adopted by federal authorities only after proposals such as establishing concentration camps or A-bombing Harlem had been rejected as "too barbaric." The approved plan centered upon a crash program to develop and market an inexpensive birth control pill. In the words of McNack, head of the president's Inner Space program, the pill would "kill the nigger babies before they're born! Fast as them black bucks can shoot 'em in! Simple as that!" If Operation Pre-Kill was a success, the government no longer would have to worry about marches on Washington. The Boy Scouts could handle any future disturbances. Within twenty years, he predicted, there would be a severe—and most welcome—shortage of black people.[106]

Alternative portrayals of the nation's movement toward an African American final solution told of plans to engage the minority population in an all-out domestic race war, to promote "behavior and aspirational changes" through psychobiochemical mind control, and to implement a Pentagon-sponsored "Forget-for-Peace" program that would induce mass amnesia and erase "militant" racial memories. One writer even predicted that all black folk eventually would be shipped off to the moon "whether they like it or not." But only if the moon proved unfit for white habitation.[107] In each case, black creative artists reiterated essential wisdom about the nation's "Dangerous Germ Culture": "Throat-cutting time" was drawing nigh and no honky could be trusted. The hateful "pink faced monkeys" considered North America a White Power enclave—and would seek to attain exclusive occupancy by any means necessary.[108]

Determined to convince doubters that these dire scenarios were reality-based, black activists of the 1980s and '90s assembled an impressive file on the whites' covert activities. Unfazed by social psychologist Michael Billig's pronouncement that "the conspiracy theorist . . . is to the professional historian what the treasure-hunter is to the archaeologist," they culled a treasure trove of incriminating data from the historical record.[109] Frequently, distrust of white people, their governing institutions, and their favored information sources caused disparities in evidence and logic to be overlooked. In the quest to connect the loose ends of causal relationships, varying amounts of rumor and speculation also were added to the mix. By century's end, the most intuitive—some would say the most easily excited and paranoid—conspiracy theorists became convinced that whites had developed "higher forms of killing" that went "beyond war, beyond genocide and into the realm of madness."[110]

Just as tall oaks grew from tiny acorns, complicated genocidal plots were shown to be rooted in individual racist acts. Over time, this festering anti-black sentiment helped shape a social and intellectual environment that was believed capable of supporting state-sponsored terrorism on a massive scale. From a mainstream perspective, the ethnosociological evidence that undergirded such notions was irredeemably flawed—the stuff of urban legend. But for African Americans, these sometimes odd, often interrelated beliefs and suspicions had great utility. Speculation on the provenance of "black genocide" provided a culture-specific mechanism for defining, interpreting, and resisting white villainy. The chief theaters of conflict in this no-holds-barred war for racial dominance were as follows:

Macabre Medical Research

To many, white medical researchers and physicians personified the modern-day genocidal personality. Their calculating, clinical manner and eagerness to garner lucrative grants from both multinational corporations and the U.S. military encouraged the belief that these so-called health care professionals had taken an oath to hypocrisy, not Hippocrates. Like the ghostly "night doctors" who were said to have prowled black neighborhoods in search of bodies for dissection during the late nineteenth century, such individuals seemed determined to advance medical science by using blacks as guinea pigs.[111]

Throughout the 1970s and '80s, negative media reports on the Public Health Service's longitudinal (1932–72) study of untreated syphilis in a group of some four hundred Alabama black men generated widespread outrage—fueling fears that these nontherapeutic experiments were part of what activist lawyer Fred Gray termed "a program of controlled genocide." Certainly, the government's cost-conscious $15,000 out-of-court settlement with the heirs of each "deceased syphilitic" set a depressingly low price on the lives of poor, uneducated folk who had been told only that they were afflicted with "bad blood."[112] Soon, health care horror stories proliferated.

In addition to expressing concern that "Amerikkkan Medical Association"—certified doctors were harvesting body parts in inner-city emergency rooms and tricking prison inmates into testing experimental drugs "for a few pieces of silver," critics of the health care delivery system complained loudly about government-sponsored birth control initiatives.[113] Convinced by Black Power–era patriarchs that there was strength in numbers, they greeted with skepticism any movement to impose white middle-class norms on black family size and structure. The most cynical viewed abortion rights activists as New Age eugenicists and considered Planned Parenthood a stalking horse for involuntary birth control and coerced sterilization. In such circles, ill-advised, medically unnecessary hysterectomies were known as "Mississippi appendectomies." Zero Population Growth was devil-speak for "no more black babies." Norplant and Depo-Provera were the social engineers' cold-blooded contraceptive solutions to "the welfare mess." Aggressively promoted by pharmaceutical companies and Medicaid caseworkers, such products, procedures, and programs seemed little more than thinly disguised attempts to deny African Americans basic reproductive rights. Collectively, these FDA-approved disincentives to procreation caused concerned students of comparative history to reflect on the fact that it was a compulsory sterilization law that foreshadowed an earlier Holocaust in 1930s Germany.[114]

Once bitten, twice shy, many of the same questioning voices were quick to charge white scientists with complicity in the rapidly spreading AIDS epidemic. A 1990 public opinion survey revealed that nearly a third of New York City African Americans believed it true or possibly true that the virus responsible for the deadly disease was "deliberately created in a laboratory in order to infect black people." At the time, blacks accounted for almost 28 percent of reported AIDS cases—more than double their share of the U.S. population. Within five years, the overall black/white percentages were equal (40%). Soon thereafter, Harvard researchers reported that it was likely that more African Americans were infected with the human immunodeficiency (HIV) virus than all other racial and ethnic groups combined.[115]

As the plague worsened, conspiracy scenarios became ever more complex and varied. One popular theory maintained that the virus was artificially engineered and intentionally spread throughout Africa via World Health Organization smallpox vaccination programs. This unleashing of biological weaponry was thought to be part of a scheme to destroy indigenous peoples and to seize control of the continent's natural resources. Purportedly designed to reduce specific "undesirable" populations, the experiment soon went awry as AIDS proved to be a far more indiscriminate killer than government scientists had imagined. Variants of this theory added Haiti to the list of targeted nations; speculated about the degree of CIA involvement; referred to the besieged European American gay community as a planned distraction— a "test batch"; and told of Jewish doctors injecting black infants with AIDS as part of a Zionist plot to seize world power.[116]

Since conspiracy theorists also held that the "AIDS establishment" sponsored a massive disinformation campaign to disguise its true intentions, no government response to the disease crisis could be considered legitimate or be permitted to serve as evidence of institutional goodwill. The experimental AIDS drug AZT, said critics, was toxic. Hypodermic needle exchange programs purportedly designed to lower the rate of HIV infection among drug users were blamed for increasing levels of substance abuse among urban youth. These, too, were thought to be components of a "genocidal campaign" that was no more accidental "than small pox was an accident with the Indians. Sending them blankets and killing them with disease."[117]

Fatal Food and Drugs

In his grimly satirical 1982 novel *The Terrible Twos*, Ishmael Reed depicted the evolution of a Hitleresque conspiracy to rid the planet of troublesome "surplus people." As noted by one high-level strategist, nothing seemed capable of stopping these doltish pests from "reproducing like mink." "We tried spermacide, and sterilization. . . . We contemplated germ warfare but ruled that out because some of the surplus people were mixed up with the vital people," he complained. A third approach to the problem was to create an artificial famine. Hopefully, elimination of free lunch programs and food stamps would end the threat of societal "mongrelization." It didn't work.[118]

As if addressing a still unmet need, other white megalomaniacs profiled by black writers were said to have developed alternative strategies for transforming the staff of life into an instrument of death. Conspiracy theorists of the 1980s and '90s voiced particular concern over reports that ghetto grocery stores were being stockpiled with tainted or highly addictive food items. According to these suspicious consumer advocates, for the USDA to find nothing wrong with recommending that lactose-intolerant African Americans wolf down two to three servings of milk, yogurt, or cheese daily was prima facie evidence of both regulatory malfeasance and conspiratorial intent.[119] Little wonder, then, that several other laboratory-tested, name-brand products seemed to be causing harmful side effects. Of far more consequence than occasional stomach discomfort or a milk mustache, the fruit-flavored soft drink Tropical Fantasy allegedly contained a secret ingredient that made African American men sterile. So did St. Ides malt liquor and Church's Fried Chicken. Rumor had it that the latter company also laced their food with chemicals that led to mental retardation in black infants. Some claimed that Church's—along with the Marlboro, Uptown, and Kool cigarette brands— was owned by the Ku Klux Klan.[120]

Consumers who were clever enough to find the three hidden K's on a pack of Marlboro's and who understood that the reason for substituting a K for the C in "Cool" had nothing to do with enhancing menthol freshness rarely questioned the likelihood of federal involvement in plots designed to induce habit-forming and potentially deadly behaviors in blacks. As if to confirm the viability of folk wisdom, conspiracy theories that posited government complicity in the spread of drug trafficking and gang warfare became front-page news during the mid-1990s. Popularized by Hollywood films such as *Boyz N the Hood, Deep Cover,* and *Panther,* the seemingly implausible notion that Ronald Reagan would say "yes" to crack cocaine in order to (1) provide funding for CIA-sponsored Nicaraguan Contra rebels and (2) permanently narcotize political insurgency within black America broke free from urban legend and came to be perceived by many as an urban reality.

In the wake of these revelations, a variety of angry voices weighed in on the issue—crafting convincing word portraits of undocumented but vividly imagined meetings between South American drug lords and South Central Los Angeles street gangs. California congressional representative Maxine Waters found it unconscionable that the U.S. intelligence community "could think so little of people of color that they would be willing to destroy generations in an effort to try to win the war in Nicaragua."[121] Nation of Islam leader Louis Farrakhan wasn't terribly surprised about the apparent degree of governmental complicity but was outraged nonetheless. "[Imitating a devilish official:] Feed them cocaine. Then make it a pure form that they can smoke and call it crack, and feed it to the young warriors among them so that they now will turn the power of their youth and their anger and hostility on themselves."[122] Less voluble critics, such as syndicated columnist Clarence Page, scored the CIA's "unholy alliances . . . with thugs and thieves," ripped the Drug Enforcement Administration (DEA) for providing aid and comfort to known enemies, and called for a full-scale congressional investigation of the disgraceful mess.[123] Ultimately, even those who held open the possibility that the West Coast drug scourge was no more than an accident of history made worse by the government's "unbridled criminal stupidity" somehow managed to feed the flames of controversy that nurtured black genocide theories.[124] As Ishmael Reed suggested in 1996, while it certainly was possible that not every word of such stories was true, "the weight of the evidence" gave credence to black America's worst fears.[125]

Fortunately, the African American worldview privileged suspicion over fear. As a result, even the most ominous rumors of a black genocide through drugs or disease were capable of energizing—not paralyzing—resistance to oppression. White America's unsavory history of enslavement, lynching, and conspiratorial scheming both strengthened the black community's resolve and mandated that its members learn the ways of whites so well that their every secretive move could be anticipated. To "know" white people, their aspirations, and their characteristic approaches to problem solving was not to love or to value them as role models. Such knowledge was, however, considered essential to group survival.

Convinced that almost any interaction with whites carried with it the potential for disaster, postbellum antilynching activists and twentieth-century conspiracy theorists labored unceasingly to provide an early warning system that could be utilized by each succeeding generation. In the process, some became expert at crafting questions that were (mis-)perceived as answers. Others developed a fondness for grand display and rooftop shouting. Still others compromised their effectiveness through unnecessary argumentation and intragroup sectarianism. All, however, believed in themselves, in the essential goodness of black folk, and in the need to convince unwary racial kinsmen to watch their backs at all times.

The possibilities for white villainy seemed endless. Somewhat more sophisticated but differing little in basic intent from earlier years, this late twentieth-century "quiet war" against people of color was said to include psychological and cultural terrorism (schools that systematically programmed African American youth for failure; mass-media promotion of negative racial stereotypes);[126] environmental racism (the targeting of minority-group neighborhoods for toxic waste dumps);[127] and police conspiracies and political assassinations (most notably the killing of Malcolm X and Martin Luther King Jr.).[128] More often than not, the "official" position on these and related issues was considered suspect. In the black worldview, alternative interpretations were preferred—at least until all the evidence was in. The following hypotheses may have seemed peculiar to those socialized within the mainstream but were fully compatible with a marginalized population's perception of white people as the most incorrigible of villains:

> The U.S. government keeps tabs on African Americans by assigning them social security numbers that contain an even number in the fifth digit. Ditto photo IDs on driver's licenses.[129]

> White-authored history texts lie: 1920s blues queen Bessie Smith and pioneering blood plasma researcher Charles Drew died from injuries sustained in automobile accidents after they were refused treatment at "whites only" hospitals.[130]

> Secret contingency plans (code names "King Alfred" and "Rex 84") exist that call for suspension of the Constitution, the unseating of minority-group members of Congress, and the relocation of blacks to detention camps in time of national emergency.[131]

> The Jonestown, Guyana, tragedy of 1978 in which over nine hundred people drank cyanide-laced grape Flavor Aid at the command of People's Temple cult leader Jim Jones was part of a mind-control/black genocide experiment.[132]

> The multirace check-off provision of the 2000 U.S. census was designed to reduce African American political clout, shrink economic benefits programs, and complicate the enforcement of civil rights laws.[133]

Naturally, whether to accept the authorized or the alternative position on a particular issue was an individual decision. The outcome was neither wholly predictable nor biologically determined. Achieving consensus was difficult and not all such stories carried the same weight of authenticity within black communities. Some were ridiculed unmercifully or dismissed out of hand. Nevertheless, to reject a specific scenario as being far-fetched did not require one to become a head-in-the-sand Pollyanna. Black America's many tragic encounters with white villainy suggested that it was only reasonable to believe that new plots were being hatched daily.

Black Social Bandits

In many cases, white people's fear and dislike of blacks was rooted in inaccurate, culturally chauvinistic assumptions about shared societal values. Accustomed to seeing their own image reflected in the social mirror, most believed that members of minority groups had to adopt mainstream views to be considered respectable. Like themselves, a "good" black person would condemn militant malcontents and studiously avoid all contact with disturbers of the status quo. To do otherwise was to abet black villainy and risk being targeted for removal from "civilized" society. Not surprisingly, relatively few people of color received high marks on this skewed white-equals-right litmus test. Most, it seems, had been studying alternative cultural texts. Socialized largely within the black oppositional culture, they experienced considerable psychic satisfaction whenever one of their own contravened institutionally imposed codes of conduct. Even individuals accustomed to donning a serviceably authentic mask of acculturation might feel empowered after learning that Mr. Charlie had been taken down a peg or two by a clever black social bandit. In such cases, transformative powers long associated with the African American worldview made it possible for disturbers of the Middle American peace to be conceptualized as folk heroes.

In the aftermath of civil war, black writers set out to reaffirm their commitment to social banditry as an avocation capable of engendering racial pride. Refusing to concede the battleground of historical memory to fallen soldiers, martyred politicians, and ex-Confederates, they canonized the wartime exploits of runaway slaves. Although guilty of gross insubordination, the fugitives were said to have evidenced "a clear common sense-like view of the evils and misery" of the system under which they labored. Indeed, the boldness, stealth, and endurance that they employed to escape the Slave Power's physical and psychological chains seemed more characteristic of "natural hero[es]" than of plantation villains. By playing a primary role in their own liberation, such self-actualized individuals "did much to make the infernal system insecure, and to keep alive the spirit of freedom in liberty-loving hearts the world over." As noted by Philadelphia vigilance committee veteran William Still, their struggles against adversity were every bit as praiseworthy as those of the more frequently memorialized white abolitionists. But, more to the point, the fugitives' determined freedom quest validated the countercultural wisdom that held that "he who would be free, himself must strike the blow." Viewed in this light, self-theft was inspirational and ennobling, not immoral.[134]

Over time, a veritable legion of admirers sought to emulate the fugitives' spirited rebelliousness. Devoted to the governing principles of the black community but considered retrograde and duplicitous by whites, these sly social bandits came in a variety of shapes and sizes. Many had overdeveloped egos or hair-trigger tempers. Bad manners and misogynist tendencies were among their more obvious flaws. Quirky, quixotic, and prone to appropriating white-owned status symbols as partial compensation for past indignities, they were wedded to the cause of group freedom and saw nothing wrong with using extralegal means to balance the scales of justice. Typically more extroverted and colorful than the average individual, the tricksters and outlaws of African American folk history won wide acceptance as risk-taking representatives of an unjustly demeaned race. Like the irrepressible protagonist of Pauline Hopkins's 1879 play, *Peculiar Sam; or, The Underground Railroad,* each seemed driven to prove the viability of oppositional norms—to show that "dis chile am no fool."[135]

Animal tricksters of the rural South owed a great deal to West African vernacular traditions that had been re-created from memory and preserved via oral narration.[136] The enduring influence of Anansi the spider and of Legba, the divine trickster figure of Yoruba mythology, was readily apparent whenever Br'er Rabbit and his anthropomorphized compatriots engaged in acts of deception in order to best stronger, higher-status foes. Employing craft, guile, and a variety of clever disguises to survive in a harsh environment, these folkloric mischief makers had considerable didactic and wish-fulfillment value. They instructed as they entertained. Although an individual character's approach to avoiding punishment or beating the odds was not always intended to serve as a literal guide for action, their proactive responses to life's challenges encouraged behaviors that were antithetical to white-determined norms. Tricksters helped shape group coping strategies and were instrumental in promoting effective use of what poet Paul Laurence Dunbar termed "the mask that grins and lies."[137] Collectively, they formed the cast of a New South shadow drama in which group representatives sought to transcend real-world social roles. By doing so, they made it clear to all that properly socialized African Americans would accept no hierarchical order or value system that was not a reflection of their own cultural identity.

Urbanized twentieth-century counterparts of the animal tricksters were no less adept at hiding their true feelings from outsiders. If, as Ralph Ellison has written, the United States is "a land of masking jokers," these characters most definitely were "in the American grain."[138] To a man, the urban tricksters loved a good joke—if played on someone else—and took great pleasure in deflating the egos of overconfident adversaries. Humiliating societal elites was their specialty. On occasion, they would goad an unwary opponent into a contest of skill—which, in truth, was no contest at all. In one frequently recounted tale, a popular trickster named Shine met the challenge presented by a hungry shark. Menaced by the creature as he departed the sinking *Titanic,* Shine bragged: "I outswim the white man, I outswim the Jew, / I know mutherfucken well I can outswim you." Making good his brash claim, he easily outdistanced the shark and reached dry land long before the doomed ship came to rest on the ocean floor. Variants of this story have the black stoker rejecting the white passengers' desperate pleas for assistance, tossing off one-liners as he turns his back on the great ship, and, ultimately, thumbing his nose at the manners and morals of high society by celebrating his triumph in sexual and alcoholic abandon. Here, an African American character whose name was used as a term of racial derision within the mainstream succeeded in changing the joke and slipping the yoke. True to his ancestral heritage, Shine turned the tables on white people and never looked back—except to survey the damage.[139]

Other subversive figures found within African American oral tradition rejected sham competitions and simply raged, threatened, and then *took* what they desired. Apparently, this trait was present at birth. A character named Dolemite, for example, was said to be a "ramping, scamping young fellow from the day he was born." At the age of one, he started drinking whiskey and gin. At two, he began "eating the bottles they came in." Prone to pitching fits and picking fights, he enjoyed "kicking asses till both shoes got shitty." By the time Dolemite was a teenager, special television bulletins were needed to warn the citizenry of his comings and goings. Undoubtedly aware that he had "swimmed across bloody rivers and ain't never got wet," even the Rocky Mountains took heed and parted whenever the young ruffian wanted to pass.[140]

Because the social bandit's displays of bravado were capable of eliciting both awe and fear, even those socialized within the African American culture sphere could find characters like Dolemite difficult to decode. Indeed, sending mixed messages was part of their oeuvre. Unlike the legendary Signifying Monkey, who used little more than clever wordplay and his enemies' gullibility to accomplish what was impossible to achieve through physical prowess, many bandits were accustomed to winning through intimidation. Well equipped by both nature and disposition to do great bodily harm, these strapping specimens constituted a force to be reckoned with by friend and foe alike. To avoid disaster, common folk had to anticipate their every movement and change in disposition. Certainly, only the most trusting—or foolhardy—felt at ease in the presence of fellow blacks who boasted of their ability to "put chains on lightning and shackles on thunder" or who could proclaim, "I measure forty-two inches across my chest / and I fear not a livin' sonofabitch between God and Death." Nevertheless, cultural norms dictated that both muscle-bound bruisers and quick-witted specialists in "lyin' and signifyin'" would be held to similar standards of accountability.[141] Irrespective of stature or modus operandi, a social bandit's behavior was considered acceptable as long as he was seeking to resolve conflicts that stemmed from disparities in power—from the strong abusing the weak. Significant problems arose only if these guidelines were disregarded and the communal nest was fouled through malicious acts directed against innocent kinsmen. Admittedly, some individuals experienced considerable difficulty measuring up to these standards. A few failed their racial loyalty test altogether and were remanded to the ranks of bad blacks and traitors. Through choice or circumstance, social bandits known as outlaws lived perpetually on the edge of this sociocultural divide.

Present in oral lore as well as in more commercial entertainments such as black-cast films, African American outlaws utilized both mental agility and physical stamina to maintain their freedom and fatten their bankroll. Ruggedly individualistic, eternally restless, and hard as nails, this diverse group of hustlers, dealers, gangsters, and pimps saw nothing wrong with employing unsportsmanlike tactics to elude and embarrass white pursuers. If not always in the best humor, they maintained a trickster-like belief in the proposition that European American assumptions of superiority were a joke. In this respect, these heroically inclined rogues resembled the cowboy-gunmen of the Old West.

Legendary outlaws such as Jesse James and Billy the Kid blurred the boundary separating folk hero from villain. Viewed with considerable ambivalence by late nineteenth-century contemporaries, they could be openly denounced for endangering the public safety but secretly admired for refusing to be bound by the constraints of "civilization." Often, even those sworn to protect society from the criminal element maintained a grudging respect for their adversaries' steely nerve, quick draw, and superb horsemanship. Of course, in certain cases, this was only to be expected. Several of the West's most famous lawmen—including James Butler ("Wild Bill") Hickok, Wyatt Earp, and Pat Garrett—were, at one time or another, fugitives from justice.

Later, as this wild and woolly era faded into historical memory, a patina of nobility was added to the outlaw's persona. Sepia-toned films and pocket-sized novels erased many a rough edge, endowing masculinist violence with idealism and transforming notorious gamblers, horse thieves, and stage-coach robbers into New World versions of England's highwaymen. Far more socially responsible than their victims ever had cause to imagine, frontier renegades placed in the service of escapist entertainment robbed only the rich and killed only in self-defense or to avenge a great wrong. They were generous to a fault when sharing ill-gotten gains with the needy. Loyal to one woman, to a favorite horse, and to a personalized code of honor, the most fortunate of the cowboy-gunmen rode into the sunset, triumphant. When they failed, either treachery was to blame or they were being used to teach an important lesson about sin's wages. At such times, good guys and bad guys, their motives, and their meaning became hopelessly confused—a situation hardly improved by the 1933 radio debut of the Lone Ranger, a champion of fair play who rode masked like a bandit.[142]

If not as well known, African American cowboy-outlaws added their own special savor to this tradition. Many, like Crawford Goldsby, aka Cherokee Bill, were as bold and clever—and as subject to romanticization—as any of the white gunmen who preyed on the settlers and commerce of Oklahoma Territory in the 1890s. Son of a Cherokee freedman and a "Buffalo Soldier" who served in the famed Tenth Cavalry, Bill was a burly man with a reputation for hard drinking, brawling, and general lawlessness. As a member of the Cook brothers gang, he developed a rapid-fire six-shooter style that was designed to intimidate opponents. Uncannily accurate with a rifle, he could bring down small game from great distances and rarely, if ever, missed a human target. As could be anticipated, mayhem ensued whenever these skills were employed to rob banks or trains. Considered by law enforcement authorities to be a conscienceless killer—"a human monster from whom innocent people can expect no safety"—Bill maintained a take-no-prisoners approach to crime. Among his victims were an unresisting Missouri Pacific station agent, a conductor who unwisely insisted that the outlaw pay his fare or exit the train, and an unfortunate wallpaper hanger who happened to be looking out a restaurant window as members of the Cook gang emerged from a nearby general store, heavily laden with booty. Rumor had it that he also shot and killed his own brother-in-law during an argument over some hogs.

Nevertheless, like many social bandits, Goldsby had a less prickly side as well. Although a man of few words and even less refinement, Cherokee Bill was a charmer—known to have a sweetheart in nearly every section of the territory. Frequently protected from harm by loyal compatriots, he was on good terms with the region's Indian nations and moved easily through their villages to avoid pursuers. According to one admirer who had known the bandit as a youth, Bill was the sort of person who made a devoted friend, but a bitter enemy. Fearless, ever alert, and "game as a hornet," he could never be accused of "shamming." True to his calling, however unsavory, Cherokee Bill was "an outlaw in good earnest" who died as he lived. Finally captured and sentenced to hang in 1896, the hardened twenty-year-old offered no excuses, no regrets, no admission of wrongdoing. On the morning of his execution, he rose at 6 a.m., singing and whistling, worried only about how the day's events would affect his mother. Like the noblest bandits of pulp fiction, Bill then distributed a small cache of personal effects among his fellow prisoners and signaled to the guard. "Well, I am ready to go now most anytime," he said calmly. "This is about as good a day to die as any."[143]

All across the South and West, African American outlaws of the late nineteenth century shared this remarkable ability to win friends and waste enemies without missing a step. Some, like north Florida desperado Harmon Murray, "mistrusted everybody" and thought nothing of sending black snitches to an early grave, but occasionally would play the role of race-conscious avenger. By threatening to "kill some crackers" if mistreatment of their people continued, they built a reputation for sheer audacity and stimulated the growth of community-wide support networks.[144] Others, such as horse thieves George Lane and Isom Dart, sought to enhance their self-image—and to disguise glaring character flaws—through outrageous boasts or by assuming romantic aliases ("the Black Fox," "the Calico Cowboy").[145] Still other rustlers, robbers, and renegades seemed content to be their own bad black selves. Exchanging evil for good regardless of race, creed, or denomination of money in a purse, these headstrong individuals could be remarkably egalitarian when it came to victimization. As was the case with John B. Hayes, "the Texas Kid," an outlaw of color might respond to an insulting "For Whites Only" sign in a saloon by shooting out the lights, but displays of this nature seldom guaranteed that a black-owned business wouldn't be targeted for robbery the following night.[146] At such times, fear and dread threatened to supersede respect and romantic attraction as the predominant emotions generated by violent deeds. Nevertheless, in a remarkable percentage of cases, the bandit's lucky streak continued.

From all appearances, a significant number of black perpetrators remained unconcerned about cultivating favorable public opinion and were perfectly willing to leave it up to their victims to decide how closely they resembled Robin Hood. Those who dodged fellow blacks' disfavor the longest, thereby avoiding the ignominy of being viewed as race traitors, were able to do so because one or more countervailing considerations helped compensate for their antisocial acts.

First, as should be obvious to all who are familiar with the dynamics of cultural projection and reception, the combination of naughty behavior and extensive media coverage has the magical ability to turn heads and alter impressions—to improve upon reality. As a result of their trickster heritage, bandits are far more resourceful than the average person when it comes to manipulating the public's perception of themselves. Moreover, a darkly handsome appearance, a swashbuckling manner, and an occasional good deed never hurt anyone's popularity rating.

Second, both folk cultural wisdom and the national history suggest that race matters—a lot. Because one of the only skin-color privileges available to an oppressed community is the ability to give its members benefit of the doubt, a black bandit's depredations are easily blamed on external agents. Here, under the influence of racial chauvinism and through the power of wishful thinking, predators become prey. Whites who have corrupted blacks and led them astray are conceptualized as both primary cause and preferred target of social banditry. African American cowboy-outlaws with few other redeeming characteristics are celebrated for confounding Uncle Tom stereotypes and contravening laws imposed by "the Man." A classic case of heart over head, all but the most glaring of the bandit's flaws may be conveniently forgotten—overshadowed by positive emblematic qualities that can be placed in the service of group advocacy and uplift.

Third, as historian Lawrence Levine has noted, postbellum African Americans rarely demand that favored folk figures mirror white counterparts in every sinew of their being.[147] Black social bandits are not required to divide the spoils or to become public benefactors in order to be immortalized in song or verse. Their supporters permit antisocial ways to be portrayed in realistic fashion, without romantic embellishment or the sugarcoating of brutality and boorishness. In the black worldview, it often is sufficient that the bandit exhibit a type of unadorned hypermasculinity normally denied the menfolk of a maligned race. Symbolizing pure force and trouble, such characters provide important lessons about placing faith in the powerful. They also serve as a negative reference point that can be used to illustrate the illogic of intragroup violence. Even those who seem unlikely candidates for either moral renewal or social redemption may be granted a type of begrudging admiration that transcends the universal fascination with risk taking. Only in rare instances are these ever-dangerous individuals equated with white villains.

Bulked up for improved stamina, stripped down for stealth, all variants of the outlaw breed could be found in the oral lore of twentieth-century urban America. Each and every one was sly as a fox and as slick as ice. Universally feared by whites but able to maintain a varied and complex relationship with the residents of black communities, they were well adapted for survival in the harsh central city environment. If not always faithful to traditional folk heroic ideals, these modern-day bandit cadres were evidence of the fact that African Americans would continue to determine for themselves what constituted adherence to group values—and which of the oppressor's cruel deeds warranted retaliatory action.

Most urban outlaws owed a great deal to frontier-era forebears. Indeed, several were Old West transplants whose legendary feats had been embellished over time. Tales centering on rough-and-tumble characters such as Missouri saloon brawler Stagolee ("a mean son-of-a-bitch"; "a bully frum his birth"), train-robbing desperado Railroad Bill ("so desp'rate an' so bad, / He take ev'ything po' womens had"), and murderous Ohio riverboat rouster George "Devil" Winston ("killed po' Vinie, about a Duke cigarette") melded violence, lust, and an occasional supernatural feat into a compelling folkloric archetype.[148] Although unlikely to have been "baptised in the dust of a Colt forty-five" like Two Gun Green or to be as gifted in taming bobcats and diamond-back rattlers as Wild Negro Bill, black city dwellers found much to admire in these fantastic figures.[149] Hoping to build upon the bandits' many contributions to psychological resistance, they updated the lore of earlier times by having outlaws don the garb of urban hustlers, gangsters, and mackmen (pimps). Instead of a territorial marshal or Stagolee nemesis Billy Lyons, adversaries included Goldberg, Vanderbilt, and other members of the white power structure.

As was the case with their predecessors, urban social bandits were experts in ego enhancement. Taking great pleasure in exceeding traditional limits of good taste and behavior, they became crude and colorful representations of black wish fulfillment. With great gusto, they tasted the "good life" and the luxuries they had acquired by extralegal means. Mackman Long-Shoe Sam, for example, boasted of his "sharkskin vine in a powder blue, / Black wingtips from Bendette's, sparkling new." He wore "a hat from Disney with a fifty-dollar tag" and carried a snakeskin billfold that was "loaded with swag."[150] Ex-con Hophead Willie, on the other hand, invested his considerable disposable income in durable goods and real estate: A "yacht on every ocean" and "a flock of seaside grills"; "fourteen furniture companies and twenty-eight lumber mills."[151] Whatever their preference in creature comforts, bandits such as Big Boy Pete and Honky-Tonk Bud knew that to display great wealth with soulful panache helped establish a reputation as a "hipcat stud."[152]

As self-taught experts on the inner-city job market, these specialists in shady dealings also were aware that the quickest way for people like themselves to amass "more dough than John Ford and Rockefeller back to back" was to develop a repertoire of scams and hustles. These trickster's games were to be supplemented with heists, harlotry, and an occasional homicide for hire. According to the requisites of this ghetto-specific career ladder, an individual could aspire to outlaw greatness only if their credentials included "a tombstone disposition" and a "graveyard mind"; a fear-inducing public image; and the proven ability to separate "chumps," "suckers," and "hicks from out in the sticks" from their hard-earned cash. Like the fast-living Great MacDaddy, every stylish social bandit who was good at his trade also was "a bad motherfucker" who feared neither death nor white America's opprobrium.[153]

Transmitted through the subculture in vernacular Black English, urban outlaw tales often were deemed too "raw" for mass consumption. As a result, relatively few reached the tender ears of white suburbanites in the original organic idiom. From a black perspective, this was all according to plan. The essence of these subversive street-corner amusements was preserved more easily when mainstream meddling was kept to a minimum. Equally important, by limiting the general public's access to basic storylines summarized in academic publications or shared selectively via black comedy albums and national magazines such as *Ebony*, African American storytellers could aspire to become gatekeepers of their own culture.

In urban black America, the ingenuity, originality, and verbal dexterity essential to effective storytelling were considered valuable social skills. They were especially useful in shaping a distinctive cultural identity. The ability to recite a lengthy narrative poem (the toast), to best one's peers in verbal duels (sounding, signifying, playing the dozens), or simply to talk with a high degree of style (rapping) brought considerable recognition and status. Through taunt, boast, and banter, an adept wordsmith could hope to influence others—to become the controlling agent of any situation.[154] Viewing their folkloric creations—and by implication themselves—as dynamic, even superior, beings, storytellers claimed the authority to name, describe, indict; to contravene the mores of "polite" society; and to seize power whenever the opportunity arose. Eager to place their glib tongue and expressive body language in the service of liberationist initiatives, such individuals were as capable of confuting assumptions of white superiority as any of the outlaws they celebrated.

Eventually, during the turbulent Black Power years of the late 1960s and early 1970s, social bandit affinity groups formed within the West Coast film community. Influenced greatly by the era's separatist politics, Hollywood filmmakers looked to African American oral tradition for subversive scenarios and stylistic cues. The resulting pop culture confections gave black bandits unprecedented national visibility, enhanced their reputation as promoters of activist ideals, and helped spread messages of self-definition and group empowerment far beyond the political arena. Employing a variety of direct confrontational techniques as well as a constantly changing array of artful deceptions favored by folkloric tricksters, they sought to divest whites of both symbolic and actual power. Invoking the memory of Cherokee Bill, Shine, and Stagolee, the outlaws of black popular culture asserted that both were theirs by right and would be reclaimed from usurpers by any means necessary.

Throughout the first half of the 1970s, brash, colorful blaxploitation films provided invaluable support for the outlaws' agenda. Joining the grittiness and first-take inexactitude of the earliest full-length features made especially for African American audiences with the didacticism and social consciousness of postwar message movies like *Intruder in the Dust* and *No Way Out*, the blaxploitation cycle consisted of well over a hundred titles.[155] Especially popular in inner-city venues, these low-budget action-adventure dramas forwarded a pop culture version of real-world dissatisfaction with the status quo. Whether the work of an independent filmmaker committed to "the decolonization of black minds" or a more overtly commercial vehicle that reached theaters only after receiving input from white producers and directors, such entertainments drew much of their attractive power from an "insider" portrayal of the black urban condition.[156] Here, in a context shaped at least as much by wish fulfillment as by plot structure, bold and beautiful representatives of the grassroots repeatedly succeeded in unleashing insurgent political impulses on grossly stereotyped white evildoers. Significantly altering dominant paradigms of representation, most deified the black male, vilified the white male, and objectified women of all races.

In this make-believe world shot on location in true-to-life settings, a social bandit's display of principled outrage at social injustice conveyed an unmistakable message of racial militance. In the context of the times, this was considered a wise career move. Capitalizing on moviegoers' growing infatuation with both black macho and the sort of tight-lipped, violence-prone characters made popular by Clint Eastwood and Charles Bronson in films such as *A Fistful of Dollars, Dirty Harry,* and *Death Wish,* blaxploitation outlaws were well positioned to garner pan-racial recognition as scene-stealing tough guys.[157]

First glimpsed in iconoclastic depictions of rough-hewn rakes played by Brock Peters, Yaphet Kotto, and Jim Brown, they scowled a lot and avoided intimacy, but their true emotions were hard to gauge.[158] Guided by idiosyncratic codes of honor, most evidenced their masculinity through good looks, feats of daring and endurance, and sound-bite-length speeches laced with sarcastic wit and braggadocio. Ultimately, this combination of stoicism, survivalism, and sensuality proved extremely attractive at the box office.

Offering audiences a good deal more than what critic Pauline Kael has termed "a funky new twist" on tired story lines, blaxploitation films addressed a variety of commercial and institutional, psychological and personal agendas. They turned a handsome profit for an industry awash in red ink; provided a training ground for neophyte actors, screenwriters, and technicians; and fostered the growth of racial self-awareness. As noted by actor/filmmaker Fred Williamson, by focusing intently on African American subjectivities and bringing into the foreground issues central to the survival of the black community, blaxploitation movies instructed as they entertained—conveying the important message that people of color no longer would be "knocked down and stepped on" with impunity. For as long as they remained marketable commodities, the black outlaws of Hollywood were fully committed to this activist educational initiative.[159]

Typically, blaxploitation films portrayed the outlaw as an unbought, unbossed helpmeet of the oppressed. The most effective elaborated upon black bandits' support of psychological revolution. Effortlessly turning alleged racial debits into assets, they engaged their audience's most wistful dreams of standing up to the Man—and winning. As filmmaker Melvin Van Peebles noted, movies featuring such fearless characters were, by definition, "victorious." Despite their shortcomings and excesses, they allowed African American theatergoers to "walk out standing tall instead of avoiding each other's eyes." Here, courtesy of Hollywood's attraction to the bottom line, inner-city residents finally were getting a chance to see "some of their own fantasies acted out." As Technicolor embodiments of common folk "rising out of the mud and kicking ass," social bandits spurred the growth of racial pride and encouraged fans to adopt a proactive approach to surmounting life's adversities.[160]

Whether they were tooling around the city in a dazzling, whale-sized town car, luxuriating in the crushed velvet splendor of their penthouse apartment, or consuming conspicuously at the clothiers, blaxploitation bandits showcased the many advantages of rejecting both white societal expectations and a "square" lifestyle. With wardrobes filled to overflowing with silk shirts, wide-brimmed hats, long leather coats, and platform shoes with four-inch heels, the flamboyantly attired outlaws let it be known that high ideals and high living were in no way incompatible. They would seek to liberate black minds from white-imposed negativity and self-hatred. But many worked equally hard at liberating stacks of swag from white people's wallets and wall safes.

Updating a time-honored outlaw strategy, the bandits sought to profit from the naïveté and moral frailty of societal elites. In general, they were very successful at such endeavors. Although rarely offering any sort of coordinated approach to "getting Whitey," blaxploitation outlaws caused numerous problems for nonblacks. Conceptualizing themselves as disadvantaged strivers struggling for survival against corrupt agents of mainstream power, they swindled or addicted any white person foolish enough to venture into the urban jungle. Those who arrived from Little Italy with plans for exploiting the resident population were issued stern warnings. As one outlaw soldier of fortune asserted in *The Black Godfather,* a line would be drawn in the dust of ghetto streets whenever African American interests were threatened. "Ain't no room for the both of us," he boasted—responding to a white racketeer's economic challenge. "I want to control my own destiny. . . . His power ends where he sees the first black face."[161]

If such macho declarations of crime world territorality elicited cheers from inner-city theatergoers, they also provided food for thought. In seeking to exclude nonblack competitors, were the outlaws striking a blow for racial empowerment or reserving a lucrative market for themselves? Was it reasonable to overlook the fact that the bandits' acquisitive, antisocial behavior frequently victimized the poorest of ghetto dwellers; to buy into the notion that most bandits were societal underdogs driven to a life of crime by exclusion from mainstream career ladders? Could it be that these cagey criminal types were toying with their audience—purposely misleading impressionable young people with a self-serving apologia? In certain cases, skepticism as to the legitimacy of the black outlaws' claims was fully justified. Their vengeance sometimes seemed to differ little from wanton cruelty. Often, violence was employed more for titillation than for group liberation. Attractive female characters in supporting roles were treated as ornamental, erotic objects to be desired and possessed. With good reason, common folk of all backgrounds and ethnicities quaked in the outlaws' presence.

Perhaps because social banditry always has been difficult to distinguish from other, far less noble acts of avarice and aggression, blaxploitation bandits rarely fretted over questions of character. Most never pretended to be full-time altruists or professional race men. Typically, they sought rewards more tangible than an admiring gaze or a plaque given in recognition of devoted community service. Unwilling to sacrifice luxuries obtained by exploiting the weaknesses of racial kinsmen, black outlaws refused to loosen their control over inner-city markets in illicit goods and services. Some of the more violent criminals couldn't even give up the habit of garroting a disobedient underling or two from time to time. Given the dog-eat-dog environment in which they operated, such behavior seemed no more than a rational business practice. On the other hand, the wisest also understood that overzealous exploitation of black brothers and sisters made for bad public relations and threatened profits. Whenever possible, the outlaws attempted to forestall communal backlash by cultivating a user-friendly public image. Like frontier forebears, they were remarkably adept at working this sleight of hand.

First, bandits who aspired to more positive forms of racial representation sought to convince critics that they *did* have standards. Specific behavioral guidelines were attached to each underworld job description. For example, drug dealers understood the need to appear tough but always to play it cool; to maintain their independence from outside suppliers while remaining loyal to the members of local distribution networks. Pimps rarely displayed emotion and never let a prostitute—or any other woman—get the upper hand. Intimations of disrespect for black manhood were to be addressed promptly via slaps, kicks, and verbal abuse. Hit men kept their true identity a closely guarded secret, watched their back at all times, and avoided shooting cops or civilians—it brought too much "heat." Policy men involved in the numbers racket recognized the wisdom of making few promises, but keeping them all and paying winners promptly. Most also found it advisable to maintain cash reserves for "administrative expenses" (i.e., bribing police and public officials). Confidence men had to remain composed and mentally alert under the most trying conditions. They also were well advised to avoid marks who stuttered, were cross-eyed, or were returning from a funeral.[162] None of the outlaw guilds knowingly accepted rapists, hypocrites, or warmongers into membership. All believed their own value system superior to that of white underworld counterparts.

The blaxploitation bandits' customary codes of conduct served to regularize relationships both within the urban crime network and between criminals and "straights." As substitutes for statutory guidelines followed by the law-abiding mainstream, they helped outlaws distinguish between approved, forbidden, and value-neutral acts. To be sure, none of these precepts were sacrosanct. Nevertheless, even if they only abided by the spirit of the black bylaws, outlaws gained an important psychological victory by having them in place, available for ready reference. Those who were so inclined could point to the various underworld guidelines as examples of self-definition and self-governance. Whenever such codes were contrasted with the callousness, greed, and hypocrisy thought to be endemic in mainstream communities, black bandits (and their admirers) were provided with a sense of moral superiority. However simplistic and overdrawn, the comparative perspective forwarded in blaxploitation films allowed viewers to observe the world through a funhouse mirror in which even the toughest ghetto thug possessed a touch of nobility.

Additional image enhancement was derived from the outlaws' willingness to maintain close community ties. Upwardly mobile yet grounded in values assimilated during their early years in an inner-city neighborhood, black bandits never really left this spiritual home. The glamour, adventure, and danger of their romanticized lives separated such ideal types from the masses, but their worldview was broad enough to encompass the everyday concerns of family and friends. The most sincere were perceived as fellow strugglers against "the system." Their image within the 'hood was that of a somewhat more dashing, more successful co-conspirator whose "crimes" were not always considered socially harmful.

An outlaw's first loyalty was to self, but fealty to family often was a major concern. Criminal careers supported younger siblings and provided aged parents with a few well-deserved luxuries. Here, the social bandit's aim was to break through societal constraints and seize a piece of the American dream. Their share could be substantial. In *The Mack*, for example, one underclass mother received a yacht basin condominium from her doting pimp son. *Black Caesar*'s game-legged mobster, Tommy Gibbs, bought his mother the posh Upper East Side apartment in which she had worked as a maid. If not exactly the Waltons of Watts, struggling family units such as these retained a modicum of cohesion and stability—thanks to the efforts of social bandit kin.[163]

Extended families benefited as well. Typically, ghetto streets had served as the youthful outlaw's playground and classroom. Having learned many important survival techniques during their earliest years in the community, adult bandits vowed to return the favor. In the spirit of black brotherhood, they developed programs to improve the living standard of long-suffering inner-city residents. "We intend to do more than just organize the rackets in Harlem," proclaimed one such altruistic mobster. "We're going to see that black people get a fair shake—a chance to live better."[164] Uplift efforts included feeding the poor, delivering antidrug messages to urban teens, and waging war against police brutality. In MGM's *Cool Breeze,* the proceeds of a $3 million diamond heist were earmarked to help local "soul" brothers establish a people's park. In *The Mack,* a splendidly caped and coifed hustler distributed monthly cash awards for regular school attendance while lecturing young admirers on the evils of pimpdom. To appreciative recipients of the outlaws' largess, such characters were "enterprising young brothers," not dangerous criminals.[165]

Despite occasional derelictions, these colorful protagonists of Hollywood's blaxploitation era proved able conservators of the traditions inherited from earlier historical and folkloric outlaws. In some cases, they even managed to exceed all previous standards for outrageous behavior. Specialists in beating the odds, they took great pleasure in besting technologically sophisticated foes, using racial stereotypes as disguises, and tricking obtuse enemies into saying incredibly stupid things like "Who do you think you are, nigger?"[166]

In truth, the outlaws knew exactly who they were—and more than enough about the workings of white America to make the Establishment uncomfortable. While law enforcement officials considered them bad examples, bandits preferred to be viewed simply as *baadd*—quick-witted scoundrels with a penchant for risk taking and a commitment to the vindication of black manhood. In accordance with the African American worldview, they held that white-on-black crime, not social banditry, was the greatest problem facing inner-city neighborhoods. Through deception, coercion, and the long con, these spiritually liberated hoodlums sought to thwart white villains' disingenuous schemes for exploiting the ghetto and thereby further emasculating black male breadwinners.

Although their heyday was brief, the blaxploitation outlaws made a lasting impression. During the 1980s and '90s, their subversive cinematic spin on the criminal mind was evident in ghettocentric action-adventure films such as *A Rage in Harlem* and *Hoodlum* while *I'm Gonna Git You Sucka* and *Original Gangstas* paid tribute to the most colorful members of the clan.[167] With the able assistance of real-world wannabes and pulp fiction counterparts like Whoreson Jones, Daddy Cool, and Eldorado Red, the essence of African American social banditry survived difficult times.[168] Carried into the new millennium on the shoulders of a hip-hop generation that found the cocky, in-your-face approach to life both stylish and utilitarian, black outlaws and tricksters remained in vogue, living large. As cultural critic Nelson George has recognized, to all but "church ladies and NAACP spokespeople," their "tough, no-nonsense, and as cool as the other side of a pillow" persona constitutes a guilty pleasure that can be enjoyed without guilt. Going about their lives "as we all dreamed we could," social bandits are unembarrassed to proclaim themselves the noblest of rogues.[169] If caught and punished for their crimes, they know how to roll with the punches. In the black worldview, whenever bandits utilize these survival skills to even the odds, they become forces for good. Despite (or because of) white disapproval, all have the potential to be seen as modern-day embodiments of a venerable folkloric tradition.

Bad Blacks, Race Traitors, and Toms

More numerous and infinitely more varied in their antisocial behaviors than antebellum counterparts, the spiritual heirs of African American exploiters, informants, and thieves have generated considerable discord ever since they were released into the general population on the Day of Jubilee. As victims of cultural dislocation and misplaced identity, bad blacks are experts at duping the unwary. They love to play the race card in mind games with their own people. Many have little understanding of grassroots concerns but are so frequently lauded by high-status whites that they aspire to universal acceptance as racial standard-bearers. Others mimic certain of the social bandit's mannerisms but neglect to honor any recognized code of conduct. Such deceptions are artful but rarely appreciated. Once brought to light, violations of communal mores are roundly condemned. To those whose trust has been betrayed, the postbellum race traitor is perceived as evil rather than *baadd*—an individual to be feared, never emulated. Persistent transgressors are shunned by the community whose standards have been compromised.

Affirming former Missouri bondsman Henry Clay Bruce's claim that blacks were "much truer to one another in [slavery] days than they have been since made free," activist contributors to the shaping of the African American worldview have linked race traitors to a select number of occupational categories.[170] Brutal cops and jackleg preachers rank high on many such lists. More moderate voices speak of "poor racial examples" and "angry black militants" in the same breath—and with equal disfavor. Both Afroworld constituencies tend to find white people hiding in the woodpile. Allegedly, these unscrupulous villains either corrupt the innocent or create living environments that corrode minority-group values and promote self-hatred, rage, and a me-first mentality. Here, European American culpability is recognized and condemned, but African American perpetrators are given fair warning: neither gullibility nor victimization automatically excuses black-on-black crime. A jury of the bad black's peers will determine whether questionable deeds were committed to "advance the race."

By the early years of the twentieth century, those unable to escape censure found themselves in dire straits and even worse company. Black writers crafted many unflattering character studies of these pathetic, maladjusted individuals. Some authors hoped to promote racial virtue through the depiction of negative role models. Others sought to encourage the growth of egalitarian attitudes within the mainstream by reminding white readers that "the negro is not inherently different from other men." All racial communities, it was said, contained both moral giants and people who were "doing far more mischief than good in the world."[171]

Bad blacks who appeared in these literary works displayed little of the social bandit's sly charm. They were "shallow, selfish soul[s]" whose "lurking brutality" was imperfectly masked by overdone politeness. Habituated to strong drink, games of chance, and fast-buck schemes designed to defraud the working poor, such "biggity, braggin' niggers" were "engrossed in self love" but inordinately fond of imitating white people's ways. Like Charles Van Courtney and Solomon Ruggles, colorfully despicable characters created by George Langhorne Pryor and Paul Laurence Dunbar, their moral compasses had been damaged—some beyond repair. Convinced that "the forum of conscience was a tribunal for fools," they seemed a law unto themselves. With "shifty eye[s]" and "thick, tobacco stained lips" the hardened reprobates proceeded through life in predatory mode.[172]

Theatrical treatments of this retrograde lifestyle had bad blacks revealing slave community secrets in exchange for "scraps off'n the table in the big house," committing parricide, taking addictive drugs, and mouthing impieties about God's "cruel laws . . . made up wholly of mistakes and flaws."[173] The early black-cast films *Body and Soul* and *The Black King* added portrayals of preacher/con artists who claimed to be "bringin' enlightenment to the brothers," but who in truth were "the biggest backslidin' sinner[s] in the church." So that the moral of the stories would be apparent, upright stage and movie characters who came into contact with such individuals were quick to label them "contemptible cur[s]"; "white-livered, lying, hypocritical beast[s]."[174]

Fictional portrayals reinforced community-based ethical standards and provided an early warning system that could be used to identify evildoers. Nevertheless, in the real world, it often took more than a thespian's condemnation of aberrant lifestyles to alleviate the threat posed by bad blacks. On numerous occasions, community reaction to the race traitors in their midst became violent. Between 1882 and 1930, 148 southern blacks died at the hands of lynch mobs that either were integrated or composed entirely of African Americans.[175] Those who perished at the hands of aggrieved neighbors included:

John Brown, lynched in Talledega County, Alabama, in 1891 for implicating two black men in a barn-burning incident.

A Baptist preacher known as "Lightfoot" who was shot to death in 1908 for defrauding some eight hundred residents of De Soto County, Mississippi, in a bogus "back-to-Africa" scheme.

David Scruggs of Jefferson County, Arkansas, abducted by a black mob and "carved to pieces with knives" in 1885 for committing incestuous acts with his daughter.

Josh Ruff, an incorrigible "desperado" executed by residents of Glascock County, Georgia, in 1897 after years of persistent thievery.

In other cases, popular justice was levied on individuals who stole livestock and farm produce, got "too thick" with a relative's wife, or assisted white mobs in brutalizing fellow blacks.[176] With every retributive act, outraged African Americans reiterated a chilling message: Violence would be met with violence as long as the white justice system persisted in devaluing black life by failing to protect the innocent or punish the guilty.

However charged with emotion, physical retaliation against race traitors was only one of several approaches that were developed to deal with an intractable problem. Typically, less precipitous measures were employed to identify, isolate, and punish troublesome individuals. Because dark pigmentation was an unreliable predictor of bad behavior, other variables had to be tested for their ability to do for black people what the color black did so readily for white people. Over time, social class and political ideology became widely accepted indicators of an individual's proclivity to black villainy. To be sure, W. E. B. Du Bois's assertion in 1903 that "the problem of the twentieth century is the problem of the color-line,—the relation of the darker to the lighter races of men" proved prescient when placed in the context of multicultural affairs.[177] But, internally, class-based animosities and ideological fundamentalisms presented black Americans with equal, if not greater challenges—pitting brother against brother and disrupting efforts to present a united front against white villainy.

Elites known as "blue veins" were among the most frequently scrutinized for signs of racial disloyalty. During the first two decades of the twentieth century, the members of this fair-skinned subgroup conceptualized themselves as a progressive force capable of leading black America out of the social wilderness. Gilded Age success stories proved that individual initiative could generate status-enhancing wealth, suggesting that even greater opportunities awaited those who were prepared to cultivate their acquisitive tendencies. As the promised land of inclusiveness drew nigh, these strivers expected to assume their rightful place as a "colored aristocracy"—a "black 400" composed of the "best" people from "old families."[178] Acting as role models and racial intermediaries, they would encourage the submerged masses to acquire refined tastes; to adopt more gracious manners; to view themselves as "lampblacked Anglo-Saxon[s]."[179] This decorous vanguard would show white people that blacks were *not* all alike. Ultimately, it was hoped that longtime foes could be moved to judge the race by its most outstanding representatives, not its worst examples.

Critics took umbrage at the smugness and materialistic bent of both the blue veins and their post–World War I cousins who occupied the upper ranks of an incipient black bourgeoisie. It was said that these self-proclaimed "exceptional Negroes" were more eager to "run away spiritually from [their] race" than to assist in advancing group fortunes. While adopting a noblesse oblige attitude toward the less fortunate, they nevertheless deigned to patronize black-owned businesses and distanced themselves from traditional folkways whenever possible. Under the influence of a secular theology in which self-aggrandizement was the first commandment, blue-vein homes became shrines to personal possessions; gathering places for preening parvenus. If the collective welfare of black America was on their minds at all, it rarely seemed to take precedence over "vanities," "tomfoolery," and a preoccupation with the mood swings of white benefactors.[180]

An extreme color consciousness was among this group's most problematic traits. Even as they professed to hold character and culture in high esteem, the guiding lights of African American society utilized a variety of complexional tests to determine eligibility for elevation to elite status. As noted in a Charles W. Chesnutt short story entitled "The Wife of His Youth," the most prized recruits were "generally speaking, more white than black . . . white enough to show blue veins." Unkind observers referred to such individuals as "mongrels." Allegedly, they possessed the vices of both races and the virtues of neither. The vast majority were believed to be more loyal to their "white half" than to the "mother race." Finding such views compatible with their own, the upper-crust leadership cohort readily accepted these mixed-up, mixed-race applicants into membership.[181]

Darker-skinned African Americans were examined more thoroughly. For example, early in the century, those hoping to join a blue-vein church might first be required to pass a "paper bag test." This involved placing one arm inside a brown shopping bag. Only if the prospective communicant's skin was lighter than the color of the sack would they be invited to attend services. Some congregations found this exercise too time consuming and simply painted front doors a light shade of brown. Anyone whose skin was darker than the door was encouraged to seek religious instruction elsewhere. If rejected, one could consider taking a retest at a later date—presumably after investing in skin bleach and hair straightener.[182]

African American authors who believed that the black aristocrats lived in a world of make-believe did their best to convince blue veins that their behavior was at odds with group goals. By drawing an artificial color line within the race, they were said to have undermined black solidarity and weakened efforts to combat colorphobia throughout the larger society. According to writers such as Wallace Thurman and Dorothy West, the blue veins' "bleachings, scourgings, and powderings" rarely had the intended effect. After considerable effort and expense, most remained "black—fast black—as nature had planned and effected." Equally foolhardy were attempts to escape association with the more darkly pigmented classes by vacationing at far-distant resorts where they "wouldn't need to feel like Negroes" or, alternatively, by relocating to a neighborhood that had not yet experienced an influx of "second-class niggers from way down South."[183] Ultimately, said the critics, all such efforts to become insulated from reality were doomed to failure. Entered into at the expense of self-respect and true manhood, they seldom permitted black elites to escape what was perceived as "the mire of color"—to pass for white. Instead, blue veins became trapped in a sociocultural no-man's-land where, on rare occasions, light skin and "good" hair caused them to be mistaken for an Italian or a Latino. At all other times, it was obvious that "no one would take them for anything but colored."[184]

Abandoning all claims to their African birthright yet unable to be considered "truly white" by those whose acceptance was most highly coveted, snooty, colorphobic black social climbers stood "individual and aloof, never a part of a component whole." As a result, they were denied the soul-satisfying sensation most blacks felt whenever members of the extended racial family got together to share "the gifts from God of laughter and song." Consumed by a desire to be something they weren't, such individuals had to be reintroduced to reality. If sufficiently embarrassed by scathing sociological critiques and literary caricatures, perhaps they could be convinced to reconsider their options; to make amends to those whom they had ridiculed. As revealed in the story of Vera Manning, a penitent blue-vein Harlemite who appeared in

Jessie Redmon Fauset's 1924 novel *There Is Confusion*, intraracial reconciliation could be hard on bloated egos but was well worth the effort. "Oh, I hated
myself so for having spent all those foolish months, years even, away from
my own folks when I might have been consecrated to them, serving them,
helping them, healing them," she confessed after an unsatisfying attempt at
"passing." "I'm glad I'm colored—there's something terrible, terrible about
white people."[185]

Class-based disputes were even more difficult to resolve when they became entangled in racial politics. During the early twentieth century, conflicts over competing programs to improve the prospects of the race raged
unchecked. Concerned observers feared that this unseemly wrangling over
ideologies, agendas, and timetables would cause black leaders to "lose half
their strength in internal strife," thereby forestalling a coordinated assault on
the "citadel of prejudice."[186] Of course, public policy always had been shaped
in this fashion. Disinformation campaigns, character assassination, and reliance on sweeping claims to promote narrow interests were all part of the
process. Thus, in many respects, the slings and arrows launched by disputa-
tious African Americans were no more than race-specific variants of the
rhetorical savaging of opponents that took place at virtually every election-
year campaign rally.

On the other hand, black America was a special case. Effectively disfran-
chised in most of the states where their numbers had the potential to make a
difference, the black electorate was less interested in analyzing planks in the
Democratic or Republican platforms than in scrutinizing the bona fides of rival race men. To throw one's support behind a particular "candidate" was
akin to voting in a hotly contested blacks-only primary election that would determine whether a moderate or militant, plural or sovereign nationalist, leftist or pan-Africanist would represent the race in subsequent contests to restore black civil rights. Throughout this era, the stakes were high and
tempers short. By maligning ideological adversaries and impugning their
motives, African American politicos created several highly partisan slates of
villains.

In later years, those who survived the backstabbing and mudslinging recalled how the "bumptious, irritated, young black intelligentsia of the day" responded to the many challenges of racial politics. Seasoned veterans described "violent outbreak[s]" of principled opposition to what, at the time,
were considered unimaginably wrongheaded notions. Lamenting the fact
that such disputes "divided friends" and made "bitter enemies," they likened
this factionalized political elite to "crabs in a barrel." None of the "so-called

negro leaders" would allow their competitors to escape. Instead, on any such attempt, they "all would continue to pull back into the barrel the one crab that would make the effort to climb out." Refusing pleas to put aside what NAACP president Moorfield Storey termed "personal ambitions, personal hostilities, differences of opinion on minor points," political combatants campaigned aggressively—tar brush in hand—to win public favor.[187] As a result, invective that otherwise might have been directed toward white oppressors was, instead, heaped upon intraracial adversaries. Over time, this negativist mind set cast a pall over the black public sphere. To those who had not yet pledged fealty to a particular political philosophy, it seemed as if all approaches to racial advancement were suspect; that no black leader was without taint.

It soon became apparent that this generation of race men was unlikely ever to stand, arm in arm, for a celebratory unity portrait. To the African American Left, black NAACP officials were a "hand-picked, me-too-boss, hat-in-hand, sycophant, lick-spittling group of Negroes." Hampton and Tuskegee Institute administrator Robert Russa Moton advocated submission to "the system of lynching and mob-law." Illinois congressman Oscar DePriest was a traitorous agent of international capitalism.[188] Elsewhere on the political spectrum, such claims were denounced as "baseless and unreasonable." Motivated by envy—the "disappointment of displaced demagogues and the spite of narrow minds"—these falsehoods were said to be concocted by individuals suffering from a "mental malady" and "utterly wanting in truth or honor."[189] Unfortunately—to the everlasting detriment of racial unity— none of the principal combatants would consider submitting themselves for clinical observation. Each ideological cluster believed its adherents to be in excellent health—fit as a fiddle and eager to treat opponents to a dose of their own medicine.

There were no sacred cows on the political landscape. Scoundrels were everywhere—in voluntary organizations, throughout the fourth estate, and ensconced within learned circles where they were "prostituting their intelligence, under the direction of the white man."[190] Nevertheless, the three most visible representatives of the leading political philosophies of the era received more than their fair share of vilification. Much of it came from supporters of the other two.

Jamaica-born Pan-African nationalist Marcus Garvey may have convinced large numbers of working-class followers that he was the "Provisional President of the African Republic," but competing race men considered him a "scoundrel and bubble-blower." A more appropriate honorific title, they said, would be "demagogue," "ignoramus," or "Supreme Negro Jamaican Jackass." In order to protect decent people from being fleeced by his "moonshine schemes," it was recommended that Garvey be "locked up or sent home."[191]

At Alabama's Tuskegee Institute, where influential educator Booker T. Washington taught that there was "as much dignity in tilling a field as in writing a poem" and urged southern blacks never to allow grievances to overshadow opportunities, moderation in all things and working within the system were hallowed concepts. Elsewhere, this conciliatory stance was viewed as submission to prejudice. Described as "wary and silent"—"not an easy person to know"—by those who considered him the "Benedict Arnold of the Negro race," this mild-mannered "political dictator" was adjudged guilty of "relegating [the] race to serfdom" in order to advance his own "special scheme." Some even accused Washington of telling anecdotes belittling "Negro character."[192]

Not even the multitalented intellectual W. E. B. Du Bois could escape this blizzard of bad press. A thorn in the side of both Washington and Garvey, he was optimistic that either an African American "Talented Tenth" or a biracial coalition of NAACP activists could jump-start the engine of equality. Such beliefs moved one group of political adversaries to label the light-skinned, Harvard-educated civil rights crusader "the Negro 'misleader'"—a "white man's nigger" and "hater of dark people" who served as the titular head of a "bastard aristocracy." No less disdainful of Du Boisian ideology, the competing camp held that his mere presence was capable of awakening "evil tendencies" in normally upright individuals.[193]

One of the most unattractive characteristics of the black worldview, this habituation to infighting caused character assassination and literary lynching to be legitimized as tools of political persuasion. So busy demonizing one another that whites sometimes escaped censure, competing African American leadership cadres dissipated their energies unnecessarily and at considerable expense to group self-esteem. Believing that it was "bad enough to be enslaved by white men without being put under thraldom to a Negro," they propagandized aggressively—creating caricatures of political adversaries that bore a striking resemblance to the corrupt, cartoonish blacks drawn by mainstream pundits. As noted by historian Kevin Gaines, these negative portraits were difficult to erase, or even to modify. Mutually reinforced and frequently reiterated, some became permanently embedded in the collective racial memory. By midcentury it was clear that none of the "crabs" were going to escape the barrel unscathed. Black leaders continued to greet each of their opponents' determined attempts at racial uplift with charges of malfeasance, meanness, deception, and betrayal.[194]

During the civil rights and Black Power years, factional feuding generated considerable national attention as proponents of the nonviolent direct-action program favored by Martin Luther King Jr. and other "moderates" crossed swords with a variety of outspoken black "militants." The movement of the late 1950s and early 1960s had spurred unprecedented federal interest in black affairs, but, said critics, its "brainwashed" leaders were too eager to claim success. Easily placated with localized victories and "a few crumbs of token recognition and token gains," the civil rights establishment was accused of failing to make significant inroads against two key components of oppression—dependence and powerlessness. While southern blacks no longer were forced to take seats in the rear of the bus and benefited from landmark legislation such as the Civil Rights Act of 1964 and the Voting Rights Act of 1965, years of marches, speeches, and petitions had little effect on de facto segregation in the North. Despite all efforts at reform, the urban ghetto continued to replenish itself with new victims daily. Out of touch with the impacted black masses and transfixed by the illusion of progress, "eunuch leaders" remained content to "peddle the Negro's welfare" for small favors. They exercised nothing more than "pawnshop power." All too frequently, they were obliged to "run begging, apologizing and whimpering to white people for help."[195]

This litany of shortcomings was accompanied by a reexamination (and eventual refutation) of the moderate's dream of societal integration. According to this long-cherished civil rights goal, integration would offer blacks full and equal participation in American society. In a just social order, dominant and submissive roles no longer would be assigned by race. Dissimilar peoples would banish fear and hatred, learning to accept and love one another. Such was the ideal. The reality, said critics, was that the moderates had been unable to achieve interracial community. Nevertheless, they continued to promote their threadbare ideology without acknowledging its potentially harmful implications. To a frustrated and angry mid-1960s black nationalist, integration appeared to be a synonym for cultural assimilation.

It was believed that a committed integrationist would barter racial identity for a nice house in the suburbs. Hoping to prove themselves worthy of whites' respect, they appeared anxious to part company with less upwardly mobile neighbors and to adopt the European Americans' consumption-oriented value system. Finding it easier to mimic than to change the main-stream, such individuals permitted the myth of the melting pot to obscure black America's colonial status. Their own self-hatred was less easily con-cealed. According to this view, the integrationist's program led not to libera-tion, but to continued dependency. As "acceptable" people of color were si-phoned off into the whites' world, they were encouraged to downplay cultural distinctives and to disparage the underclass. Those left behind by the exodus possessed few of the black professionals' talents and leadership skills. Indeed, the whole scheme seemed a subterfuge to maintain white supremacy.[196]

Militants joined this critique of integration with a strident denunciation of nonviolence. Here, again, their frustration stemmed from the moderates' inability to change majoritarian behavior. Although the early 1960s freedom movement had mobilized blacks and placed important issues before the na-tion, it had not put an end to white-initiated terrorism. By mid-decade many African Americans seemed convinced that white people were incapable of love. Whenever it had been proffered by representatives of the NAACP or the Southern Christian Leadership Conference, racists returned hatred. Increas-ingly, the belief that white adversaries possessed either a modicum of com-passion or a sense of justice seemed a naive and dangerous assumption. As a result, nonviolence became stigmatized as little more than a moral exercise. Whites, most assuredly, needed to partake of the doctrine. Blacks, however, risked being rendered psychologically impotent by it. More often than not, their expressions of love had been mistaken for weakness. By transforming nonviolence into a way of life, moderate leaders appeared to be closing the door to all other approaches—including those that viewed civil disorder as a cleansing, empowering social force.[197]

Given their middle-class values and aversion to modifying traditional ap-proaches, it is scarcely surprising that the African American moderates found themselves skewered by militant rhetoric. To some, they composed a fading generation of idealists chasing an impossible American dream. Oth-ers saw them as calcified Uncle Toms who had to be eliminated before real change could occur. They were modern-day Booker T. Washingtons who stood accused of failing to question the controlling values of U.S. society. The NAACP's Roy Wilkins was "a white man who somehow came out the wrong color"; Quaker direct-action strategist Bayard Rustin, a "freak" who was "pro-jected by the press as a leader of black people." Even the hallowed name of Martin Luther King was dragged through the dirt. Allegedly, his attempt to involve the masses in the "sham ethic" of passive resistance was a flawed attempt to disguise the fact that he was an agent for "white Intelligence." Surely, the times were proving "Reverend Dr. Chickenwing" and his ilk to be as irrelevant as their outmoded ideology.[198]

Eventually, black nationalist truth squads expanded their search for race traitors to other areas of society. Reports from the field warned that suspected Toms were everywhere and should be approached with extreme caution. Many suffered from cultural dislocation and had become slaves to white aesthetic imperatives. The most seriously debilitated were prone to using affected Oxfordian accents and "big horseshit doctor words." Such individuals believed that "blackness is a Dirty Disgraceful ugly thing." A major hindrance to psychological liberation, traitorous Toms were said to constitute a bourgeoisie in blackface who were leading African Americans in "the opposite direction of peoplehood." Like "a monkey with [a] straight razor," they posed a danger both to themselves and to others. Potentially, their urge to become "white as snow" could destroy the spirit of an entire generation.[199]

Tomish blacks' purported racial disloyalty created numerous problems for those seeking to transform a movement into a revolution. Unlike the militants, they rarely spoke of the need for armed self-defense and maintained an unassailable faith in nonblack allies, big government, and the efficacy of civil rights legislation. More accustomed to turning the other cheek than striking out against the oppressor, Toms displayed little interest in pressing insistent demands. Upon reaching the upper echelons of their truncated caste-based world, many seemed content to retreat to their ranch-style homes, venturing out only to display a new sailboat or luxury car. Convincing "Uncle Thomas Wooly Heads" to abandon the occasional "Love your Brother" fund-raiser and polite protest march for in-your-face activism presented a major challenge. Within Black Power circles, there were two schools of thought on how to address this untenable situation and thereby reduce the incidence of intraracial villainy. One advocated force, the other forgiveness.[200]

As one of playwright Ed Bullins's militant characters asserted, there was none more vicious than "a nigger who is threatened by the Blackman with losing his imaginary place beside the whiteman." Once the revolution began, these treacherous Toms would be the first to go. In their cautionary tales of societal upheaval, Black Power–era writers told of how scores were to be settled. Chanting "Death to the house niggers," psychologically liberated warriors would swoop down and round up all "bushwa" malefactors. If found guilty of carrying out the slave master's will or otherwise keeping the race down, the accused's traitorous tongue would be removed. Those posing the greatest threat to the people's cause faced summary execution. The message was clear: "NEGROES THAT LEAN WHITE, LOVE WHITE, WILL HAVE WHITE/ NIGHTS OF DEATH."[201]

But even the most committed activist understood that this course of action was fraught with danger. As if afraid to confront the real enemy, black folk always seemed to be killing their own, diluting their power. What if black Anglo-Saxons could be reclaimed from mental servitude? After all, their ill-advised behavior was learned, not genetically determined. Upon reflection, some black writers urged restraint in dealing with the Toms. It was even suggested that all but their most heinous crimes be forgiven. Affirming faith in the potential of each and every African American, the authors of black fiction and drama asserted that "all Black People are Black in one way or another." This being the case, it was the duty of creative artists within the movement to help unfortunate Toms "straighten out the shit in their heads."[202]

Unfortunately, Toms were slow to recognize the seriousness of their plight. They saw no need to transcend what others viewed as an inglorious history of sleeping with the enemy. As a result, there was no headlong rush to truth seeking and redemption. Instead of integrating into blackness and celebrating victory over Whitey with new nationalist friends, most remained bitter enemies of those who sought their release from spiritual servitude. Adding insult to injury, factionalism eventually split the Black Power ranks into competing fiefdoms, diluting whatever gains the tough-minded yet structurally fragile coalition had managed to wrest from vested interests. This clash of incompatible fundamentalisms so seriously compromised the activists' agenda that external foes had little difficulty separating stragglers from the pack. Thus, even before leaders of the most militant cadres either were exiled, "rehabilitated," or permanently silenced by the Establishment, they were rebuked by black moderates and drained of the capacity to sustain insurgency by infighting and parochialism.

During the Black Power years, numerous publications carried spirited critiques of the movement. From the pages of the *Crisis* and *Liberator*—as well as *Ms.* and the *National Review*—critics made it appear that *none* of the militants' programmatic approaches to empowerment were viable. Failing to meet their adversaries' high standards of acceptability, each variant of the radical empowerment ethic was believed to have its own set of irredeemable flaws.

Territorial Nationalism

Separate political development, said the critics, was an escapist fantasy, a coward's way out of the black American predicament. Promoters of this ideology were thought to be seeking a cocoon of refuge from reality. Proof of the extent to which white America's "racist disease" had affected its victims, the tough talk of separatists like the Congress of Racial Equality's Roy Innis and Republic of New Africa cofounders Gaidi and Imari Obadele was interpreted as a wail of defeat, their exclusionist organizations a sign of insecurity. To nonbelievers, chimerical ideas about sundering ties with "responsible" African American leaders and "decent" working-class whites in order to campaign for a black nation-state seemed a plot from a third-rate farce. The basic task, they asserted, was coalition building, not disengagement.[203]

Revolutionary Nationalism

Because they were held to encourage antiblack sentiment, calls for violent confrontations with white power were considered foolhardy. If implemented, said the moderates, precipitous schemes favored by groups such as the Revolutionary Action Movement and the Black Liberation Army would be suicidal. Outnumbered ten to one, blacks hoping to overthrow the government by force would find themselves trapped in a descending spiral of destruction and death. The white majority—spearheaded by its fanatical right wing— would triumph over ragtag guerrilla forces quickly and easily. African American history, asserted the skeptics, proved that armed rebellion was doomed from the start. One only had to tour riot-torn neighborhoods in Watts, Newark, or Detroit to realize that such "disruption for disruption's sake" was the "antithesis of creativity and wholeness." At best, nihilistic acts of revolutionary intent provided only a few additional antipoverty palliatives and a water sprinkler or two to cool overheated ghettos.[204]

Cultural Nationalism

This variant of the Black Power enthusiasm was likened to a sugary treat that provided momentary satisfaction but no lasting strength for the fight. Indeed, the neo-African rituals adopted by "back to black" groups like the Los Angeles–based US Organization were thought to be a drain on the storehouse of communal energy. Instead of working for social change, they engaged in endless sloganeering and meaningless posturing—"flying around the country in . . . dashiki[s]" to promote a "goon squad aesthetic." By reducing artistic expression to shrill, inarticulate propaganda, these misguided writers and creative artists had succeeded only in "vulgarizing" their own skills, thereby making it unlikely that they would leave anything of value to posterity. Surely, said traditionalist critics, a poem for the ages should enlighten and elevate. It should be more than a "piece of writing with choppy non-sentences, perverted word order and four-letter words set in stanzaic form."[205]

Ideology aside, militants of all stripes—particularly those of the macho male variety—were implicated in a series of grievous crimes against "the people." The most damaging charges were filed by female activists who no longer would tolerate gender-based discrimination or remain silent when militant artists portrayed women as bitches, bimbos, or baby makers for the revolution. Accusing their male counterparts of "acting like white-sexist bastards," feminists within the movement claimed that it made no sense for the men of the Black Power generation to reject mainstream mores in most areas while taking instruction in male-female relations from the pages of *Good Housekeeping*. This outmoded model had to go, they said, not only because of its effect on the feminine self-image, but also because the relegation of women to domestic support duties weakened the revolution. Certainly, no black woman could aspire to become a Harriet Tubman when burdened with child care and chained to an ironing board. None could transcend patriarchal norms and expectations if continually degraded by claims that the proper place of women in the movement was "prone." To believe otherwise was said to promote "revolutionary servitude" and encourage belief in the antiquated notion that a black man's attempt at self-definition presumed the right to define women as well. After receiving fair warning that the black feminist vanguard no longer would take "unending shit off Black men," those who stubbornly refused to share leadership roles risked being labeled chauvinistic and counterrevolutionary.[206]

By the mid-1970s, heated debates over whether the movement represented a protest against inequality, an adjustment to it, or an overcompensation for it contributed to the belief that Black Power was a fractured, ineffective enthusiasm. Brought low by the programmatic, stylistic, and gender-based critiques of both declared enemies and professed friends, black militants retreated to their separate ideological enclaves amidst what one seasoned activist later characterized as "beaucoup dissention and disunity."[207] Soon surviving cadres showed signs of developing a cloistered siege mentality. Some leaders decried the loss of "revolutionary initiative" but nevertheless continued to castigate ideological adversaries. Other Black Power stalwarts entered into a period of introspection and self-criticism. On occasion, these movement postmortems bordered on self-flagellation. Deeply shaken by their failure to achieve liberation according to plan, militants responded to the critics' most damaging claims by confirming their accuracy.[208]

If, at the time, the strength and staying power of the historical revolt against white domination were undervalued, it nevertheless was obvious that considerable damage had been done to the ideal of black unity. During the Black Power years, the various ideological clusters expended an inordinate amount of energy on petty turf disputes and attempts to discredit one another through the airing of dirty laundry. In effect, ongoing internecine quarrels substantiated the opinion that each of the major political factions harbored a group of scoundrels who were willing to compromise sacred principles for narrow self-interest. Prone to fuzzy thinking and paranoia, the worst malefactors stood accused of shortchanging the very movement their rhetoric claimed was central to the advancement of the race.

By 1980 there was little call for journalists to prepare probing exposés of the "Black Mystique Pitfall"; to ask "What's Left of the Black Left?"[209] As the nation experienced a welcome hiatus from angry nationalists waving lists of non-negotiable demands, the Black Power movement vanished from the public consciousness. Like hippies, yippies, and other period-piece oddities, the militants no longer made front-page news and were consigned to paragraph-length treatments in history texts. In their stead, Young Republicans were seen celebrating Ronald Reagan's stunning electoral victory over Jimmy Carter. Serving as a rallying point for all who were tired of conflict, hard questions, and the relentlessness of change, the "Great Communicator's" ascendancy signaled the beginning of a dark night of the soul for remaining activists. To many, it now seemed certain that the societal pendulum would return to its more customary right-of-centrist position. Those excluded from the shaping of the "Reagan Revolution" feared that the new administration's attempt to reconstitute midcentury bourgeois normalcy would have a negative impact on the growth of white American social consciousness, thereby making racism more palatable.[210]

This eclipse of the mind-altering visions of yesteryear was accompanied by the rise of an unprecedented number of outspoken, right-leaning African Americans to positions of influence and power. Dubbed neo-conservatives by ideological opponents, many within this group of upper-middle-class writers, politicians, and media figures had rejected what now were considered youthful black nationalist indiscretions. As a result, they became a lightning rod for controversy. During the century's final two decades, high-profile Republican appointees such as U.S. Commission on Civil Rights chairman Clarence Pendleton, Housing and Urban Development secretary Samuel Pierce, and Supreme Court justice Clarence Thomas joined with talk-show hosts Armstrong Williams, Ken Hamblin, and Star Parker; policy-oriented public intellectuals Walter Williams, Thomas Sowell, and Shelby Steele; and the publishers of *Issues & Views,* the *Lincoln Review,* and *Headway* magazine to advance a conservative agenda within black America.

Adhering to the early civil rights movement concept of a color-blind society, conservative blacks celebrated the bounty of equal opportunity wrought by their forebears' nonviolent crusade. They lamented the "loss of genuine innocence" that accompanied Black Power and urged that late-century African Americans stake their claim to a "piece of prosperity from the American mainstream" by disavowing race as a source of privilege or entitlement. Demands for "eternal reparations" made by the current generation's most vocal "poverty pimps" and "pseudo-community leaders" were considered déclassé and detrimental to minority-group self-confidence. Preferential treatment of any kind was held to sap personal initiative, to imply inferiority, and to keep the lower classes secure in their "cocoon of victimhood."[211] It was one thing to be victimized, said the neo-conservatives, but quite another "to make an identity out of it." As noted by affirmative action opponent Clarence Pendleton in 1985, civil rights legislation enacted during the Kennedy and Johnson years established the right of any black American to stay in a white-owned hotel but made "no commitment to pay for the room."[212]

Encouraged by mainstream support for self-help, accountability, and "traditional" values, conservative blacks broadened their focus to encompass a variety of hot-button issues. In addition to launching spirited attacks on white liberal paternalists, black essentialists, and "political correctness," representatives of this new black elite came out against abortion, minimum-wage laws, gay rights, and sex education in schools. With equal or greater enthusiasm, they championed the death penalty, school prayer, supply-side economics, and the privatization of government services. In all cases, neo-conservative opinion shapers let it be known that they considered it a sworn duty to take "tough positions" on controversial issues; to resist the "herd mentality."[213]

Refusing to believe that equal *opportunity* mandated equal *outcomes* or that racism and discrimination were the primary determinants of the era's endemic urban poverty, black conservatives rarely passed up a chance to counsel the poor in free-market solutions to their plight. Individual responsibility was the sine qua non of upward mobility. Reliance on government handouts and the cross-generational transmission of pathological behaviors guaranteed continued failure. In conveying this essential wisdom, neo-conservative teachers sometimes related personal success stories—inspirational accounts that highlighted the benefits of de-emphasizing one's racial identity in favor of an "American" identity. Presumably, the latter was better adapted to the task of infiltrating mainstream meritocracies. On other occasions, a more direct approach was employed. For certain political figures and talk-show hosts like Larry Elder of Los Angeles station KABC, this meant telling target audience members to "get off your ass and work hard, stop blaming the white man, stop bitching and moaning." With either approach, conservative pedagogues risked censure both for neglecting to mention that affirmative action programs had been key to their own rapid advancement and for contributing to the vilification of fellow blacks.[214]

Echoing class-based beliefs about role modeling and refinement long held sacred by the black bourgeoisie, this focus on the ghetto dwellers' need to undergo psychological, moral, and cultural rehabilitation had the effect of forcing victims of racism to become their own scapegoat. Stigmatized as shiftless beggars lacking in self-respect, poor blacks were adjudged guilty of refusing to capitalize on available opportunities. In black neo-conservative thought, poverty was a self-inflicted wound; welfare dependency, a sign of one's inability to resist the temptations of drug use and irresponsible sex. According to finger-wagging Harvard University economist Glenn Loury, those who believed otherwise had been misled by the "welfare-state philosophy that says what happens to you is out of your control." They were "taking the wrongs of the past as an excuse for the failures of the present."[215] In other words, such individuals were post–civil rights–era dupes whose habituation to left-liberal ideas prevented them from recognizing that what poor blacks did to themselves was the chief cause of their inability to do for themselves.

On a crusade to rekindle the entrepreneurial spirit, black conservatives gave little consideration to how their hypercritical explication of urban poverty's origin and intractability might negatively affect the racial self-image. Most seemed unconcerned that their proposed solutions to contemporary social problems gave aid and comfort to white reactionaries. Instead, they worried about the immediate threat posed by African Americans whose class, political affiliation, or lifestyle made them the enemy. To true believers, it seemed as if hell's gates suddenly had been flung open and a vast horde of miscreants unleashed to torment the righteous. Their number included "government parasites" and "manipulators of racial paranoia" like Marion Barry, Al Sharpton, Maxine Waters, and Jesse Jackson; pseudo-intellectual "professor[s] of alienation" Leonard Jeffries, Angela Davis, and Derrick Bell; and cultural figures such as "literary conjure woman" Toni Morrison, "Afro-fascist" rap musician Chuck D, and filmmaker Spike Lee ("a pop, agitprop black nationalist with a gift for self-promotion").[216] According to staunch conservatives, these and other "enemies of the truth" constituted a clear and present danger to the "good folks" who still believed that "America works for black people too." They were rabble-rousers who preached racial xenophobia to their morally deviant constituents regardless of the consequences. Under the tutelage of "community-activist loudmouths," said syndicated columnist and radio personality Ken Hamblin, it was unlikely that such "black trash" ever could be motivated to take responsibility for their own "shiftless attitude and sorry predicament." If permitted to spread among those who persisted in viewing themselves as victims of racism, the liberals' "lies and . . . disinformation" would confirm millions in the belief that it was perfectly acceptable "to make parks unsafe, to terrorize senior citizens, and to denounce the American Dream."[217]

Throughout the 1980s and '90s, the neo-conservatives' campaign to discredit "quota blacks" and their "menacing black brethren" from the ghetto garnered considerable media coverage, attracted numerous flag-waving initiates, and earned key spokespersons fellowships and staff positions at foundation-funded think tanks.[218] It also elevated character assassination to a fine art and threatened to diminish the accuser's reputation for intellectual integrity almost as much as it did that of the accused. Quick to respond to what were considered serious libels, ideological enemies seized upon every noteworthy contradiction and character flaw. To paraphrase and redirect *New York Daily News* columnist Stanley Crouch's caustic characterization of activist Jesse Jackson, this not-so-loyal opposition believed that the neo-conservative movement was "besmirched" by arrogance, ambition, and an apparent "willingness to make pretzels of the truth."[219]

As if to deflect claims that their supporters had "stayed too long at the barricades," the black Left parried right-wing blows with an alacrity seldom seen since Black Power's heyday. Like a contingent of New Age "Great Black Hopes," movement veterans even came out of semiretirement to join the fray. However predictable, their rejoinders were steeped in conviction. Neo-conservatives, they claimed, were "house Negroes" whose fear of being taken for "*common* field niggers" caused them to ally with those who maintained a vested interest in perpetuating the status quo.[220] More out of touch with the grassroots than elites of previous generations, such individuals were depicted as "handkerchief heads" and "lawn jockey[s] for the far right." Allegedly, an insatiable hunger for power had caused them to become paid provocateurs—mouthpieces for white conservatives afraid of being accused of hatching racist schemes. While professing concern for poor people's "enforced dependency" on big government, most were considered false friends who held the "proxies of no identifiable groups of black citizens anywhere."

Some were said to evidence such "breathtaking hypocrisy" that they could be compared to "Jews who led their brothers and sisters into the ovens of the Holocaust." Surely, simultaneous support for private-sector investment in pre-independence South Africa and public-sector disinvestment in urban black America revealed their duplicitous nature. Eventually, vowed the re-energized activists, leaders of this "New Negro cabal" would be discredited and sent packing to the "Uncle Tom sanitarium."[221]

Astute enough to make political capital out of opponent's threats, leaders of the African American Right wrapped themselves in the flag and regaled reporters with accounts of their own victimization. They complained loudly of being subjected to shuns and scolding, ad hominem attacks, and "lies out of whole cloth"; of being abused by liberal moderators during public policy debates; and of their detractors' attempts to "de-black" them as punishment for remaining true to conservative principles. Nevertheless, refusing to cower before "Mau Maus" or bow to the will of "racial bluenoses," they persevered. As noted by the ever-implacable Clarence Thomas in 1987, accusations that African American conservatives opposed "all that was good and just and holy" and were "hell bent on returning blacks to slavery" stung but were by no means fatal. "Dissent," he said, always bore a price—"one I gladly paid."[222]

Ultimately, the deep-seated hatreds and factional intransigence evidenced in late-century policy debates worked against black unity. Only the most optimistic could maintain that a lasting reconciliation was imminent. At best, olive-branch entreaties to cease "frivolous division" or to "put aside our egos and save our children" served only to smooth ruffled feathers for a brief season. All too soon, this forced civility was eroded and accusations of "intellectual totalitarianism," political double-dealing, and economic self-aggrandizement resurfaced.[223] At the end of the millennium, fractious, mudslinging "crabs" were still trapped in their "barrel" of ideological and class-based self-absorption, tenaciously striving to keep each other from climbing out with dignity.

Gangland: Crime and Culture in Contemporary America

As the contention-ridden parade of tricksters and traitors, neo-conservatives and retro-nationalists made its way through the collective consciousness of late twentieth-century America, white people became anxious and confused. Tragically, the vast majority were ill prepared for diversity. Because a century of freedom had moved only a small number of blacks into the mainstream, relatively few European Americans could conceptualize African Americans as fully formed individuals. Despite unconvincing claims of having "friends" within communities of color, many whites continued to obtain the bulk of their insight into contemporary racial affairs from secondhand media sources. Here, the legacy of '60s activism and the entertainment industry's concern for a healthy "black box office" made it increasingly difficult to find traditional forms of reassurance. Soothing black images popularized during bygone eras were attacked whenever they surfaced within the popular culture. Comic minstrels still played the main room but now had a surly attitude and an X-rated vocabulary. Unsmiling macho dudes wearing gang colors and gold jewelry shamed the last of Hollywood's docile domestics into taking early retirement. By the end of the century, even that fabled provider of Caucasian creature comforts, Aunt Jemima, had opted to exchange her checked bandanna for a sleek new coif. Then, thinking the makeover both overdue and incomplete, mixed-media artist Betye Saar added insult to injury by depicting the beloved plantation cook with a broom in one hand and a gun in the other.[1] Was nothing sacred? Apparently not, because only the profane seemed to remain in vogue.

Denied access to cultural security blankets, late-century white Americans at last were obliged to confront what people like themselves always had feared and had tried to explain away or eradicate. With high-living outlaws in vogue and burnt cork bromides in short supply, they were made to look square in the face of the hideous black demon who lived just on the other side of the "model" Negro's bemused smile. The cacophony of black factions quarreling among themselves couldn't drown out the gasps of horror as whites recoiled at the prospect of joining the Dark One's minions in battle on central city turf. Because majority-group psychological defenses had been weakened by charges of genocidal intent and by the nagging suspicion that not even Uncle Tom could be relied upon at Armageddon, many within the mainstream appeared to approach emotional meltdown. For these tormented souls, neither current events nor contemporary cultural expression contradicted the ancient wisdom that held that blacks were born evildoers.

The account of white America's forced march to the corner of Fire and Brimstone streets in the rough-and-tumble neighborhood known as gangland constitutes the latest chapter in an ongoing morality tale that is filled with essential wisdom for students of both colorphobia and color consciousness. With a true rogue's gallery of characters—shape-shifting social bandits, black New Wave filmmakers, crackheads, gangsta rappers, suspected sociopaths, racial hoaxters, welfare "queens," and a variety of authority figures under siege—it is a story for the ages and contains many defining moments for black as well as white Americans. As is the case with most epic narratives, this one is steeped in the folk beliefs of its subjects and requires a certain amount of contextualization. Here, it is especially important to understand the dynamics of interracial rioting and how such historical conflicts have shaped—and have been shaped by—societal notions of villainy.

THE RIOTS

Earlier in the century, white Americans didn't need a Black Power–era poet like Sonia Sanchez to tell them that their dark-skinned countrymen were "a baddDDD people."[2] If born too early and too privileged to understand that, for some, "bad" could mean "good," they nevertheless were confirmed in the inherited belief that ex-slaves and their offspring were indolent and immoral. Periodically, it seems, black living spaces had to be cleansed by fire to ensure that such dens of iniquity did not pollute surrounding districts. It was upon the scorched earth created by these "white" riots—and by the far better reported "black" riots of the mid- to late 1960s—that the foundations of gangland were constructed.

Collective displays of outrage against real and imagined threats to white supremacy were a frequent occurrence in postbellum society. State-sanctioned disfranchisement and segregation never successfully calmed deeply rooted Negrophobic fears. Indeed, even as they waxed poetic about Old South folkways, mainstream cultural commentators reinforced the notion that physical freedom had done little to rid the ex-slave population of spiritual darkness.

Awash in nationalism, romanticism, and local color, late nineteenth-/ early twentieth-century novels affixed the bar sinister to African American portraiture by contrasting "world-conquering [white] men" with blacks who were unctuous or insolent, but never legitimately honorable or heroic. Descended from "a long line of savage spell-binders," such characters had been released from slavery's close-order supervision before their time. The most dangerous were distinguished by "gleaming jungle eyes," a "cunning intelligence," and the facility with which they masked rage with obsequiousness. Like Moses, the menacing "trick-doctor" of Thomas Nelson Page's 1898 novel *Red Rock,* these villains considered themselves to be "jest as good as any white man." They longed to marry a "white 'ooman" and to make former overlords their servants. Half child, half animal, the lustful African American freedman sought to "reverse the order of Nature" by mongrelizing Anglo-Saxon civilization.[3]

Social Darwinist popularizers added pseudoscientific validation to these dire literary scenarios. The color line, they said, was the Caucasian's last, best defense against the curse of "foul and fatal blackness." It had to be guarded with "more than vestal vigilance, with a circle of perpetual fire" if the "absolute and unchangeable superiority of the white race" was to be maintained. Blacks posed a threat because they were seen as members of a declining race that was reverting to barbarism. Hereditarily disadvantaged by "inferior organisms" and prone to criminality, lasciviousness, and a variety of communicable diseases, their failure to make significant advances during an era of competitive race relations foreshadowed complete "fossilization." All who dared tinker with the process of natural selection by mingling their blood with these unchaste pariahs risked sharing a most unhappy fate. To be completely safe, it was recommended that black America's "unsanitated throngs" be segregated and subordinated until the last of the defective, "dingy-hued" breed had met their "organic destiny."[4]

While rejecting the social Darwinists' "atheistic theory of Natural Development," theological minds of the day entertained highly speculative interpretations of early world history that reinforced the connection between dark skin color, sinfulness, and seduction. Replacing Ham's curse with a pre-Adamic creation story, revisionist authors such as Buckner Payne and Charles Carroll claimed that Eve's tempter was a beast—a Negro. Various permutations of this strange tale held that, like other animals, blacks had no moral faculty, soul, or hope of immortality; that transracial sexual intercourse was the "forbidden fruit" mentioned in Genesis 3; and that the offspring of such unions had so "outraged the very design of God in creating man," he attempted to eradicate them en masse via the Great Deluge. In such accounts, it was the earliest Caucasians' granting of sexual and social equality to black "talking beast[s]" that brought sin into the world. Clearly, for contemporary white society to abide amalgamation—"the most infamous and destructive crime known to the law of God"—was to invite divine displeasure.[5]

Reified again and again in darkly humorous songs like "The Mormon Coon" ("I've got a big brunette, and a blonde to pet, / I've got 'em short, fat, thin and tall, / . . . They come in bunches when I call");[6] in minstrel burlesques of interracial couplings that produced offspring who were "black one side de face an' white todder";[7] and in sensationalistic newspaper accounts of razor-toting "colored ruffians" menacing white women, mainstream disquietude over the genetic threat posed by black male sexuality was central to the shaping of a mobocratic social order.[8] Adding a sense of urgency to concerns about the ex-slaves' habituation to thievery and sedition, colorphobic insecurities over miscegenation promoted a negative response to the presence of those who postbellum polemicists conceptualized as "night-born ogre[s]"— "monstrous representatives of blackness and abomination."[9]

Shaken by the realization that key defense mechanisms once provided by the plantation regime had vanished with its passing, whites tried to stem panic, limit the spread of black contagion, and educate against racial intermixture. Some approached these daunting tasks by campaigning for rigorous enforcement of local segregation ordinances. Others relied upon the opinion-shaping power of negative race-linked attributions (park signs noting "Negroes and dogs not allowed"; department store prohibitions against "unclean" African American women trying on hats or gloves) and linguistic differentiation (white *people* vs. the colored *race;* southern lady and gentleman, boss, or cap'n vs. "asp-eyed negress" and "bullet-headed buck"). Still others sought to massage the European American ego by adopting rigid orthodoxies of racial etiquette. Unfortunately, none of these social stratagems guaranteed the sort of psychic security that fearful whites demanded. In such confused and trying times, more direct, far more invasive coercions were mandated.[10]

Racial rioting provided an alternative course of action for those who held that vigilantism was a legitimate instrument of social control. More dramatic and spontaneous than extralegal policing by quasi-military patrols, "home guards," or "committees of safety"; less piecemeal than the sacrificial rite of lynching, sudden outbreaks of popular disorder were believed by many to reinforce rather than subvert communal standards of justice. Indeed, from the nation's earliest years, bloody civil disturbances had provided incontrovertible evidence of the commoners' aversion to unmerited privilege, their determination to defend local interests against government intrusion, and their tendency to confuse acts of nativist, racist, or religious persecution with the sacred duties of true patriots. Thus, unless one was counted among the victims, postbellum whites' utilization of collective violence against subversive and sexually threatening black villains was easily understood and readily defended. Theirs was a time-honored approach to shielding beleaguered communities from both real and imagined dangers. Like "Negro barbeques" and the raids of robed night riders, white riots employed the temporary chaos of physical violence to preserve prevailing caste and gender hierarchies, thereby averting far more convulsive societal upheavals.[11]

As was the case with the ruffians who looted or burned free blacks' homes, schools, and churches in the years before the Civil War, postbellum mobocrats were motivated largely by fear and jealousy. Nevertheless, many claimed to be engaged in the noblest of reformist endeavor. In certain circles, the periodic storming of African American neighborhoods by white mobs was seen as evidence of progressive ideals and civic pride, not racial bigotry. To make this self-exculpatory tale ring true, outbreaks of antiblack violence in Wilmington, North Carolina (1898); Atlanta, Georgia (1906); Springfield, Illinois (1908); Tulsa, Oklahoma (1921); and other cities were blamed on the victims' persistent wrongdoing and social deviancy. Allegedly, the disturbances were a result of "the negroes' own misconduct, general inferiority or unfitness for free institutions."[12] If African Americans tended to view these deadly assaults as police riots, pogroms, or convenient excuses to brutalize and pillage, many whites maintained that extraordinary measures had to be taken to defend the larger society against evils spawned in vice-ridden black urban enclaves.

Targeted behaviors included cockiness and conspicuous consumption; criminal activity and the corruption of community morals. Also scored were the African Americans' apparent eagerness to serve as strikebreakers, stand for public office, and entertain the seditious beliefs of Bolsheviks and Wobblies. Some municipal leaders feared that the speakeasies, gambling dens, and houses of ill repute found in central city districts such as East St. Louis's "Black Valley" and Atlanta's Decatur Street were serving as staging grounds for armed invasions of white neighborhoods. Others evidenced more immediate concerns about blacks lowering property values by purchasing homes outside the overcrowded ghetto. All were influenced by a widespread belief that the lasciviousness of dark-skinned males posed a serious threat to the future of the White Republic.[13]

Even when conducted in broad daylight, the early twentieth-century riots were inextricably connected to darkness. Sexually charged paranoia provided a perverse subtext for many of these orgasmic rampages. For example, in Tulsa mass hysteria erupted after a white teenager named Sarah Page accused a bootblack known as "Diamond Dick" Rowland of tearing her clothes and attempting to assault her in a downtown office building. While it is likely that the alleged rapist had done nothing more than accidentally step on the female elevator operator's foot, subsequent mob violence left an estimated 250 people dead, some 6,000 blacks forcibly interned under armed guard, and over 1,000 homes and businesses in ruins.[14]

Atlanta's four-day riot was preceded by press speculation that a series of brutal sexual assaults had been fueled by strong drink laced with cocaine and by pictures of scantily clad white women displayed on the walls of "colored only" saloons. Citizens concerned about maintaining the "Christ-like" chastity of southern womanhood held that "Caucasian virtue" was being threatened by the "low-browed, whisky loving Guinea Negro from which comes the rapist." Before an estimated ten thousand people took to the streets and an orgy of butchery and plunder interrupted debate, proposed solutions to the problems caused by African American hypersexuality included substantial monetary rewards to women who shot and killed would-be assailants, castration and branding of rapine-prone black males, and sterilization of black baby girls who, as adults, were suspected of seducing European American men in order to have mulatto children.[15]

Equally perverse conceptualizations of blacks as a race of sexual predators helped to justify the actions of vigilante "reformers" in other cities. Reports of presumptuous young "rakes" making indecent proposals in parks and on streetcars, inflammatory newspaper headlines that screamed "NEGRO GRABS GIRL AS SHE STEPS OUT ON BACK PORCH," and rumors that mass seductions would occur after white men were conscripted into the military brought tensions to the boiling point. The fact that volleys of gunfire were exchanged with marauding mobs in several locales only made matters worse. Militant responses encouraged the belief that blacks would use deadly force to effect racial mongrelization. Consumed by animalistic lusts and "rotten" with venereal diseases, such "two legged monster[s]" had to be destroyed lest the white community's ability to protect its female citizens from unspeakable horrors be called into question.[16]

For those who considered proposed federal antilynching legislation "a bill to encourage rape" and maintained that voluntary interracial sex was impossible due to white women's universal aversion to black men, the omnipresent fear of "Negro Domination" went far beyond obvious concerns over school and housing integration, loss of political power, or an increase in black business competition. To dominate white women sexually was to degrade a key symbol of European American domesticity. It was "the greatest wrong, the blackest crime"—one that seemingly could be combated only by the terrible forces unleashed during lynching bees and white riots.[17] Influenced greatly by Victorian moral teachings that condemned uncontrolled sensuality and carnal self-indulgence; born too early to conceptualize rape as an act of masculinist violence divorced from sexual passion, many within the early twentieth-century mainstream were unable to look at a black person without seeing the incubus that would permanently pollute their gene pool. To besieged whites living in increasingly diverse and secularized cities, the threat that physical darkness posed to inherited standards of beauty, customary notions of racial superiority, and the stability of the existing social order was no less terrifying than the spiritual darkness earlier generations had attributed to the children of Ham.

As the century progressed, the various malignancies associated with blackness were conflated into a fearful specter of death and destruction. The "bad class of Negroes" seemed to grow larger each year; their criminal appetites and deviant sexual desires less easily sated than ever before. Like Methodist Bishop Warren A. Candler, some social critics believed that a "danger to women is inherent in every offense against white men." Others, influenced by the pro-"Nordic" writings of eugenist Lothrop Stoddard, warned that "excessive multiplication" of "colored" races worldwide threatened to "obliterate" white civilization. Certainly, World War II–era rumors that African Americans were organizing Black Dragon Societies and Swastika Clubs, ordering firearms and ammunition from the Sears catalog, and intentionally contracting venereal diseases to more easily dodge the draft encouraged feelings of dread.[18]

Because government statistics and academic studies that could have calmed frayed nerves typically were overlooked or ignored, scores of anxious whites rushed pell-mell to find a new Eden—a pristine racial homeland far removed from the black peril. If, for a time, the Golden State of California met these requisites quite nicely, African American in-migration eventually forced postwar frontiersmen to revisit the troublesome topic of black villainy. By the mid-1960s, Los Angeles contained ethnic neighborhoods so crime-ridden and hostile to outsiders that incursions by European American mobs were considered foolhardy. When, in 1965 and again in 1992, mutual hatred caused violence to engulf Watts and surrounding districts, black rather than white Angelenos assumed the role of racial aggressor.

Like the September 11, 2001, terrorist attacks on Manhattan's World Trade Center complex, the far more spontaneous assault on American symbols of authority and power that began in Watts on the evening of August 11, 1965, had a decidedly negative effect on the nation's sense of internal security. Contrary to established principles of optics, but in line with the workings of blind prejudice and mass hysteria, light from the fires set by Afro-American insurgents occluded the vision of terror-stricken white people. For those most susceptible to urban myth and media manipulation, the black riots were seen as nothing less than the long-anticipated rising from the depths. The end times seemed to be drawing nigh for Whitey. Long before the last fires were extinguished and a modicum of order restored on August 18, it was clear that emotional tremors stemming from the violence would be slow to dissipate.

Even a cursory accounting of the chaos wrought by this five-day uprising reveals why both European American comfort levels and the complacency born of self-satisfaction were destined to experience a precipitous decline after Watts. Within the 46.5-square-mile curfew zone, between 2,000 and 3,000 alarms tied up the county's firefighting equipment and necessitated the deployment of 13,900 National Guard troops, 934 police, and 719 sheriff's deputies. Overall, almost 1,000 buildings were burned, looted, or destroyed, and total property damage exceeded $40 million. By one count, rioters numbered between 31,000 and 35,000—the equivalent of three combat infantry divisions—while another 64,000 to 72,000 were involved as "close spectators." Of 3,438 adults arrested, 2,206 had prior criminal records, as did almost 50 percent of the 514 juveniles taken into custody. Thirty-four people died and 1,032—including 226 police and firefighters—were injured seriously enough to require medical treatment.[19]

In an attempt to contextualize these grim statistics, government officials, press and television commentators, and members of the affected community weighed in on the subject of civil disorder. Some opinions carried more weight than others. Understandably, those that pinpointed the root cause of black unrest while promoting respect for the law proved attractive to a mainstream public beset by upheaval and uncertainty. Thus, when blustery, hardline Police Chief William Parker claimed that "you cannot ignore the genes in the behavior pattern of people" and compared "Negro hoodlums" to "monkeys in a zoo," his unapologetically outspoken views on the connection between racial character and rioting were guaranteed a favorable hearing. After predicting (inaccurately) that 45 percent of metropolitan Los Angeles would be black within five years, Parker urged white residents to protect hearth and home by supporting a strong police department. "If you don't do that," he told a local television audience, "God help you." At a time when the northernmost point of the curfew area was only four miles from Beverly Hills and reports of an imminent black strike on the all-white municipality of Lynwood circulated widely, this seemed like sound advice.[20]

Adding credibility to Parker's warning was white Californians' view of Watts as a once-peaceable New West promised land that was being despoiled by unproductive, ungrateful, and increasingly dangerous black migrants. Incorporated in 1907 and annexed to the city of Los Angeles in 1926, Watts had always been a low-income, working-class community. Between 1940 and 1960, wave after wave of unskilled, often illiterate job seekers from southern states permanently altered the racial balance of the 2.5-square-mile district. Once-dominant Anglos fled to the suburbs and Mexican American residents relocated in East L.A. By 1965, 87 percent of Watts residents were African Americans, population density was the highest in the county, and joblessness topped 13 percent. Nevertheless, with wide main streets, numerous public parks, and clusters of small but neat and attractive frame houses, much of the area continued to give outsiders the impression that they were passing through a fairly comfortable residential neighborhood. As the commission appointed by Governor Edmund "Pat" Brown to investigate the 1965 disturbances noted in its final report, "A Negro in Los Angeles has long been able to sit where he wants in a bus or a movie house, to shop where he wishes, to vote, and to use public facilities without discrimination. The opportunity to succeed is probably unequaled in any other major American city." That an urban rebellion should begin here seemed unlikely—unless one assumed that purposeful subversion by black villains was involved.[21]

Mainstream media coverage confirmed the presence of these diabolical troublemakers throughout the riot zone. Allegedly, they had taken "thousands of rifles, shotguns, pistols and machetes" from pawnshops and war surplus stores and were using secret hand signals as passwords. It was said that they made a practice of luring rescue workers into harm's way by phoning in false fire and personal injury reports. If some rejected reporters' requests for interviews with the angry retort, "I ain't got no time for you white demons," others were emboldened by the prospect of appearing on TV news broadcasts—regaling bystanders with sound-bite-ready encapsulations of plans to take the violence to "the white man's neighborhoods tonight." Such displays, said one outraged member of the Fourth Estate, proved that the Watts revolt was caused by "weak character traits in uncivilized human beings who yielded to their savage emotions in a barbaric display of ill will and hate."[22]

Handicapped by broadcast and publication deadlines as well as by an embarrassing shortage of African American staff members, media outlets aided and abetted the city's more informal networks of rumormongering. Unconfirmed reports and hysteria-inducing film footage helped disseminate malicious gossip while showcasing the worst examples of black villainy. The following were among the more tantalizing rumors in general circulation:

> Urban rebels had armed themselves with machine guns and were storing large quantities of conventional weaponry underground for use in future uprisings. Some had adopted a quasi-military uniform of black pants and turtleneck sweaters. Others were busy disguising Molotov cocktails by sucking out eggshells and filling them with gasoline.[23]

> Leaders of the Nation of Islam had ordered the disturbances to stop until National Guard troops left—and then to begin anew with attacks on Jewish-owned businesses. Black Muslim assassins were prepared to kill Martin Luther King Jr. if he came to Los Angeles as a peacemaker.[24]

> Roving groups of rioters who had been spotted wearing red armbands were in league with the Vietcong.[25]

However vivid, none of the riot scenarios that imputed blame via unsubstantiated rumor did an acceptable job of explaining how a specific "riot climate" was formed. Typically left out of the equation were the many ways in which mainstream institutions and practices fostered racial division. In Watts such an accounting would include overcrowded, understaffed public schools; a police force that was 96 percent nonblack; lack of reliable public transportation to industrial plants with high-salary union jobs; exploitative shopkeepers; and uncaring, absentee landlords. Thus, unless one reserved judgment until the inevitable spate of statistics-filled studies appeared in academic journals, it was easy for a white Angeleno to essentialize guilt. As one LAPD officer concluded, "Say all you want about social causes, I don't believe they accounted for what occurred. Face it, people gorged themselves with a heady diet of unrestrained conduct . . . flouting the authority of government . . . , burning and looting just for the sheer hell of it." According to this interpretation of events, all of the "marauding" and "guerrilla warfare" that occurred during the Watts Riot was attributable to villainy spawned within the African American community.[26]

As if transfixed by an evildoer's hypnotic gaze, whites modified their beliefs only with great difficulty. Disregarding the fact that relatively few civilians were attacked and most neighborhoods outside the curfew zone were spared serious violence, nonblacks continued to exaggerate both the scope and participation level of the disturbances. Even after early impressionistic data had been refined, European Americans had trouble comprehending how blacks who were philosophically opposed to armed confrontation could sympathize with the insurgents or view Watts as a symbolic protest against deteriorating ghetto social conditions.[27] To Californians whose understanding of urban sociology was hindered by spatial separation as well as by victim-bashing headlines that screamed, "RACIAL UNREST LAID TO NEGRO FAMILY FAILURE," such reasoning seemed little more than a villain's rationalization of antisocial behavior. Like former president Herbert Hoover, many felt compelled to question the legitimacy of loudly voiced black protest at a time when "our 19 million Negroes probably own more automobiles than all the 220 million Russians and the 200 million African Negroes put together."[28]

Ultimately, central city car registration proved an unreliable indicator of societal equilibrium; mainstream opinion that considered black protest to be illegitimate did little to improve interracial understanding. Grievances remained unaddressed. Mutual suspicion and hatred festered. As a result, there were more uprisings. During the late 1960s, frustrated black residents of Detroit, Newark, and a host of other cities took to the streets in what the author of one Midwest civil arrest study aptly termed "summer mockery."[29]

While social scientists diligently mapped "riot phases" (precipitating incident, street confrontation, Roman holiday, siege), searched for commonalities, and sought to provide a definitive answer to the question "Who riots and why?" nonacademics composed their own informal indices of importunate behavior. Influenced greatly by studies detailing inner-city residents' "social disorganization"—high rates of juvenile delinquency, narcotic addiction, homicide, illegitimacy, and female-headed households—middle-class whites were appalled at the degree to which underclass lifestyles differed from their own. The most unsympathetic refused to believe that those trapped in a "tangle of pathology" were making a concerted effort to escape. Unlike earlier generations of European American strivers, they had become "cop-outs and dropouts," "welfare rights ruffians," and "24-carat specimens of worthlessness." Loudly voiced in the aftermath of the '60s uprisings, these negative characterizations enabled outsiders to stereotype poor urban blacks as an undifferentiated cohort of villains. By the time Los Angeles once again experienced a major civil disturbance in 1992, many nonblacks conceptualized the prototypical ghetto evildoer as a youthful African American male who claimed to be "deprived" and "disadvantaged"—scarred by the "mutilating marks" of oppression. Perpetually offended, easily angered, and driven by a deep-seated "lust for destruction," such individuals considered it their right to "take what is not theirs," to "destroy what they have not produced," and to "hate what they refuse to understand." In other words, these modern-day black villains seemed a lot like Rodney King.[30]

On May 1, 1992, twenty-seven-year-old King emerged from his lawyer's office in Beverly Hills to deliver a halting, somewhat rambling plea for interracial understanding. "Please, we can get along here," he said nervously—barely audible over the noise of helicopters hovering overhead. "We all can get along. We've just got to, just got to. We're all stuck here for a while. . . . Let's try to work it out."[31] As would be noted by the more analytical of the hundred or so reporters in attendance, what needed to be "worked out" was the complex tangle of intergroup antagonisms that was fueling a deadly conflagration in South Central L.A.

Variously perceived to be either the cause or the conscience of this five-day riot that took more than fifty lives and destroyed an estimated four thousand Los Angeles businesses, Rodney Glen King had the great misfortune to enter the public consciousness as both victim and villain—a "disadvantaged" and brutalized black man whose alleged animalistic behavior initiated a downward spiral of events culminating in unprecedented social disorder. Frequent rebroadcasts of King's videotaped manhandling by police on March 3, 1991, generated considerable sympathy—especially among young African American males whose own experiences with the LAPD were overwhelmingly negative. By being clubbed, kicked, and jolted repeatedly by a 50,000-volt Taser stun gun, he bonded spiritually with all ghetto dwellers who had reason to claim hardship reparations. Elsewhere, individuals so thoroughly insulated from street-level reality as to be unaware that the city was spending upwards of $9 million a year to settle lawsuits alleging police misconduct puzzled over the incident.[32] Why, they asked, would an otherwise innocent speeder be abused? Weren't each of the twenty-five officers present at the time of the arrest sworn to preserve and protect? If both the videotaped evidence and King's medical report (nine skull fractures, a broken cheekbone, a shattered eye socket, a broken leg, and assorted contusions, abrasions, and bruises) elicited widespread condemnation, neither offered conclusive proof that the beating was unprovoked. Indeed, the only incontrovertible fact seemed to be that even King's mainstream sympathizers had been socialized to believe that rogue blacks posed a far greater threat to law-abiding citizens than did rogue cops.

As if to validate white fears and discredit official assurances that the police were well equipped to prevent another Watts-style disturbance, the April 29, 1992, acquittal of four of Rodney King's assailants in a Simi Valley courtroom sparked black rebellion. It also confirmed that yet another African American victim had been subjected to villainization in the court of public opinion. Trial testimony, insider accounts, and talk-show interviews with former jurors focused on the ferocity with which King resisted arrest. Said to have "dictated all of the actions"—to have been "in full control" of the situation that resulted in his own beating—the powerfully built black man was portrayed as a serious threat to investigating officers and innocent civilians alike.[33] After being stopped in the early morning hours for allegedly driving his two-door Hyundai Excel 115 miles per hour on the Foothill Freeway, King began to behave in a most bizarre fashion. Talking gibberish, laughing, and dancing about, he waved into the spotlight of an LAPD helicopter and then got on all fours, giggling, and patting the ground. After ignoring a female officer's order to stop, King grabbed his buttocks with both hands and began to gyrate suggestively. The police were not at all amused. They believed that the "buffed out" six-foot-three, 225-pound suspect was acting under the influence of the strength-enhancing hallucinogenic drug PCP and feared what later was referred to as a "Mandingo sexual encounter." To diffuse the situation, four officers "swarmed" King, but continued resistance mandated the use of "escalating force"—in this case, metal PR-24 batons and Taser darts. As was revealed by the now-infamous eighty-one seconds of graphic violence captured on videotape by an amateur photographer, fifty-six powerful blows eventually sapped King's "Hulk-like strength." He was double-cuffed, hogtied with nylon rope, and taken into custody.[34]

Officers on the scene discounted charges of police brutality and spoke glowingly of the high level of professionalism evidenced while "subduing a really monster guy." Subsequent record checks confirmed that their prisoner was no Boy Scout. A junior high school dropout who suffered from a learning disability, King habitually displayed poor judgment and a confrontational attitude after overindulging in Olde English 800 malt liquor. At the time of the Foothill Freeway incident, he was unemployed and on parole in connection with a 1989 armed robbery. Earlier brushes with the law involved retail theft, misdemeanor battery, reckless driving, and soliciting sex from an undercover Pasadena policewoman. With a record like this, it was hard to fault veteran LAPD officer Theodore Briseno's characterization of the violence-prone ex-con as "a bad ass."[35]

Ultimately, the twelve nonblack Simi Valley jurors accepted the essential accuracy of this description. Unmoved by the prosecution's efforts to humanize the burly black man, they opted for objectification. Described as a bear and his groans as bearlike, the brutally savaged Rodney King came to be perceived as a savage brute, a wounded beast. "He wasn't an animal, was he?" asked a deputy district attorney at one point. "No, sir," replied officer Laurence Powell. "He just acted like one." It was a fine distinction, easily lost amidst repeated recountings of how King's belligerence and near superhuman strength had endangered the lives of career public servants who constituted the "thin blue line" separating civilization from chaos.[36]

Transcripts of communications sent via LAPD Mobile Data Terminals on the night of March 3 revealed that some patrol officers were of the opinion that "a big time use of force" was a virtual prerequisite to dealing effectively with animalistic black "mo fos" and "gorillas in the mist."[37] Whether the product of racism or darkly humorous occupational cynicism, this crudely stated thesis was tested repeatedly during the 1992 rebellion. From the start, young blacks defying all attempts to restore order identified with Rodney King and, in turn, were linked by the media and general public to negative racial stereotypes. "This is for Rodney," one man declared triumphantly as a Korean liquor store employee was struck in the head with a bottle of Olde English 800. "Rodney King?" exclaimed another. "Shit, my homies be beat like dogs by the police every day. . . . Rodney King just the trigger."[38] If, as noted by Jesse Jackson during a speech in Pasadena, local African Americans viewed the beating as "the caboose on a long train of abuses," a nationwide television audience received the unmistakable impression that roving bands of young blacks constituted a powerful engine of destruction speeding out of control.[39] To many, it seemed that sanity could be restored only by resorting to extreme measures, that is, "a big time use of force."

Without question, the situation in Los Angeles was grim. Given unprecedented immediacy by continuous live coverage beamed from a fleet of mobile broadcast units and a dozen or more "telecopters," the escalating violence transfixed viewers. More than a decade later, indelibly ingrained images from this nightmare scenario continue to generate feelings of sadness and repulsion:

Slightly built thirty-six-year-old Reginald Denny pulled from the cab of his eighteen-wheeler, kicked in the stomach, beaten with a claw hammer, and knocked unconscious with a chunk of concrete; his assailants flashing gang signs, rifling through his pockets, and performing an impromptu victory dance in the middle of the street.[40]

Sooty, bone-tired firefighters being pelted with rocks, bottles, and projectiles made from pieces of smashed bus benches as bystanders jeer, "Kill 'em, shoot 'em!"[41]

Guatemalan immigrant Fidel Lopez having his face and genitals sprayed with black paint by an attacker who robbed him of $2,000 and then crowed, "He's black now."[42]

A crowd of African American teenagers laughing and mugging for the camera at the scene of a grisly shooting; the mortified KCAL-TV staffer reporting, "There's a dead person here and it's a big joke. Back to you."[43]

Incidents such as these shocked the nation, spurring handgun sales and memberships in suburban rifle clubs. When violent reaction to the police acquittals spread beyond Los Angeles County—to San Francisco, Las Vegas, and other cities—black and white never seemed so far apart. "I just couldn't believe humankind had sunk to such depths," said a female police officer, speaking for many caught within the riot zone. "I thought, 'animals.'"[44]

Print and broadcast news professionals did little to discourage others from arriving at the same conclusion. On the whole, media coverage tended to privilege dramatic episodes of violence over thoughtful analysis of foundational social issues. The total number of fires set by arsonists was overstated. Minimized or downplayed was the fact that more than half of all those arrested were Latinos and that many African American residents were appalled at the carnage—the boldest placing themselves in harm's way to aid the injured.[45]

This skewed news coverage virtually guaranteed that the temptation to demonize would increase with each new outrage. With minority viewpoints remaining ill reported, the events of May 1992 came to be interpreted and understood as a black-initiated race war. Thus, when Rodney King made his famous plea for interracial peace, whites were in no mood to parley. Most couldn't understand that within black America *they* were considered to be a significant part of the problem. The vast majority were mystified at the ability of their black neighbors to make a clear distinction between the savaging of a European American truck driver by an unrestrained mob and the savaging of an African American motorist by unrestrained public servants. And virtually none could fathom how it was possible for some Los Angeles blacks to believe that "justice" had been meted out to Reginald Denny but denied to King.[46] As had been the case during times of slave unrest and lynching fever, the twentieth-century urban rebellions inhibited white Americans' ability to learn from the past, empathize with the oppressed, or effectively employ logic and reason in addressing issues of race and power. When confronted with scenes of social disorder, critical faculties failed and they were unable to engage in problem solving without profiling or scapegoating.

Unquestionably, the problem of black villainy had become ever more complex. Having delegated the task of policing the "bad class of Negroes" to trained law enforcement professionals, late-century white Americans were denied both the temporary psychological security and the illusion of effective hands-on community control once provided by vigilante-led white riots. To postsegregation-era whites, the option of addressing perceived social wrongs through collective violence now seemed reserved for ghetto toughs. And the proverbial "taste of their own medicine" was proving all too bitter. Thrust into what Los Angeles police chief Daryl Gates described as "a world of guns and violence and sociopathic behavior that is almost beyond human understanding," a numerically declining and increasingly insecure majority population imagined that they saw clusters of predatory black villains rising, Phoenix-like, from the ashes of riot-torn neighborhoods.[47]

* * *

Because their understanding of urban sociology was hindered by spatial separation as well as by an overreliance on inherited stereotypes and mass-mediated images, white Americans who came of age between 1965 and the 1990s experienced considerable difficulty distinguishing between the various community-based entities that were said to harbor African American villains. When asked to differentiate between the Black Panthers, the New Black Panthers, the New Panther Vanguard Movement, and the Black Panther Militia—or to assess the relative threat posed by RAM, MOVE, or DRUM—severe intellectual distress set in. Whether conceptualized as "urban terrorists," "hate-mongers and rabble rousers," or "an outlaw political gang," each faction of this militant confraternity appeared equally malevolent.[48] John Africa, Assata Shakur, Kwame Ture, and Imari Abubakari Obadele—exotic "movement" names adopted by an activist vanguard—conjured up primal fear by way of the Dark Continent. Confrontational and prone to rhetorical excess, all were suspected of hatching subversive schemes against the established world order. Somehow, they had to be stopped.

African Americans who had become disenchanted with "revolutionary politics" were inclined to agree—at least in principle. Periodically, overzealous ideologues were driven from their soapbox and subjected to ridicule and rebuke. Nevertheless, because urban blacks possessed specific, detailed knowledge of the villains' depredations, they were better able than their white contemporaries to separate real from imagined perils. Less concerned about the rise of a revolutionary "messiah" than about getting to and from the corner grocery store safely, many continued to honor a select number of charismatic "political" operatives while reserving their harshest condemnation for confirmed criminal types. As the national learning curve improved and white Americans became more adept at recognizing and rewarding black achievers, it was understandable that black Americans would grow less hesitant to acknowledge that there were villains in their midst. When exculpatory claims of "deprivation" rang hollow and no manipulative white "boss" or liberation-oriented ideology could be found guiding their actions, such individuals were denied the coveted status of social bandit. Thereafter, they were treated as social pariahs.

By the end of the millennium, black-on-black crime was a major concern and both European Americans and African Americans entered into a long overdue dialogue over how to address the problems of central city neighborhoods. In fits and starts, with countless setbacks and frustrations, the two traditionally adversarial racial constituencies moved a bit closer as it became apparent that mutual self-interest called for urban ganglands to be transformed into fully habitable communities. A variety of short-fused hard cases opposed this noble endeavor. Formidable adversaries, they joined an obstructionist mind-set with criminal intent and the ability to marshal deadly force. Determined to uphold the bad black tradition at all cost, most didn't seem fazed in the least by communal condemnation. In his 1998 work, *Two Cities,* African American novelist John Wideman accurately encapsulated the danger posed by modern-day black villains. Simply but vividly put: "They got guns and like to use them and don't give a fuck who they hurt."[49]

THE CRIMINAL ELEMENT

Over the years, it had been rare for perpetrators of black-on-black crime to receive full pardon from the persons they had harmed. However, less immediately affected members of the community often practiced what has been termed "reflexive absolution"—exempting African American perpetrators from thoroughgoing censure in the name of brotherhood. On such occasions, an "extenuating circumstance"—such as a rumored white conspiracy—would be used to redistribute blame. Through this clever sleight of hand, the burden of guilt was relieved and a semblance of racial unity preserved. For example, after 1975 the "I-told-you-so's" emanating from the Afroworld reached an ear-shattering crescendo as documents released under the amended Freedom of Information Act confirmed that infighting between '60s militants had been fomented by the federal government. True, cultural, territorial, and revolutionary nationalists frequently had been at each other's throats as a result of ideological differences. But J. Edgar Hoover's covert action campaign of dirty tricks, "snitch jacket" infiltration, and harassment arrests sowed discord, frayed nerves, and, eventually, drew blood. Corroboration of the fact that FBI operatives had produced and distributed incriminating correspondence, defamatory cartoons, and bogus "underground" newspapers charging activist leaders with ideological, financial, and sexual improprieties helped vindicate the accused parties. Thereafter, it became more tempting than ever to believe that white villainy was responsible for many, if not most, of the criminal acts committed against blood brothers.[50]

Periodically, these lingering suspicions that the "official line" was a lie were reinforced by fresh evidence of duplicity—that is, high-profile racial hoaxes in which European American murderers, thieves, and rapists attempted to shift blame to nonexistent criminals of color. By tapping into widely held beliefs about black deviancy, Charles Stuart, Susan Smith, Jesse Anderson, and other manipulators of societal stereotypes hoped to escape punishment for their own misdeeds. For many African Americans, the fact that these schemes were thwarted and the perpetrators arrested brought only temporary relief from the psychological burden of blackness. Understandably, they felt abused and angry. It seemed that little had changed. White Americans still assumed that skin-color privilege enabled them to cry "The niggers did it" and everything would work out fine. The most skillful convinced authorities that their "invented" alibis were plausible—weaving elaborately fabricated tales to cover up an extramarital affair or collect an insurance settlement; to escape a failed marriage, disguise retail theft, or hide gambling losses. Within black America, white-on-black hoaxes—as well as continuing revelations regarding unethical FBI practices—encouraged the belief that instances of black villainy were greatly exaggerated; acts of white criminal behavior purposefully underreported.[51]

During the century's final three decades, inquiries into the nature and genesis of black-on-black crime led to even more unnerving discoveries. Reports indicated that the number of serial murders had risen markedly in recent years and African American communities were found to have more than their fair share of both predators and victims. A peculiarly American phenomenon, serial killings accounted for nearly fourteen hundred deaths during the period 1975–95. Averaging 7.7 cases per year with six to nine victims per case, this category of violent crime made up a minute percentage of all homicides but created unparalleled anxiety and fear in affected locales.[52] Central to the phenomenon was its seeming randomness. Frequently "ordinary" in appearance and demeanor, the various sociopaths who killed repeatedly, methodically, and without apparent motive kept their deadly timetable a closely guarded secret. As a result, tension mounted incrementally during the sometimes-lengthy "cooling off" periods between attacks.

At times, the public's attraction to these "werewolves of the modern age" bordered on the grotesque. Evidencing addictive behaviors that the criminals themselves would fully understand, some became morbidly involved with the minutia of a particularly well-publicized case. They corresponded with imprisoned killers, sent them gifts, and created a lucrative market for questionably tasteful T-shirts, trading cards, and comic books. Those unable to afford the pricier items—such as a $20,000 clown painting by Chicago-area murderer John Wayne Gacy—had numerous options. Academic studies, lurid true-crime accounts, and fictional potboilers competed for space on bookstore shelves while Hollywood rushed to meet the demand for ever-higher body counts with films like *Manhunter, Copycat, Kiss the Girls, The Bone Collector,* and *Seven.* This proliferation of multiple-homicide mayhem throughout the popular culture had potentially dangerous consequences. "Our society is actively breeding serial killers," warned crime writer William J. Birnes. "And society's fascination with them is only adding to that." Uncomfortably familiar to all of us, these two-legged monsters remain both perversely appealing and utterly appalling.[53]

No one really knows how many serial murderers are active in the United States in any given year. Experts believe that most start their grisly careers in their late twenties and target strangers almost exclusively. Nevertheless, strangling, stabbing, and other methods of attack that put them in close contact with their victims are preferred. They are overwhelmingly white males, but perhaps one in five is African American.[54] Among the best known within the latter cohort are individuals who were committed to crossing racial boundaries in search of prey.

During the early 1970s, a skewed take on revolutionary ideology and an intense hatred of white people combined to provide a serviceable rationale for mass murder. On New Year's Eve 1972, twenty-three-year-old Mark Essex sought to avenge the November 16 shooting of two African American students at a campus demonstration in Baton Rouge by ambushing a group of officers outside New Orleans's police headquarters. Before he was killed in an intense firefight a week later, the navy veteran left ten dead and twenty-two wounded. Although one of the victims was an African American police cadet, Essex—whose Swahili name was "Mata" or "bow and arrow"—made a concerted effort to avoid harming racial kinsmen. "Don't worry, I'm not going to hurt you black people," he told a group of hotel workers during the final standoff. "I want the whites." Later, when investigators searched his apartment for clues that might provide a motive for the rampage, they found a cache of incendiary literature and a graphic display of Essex's perspective on race. Nearly every available inch of wall and ceiling space was splashed with slogans declaring: "Hate white people—beast of the earth"; "Revolutionary justice is black justice"; or simply the words "hate," "blood," and "kill." Most disturbing of all was a statement carefully penciled inside the three-foot-tall "C" of a boldly painted "AFRICA." It read: "The quest for freedom is death— then by death I shall escape to freedom."[55]

The difficulty of fathoming this apocalyptic mind-set was driven home later that year as San Francisco police conducted the most extensive manhunt in the city's history. Already overextended by efforts to locate newspaper heiress Patty Hearst and bring members of the underground Symbionese Liberation Army to justice, law enforcement officials were confronted with a wave of random execution-style street shootings. Dubbed Operation Zebra after the special radio band assigned for the investigation, controversial stop-and-search sweeps of the African American community eventually netted a core group of seven suspects. After a marathon trial that lasted more than a year, four black men, ages twenty-four to thirty-one, were convicted by a grand jury of assault, kidnapping, robbery, and murder. The 181 witnesses who were called upon to provide nearly fourteen thousand pages of transcribed testimony drew a nightmarish portrait of the accused killers. Said to be members of a "fanatical black sect" known as the Death Angels, their modus operandi was to seek out "white devils" standing at an out-of-the way bus stop, using a public telephone, or hitchhiking; flash them a "zombie-look"; and then either shoot them at point-blank range or take the unfortunate individual to a deserted building for torture and dismemberment. Pleas for mercy had no discernable effect on these cold-blooded criminals. They took Polaroid snapshots of their bloody handiwork and were said to fantasize about someday raiding a white orphanage or nursing home—"just go through a place like that and off them all. . . . Use a blade and really hack them up."[56]

When asked by a reporter to describe the sort of person who would be capable of committing such unspeakable crimes, noted African American psychiatrist Price Cobbs was quick to respond. "Bad niggers," he said simply. "It seems that every community has had one or was afraid of having one. They were feared as much by blacks as by whites."[57] This encapsulation of the threat facing all late-century urbanites proved prophetic. In recent times, the appearance of African American serial killers who targeted black as well as white victims made it far more difficult for sociopaths to masquerade as liberation-loving social bandits. Certainly, child molester and murderer Alton Coleman; Charlotte, North Carolina, strangler Henry Louis Wallace; and the notorious Beltway snipers, John Lee Malvo and John Allen Muhammad, were unlikely to convince even the most devoted race man that they were on a crusade to "pay back" Whitey.[58] Evidencing an unlimited capacity for evil, such monsters in human form knew neither compassion nor racial loyalty.

The most widely reported case thought to involve one of these traitorous blacks brought near pandemonium to the urban South. For twenty-two months between July 1979 and May 1981, Atlanta parents kept close watch over dooryards and school playgrounds as more than two dozen of the city's youth were lured away to be killed by a person or persons unknown. Ranging in age from seven to twenty-eight, most of the victims were smallish, slightly built males who had died of asphyxiation. Some disappeared while running errands; others likely had been hustling for pocket change. All were black and poor.[59]

In the absence of firm evidence, many within the African American community believed that the elusive villain was a white supremacist or Satan worshipper. In their experience, racial killings were racially motivated. Thus there was considerable surprise and widespread disbelief when a twenty-three-year-old self-employed black talent scout and aspiring record producer named Wayne Bertram Williams was arrested as the Atlanta Child Murderer. Neither the elaborate array of forensic evidence amassed by authorities nor sworn testimony by witnesses who claimed that Williams was consumed by hatred for "sorry" fellow blacks could convince skeptics that the "real" killer was in the dock. Even after he was found guilty and sentenced to two consecutive life terms in prison—with an African American judge presiding and a two-to-one black majority on the jury—a core group of supporters maintained Williams's innocence. Refusing to believe that the monster who had stalked their neighborhoods was one of their own, some of the still-grieving families filed suit to have the cases involving their loved ones reopened. In later years, they would support the petitions of celebrity attorneys Alan Dershowitz and William Kunstler to grant the convicted killer a new trial.[60]

Other blacks simply struggled to make sense of what seemed a wholly implausible series of events. Indeed, the confusing mixture of fact, fiction, rumor, and speculation that circulated throughout Atlanta contained all the essential elements of urban legend. It was said that the killings were part of a sinister Ku Klux Klan plot; the handiwork of pornographers producing "snuff flicks"; a new way for federal agencies to obtain human specimens for top-secret research. Talk of FBI involvement and white genocidal intent were by no means considered idle gossip. Those who fixated on the legend lived in fear—wondering when and where the next serial murderer would strike.[61]

But street crime took a variety of other forms that demanded immediate attention. When the perpetrators were found to be garden-variety hoodlums rather than mysterious serial killers, central city residents came to question the plausibility of the more elaborate conspiratorial scenarios. Although some African Americans still sought to avoid intraracial controversy by attributing the ills of urban life to white people—as if this approach would make their neighborhoods safer—a growing number refused to accept implausible alibis for inexcusable behavior. Without question, crime statistics are easily manipulated. Nevertheless, even when "Establishment" control (and possible misuse) of key databases was factored into the equation, late-century black urbanites were forced to admit that the traditional social bandit/bad black ratio had changed dramatically—and not for the better.

Widely disseminated studies documented the growing crisis. By the early 1990s, blacks made up 12 to 13 percent of the U.S. population but accounted for about one-half of all arrests for crimes carrying the threat of bodily injury. Data on victimization compiled by the Census Bureau showed that in cases where the assailant's race was known, African Americans were reported to have committed 65 percent of all robberies, a third of all rapes, and 54 percent of all criminal deaths.[62] Because four-fifths of violent crimes were perpetrated by individuals known to be of the same racial group as the victim, there was little hope of justifying a predatory act as a "revolutionary" strike against white power. If, as was the case at mid-decade, African American males were being killed at a rate double that of U.S. servicemen during World War II and a black teenager was nine times more likely to become a murder victim than a white peer, exaggerated claims of principled social banditry were certain to ring hollow.[63] Although close study of the data revealed that whites typically experienced high rates of arrest for serious offenses such as arson, driving under the influence, burglary, and vandalism—and that in any given year only about 2 percent of the U.S. African American population was arrested for committing *any* crime—urban blacks came to represent what University of Maryland law professor Katheryn K. Russell has termed "the public face of street crime." Certainly, the fact that the national homicide rate for black males ages fifteen to nineteen skyrocketed from slightly over 80 to more than 180 deaths per 100,000 between 1984 and 1992 bode ill for the future.[64] Black communities seemed to be in self-destruct mode, intent on devouring their own.

Those who took a clear-eyed approach to urban crime condemned the acts of black criminals while stating emphatically that such misfits were in no way representative of the race as a whole. With heightened conviction, they maintained that the pathological conduct of these lawbreakers was the hallmark of a distinctive social class—one whose misguided attempts to survive and prosper in a rapacious social environment posed a threat to every law-abiding citizen. By adopting this utilitarian, class-based approach to a problem that many whites still attributed to caste, African Americans were able to affirm group values while distinguishing themselves from black villains.

During the 1980s and '90s, studying the black underclass became a cottage industry among academic and government researchers. There was much to learn. Little understood even by those familiar with the underclass lifestyle, these children of the children of the poor were the people filmmaker Spike Lee chose *not* to include in his richly detailed movies set in a kinder, gentler Bedford-Stuyvesant. Prone to antisocial acts and seemingly incapable of escaping welfare dependency, their ranks included delinquents, drifters, and derelicts; street hustlers and school dropouts; addicts and alcoholics; ex-convicts and mental patients. Many were totally alienated from mainstream institutions. Unprecedented levels of geographic isolation, or "hypersegregation," prevented most from being influenced by the positive values of a rising African American middle class. Collectively, they proved a racial embarrassment to the sort of ghettoites the black bourgeoisie always had viewed as racial embarrassments.[65]

When subjected to close scrutiny by investigative journalists and social scientists, the most maladjusted members of the underclass revealed a decided aversion to conventional understandings of "community," "responsibility," "decency," and "achievement." Central to the smooth functioning of any social contract, such norms prevented amorality and predatory violence from becoming accredited pathways to upward mobility. Rejection of community-sanctioned mores by even a relatively small proportion of the population posed numerous problems for residents and nonresidents alike. If these perversities were continually replicated—remaining unchanged over several generations—it was feared that black criminal activity would become intractable.

As could be seen in case studies penned by Leon Dash and Fox Butterfield in the mid-1990s, conditions were ripe for what black America's critics were sure to identify as a major outbreak of recidivist villainy. Certainly, Dash's Rosa Lee Cunningham and Butterfield's nightmarish Bosket clan seemed less the repositories of folk wisdom than perpetuators of an urban crime wave. Instead of cadres of noble social bandits, their family trees were populated with a creepy-crawly collection of drug traffickers and abusers, prostitutes, gang members, and borderline psychotics.

Described as "welfare dependent, marginally educated, chronically unemployed, and engaged in repeated patterns of criminal deviance," three generations of the Cunningham brood shared a cramped two-bedroom apartment in a Washington, D.C., low-income housing complex. When not strung out after passing around the communal hypodermic needle, they burglarized homes, schools, and churches or shoplifted from downtown stores to support a variety of addictions. Each family member had a role to play. The youngest acted as lookouts or distracted security guards. Sometimes they would "help Grandma" by ferrying heroin through nearby open-air drug markets. Older siblings included Patty, an HIV-positive hooker who "makes no attempt to protect herself or anyone else"; Junior, a teenage crack dealer, enforcer, and car thief; and a thirty-six-year-old parolee named Richard, who supported his drug habit by stealing telephones from empty Howard University Hospital rooms and selling them to liquor stores and beauty parlors. By the time Rosa Lee succumbed to AIDS-related pneumonia in 1995, there was little prospect of this profoundly dysfunctional group adopting traditional working-class values. Locked in desperate circumstances, each appeared to have thoroughly assimilated "Mama Rose's" governing philosophy. As the frequently jailed matriarch told her biographer, rehabilitation schemes were totally useless. "I attended those programs so it would look good on my record when I went before the parole board," she said. "What they were talking about didn't mean anything to me."[66]

The family of convicted "mad dog" killer Willie James Bosket Jr. was even less likely to encourage belief in the ability of reformist endeavor to improve the life prospects of underclass blacks. Told from an early age that continued misbehavior would cause him to "end up just like [his] father," young Willie seemed determined to meet these low expectations. Himself the son of an unschooled, alcoholic thief who had spent a year in New York's Rikers Island city prison for kidnapping and sodomy, Willie "Butch" Bosket Sr. was a terrible parent and a worse role model. After being deemed "completely uncontrollable" by a juvenile court probation officer, he was abandoned by his mother and began a lifelong quest for rank and reputation among those to whom impulsiveness and aggression were considered requisites for survival. He also started to hallucinate and to hear voices. Diagnosed by psychiatrists as being afflicted with either schizophrenia or psychopathy, Butch was in and out of mental institutions for years. Between visits he ran numbers, pimped, sold porn, delivered drugs—and became the most notorious murderer the city of Milwaukee would see until Jeffrey Dahmer.[67]

Willie Bosket Jr. was a chip off the old block—a real piece of work. So violent and unfeeling that New York state prison officials likened him to *The Silence of the Lambs*' Hannibal Lecter, this slightly built, puckish-looking inheritor of the Bosket legacy claimed that he had committed some 2,000 criminal acts—including 25 stabbings and 200 armed robberies—by the age of fifteen. Cursed with what social workers said was a Jekyll and Hyde personality, Willie could be courteous and charming one moment, utterly cold-blooded the next. On one occasion, he lit a fire under a black man dozing on a bench in Central Park. On another, he mugged an elderly woman and then "gave her a good push" because "she was old and going to die anyway." Eventually, he was found guilty of participating in a series of strong-arm robberies and murders on the IRT. His response was chilling. "I shot people, that's all," he said, laughing. "I don't feel nothing."[68]

Was this ticking time bomb who boasted about "cut[ting] a man's eyeball out of his head" and who once addressed an African American judge as "Mr. Nigger" everything that he claimed to be? Was he to be viewed by the larger society as "a monster that the system created—a monster that's come back to haunt the system's ass"?[69] Did familial factors—violent, neglectful, emotionally maladjusted parents, for example—launch the Boskets and similarly troubled individuals on what one researcher has described as "an inevitable trajectory toward a criminal lifestyle"?[70] Was this sort of aberrant behavior adaptive or culturally determined; evidence of a flawed social order or of a deformed personality; cause or effect of being black and poor? As the new millennium dawned, inquiring minds demanded immediate informed responses to these vexing questions.

Sadly, few responses proved satisfactory to all interested parties. Influenced greatly by conservative politicians' coded appeals to media-driven fears, white opinion on the black underclass remained hopelessly confused. Typically, introduction of the racial variable transformed academic debates over nature versus nurture into exercises in frustration as the politically correct of all ideological persuasions locked horns. The result was an intellectual impasse that frayed tempers but did little to discourage the notion that all "at-risk" youth resembled the societal detritus profiled on "reality-based" TV shows such as *Cops* and *America's Most Wanted*. Meanwhile, black America remained on the defensive, hesitant to probe too deeply within the racial subculture for answers lest such inquiry result in self-incrimination.

Obviously, the launching of a joint problem-solving initiative would be a Herculean task. Because African Americans and European Americans had experienced and interpreted key events in the nation's racial past in radically different ways, it could be anticipated that the two groups would have difficulty coordinating efforts to address common concerns. But without mutual trust and basic agreement on foundational definitions, operative principles, and ultimate goals, there could be no united front to combat underclass-related problems. Thus, during the early years of the twenty-first century, there was a pressing need to resolve traditional disagreements over the relationship between skin color and virtue; social banditry and villainy; the black community and the criminal element.

To gauge the probability of achieving favorable outcomes in these areas, it is useful to explore the history and popular cultural representation of three specific groups within contemporary urban society that have been linked in the public mind to negative underclass values and behaviors. The study of black mob and gang members, prison inmates, and gangsta rappers also can help answer two interconnected questions relating to matters that long have troubled the nation's soul. First, whether black villains are necessary for whites to define themselves as virtuous. Second, if unmerited slander and abuse persists, whether blacks ever can hope to win release from the temptation to treat bad as good for purposes of argumentation and psychological survival.

MOBSTERS AND GANGBANGERS: FROM HOLLYWOOD TO SOUTH CENTRAL

Most Americans' impressions of mob and youth gang members have been shaped both by real-world events and by Hollywood's approximation of them. Tabloid journalism and Saturday matinees are equally important in bringing noteworthy malefactors to our attention. Seldom are we able to avert our gaze. Torn between feelings of revulsion and envy, we have difficulty deciding whether to condemn the badman's methods or to admire his forthright, self-assured manner. Like other villain variants, these denizens of the urban underworld often receive points for style and are seen as social bandits by the romantic and the unmolested.

Organized criminal networks are ancient institutions. Some say the earliest gangs guarded the pyramids of Egypt and that the term itself can be traced back at least to the Middle Ages. A character in Shakespeare's *The Merry Wives of Windsor* complained of "a knot, a ging, a pack, a conspiracy against me."[71] In the nineteenth-century United States, Wild West outlaws and Irish immigrant combinations like New York City's "Forty Thieves" helped shape the social parameters of gangland. The latter even had an adolescent auxiliary—"Forty Little Thieves"—which provided cross-generational transmission of street wisdom and criminal skills to boys and girls alike. By the time of the Great Depression, key connections between mobsters and the star-making machinery of popular culture already were in place. Eager to increase circulation, metropolitan newspapers gave racketeers catchy nicknames and embellished their deeds. Bootleggers, in particular, came to be viewed sympathetically—as simple working-class stiffs who provided a useful public service. Their reward? Toleration of unsavory techniques and a fair share of the ill-gotten gains.[72]

As portrayed in cultural texts provided by Hollywood screenwriters, these idealized criminals sometimes seemed less public enemies than somewhat tarnished national treasures. Perpetually surrounded by fawning subordinates and female admirers, the big-screen gangsters of the 1920s, '30s, and '40s radiated an energetic, swaggering masculinity. They dressed well, possessed a razor-sharp wit, and spoke authoritatively, in a breezy, colorful manner. Most pursued the American consumerist dream in a pugnacious, sometimes ruthless fashion but were capable of charity and compassion. They were loyal to friends, loved by their mothers, and remained receptive to the transformative influence of a "good woman." Well aware of the genre's subversive potential—and of the power wielded by state and municipal censorship boards—creators of films such as *Dressed to Kill, The Racketeer,* and *All through the Night* depicted square-jawed brawlers befriending the urban poor and battling foreign agents. They championed the cause of the "little guy," defended the virtuous, and worked to rehabilitate alcoholics and delinquent youth. Many a happy ending found the mobster himself altered forever by romance or religion.[73]

Nevertheless, prior to redemption, even sympathetically drawn characters provided moviegoers with a harrowing glimpse of underworld evil. The mobster's negative characteristics and behavior were central to his attractive power. Advertisements for films with titles like *Sinner's Holiday*, *The Unholy Three*, and *The Doorway to Hell* promised storylines "Snatched from Today's Headlines," warning ticket-buyers to "come prepared to see the worst of women and the cruelest of men—as they really are!"[74] Once inside, audiences were treated to seventy-five minutes or more of decadence, deceit, and disorderly conduct. Little wonder, then, that Depression-era critics like the Catholic Church's Legion of Decency condemned Hollywood for encouraging unwholesome behavior—for presenting the criminal's "filthy philosophy of life as something acceptable to decent men and women."[75]

Part Robin Hood, part robber baron, the silver-screen crime boss combined hero and villain in a single character. Blurring the boundary between good and evil, he could contribute generously to the local orphans' fund and then, without pause, murder a suspected snitch in cold blood. Such behavior provided the movie-going public with vicarious thrills. But the gangster's ambivalent actions also suggested the existence of a suppressed humanity that, if cultivated, might flower into full-blown virtue. Beset by inner turmoil, pretty boy crooks with steely eyes and soft hearts provided audiences with a romanticized view of gangland's most dangerous residents.[76] Ultimately, Hollywood's desire to drive home the message that virtue invariably triumphs over vice and that crime doesn't pay left both black and white Americans unprepared for real-world encounters with those who had no intention of "going straight."

These moralistic themes were mirrored in early black-cast films. Like other race movie genres, independently produced crime dramas differed little from white archetypes. Lead actresses were only slightly darker in skin tone than their mainstream counterparts. Top male screen personalities were provided with white "reference points" for promotional purposes. During the 1920s and '30s, Lorenzo Tucker was known as "the Black Valentino"; Ralph Cooper as "the Bronze Bogart." In this manner, African American newcomers could hope to enhance and solidify a preselected "image" via association with well-known white celebrities. Established conventions remained largely undisturbed and films featuring suavely sensual tough guys and floridly dressed femme fatales were expected to serve reformist ends. When they didn't provide "elevating" stories that would contribute to the "upbuilding" of the race, movie critics could be *very* unkind.[77]

Like all who aspired to entrepreneurial greatness in this field, the not-always-black makers and distributors of pre–World War II race movies attracted audiences with sex and sensationalism. Firm believers in the Fourth Estate adage "If It Bleeds, It Leads," they focused their small-budget ad campaigns on the prurient and the polemical. Colorful posters featuring back alley shoot-outs, menacing thugs, and scantily clad women promised to reveal "The Shame Story of Colored America" in which "Guns Bark as Rival Gangs Fight for Power" and "Negro Youth Runs Wild."[78] Typically, this mayhem was wedded to storylines featuring variations on familiar mixed-message themes. Syndicate bosses with names like "Bull" and "Mugsy" stole from the rich, scammed the poor, intimidated witnesses, and roughed up their molls with reckless abandon—only to experience a moral epiphany or have their reign of terror short-circuited by a crusading minister or district attorney. When the script called for a hoodlum to pay the ultimate price for his sins, the message was driven home in an even more obvious fashion. Struggling in death's clammy grip, conscience-stricken thugs inevitably saw the error of their ways and implored associates to "find my kid and educate him so he doesn't grow up like me." A criminal's abrupt fall from temporal power helped shore up a threatened moral universe.[79]

In more recent times, creators of popular entertainments featuring black lawbreakers have been privileged to work with larger budgets and vastly improved technologies. Nevertheless, the problem of meeting community standards for moral content and racial representation remains as vexing as ever. The issues facing modern-day filmmakers are multifaceted, making decisions difficult. Often all of the suggested alternatives seem fatally flawed. For example, should black-cast films provide spectacle or social commentary; feature oppositional or hegemonic imagery; critique or reinforce the dominant racial discourse? Must they strive to balance the sacred and the profane or to present precisely the same message to both black and white viewers? Can one glorify violence in order to condemn it? And when does the portrayal of black anger become patronizing; preachy; dangerously reductive? How does one go about distinguishing villains from social bandits?

During the civil rights and Black Power years, selected African American mob and gang members were enlisted in the era's activist vanguard. Adhering closely to blaxploitation guidelines for socially conscious behavior, they supported community uplift initiatives and did their best to thwart the designs of European American rivals. Unless one was an overly exploitative, pug-ugly thug who lacked the common sense not to stand in the way of a Virgil Tibbs or a John Shaft, such characters were permitted to maintain the traditional tough/tender mix of swagger and sweetness. If they adhered to customary codes of conduct for their underworld specialty, sought to "stick it to The Man," and voiced a desire to abandon outlawry after "beating the System" just one more time, they were considered social bandits by true fans. Minor errors in judgment were forgiven in the spirit of racial brotherhood. It was hoped that the crime boss's superlative *baaddness* would assist in combating black male emasculation and in sparking a psychological revolution capable of bringing real "power to the people."[80]

But this was not to be. Blaxploitation con men, pimps, and dealers rode into the sunset with agendas incomplete, liberationist dreams unfulfilled. During the latter half of the 1970s, it was obvious that there still was plenty of "Hell Up in Harlem." The problems that were endemic "Across 110th Street" had not been eradicated by either the strong-arm tactics or the slick martial arts skills of a Black Caesar or Mister Mean. In this unfavorable environment, claims to be the "baddest cat that ever walked the earth" rang hollow.[81] Although fondly remembered by fans of the genre, by 1980 they had been superseded in the public mind by *The Godfather's* wiseguy banter, by the deadpan quips of Dirty Harry Callahan, and by the cheers accompanying boxer Rocky Balboa's gutsy quest for self-affirmation. Committed to what film historians have termed "the cinema of recuperation," Hollywood chose to play it safe with salt-and-pepper buddy films (*48 Hours*), white actors masquerading as black (*Soul Man*), and blacks acting the fool (*The Toy*). Because the film industry was averaging only six or seven black-focused productions per year, African American bad guys had little chance either to alter or reaffirm familiar mixed messages—or to deliver any message at all.[82]

Beginning in the mid-1980s, youthful filmmakers like Spike Lee, John Singleton, Matty Rich, and Mario Van Peebles parlayed their intimate understanding of a "New Black Aesthetic" into a series of projects that constituted a black-cast film boom. At times avant-garde and brimming with social urgency, more often sufficiently commercial to benefit from crossover marketing aimed at suburbia, these insider depictions of contemporary urban landscapes were both fresh and financially viable. Lauded by rapturous critics as a rebirth of modern American cinema comparable to the "Nouvelle Vague" movement in early 1960s France, "Black New Wave" films were said to combine style and substance in exemplary fashion. According to *Chicago Sun-Times* critic Roger Ebert, movies such as Bill Duke's *A Rage in Harlem* and Lee's *Do the Right Thing* and *Jungle Fever* were noteworthy because they succeeded in moving "beyond the ritual charges of racism, beyond the image of wronged and angry black characters, to a new plateau of sophistication on which there is room for good and bad characters of all races."[83] Seeing no pressing need to lecture Whitey, to showcase only exemplary blacks, or to forward any specific revolutionary ideology, African American filmmakers of the 1990s were free to break with convention. As they did so, formerly taboo treatments of seldom-seen subjects proliferated. The crime film genre became grittier and less self-conscious than ever before. Featured prominently in this newly revamped cinema were overt displays of black villainy.

Variously described by those who knew them best as "the worst type of nigger," "a fuckin' maniac," and "America's nightmare," villainous characters such as O-Dog (Larenz Tate) in *Menace II Society* and Nathan (Glenn Plummer) in *Tear It Down* earned their unsavory reputations the old-fashioned way. They were cruel and conscienceless, unpredictable and unfathomable. Guided by neither a recognizable political agenda nor a coherent code of conduct, these homicidal homies had "no respect for life." Their foul-mouthed, sullen presence eroded the moral universe.[84]

Evidencing a willingness to "kill for nuthin'" and "murder people for fun," brutal criminals like *Belly*'s wealthy Jamaican drug lord Lennox (Louie Rankin) were unmoved by human suffering. They would seek to permanently silence anyone who threatened their livelihood, challenged their authority, or had the misfortune to get in their way during a fit of pique. As a result, many hapless junkies and hookers, "disrespectful" Asian American convenience store clerks, and unwitting witnesses to illegal business transactions met horrible fates. It was like "swattin' flies." Even the wails of widows and wounded bystanders were met with cynicism and smart remarks. "That boy's toast"; "Smoked his ass, looked like bloody Swiss cheese"; and "What's the deal, man, they were just Koreans" typified their cold-blooded retorts. It was obvious that the killers felt neither compassion nor responsibility for the most vulnerable members of their inner-city communities.[85]

In many respects, these Black New Wave–era cinematic portrayals approached the demonic. Communicating with compatriots via a mysterious glossolalia in which "bitch" was employed as a genderless modifier and "my nigger" considered a term of approbation, African American villains touted the value of high living in the here and now over hope in the hereafter. Some, of course, were simply questing for creature comforts—gold chains, sports cars, palatial homes—in the time-honored manner of underclass strivers. Like Nino Brown, the cracklord and ex–youth gang member played by Wesley Snipes in *New Jack City*, they were thick-skinned pragmatists whose guiding philosophy could be summed up as follows: "Money talks. Bullshit runs the marathon. . . . You gotta rob to get rich in the Reagan era."[86]

Others offered a more metaphysical take on criminality and conspicuous consumption. The need to acquire "juice" (i.e., power and respect) tempted some inner-city villains to privilege hardness and violence over more traditional ethical and behavioral guidelines. A satanic brotherhood in Starter jackets, they ridiculed key elements of the conventional morality, purposely profaning all that was holy. In conversations with their henchmen, mob and youth gang leaders questioned the existence of a higher power ("If there was a God, why he be lettin' motherfuckers get smoked every night—babies and little kids?");[87] rejected the church as an option for personal transformation ("Man, black people got too much damn religion as it is");[88] and claimed various aspects of the deity for themselves. Having survived numerous drive-by shootings, they seemed all-knowing and invincible—perhaps even immortal ("The bullets just go around me. I ain't a scared of nothin'").[89] The powerful Cincinnati underworld boss played by LL Cool J in the crime drama *In Too Deep* was nicknamed "God," and one of the main characters in *Belly* claimed to have sold his soul to the Devil in the hope of reaching similar heights in the New York–to–Omaha drug trade.[90] Without question, something sinister was afoot in the nation's heartland.

Compounding the evil of these blasphemies, gangland villains schemed endlessly to corrupt black American youth. As noted by Eric Walker (Tim Taylor), the hustler/narrator of *Streetwise*, "that old Godfather-type shit" was their secular religion. The purpose of life, they maintained, was "to fuckin' die, man. In the meantime, get money." A major mobster watchword was "don't give nothin' to nobody." Alternative outlooks and pursuits, such as aspiring to a college education or holding down a regular 9-to-5 job, were discouraged. Indeed, sweet-talking crime-world recruiters held that only a "zero nigger" would turn down a chance to get rich by marketing the "world's greatest product"—crack cocaine. There was risk involved in this underworld career, but selling hard drugs guaranteed a full complement of "the finer things in life."[91] Just try it, the sly tempter/dealers in films such as *South Central, Fresh,* and *Clockers* purred, "You know this is an honor, right? . . . You get bigger, you gonna be the man. . . . You know its me and you, right?"[92] Socialized to believe that "word is bond and bond is life," the innocents were trapped.[93]

Gangland acolytes who dodged bullets successfully enough to become negative role models in their own right were well versed in the art of deception. In order to outwit law enforcement authorities—as well as to calm community-based criticism—the cleverest appropriated a romanticized roughhouse persona from the annals of social banditry. However contrived, this image enhancement could be remarkably convincing. Selectively pilfering blaxploitation-era plot devices, crime film protagonists of the 1980s and '90s trafficked in tropes that were proven crowd-pleasers. Apparent moral failings were traced to (1) peer pressure; (2) pervasive job market discrimination; and (3) a desire to provide for dependant family members. "White folks ain't left me nothin' out here but the underworld"; "I had to do what I had to do to survive"; "They say I'm a thug, but I say I was made into one," they complained, attempting to deflect blame from themselves. Claiming to be "home-grown" businessmen rather than exploitative hoodlums, crime bosses boasted about creating jobs for the ghetto poor and promised to sever ties with questionable associates as soon as they had made "some real money"— enough to buy "a first-class ticket outta here."[94] But, one suspected, it was all for show. With unnerving frequency, removal of a mobster's Good Samaritan disguise revealed the demon within. In the opinion of Scotty Appleton (Ice-T), an African American cop in *New Jack City,* this "Robin Hood bullshit" was simply one more clever ruse designed to deceive. Inevitably, the unwary became economically exploited, chemically addicted "living hostages."[95]

Low-budget, high-profit ghettocentric movies reinvigorated the gangster genre and created second careers in "rapsploitation" for recording artists such as Tupac Shakur, Snoop Dogg, Ice-T, Ice Cube, DMX, Nas, and Silkk the Shocker. While certain of these "guilty pleasure" entertainments were deemed critic-proof because of their slapdash production values and indecipherable dialogue, many 'hood films were clinically dissected and condemned. Fearing that the ghetto-theme action pictures represented a regression rather than a renaissance in black-cast filmmaking, unsympathetic reviewers scored actors, producers, and financial backers for pandering to the most sensational aspects of contemporary urban mythology. Hollywood gangland "pop crap," they said, alternately patronized and exploited black anger while confirming the belief that young black men were habituated to lives of senseless violence. Unlike the most socially conscious of the '70s blaxploitation epics, these films were deemed to be obsessed with victimization—offering no clear guidelines to personal or group empowerment. Considered socially irresponsible and artistically fraudulent, wide-screen depictions of black-on-black crime suggested that mob- and gang-related suffering was self-induced.[96]

Hoping to ward off further "bad press," thereby prolonging the genre's life span, supporters responded to criticism with a variety of counterclaims. Studio spin doctors maintained that the most skillfully crafted 'hood films introduced audiences to a variety of character types and to stories that highlighted what *Hoodlum* director Bill Duke termed "the testing of the human spirit . . . those challenging moments when you find out who you are [and] where you stand." Striving to consider both inspirational and confessional themes, filmmakers disavowed any intent to promote antisocial behavior. According to *New Jack City*'s Mario Van Peebles, the industry was well aware that there were "obvious dangers" in glorifying "the wrong equation." Every effort was being made to employ gangland spectacle as "edutainment"— to engage black teenagers in an Afrocentric critique of self-destructive lifestyles.[97]

When this soft-sell approach failed to quell discontent, alternative strategies were adopted. In the hope of maintaining access to lucrative theatrical and video markets, major studios labored to make their products more user-friendly. Paramount airbrushed a gun from Tupac Shakur's hand in their advertising posters for *Juice* and opened the VHS version of the movie with an AIDS/HIV awareness message from Magic Johnson and Arsenio Hall. Columbia and New Line Cinema followed suit, prefacing gang-related fare with didactic entreaties to "Increase the Peace" and promotional clips urging viewers to support the work of the Institute for Black Parenting and the United Negro College Fund.[98] Elsewhere, solemn warnings about the dangers of hard drugs and handguns were inserted before opening titles. In certain cases, screenplays came to resemble infomercials for prepackaged truisms such as "A bullet ain't got no name on it" and "I make bad decisions when I'm high."[99]

However well intentioned, filmmakers' directorial and marketing strategies failed to convince critics that ultraviolent 'hood movies were serving the best interests of inner-city youth. Not even charges that black directors were being held to higher standards than those applied to the creators of Italian American gangster films generated much sympathy.[100] In part, this can be attributed to the fact that entertainment industry movers and shakers made less than convincing moralists. To many, their earnest but often self-conscious and superficial encouragements to law-abiding lifestyles rang false. Certainly, it was not unreasonable to believe that after witnessing ninety minutes or more of fast-paced criminal activity perpetrated by colorful, worldly-wise protagonists, viewers would have difficulty remembering *anything* contained in the film's bland public service messages. A moviemaker's moral high ground stood in constant danger of being eroded by the attractive power of graphic gangland violence.

Given the emotionally charged atmosphere, claims to verisimilitude only heightened suspicion, fueling the controversy. African American filmmakers who told journalists that they aspired to make "extremely personal" studies of ghetto life or who brought in gang members to act as technical advisers set themselves up for additional criticism when violence erupted outside theaters showing their "autobiographical" slice-of-life productions. After thirty-three people were wounded and one killed on the opening night of John Singleton's *Boyz N the Hood* in 1991, some feared for the future of black film—and for the viability of movie houses whose management felt compelled to install metal detectors and to ask gang members to check their colors at the door.[101] Perhaps assuming that pop culture consumers would understand the necessity of permitting art to imitate life, Hollywood insiders underestimated the depth of concern among those who warned that (street) life was, in fact, imitating art. By the end of the decade, not even *Don't Be a Menace to South Central While Drinking Your Juice in the Hood*—Marlon and Shawn Wayans's comedy spoof featuring characters with names like Doo Rag, Loc Dog, and Dave the Crackhead—could brighten the mood of critics who felt that gangbangers, real and imagined, were conspiring to destroy the life chances of black youth.[102]

* * *

Although there was a lack of consensus as to whether the documentary quality of ghettocentric action films heightened awareness of contemporary social problems, provided an escapist diversion from them, or made them more intractable than ever by glamorizing criminal lifestyles, most observers of the late-century urban scene agreed that there was enough "drama" taking place on the streets of black America to script a multitude of movie projects. Sociologists and filmmakers alike recognized that the structural changes in the postindustrial ghetto that served to expand the ranks of the black underclass and to increase the frequency of black-on-black crime also altered the character of black gang activity. As noted by wistful Old School veterans in films such as *Squeeze, Sugar Hill,* and *Original Gangstas,* macho aggression no longer seemed to be tempered with reason. "Back in the day . . . we didn't have nines and 45s," they reminisced. "We didn't kill people. . . . Now it's all about drive-by shootings. . . . It isn't about rocks and bottles anymore. It's about automatic weapons."[103] The social scientists' research confirmed these observations. During the 1980s and '90s, attitudes hardened, violence escalated, and an epidemic of gang-related villainy threatened to overwhelm the resources of law enforcement agencies nationwide. According to one study, over 90 percent of U.S. cities with more than 200,000 residents reported having a gang problem. National Institute of Justice data showed that 555,181 gang members in 16,643 gangs committed 580,331 crimes in 1993 alone.[104]

The early movers and shakers of African American organized crime would have been amazed at the changes that had taken place in gangland. Schooled in traditional underworld mores by the most demanding teachers the dominant white ethnic mobs had to offer, black crime bosses of the 1920s, '30s, and '40s amassed great wealth by cultivating human weaknesses but did their best to appear as community benefactors. Racketeers like Harlem numbers bankers Casper Holstein, Wilfred Brunder, and Big Joe Ison understood that it made good business sense to share a portion of their profits via acts of philanthropy. Their achievements as entrepreneurs, loan officers, and employers of last resort were well publicized, eventually becoming the stuff of legend. Upon their demise, loyal cronies mourned while eulogists recounted the deceased criminal's many virtues.[105] Part reality, part romanticized ideal, this was a hard act to follow. Subsequent generations of black gangsters never quite measured up.

Contemporary crime lords substituted force for finesse and let community relations slide. If, as described by poet Gwendolyn Brooks, Chicago's Blackstone Rangers and other youth gangs of the 1960s were "sores in the city / that do not want to heal," their successors were malignancies and social toxins.[106] Benefiting from federal prosecution of the La Cosa Nostra hierarchy and eager to control street-level marketing of an illicit pharmacopoeia that included heroin, cocaine, marijuana, PCP, and fentanyl ("China White"), prison-hardened veterans known as "O.G.'s" solidified connections with Latin American suppliers beginning in the mid-1980s. Soon thereafter, smokable crack cocaine selling for as little as five dollars a "rock" became the inner-city drug of choice. Easily produced by cooking down a mixture of powder cocaine, baking soda, and water, crack created what law enforcement authorities and journalists referred to as a "plague" of addiction. According to an April 1988 *ABC News* estimate, Americans were spending $20 billion a year on cocaine. By the fall of 1989, 64 percent of those polled in a *New York Times/CBS News* survey claimed that drugs were "the most important problem facing this country today."[107] In the epidemic's wake, turf conflicts were transformed into guerrilla warfare. As scores came to be settled with Uzis and AK-47 assault rifles rather than with fists or knives, it became clear that this proliferation of aggressive drug traffickers threatened to destroy the already-tattered social fabric of urban black America.

In various locales, drug money supported growth of a "quisling culture" in which car dealers, clothiers, and landlords profited indirectly from the gangs' illegal activities.[108] But such endeavor also eroded traditional values, widened the generation gap, and caused incalculable pain to thousands. Even if its monetary benefits had been equitably distributed, the underground economy centered on drug dealing and street crime could not hope to compensate inner-city residents for social costs associated with the crack contagion. Gang infestation discouraged investment in legitimate business enterprises, decreased senior citizens' sense of personal security, and served as a negative inducement for middle-class (re-)settlement of blighted areas. As the crisis deepened during the 1990s, mothers were forced to put their babies to bed in iron bathtubs for protection against stray bullets. Gang graffiti usurped and degraded public spaces. Antiloitering ordinances effectively placed all who fit the gangbanger profile under police surveillance.[109]

Quite literally, there was no hiding place. Youngsters growing up in this environment became tainted by their neighborhood's unsavory reputation. At the same time, they faced the constant temptation to get "caught up in the rapture" of underworld lifestyles. Around every corner, it seemed, drug culture Pied Pipers were waiting—seeking to convince unwary youth that the "academy of the streets" should be their classroom.[110] For parents and other concerned adults, these prospects were disheartening. A handful of villains were proving powerful enough to hold entire communities in virtual thralldom.

Reasons given for rejecting more conventional adolescent pastimes and casting one's lot with a youth gang were numerous and varied. A short list of the most frequently voiced would include

1. The desire to enhance one's chances of self-preservation in a kill-or-be-killed world where "nobody wants to give up their grudges."[111]
2. An eagerness to win reputation and respect, "to fulfill my name," and to be granted one's "props"—the deference one deserved.[112]
3. As "a way to get over" (i.e., gain access to money, alcohol, drugs, and women).[113]
4. To establish independence from parental directives, lifestyles, beliefs, or icons. ("[Martin Luther King Jr.] can't do nothing for me. He ain't on a dollar bill.")[114]
5. Because powerful images of West Coast street gangs in films such as *Colors* "just fired niggers up," serving as a catalyst for emulative activity.[115]
6. Gang membership had become conventional in many inner-city neighborhoods. Like other living folkways, the practice of wearing gang colors was being passed on from generation to generation.[116]

While each of these factors figured prominently in recruitment, one inducement overshadowed the rest. As male-oriented membership organizations, gangs provided essential socialization and support mechanisms for at-risk youth. It was this prospect of joining with one's peers in "manly," sometimes violent, defense of the communal 'hood that many found irresistible. To be sure, living "fast and large" was an attraction. But as one sixteen-year-old member of St. Louis's Thundercats noted, the importance of having "a family away from home" who all "stick together" in times of adversity should not be undervalued.[117] Unshakable male bonding was essential to the viability of modern-day gangs and played a key role in ghettocentric rites of passage. The specific "family values" learned through subcultural socialization were foundational to modern-day black villainy.

As in the larger crime community, shared beliefs about appropriate gender roles helped establish guidelines for African American gang membership. Typically, women were marginalized via exclusion or subordination. Viewed as "male love pushed to its limits . . . brothers bonding together to the death," gangbanging was a testosterone-soaked proving ground for racial toughness.[118] Women who earned enough respect to be known as a "down sister" did so on male terms. Those who aspired to leadership roles had to be bright, athletic, and exceptionally hard-nosed to garner recognition. Milwaukee gang operative and bank robber Mama Sheik required female initiates to demonstrate their nerve by tussling with men far taller and heavier than themselves. According to urban legend, on one occasion she also used her kickboxing and karate skills to toss a half-dozen policemen off a bridge. But this was unusual. Where they existed, female auxiliaries were far more likely to participate in "cafeteria-style delinquency" than in violent criminal acts.[119] An unintended consequence of female marginalization was that charges of gang-related villainy almost always were leveled against young black men.

As the bonding process proceeded, expectations regarding proper comportment were conveyed to newcomers by word and, more commonly, by deed. Gang-initiation rituals varied greatly but often involved tests of physical endurance (taking "six to the chest" without flinching), assignment to a dangerous "mission" in enemy territory, stealing a car, or selling a certain quantity of drugs. Successful initiates were regaled with vivid accounts of the gang's history and instructed in the fine art of "flaggin', saggin', and braggin'" (throwing signs; wearing one's pants hanging low; boasting about past exploits). Some elected to seal the bond of solidarity by auditioning their newly developed "mad dog stare" or by getting "tagged" (tattooed). Collectively, these rituals delineated the boundaries of black manhood, teaching that only those who exhibited a physically and emotionally tough supermasculinity were worthy of respect.[120]

Promotion of this ideal within gangland had numerous negative consequences. Male/female relationships and traditional notions of fatherhood were skewed; commonplace understandings of "work" and of "community" drastically revised. The hyped-up sense of machismo deemed necessary for group bonding overwhelmed critical thought processes, short-circuiting internal monitors governing empathy and fair play. The effects were most apparent among members of an age cohort that was in the midst of developing coping strategies needed to negotiate harsh inner-city environments. Thus, unlike social banditry's far more complex code, the minimalist guidelines that regulated youth gang attitudes and behaviors were decidedly apolitical. They rarely considered the greater good. "Love your set and hate your enemy"; "Watch your back"; "Be devious, do anything, be bad to the fullest" were the watchwords of those who thirsted for a hard-core reputation. Compassion and remorse were not in their repertoire of emotions. Most assuredly, such sentiments never could be revealed in relationships with outsiders. To do so would violate the black macho ethic. It would invite trouble and provide evidence of latent homosexuality. Even the ancient concept of "an eye for an eye" fell into disuse and was replaced by "one-up"—that is, "You beat our homeboys, we kill yours." "Killin' and not caring, and dyin' without fear" was the gang members' fatalistic take on the ultimate purpose of existence.[121]

Even as this law of the urban jungle was being tested and refined, attempts were made to manipulate reality. Hyper-aggressive gang members claimed they were affiliated with "defensive club[s]." Senseless acts of violence were endowed with great purpose—allegedly deriving their meaning from challenges to group authority. "We ain't what you call real bad people," asserted a fifteen-year-old 107 Hoover Crip known as 8 Ball. "We down. It ain't like we a lynch mob hanging together." But actions speak louder than words and the general public wasn't buying this line of reasoning. They recognized true villainy when it hit them between the eyes and emptied their pockets.[122]

In their quest to realize the supermacho ideal, alpha-male O.G.'s and their sets committed atrocities that dehumanized both victim and assailant. Stomach-turning incidents involving carjackings and home invasions, drive-by homicides and pit bull attacks became daily occurrences. Crossed-out initials on graffiti-scarred walls both denigrated enemies and foreshadowed their demise.[123] To make matters worse, status-seeking gang members elaborated on their exploits in the presence of reporters. With normal human feelings narcotized by drugs or alcohol, the victors of intragang confrontations boasted of "doggin'" and "beasting on" their rivals. Deadly incidents were so frequent, they said, "it don't faze me no more." Unafraid to die, they claimed to have no qualms about taking another's life: "I lit his ass *up*! I killed him—shot his baby in the leg—crippled his wife!" For those seeking recognition and respect in gangland, cold-blooded deeds were considered to be both vocational and leisure time activities—"putting in work" and "our way of having fun."[124]

Throughout the 1980s and '90s, first-person accounts of this sometimes-mythic violence were incorporated into news coverage of current events. Rampant sensationalism ensued. Banner headlines and grisly photo spreads kept the public up-to-date on what seemed to be a nationwide decline into anarchy. TV interviews with hooded young hoodlums and educational forums featuring traveling "drug culture experts" stigmatized black communities and heightened fears of African American men throughout suburbia. As a result, revitalizing the economic infrastructure of urban America took a backseat to fathoming enigmatic ghetto toughs. Over time, media fascination with inner-city crime caused worst-case scenarios to appear normative. As the episodic became the epidemic, many incorrectly assumed that they could understand gang-related activity in their own town by watching a documentary on crack house busts in New York or Los Angeles.[125]

By touting the allure of "total lawlessness" at every (photo) opportunity, gang leaders encouraged the belief that ghetto teenagers were afflicted with some sort of bizarre psychopathology. At minimum, the "every man for himself" mind-set that enabled them to commit brutal acts without concern for negative consequences suggested severe social maladjustment.[126] Experts traced the condition to early life experiences with lovelessness and poverty, aggravated by adolescent drug use and intense peer pressure. "They are already . . . driven by a sociopathic mentality that kind of permeates the group," asserted LAPD chief Daryl Gates in 1990. "And they have a few beers and snort some coke and they are on their way. 'Why don't we have some fun? Let's go shoot somebody.'"[127] A gangbanger's self-diagnosis could be even more frightening. According to Steel, a sixteen-year-old second-generation Crip, some of the most violent homeboys were "born messed up . . . nuts right from the start." They were "crazy, like . . . just automatically crazy." All they could think about was "killin'."[128] Whatever the root cause, late-century gang culture's nihilistic tendencies discouraged optimism. As noted by Princeton University's Cornel West, black people were accustomed to searching for a promised land in "America's wilderness" but now found themselves trapped "in a jungle with a cutthroat morality devoid of any faith in deliverance or hope for freedom." If unaddressed, this "disease of the soul" threatened to spread lawlessness and "collective clinical depression" throughout the Afroworld.[129]

In reality and as imagined by Hollywood, gangland was the epicenter of black-on-black crime. During the 1990s, studios packaged and marketed their approximations of life in the 'hood with such flair that aberrant youth gang behavior became a nationwide curiosity. Although the depth of inner-city despair and alienation never was fully captured on film, a slightly diluted essence of the ghetto oeuvre may have been all that most middle-class Americans could stomach. It was through these Black New Wave–era productions that many learned of the social bandit's cinematic fall from grace. Pushed out of the spotlight by changing times and altered sensibilities, their liberationist dreams were put on indefinite hold. In their stead, the creators of ghetto-theme action pictures adopted revised guidelines for black portraiture. Predominantly negative portrayals of young black men were essentialized and made formulaic. Without a mix of what director Mario Van Peebles termed "interesting, alternative role models," the message sent to moviegoers was that "The brother is a villain. The villain is a brother." To many in the audience, this seemed no more than fair warning. Beyond the back lot, casting calls were being held for a cinema verité sociodrama that some said was adapted from *Lord of the Flies*.[130] Here, rival gangs stalked one another in a never-ending quest to displace inner rage, to earn the respect of peers, and to meet or exceed the standards for sadism set by big-screen O.G.'s. As life imitated art (and vice versa), the mutually reinforced threat posed by underclass villains, real and imagined, grew more ominous.

Although newscasts and feature films heightened existing fears, they also suggested a possible solution to the drug culture plague: remediation through incarceration. Fed up with crime and hoping to free their neighborhoods from gang control, even African Americans who entertained a healthy suspicion of the American judicial system considered adopting a hard line on sentencing. "We have to realize that there are criminals among us," Berkeley sociologist/activist Harry Edwards told a reporter in 1988. "I'm for locking 'em up, gettin 'em off the street, put 'em behind bars."[131] But there would be no quick fix. Public policy debates over whether U.S. prisons were more recidivistic than rehabilitative were complicated by the testimony of ex-convicts who maintained that imprisonment enabled them to "bulk up," to learn new criminal skills, and to develop a "thirst" for lawbreaking. Upon release, the supposedly chastened gangbangers claimed they had returned to the 'hood stronger and more devious than ever.[132] Like a B-grade science fiction film intent on foreshadowing its sequel, the monster never really died.

BLACK INMATES: "RE-CREATING THE MAN IN PRISON"

Ever since they replaced far more draconian measures of "correction" in the years following the American Revolution, U.S. prisons have served multiple purposes. As the roster of capital crimes was thinned and stocks, pillories, and court-ordered banishment employed less frequently, incarceration in a state-funded penal institution became the preferred mechanism for meting out punishment to dangerous criminals—but also for rehabilitating them. Ideally, both the retributive and reformative aspects of this program were to be carried out in an atmosphere far removed from the temptations of vice. These nineteenth-century penitentiaries promoted attitudinal change via disciplined routine and religious instruction. In solitary cells, inmates were encouraged to read the Bible and to reflect on the error of their ways. Outside, at hard labor, they learned that idleness was equally symptom and cause of antisocial behavior. Even the guards were groomed to be role models for reformation. As specified in rules adopted at Fort Leavenworth prison in 1898, they were to act at all times as moral beacons, refraining from "whistling, scuffling, immodest laughter, profanity, [and] boisterous conversation."[133] While frequently subverted by overcrowding and understaffing, the maxim that held that a prison without a redemptive influence could be little more than a nursery for crime helped shape the policies and programs adopted by several generations of corrections officials, chaplains, and benevolent society volunteers.

During the early twentieth century, this velvet glove approach to what specialists in correctional therapy termed "re-creat[ing] the man in prison" was modified by Progressive-era reformers. Organized sports and other group activities were encouraged in the hope that inmates would learn to forge positive interpersonal relationships.[134] When consistently cooperative behavior was evidenced, the possibility of parole could be entertained. A rarity at the turn of the century, in 1923 almost half of all criminals sent to state prisons were given an indeterminate sentence and slightly more than 50 percent of all who left such institutions did so under supervised parole. By 1930 thirty-six states and the federal government had expressed their belief in the benefits of extended intervention by enacting adult probation laws. Rather than languish in unending confinement, parolees were returned to society with the expectation that their moral growth would be ongoing. Caseworkers, vocational counselors, and rehabilitative therapists were assigned to keep the ex-offender on the straight and narrow. In most cases, this meant that idleness, alcoholic beverages, "improper places of amusement," and "evil associates" had to be avoided; obedience and respect for the law, cultivated. Some probationers were even required to bank a certain percentage of their earnings for a rainy day, to attend church services, or to meet a nightly curfew.[135] Through faithful performance of these obligations, former criminals proved themselves capable of leading lives of honesty and sobriety, thereby validating the rehabilitative ideal.

By censuring and then transforming offenders, correctional institutions consecrated the moral order and made it seem inviolable. Disequilibrium resulted whenever such transformation failed to occur. In the mid- to late 1970s, U.S. prisons devolved into a state of disequilibrium as their ability to effect even a modest amount of reform was questioned by both activist-oriented inmate councils and citizens frustrated over rioting and recidivism. Violent, fractionalized gangs such as the Mexican Mafia, Black Guerilla Family, and Aryan Brotherhood made discipline impossible and greatly increased the number of cellblock extortion attempts and assaults. Opposition from organized labor and various manufacturers' associations inhibited the growth of job-training programs in prison industries. Serious overcrowding taxed recreational, health care, and educational services. Seemingly, the limits of social engineering had been reached. The reformative approach had proven insufficient to the task of human reclamation.[136]

As the nation took an ideological turn to the Right under the Reagan administration, calls for public officials to launch a no-holds-barred "War on Crime" were heard far more frequently. Soon, resistance to the warehousing of prisoners declined and legislative proposals to adopt mandatory minimum sentences for serious crimes proliferated. Throughout the 1980s, enthusiasm for "truth in sentencing" laws and big-budget prison expansion far surpassed that which could be generated for diagnostic and vocational training programs. In the public mind—as well as in public policy—incapacitation and retribution superseded deterrence and rehabilitation as the principle justifications for imprisonment. This punitive response to crime reflected a loss of faith in the ability of criminals to transform their lives—disqualifying them from entering law-abiding Americans' moral universe. Significantly, these critical shifts in opinion and practice occurred at a time when the nation's penal institutions were being filled to overflowing with underclass offenders. Drawn from far outside the mainstream, they were deemed unlikely candidates for successful socialization into it.[137]

Between 1970 and 1980, the population of U.S. prisons doubled. By 1995 it more than doubled again. At century's end, some 2 million people—1 in every 137 Americans—were behind bars, and the country was spending more on prisons than on foreign aid, the Environmental Protection Agency, and the Department of Education combined. With a per capita incarceration rate seven times that of whites, African Americans accounted for a disproportionate share of the total. Twelve percent of the general public—but more than half of all prisoners—were black. During the 1990s, research studies revealed that more young black men were inmates than were enrolled as full-time college students and that one in three black males between the ages of twenty and twenty-nine was either imprisoned or under the control of the criminal justice system through probation or parole.[138] From a law-and-order perspective, this was what was meant by "getting tough on crime." But prisoners' rights advocates interpreted the data differently. To them, it was clear that African Americans were being subjected to discriminatory treatment at all stages of the judicial process. According to activist academician Angela Davis, the result was both bizarre and unsettling: "One has a greater chance of going to jail or prison if one is a young black man than if one is actually a law-breaker."[139]

Those who held that the disproportionate number of African Americans in reformatories, in municipal lockups, and on death row could be traced to the "cumulative disadvantage" of their minority-group status recognized that justice was not blind. Dark skin served as an "enhancer" in criminal cases—facilitating the imprisonment of black defendants who were perceived as a danger to the community.[140] When viewed in this light, the fact that whites constituted roughly half of all crack cocaine users, but only 4 percent of those convicted under federal antidrug statutes made perfect sense. The 38 percent of crack users who were black accounted for more than 85 percent of the convictions because they had been prejudged.[141] Rife with built-in biases, America's criminal justice apparatus reflected the larger society's tendency to conflate blackness and villainy.

Best understood by those least able to effect change, such critiques were not easily translated into public policy. With drug-related convictions on the rise, interest in rehabilitation on the decline, and panicked public officials clambering to get on the super-maximum-security bandwagon, options appeared to be few and unattractive. According to U.S. Attorney General

William P. Barr, there was but a single alternative: "More prison space or more crime." But not even the construction of more than two hundred new state and federal correctional facilities during the first half of the 1990s could solve the problem. By 2000 the U.S. prison population was large enough to fuel its own growth through recidivism. Tougher penalties and more prison cells hadn't put an end to the crime wave.[142]

As was made clear by George Bush's coded appeals to racially conservative whites in the 1988 presidential campaign against Democrat Michael Dukakis, the perception that the nation's prisons were "revolving doors" for dangerous black convicts was both widespread and adaptable to partisan purposes. For many late-century Americans, to be "soft on crime"—to oppose "three strikes" sentencing laws and the death penalty—constituted moral malfeasance. Leniency in any of these areas suggested that one cared more about the rights of murderers and rapists than about the welfare of victims.[143]

Given the prevailing political climate, underclass blacks who bore the brunt of Washington's hard-line penal policies often had to serve as their own advocates. To counter the widespread belief that African American criminality was an intractable problem, convicts and ex-offenders denied that rehabilitation was a social engineer's pipedream. Awakened to the possibility of self-reform by the stark reality of prison life, they maintained that reflection on past misdeeds could be therapeutic. After evaluating available options, many were said to have committed to a regimen of spiritual enrichment and growth. Unfortunately, the punitive nature of American prisons inhibited wholesale change. Reeducation in normative modes of social interaction was believed possible. But, first, the prisoner's surroundings had to be made less dehumanizing. By articulating grievances while at the same time promising lifestyle transformation, those who had been condemned and cast aside by the system sought to generate support for institutional reform. Ultimately, they hoped to discredit villainous stereotypes and to balance the scales of justice.

Inmates and ex-offenders utilized a variety of techniques to share their message with the public. Over the years, country blues, folk, and group harmony singers have recorded numerous mournful odes derived from the firsthand experience of serving hard time in "Birmingham Jail" and of offering "A Prisoner's Prayer" that "Pardon [Wouldn't Be] Denied Again." Attracting listeners through a rough-hewn authenticity and music that "could make any good Christian move his foot," performers such as Robert Pete Williams, Big Joe Williams, Lightnin' Hopkins, and the Prisonaires won acclaim with a repertoire rich in unmannered narratives of their fight to be "Free Again."[144] Although crudely phrased, the headline gracing a 1937 *Life* magazine pictorial on brawling Louisiana songster Huddie Ledbetter (aka Lead Belly) reflected the general consensus: "BAD NIGGER MAKES GOOD MINSTREL." As historian Benjamin Filene has written, even if only superficially reformed, it was possible for such performers to be considered "both common man and convict." When suitably showcased by a clever promoter, they became purveyors of "outsider populism"—embodiments of core American values and strengths. Their songs about surviving "Thirty Days in the Work House" and then seeking redemption by going "Down in the Valley to Pray" encouraged empathetic responses from audience members—especially those in the throes of developing a left-leaning social consciousness.[145]

In like manner, novelists Chester Himes, Nathan Heard, and Donald Goines have drawn upon personal experiences to craft gritty, imaginative accounts of prison life. Their popular pulp fiction has introduced several generations of readers to colorful characters like "Brother Minister" Mustafa Abdul-Haqq, a "bully-butch" powerhouse with sparkling eyes and the self-discipline needed to do two thousand push-ups daily; a onetime "rat and . . . degenerate" named Beau Diddly who, upon seeing the light during a cellblock revival meeting, jumped out of his seat and "dived head first into a commode"; Sam Polk, a black man whose adopted Indian name, Shunka Witco, became "a prime emancipating energizer"—despite the mockery of guards who called him "Hunka Shitko"; junkie-turned-revolutionary nationalist firebrand Wally Allen; and William "Beans" Butler, a streetwise con who found "clear sightin'" on his postprison future through the study of literature and philosophy.[146] Here, in all their tarnished glory, were displayed the correctional system's prize acquisitions. Described by one-time Allegheny County Jail inmate Lloyd Brown as "the young and the old, the crippled and the whole, . . . rapists, riflers, tinhorns, triflers, swindlers, bindlers, peepers, punks, tipsters, hipsters, snatchers, pimps, unlawful disclosers, [and] indecent exposers," some posed a threat to society while others found themselves behind bars for doing little more than "being-black-and-talking-back."[147] Like "slaves on a modern slaveship," they had run afoul of the nation's "double-standard" of justice and had to rely on quick reflexes and inner strength in order to survive "a system designed to destroy them."[148]

Some real-world offenders couldn't vocalize or pen tolerable prose but were so charismatic that professionals with the skills to do so became eager to assist in telling their story. Like Virginia's Briley brothers, whose audacious escape from death row in 1984 sparked a regional outbreak of satirical cartoons and bad jokes, convicts whose exploits approximated those of folkloric outlaws could hope to be treated as pop culture curiosities.[149] A select few were even courted by Hollywood. To be sure, prison dramas of the 1980s and '90s had their share of crusading wardens (Robert Redford in *Brubaker*), unfeeling guards (Frederic Forrest as Lieutenant Weisbad in *Against the Wall*), and animalistic inmates (Raymond Kessler as "Midnight Thud" Jessup in *Penitentiary III*). But iconoclastic portrayals of African American convicts as truth seekers and reformers could be seen as well. Denzel Washington (*The Hurricane*) and Michael Clarke Duncan (*The Green Mile*) won Oscar nominations for playing murderers whose commitment to self-improvement and heartfelt concern for others enabled them to "rise above [prison] walls." In similar fashion, black convicts in *First Time Felon* and *American History X* evidenced their humanity by refusing to become desensitized cogs in the system. While struggling to avoid "institutionalization" in a psychological sense, many learned invaluable life lessons. When taken to heart, these could be used to benefit the community—shared with ghetto youngsters on the verge of becoming ensnared in the drug culture. As noted by a dedicated creative writing teacher (Sonja Sohn) in *Slam*, it was clear that prison "really isn't about rehabilitation anymore." In order to triumph over institutional constraints and develop a sense of moral worth, modern-day prisoners had to "stand up with some courage" and seek positive ways of managing anger. Ultimately, they had to be responsible for shaping their own destiny. Successful self-renewal was possible, she said, because convicts were "good guys inside." The general public was wrong to view them as "monsters."[150]

While feature films, folk ballads, and fiction all proved useful in shaping opinion, nothing was more effective than an inmate's personal narrative. Part of a noble tradition that included spiritual autobiographies and political manifestos penned by John Bunyan, Henry David Thoreau, and Martin Luther King Jr., these works were meant to move hearts and minds.[151] The most effectively presented were deeply introspective and resonated with conviction, encouraging readers to sympathize with the prisoner's plight. Like nineteenth-century jailhouse confessionals that warned "the young and ambitious" against careers in "vice and crime," some modern-day accounts focused on personal renewal.[152] Others adhered to the protest tradition in American letters by presenting nonconformist writers as political prisoners or as the victims of class- and race-based persecution. Each variant helped convict-authors to deal constructively with the isolation and obscurity of prison life.

Throughout the Black Power era, African American inmates maintained that their world of iron bars, guard towers, and "lock-downs" was a microcosm of the larger society.[153] For many, this experience served as a formal recognition that they had been consigned to the very bottom of the American social structure. Their overrepresentation in the nation's correctional institutions was proof of white society's determination to keep racial minorities powerless. "Victimized by exploitation" and denied "the celebrated due process of law," members of underclass constituencies may have been "sent to prison for what they did" but were being kept there like "caged beast[s]" because of who they were and what they believed. Prison writing of the 1970s reflected these understandings.[154]

Determined that the larger "struggle against injustice" would not be "muffled by prison walls," imprisoned revolutionary nationalists constructed an ideological foundation for resistance out of bits and pieces of Marx, Lenin, and Trotsky; Mao, Che Guevara, and "Uncle" Ho Chi Minh. In this class-based analysis, police and corrections officials were "armed guardians of the social order" who presided over "neo-concentration camps . . . pre-designed and constructed to ware-house the people of un-developed and lower economical communities." As an appendage of the capitalist state, the U.S. penal system was said to offer convincing proof that "men are brutalized by their environment—not the reverse." To remedy this situation, all such instruments of "Amerikan fascism" had to be subverted and destroyed by a broad-based prison liberation movement led by the black vanguard.[155]

During these same years, African American cultural nationalists encouraged inmates to join a highly politicized but somewhat more spiritual freedom struggle. Seeking to avoid the immolation of self—to maintain their humanity while fighting for survival within the belly of the beast—activists petitioned for the establishment of black-run cultural societies, black history study groups, and theatrical and literary workshops. Because such activities were compatible with prevailing notions of what constituted acceptable rehabilitation, prison administrators tolerated a wide variety of self-help efforts.[156] Inmates who were shackled in body, but not in spirit, responded enthusiastically, becoming standard-bearers of black awareness. Their mission was to guide others away from the psychological abyss of self-hatred and despair. The creative cultural expression of "liberated" prisoners chronicled personal histories, recounted physical burdens, and described the advance of Black Power. In poetry and prose, they told of how petty harassment, mace, electric shock, and the false labeling of prisoners as "freaks, homosexuals and black racist fanatics" were used in attempts to transform ghetto blacks into "white value-loving, incubator-bred humanoid[s]." To counter institutional attempts at mind control, they urged fellow inmates to set their thoughts on more supernal things. Highly recommended were the writings of iconic ex-convict Malcolm X, the "cosmic beauty" of black women, and the prospect of creating a "glorious black nation" for their long-suffering people. While confident that the drive for group self-determination would continue unabated, even behind bars, black writers celebrated each perceptible "lifting of the shoulders." The cultural revolution, they boasted, was "changing niggers into blackmen—/ blackmen into a—/ blackNation / black Nation into—/ blackpower / black power into—/ equality / world equality."[157]

Nationalist authors had considerable staying power. Subsequent generations of prison intellectuals looked to their ideological manifestos for guidance in developing resistance strategies while more introspective pieces continued to encourage reflection and renewal. Until American penal institutions ceased to be governed with what Rahway State Prison inmate Rubin "Hurricane" Carter termed "a minimum of compassion, and a maximum of security," black writers would feel free to subject their experiences to class analysis and to disseminate their views through the cultural arts.[158] Nevertheless, when both the Black Power movement and the rehabilitative ideal fell on hard times during the 1980s, prison writing experienced a subtle shift in emphasis. Critiques of the system's purported attempts to "break minds, to create warped and aberrated personalities" through isolation, sensory deprivation, and "subtle techniques of brainwashing" continued to appear.[159] But societal conservatism and institutional retrenchment had a noticeable effect on prisoners' rights rhetoric. Armed class struggle and nation building were put on the back burner. Increasingly, black-authored narratives adopted a confessional, sometimes penitent tone. Their focus was on self-reform and moral growth.

Fearing the wrath of betrayed cellmates far more than that of "goon squad guards," black convicts and ex-offenders who succeeded in getting their oppositional viewpoints into print during the 1980s and '90s denied trafficking in myth. As they updated earlier critiques of the criminal justice system, African American authors claimed that their portrayals of deteriorating prison conditions were more accurate than stories "reported from the safety of an observation deck." Writing from the prison experience, not about it, made their literary expression authoritative. What would be shared with outsiders was a "stripped, bare-bones, objective version of . . . reality." In the contemporary correctional institution, they said, thoughts were "contraband" and writing a "deadly, serious business."[160]

Prison exposés detailed numerous administrative shortcomings and human rights abuses. Among the most frequent complaints were enforced idleness in stark, windowless eight-by-seven-foot cells; poorly designed education programs staffed by teachers who seemed "very close to burn-out"; body-cavity strip searches "designed to destroy your self-esteem"; and visitation rules that denied physical contact, thereby severing the "emotional connection" between family members. When combined with inadequate medical care, punitive discipline, and "half-cooked cold meals," these conditions and practices caused inmates to feel violated. Until they were returned to the streets "crazed and angry"—"harder, tougher, and more callused" than ever—prisoners received little that truly could be considered "correctional." Instead, they were taught bitterness and permitted to hone preexisting hatreds to razor sharpness. Denied "any kind of compassion and love" and treated with "the ultimate disrespect" in state-run "human slaughterhouse[s]," black convicts were considered "useless, walking, dead meat." It was, they said, "a hell of a system."[161] According to "Cruel and Unusual," a poem by Marion Federal Penitentiary inmate Ra'uf Abdullah, the typical American prison was "a place where the / 'survival of the fittest' / is the law of the land!"[162]

Given these understandings, it is hardly surprising that African American prisoners who described themselves as "existing not living" would blame institutional shortcomings for the creation of a "riot climate."[163] Overcrowding, inadequate heating, strict visitation rules, and staff abuse were cited as the "spark" that led to disturbances at the Somers, Connecticut, Correctional Institution in 1981; at Perry Correctional Institution, Pelzer, South Carolina, in 1982; at Moundsville Penitentiary, West Virginia, in 1986; and at Washington's Clallam Bay Corrections Center in 1992. Indeed, throughout the era, violence that prison officials traced to inmate irresponsibility and impulsiveness was said to be the product of the criminal justice system's fundamental injustice and intractable racism.[164]

After presenting corrections officials with lists of demands containing allegations of civil and human rights violations, black prison writers started to ask hard questions of themselves. At a time when both the mainstream press and prison administrators were blaming the "new, violent-type" of inmates for major disruptions, African American prisoners were beginning a regimen of individualized instruction in self-reform. As the nation's penal institutions abdicated their responsibility for rehabilitation, prisoners claimed the right to rehabilitate themselves. They believed that lifestyle transformation could be achieved in a variety of ways—and by the most hopeless societal outcast.

Music, humor, board games, and television soap operas were utilized by black prisoners to relieve stress and provide fantasy escape. Books, however, offered both temporary release and long-term intellectual nourishment. They were "the plates on which mental food is served."[165] As pilgrims seeking self-understanding and spiritual guidance, inmate authors tended to be voracious readers. The most highly motivated had eclectic tastes but favored titles that expanded their worldview, challenged their intellect, and encouraged belief in the possibility of personal growth. Some, like Pennsylvania lifer Irvin Moore, learned that "man needs to rise above his conditions and experiences" from the autobiographies of individuals who had triumphed over misfortune. Others focused most intently on works by African American authors. Since, in many cases, their public school education had consisted largely of "learning about damned white folks, like [black] reality didn't exist," a prison library crash course that included Gwendolyn Brooks's poetry, novels by Richard Wright, and holistic works of psychologist Na'im Akbar could prove uniquely therapeutic. Each eye-opening encounter with literature helped inmates see that "if you change your self-perception, you can change your behavior." As armed robber–turned-journalist Nathan McCall wrote in his own autobiography, after developing "a fascination with the power of words," he came to experience "a range of realities . . . as vast as the universe itself." Thereafter, it was feasible to believe that "if Malcolm X, who had also gone to prison, could pull his life out of the toilet, then, maybe I could, too."[166]

Faith-based literature proved especially influential. Black writers who experienced a religious awakening while imprisoned sometimes compared their immediate surroundings to a monastery. Whenever there was sufficient solitude, they could search sacred Scriptures for insight into the human condition. Through prayer and fasting, the most fortunate discovered a heretofore-unknown sense of inner peace, a "new kind of compassion," and the desire to serve others. Instead of abusing or exploiting their brothers and sisters, converts to the various branches of major world religions vowed to seek divine assistance whenever new temptations—or old habits—threatened to redirect their moral compass. Having gotten "in touch with the Creator," they vowed to "pursue the good" and live "a meaningful life."[167]

For some, an accredited holy book was less essential. Joining with prison poet Mshairi Shujaa Maganga Alkebular, they would "chill Righteously" on "Positiveness" and on "the Beauty of / the AFRIKAN Spirit." Hostile to any organized faith that supported repressive social institutions and suspicious of jailhouse fellowships organized by "racists guised as clergy," such individuals sought to reinvent themselves with a minimum of external assistance. As noted by Texas death row inmate Toby Williams, the stultifying boredom of long-term incarceration encouraged this sort of introspection. "Every morning," he wrote, "I have to reach down into the abyss of my being to pull up the strength I need to face another day." In the process of marshaling inner resources, many convicts overcame low self-esteem and gained confidence in their ability to sort things out spiritually. This new sense of empowerment made them aware that no "middleman" was needed to keep in touch with God. As mental chains loosened further, they saw "the face of the divine" in themselves—and in others. Once a bewildered "cosmic freak," the self-reformed prisoner now recognized there was "purpose and design in creation" and wanted desperately to be "part of that grand scheme."[168]

Like convicted murderer Richard Simon, inmates and ex-offenders whose moral sensibilities had been reawakened while in confinement knew there was "a lot of wrong to correct." Once they had regained the "capacity to love," such individuals became model altruists. Prisoners showed that they believed it possible to "do something to make a difference" by supporting worthwhile community service initiatives. These included AIDS, drug, and alcohol education as well as gun control and affordable housing advocacy. At Anamosa State Penitentiary in Iowa, inmates helped repay their debt to society by translating literary and technical works into Braille. Throughout the California penal system, hundreds of incarcerated trainees worked at refurbishing computers for distribution to schoolchildren. And in Omaha, Nebraska, former inmates joined with recovering addicts and gang members as the G-Crew—a service organization that removed graffiti and mowed the lawns of elderly residents.[169]

Above all, African American prisoners championed the life prospects of black youth. Sometimes they used "tough love." Throughout the 1980s, confrontational forums at which juvenile offenders were "scared straight" received considerable media attention. Here, in an East Jersey State Prison auditorium, hard-nosed lifers informed groups of delinquents that they were being played for suckers by false friends involved in the drug culture. "Somewhere down the line," the teens were told, "a bullet is waiting for you with your name on it." To avoid this fate, they had to stop acting like "damn fool[s]" and consider the future. "You still have a chance to be anything you want to be. Doctors, lawyers, judges," intoned the inmate interrogator. "But if you want to be a convict, you can be that, too."[170]

Other approaches to aiding disadvantaged youngsters were tried as well. Poetically inclined inmates such as Arthur Hamilton Jr. penned impassioned verse urging community members to protect those who "will one day be our future," teaching them "wrong and right." At San Quentin, death row inmate Stanley "Tookie" Williams developed a series of books and a Web-based educational site designed to steer preteens away from drugs and crime. Elsewhere, prisoners supported prenatal care and Head Start classes, worked to improve the parenting skills of minority-group fathers, and teamed with local schools and social service agencies to develop gang intervention programs. Clearly, as noted by New Jersey bank robber Ahmed Ibn Muhammad, inmates believed that to place their own negative life experiences in the service of positive change was both socially responsible and therapeutic. By reaching out to those who, from birth, had "the cards . . . stacked against them," prisoners put at-risk youth on the "road to having a successful and fruitful life." At the same time, by serving as positive role models, conscientious convict-educators furthered their own efforts at self-reform. When asked whether they considered themselves "rehabilitated," such individuals invariably responded in the affirmative.[171]

Whether presented in autobiographical or interview format, in film, fiction, song, or verse, a prisoner's confessional plea had the potential to narrow—if not completely bridge—the gap in understanding between "us" and "them." Compelling accounts of spiritual struggle and emotional maturation behind bars encouraged belief in the possibility of convict reclamation. Inmate-authored critiques of the corrections establishment echoed widespread concern that coercive societal institutions were degrading the "quality of life" for all citizens. At century's end, there was hope for reaching common ground via joint initiatives in support of a rehabilitative ideal that would have salutary effects on both personal and institutional behavior patterns. Unfortunately, statistics on recidivism suggested that many more prisoners professed self-reform than actually experienced it. Undoubtedly, some were overly optimistic about their ability to break bad habits. Others simply tried to catch a break by telling sympathetic outsiders what they wanted to hear. Certainly, it was impossible to take every proclamation of newfound moral rectitude at face value. Such assertions not only went against received wisdom regarding the black underclass, but also were contradicted by verifiable incidents of "backsliding." Just as the presence of free blacks—and of black slaveholders—confused the caste system of the antebellum South, remarkable tales of self-transformation complicated the modern-day moral universe. They also blurred the distinction between African American villains and social bandits. Claiming to have triumphed over an inhumane system, the convict's every subsequent act of inhumanity was a blot on both their own record and on that of a corrections system that required the spiritually ailing to heal themselves.

HIP-HOP HARD CASES: MORAL CONTAGION AND THE BURDEN OF IRRESPONSIBILITY

During the 1980s and '90s, no cultural trend more tellingly influenced public opinion on African American villainy than the valorization of rap music and its creators by mainstream youth. Otherwise unconnected to gangland, many suburban teens materially advanced the careers of hip-hop artists through the purchase of concert tickets, compact discs, and videos. Some adopted elements of the controversial performers' lifestyle as their own. According to middle-class parents, these unsuspecting "wannabes" placed themselves in grave danger by doing so. Although almost all practitioners of the brash new style proved an irritant to afficionados of '50s rhythm and blues or '60s soul music, gangsta rappers posed the most immediate threat. Their street thug personas and lyrical celebration of drug culture violence and misogyny were said to encourage black-on-black crime—to serve as a potential catalyst for yet another wave of civil unrest. That more than a fair share of rap artists had criminal records and/or recurring encounters with the police spoke volumes about the state of disrepair into which rehabilitative ideals had fallen. If such individuals had been "re-created," their new incarnations were no less frightening. Thus, for many concerned adults, the spread of hip-hop culture was like a home invasion carried out on a grand scale. At the outset of the twenty-first century, rappers and their critics were locked in an epic struggle for the soul of the hip-hop generation. As in most morality plays, this conflict over cultural expression and racial representation pitted unblemished righteousness against unmitigated evil. Allegedly estranged from both God and good manners, offending musicians provided a convenient lightning rod for criticism of underclass mores and helped shape new millennial views on black America's spiritual health.

Equally commodity and art form, popular musical expression can reveal a great deal about time, place, and perception. Whether cast in the gospel, jazz, soul, blues, funk, or hip-hop mode, favored tunes both entertain and inform. In addition to providing release from everyday concerns, they express ideas and emotions not normally revealed in ordinary discourse, define (or attribute) good and evil, and either validate or critique customary social practices. Clearly, music is a many-splendored thing. It can wound or heal; anesthetize or invigorate; draw people together or drive them apart. Under certain circumstances, encoded musical messages may even spur efforts to reshape existing societal institutions. At such times, this normally nonthreatening form of expression can become a significant political force—stirring the psychic energies of listeners and driving them into a frenzy of activism or rage.[172]

As creator, facilitator, and disseminator of this dynamic cultural force, the musician's potential for leaving a recognizable mark on the contested terrain of mass culture is great. In minority communities, it is expected that the most gifted will serve as positive role models—avatars of group progress. Those who faithfully reflect the folk soul, striving to uplift the race through their art, are handsomely rewarded with wealth and acclaim. Dereliction of sacred duties can cause a performer to be labeled a "bad racial example" and shunned by at least a portion of the record-buying public. Just like their music, African American musicians can repel as well as attract.

In common with other art forms, black musical expression is open to critical evaluation and interpretation. Singers whose performance style or off-stage conduct is abhorred by one group routinely become heroes to another. Even oppositional cultures generate countervailing tendencies, reflecting their internal diversity. For example, during the 1920s and '30s, jazz was viewed by many as wonderfully invigorating—instinctive and infectious. This fresh musical force with the novel rhythmic swing and penchant for spontaneous improvisation held special attraction for cool cats and red-hot mamas who were alienated from the core values of a highbrow-dominated mainstream. At the same time, critics perceived only cultural peril in the music's propulsive, downbeat-driven form. Dismissed as a "common combination of unlovely tones and suggestive lyrics" by *Crisis* music editor Maude Cuney-Hare, jazz was held to promote immodest dress and casual sex, increase alcohol and drug consumption, and create a general disregard for order and authority. According to Lucien White of the *New York Age,* its primary appeal was to "the lover of sensuous and debasing emotions." Surely, black critics maintained, no true connoisseur of the classics could abide the polyrhythmic "squeaks, squawks, moans, groans, and flutters" favored by such profligates.[173]

Over the years, numerous African American blues artists and their admirers have received similar admonitions to "proper" taste and behavior. Like urban jazz fanciers who stood accused of putting the sin back in syncopation, down-home bluesmen (and -women) were considered lawless spirits. Said to be hell-bent on spreading their risqué songs about honey drippers, meat grinders, and sweet jelly rolls beyond the juke joint, over the airwaves, and into middle-class homes, such individuals became persona non grata among cognoscenti of more "serious," more "uplifting" entertainments.

Within black communities, a good deal of this aversion to the bluesmen and their repertoire can be traced to a long-standing dispute over the primacy of the sacred versus the secular in African American life. If admirers celebrated this music of heartbreak and endurance, release and transcendence as an oral art of considerable depth, critics portrayed the prototypical blues singer as a negative moral force: sensual, materialistic, individualistic; the patron saint of idlers, womanizers, and wine bibbers. For such wayward souls, living right, praising the Lord, and looking forward to a better day in the afterlife seemed to hold little attraction. To many churchgoers, blues was "the devil's music"—worldly and vulgar; spiritually malevolent with an undercurrent of eroticism.[174]

Belief in the notion that the blues stream always ran parallel to the gospel road, never intersecting or allowing for a synthesis of competing worldviews, was encouraged by folkloric accounts of musicians who conspired with supernatural entities in the hope of advancing their career. The best known of these cautionary tales involved Mississippi bluesman Robert Johnson and his dead-of-night crossroads encounter with the Devil, but other talented performers have been implicated in the "black arts" as well.[175] As the popular Muddy Waters song warned, musically gifted hoochie-coochie men who bartered their souls for acclaim (Tommy Johnson), believed in voodoo (Big Joe Williams, Mance Lipscomb), or vanished mysteriously without leaving so much as a trace of black cat bone as a clue (Blind Blake, Casey Bill Weldon) appeared to be in league with powerful and little-understood forces.[176] Some, like Sterling Magee, a contemporary one-man blues band known as "Mister Satan," openly reviled organized religion. In Magee's case, this meant mocking Christians' "worthless-ass God" and terming the church a "racket" designed to ensnare the "backwards-bamboozled."[177] Others, referencing Robert Johnson, seemed content to spread "stones" in the "passways" of believers by thumbing their noses at guidelines established by the Almighty. Having little concern over the perilous state of their spiritual well-being, they bragged openly about "smokin' dynamite" and "drinkin' TNT"; about being "just as evil as a man can be." To less "worldly" individuals, blues singers were pied pipers of the damned—ever eager to cast their spell and "pitch a Wang Dang Doodle" all night long.[178]

Throughout the twentieth century, jazz and blues acts have appealed to a vast multicultural audience, providing their fans with life-enhancing entertainments capable of nourishing what poet Langston Hughes termed the "shining rivers of the soul."[179] Nevertheless, African Americans less enthralled with these particular forms of pop culture exotica have made their position clear. As even country blues patriarch Eddie "Son" House believed, "You can't hold God in one hand and the Devil in the other. You got to turn one of 'em a-loose. . . . You can't sit straddle of the fence."[180] Clearly, musical "taste" involves more than aesthetics. Lifestyle preferences and moral concerns are reflected in the choices each listener/consumer makes. Within any given segment of the public, approval or rejection of an artist's work may hinge on personal appearance, marketing savvy, or record-industry politics as much as on talent. After decades of hands-on experience, jazz and blues performers were well acquainted with these musicological facts of life. Aspiring rap stars faced many of the same obstacles to public acceptance and would learn from their experiences.

Like their bad-boy predecessors, hip-hop heroes of the contemporary youth culture enjoyed stirring the calm waters of orthodoxy. That many had a prominent "dark side" was part of their burden and part of their subversive attraction. As was the case with the iconic James Brown, whose driving '60s dance sound they often "sampled," prominent rappers presented themselves as "bigger than life, broader than the average person."[181] The emblematic and representational aspects of their public personas were well developed and—if somewhat inscrutable—impossible to ignore. Whether their musical gifts would be used for good or for ill was a major concern. Whenever their "message" songs denounced injustice or preached self-awareness and racial unity, the controversial performers became shamanlike mediums for the transmission of essential wisdom. In the manner of traditional social bandits, they were proudly defiant and claimed to speak on behalf of the inarticulate. By rejecting pity, demanding respect, and identifying with a grassroots constituency, hip-hop acts had the potential to invigorate a liberationist ethic that had fallen on hard times. Although not as immediately accessible as Marvin Gaye's topical concept album, *What's Going On,* the inspirational, gospel-influenced sound of Curtis Mayfield, or the insistent protest music of reggae warrior Bob Marley, their abrasive post–Black Power/post-soul missives were an antidote to apathy—a musical assault on the social conscience of a new generation of record buyers.[182] On the other hand, much of this recorded output was alienating and self-absorbed. If "authentically black," the sentiment expressed in individual songs could be terribly depressing. Vulgarities and ultra-violent imagery were commonplace. Critics claimed that the typical rap composition was too crude, too perverse to serve as a soundtrack celebrating social banditry. It was, they said, more appropriately the theme song of villains.

Rap music has been categorized as a "post-apocalyptic art" and a "form of radical post-modernism" by musicologists.[183] But its roots are ancient. The rap family tree links precolonial West Africa with the South Bronx and recognizes important diasporan connections between African storytelling, the Jamaican tradition of "toasting," verbal duels known as "the dozens," and the rapid-fire patter of inner-city radio disc jockeys. By fusing orality and technology into what cultural critic Nelson George has called "a loud, scratchy, in-your-face aesthetic," rap manages to sustain historical consciousness while remaining in the moment.[184] At once playful and poetic, cacophonous and caustic, the music articulates the concerns of marginalized individuals via an ever-changing montage of sounds and images. For the culturally attuned, this so-called "CNN" of the black urban terrain facilitates the reinterpretation of received wisdom, provides a wealth of information on contemporary racial politics and gender relations, and serves as a guide to streetwise style and attitude. For good or for ill, the effect of high-volume rap music on listeners is immediate. Love it or hate it, you can't ignore it. Despite more than a quarter century of derision, the commercial juggernaut that is rap refuses to go the way of doo-wop and disco.

Like break dancing and graffiti art, rap music was a key component of the hip-hop youth culture that somehow managed to thrive amidst the despair of late 1970s ghetto life. Soon, however, this raw-boned form of rhymed storytelling broke free from the projects. Danceable tunes such as the Sugarhill Gang's "Rapper's Delight" and the biting social commentary of "The Message" by Grandmaster Flash & the Furious Five sounded fresh and "real" to a generation searching for alternatives to mainstream musical fare. After MTV, BET, and other music video outlets got on board, there was no turning back. Infectious songs like "Walk This Way" by Run-DMC and Salt 'n Pepa's "Push It" rose to the top of the national charts as teenagers everywhere opted to "pump it up" and "live large."[185]

In the ensuing scramble to divest America's youth of their lunch money, hip-hop celebrities hawked tennis shoes (Chuck D and KRS-One for Nike, Coolio and Method Man for Reebok); fast food (Young MC for Taco Bell, MC Hammer for KFC); and the latest in homeboy chic urbanwear (Funkmaster Flex and DJ Jazzy Jeff for Starter, Sean "P. Diddy" Combs and members of the Wu-Tang Clan for their own Sean John and Wu-Wear labels).[186] Promotional music videos went long form, morphing into a series of largely forgettable feature films and ultra-violent video games in which rap icons acquired superhero powers and battled space aliens.[187] Fanzines, comic books, and hip-hop noir novels targeting the fifteen- to twenty-four-year-old male demographic proliferated.[188] Eventually, Web surfers could connect with their favorite MC (the performer who spoke the words) or DJ (who was responsible for mixing the music) via Internet sites such as Davey D's Hip Hop Corner (www.daveyd.com), Support Online Hip-hop (www.sohh.com), and Hookt .com. In a remarkably short period of time, an underground musical style conquered cyberspace.

A good deal of the genre's success can be attributed to the fact that it resists easy description and categorization. According to the *Village Voice*'s Greg Tate, "arguing with hip-hop about the nature of hip-hop is like arguing with water about the nature of wetness. . . . You know hip-hop when you see it. [But] you may not see hip-hop before it seizes you."[189] Like bebop, rap deconstructs its sources and then reconfigures familiar elements—song samples, sound bites, TV jingles—into a new commodified whole. Both the resulting songs and the public personas adopted by individual acts are remarkably diverse. Streetwise impresarios realize that as much attention must be paid to packaging as to performance if they are to receive a satisfactory share of the consumer market. The result is a smorgasbord of styles: jazz/hip-hop fusion (Gang Starr), Christian (End Time Warriors), and horrorcore (Gravediggaz); cartoonish rhymers (Fat Boys) and joyously eclectic "Native Tongues" aggregations like De La Soul and the Jungle Brothers. Chameleonlike Kool Keith even chooses to reveal multiple personalities—populating his CDs and videos with bizarre characters such as Dr. Dooom, Black Elvis, and a kinky supermack named Big Willie Smith. Whether sitcom wholesome (Kid 'N Play), sexy and seductive (LL Cool J), or cybergothic (NATAS), there is a colorful alter ego designed to appeal to almost every segment of the target audience. Except for those too old to be considered Old School, the possibility of being seduced by one or more of these hip-hop heartthrobs, pop-oriented dance acts, or live-action cartoon heroes is real.[190]

Of rap music's many variants, political "message rap" and gangsta rap have been most centrally involved in the debate over whether new millennial black cultural expression would reflect a moral universe grounded in the sacred or in the profane. Although not averse to supplying fans with flavorful party grooves, politically conscious rappers prefer to skewer establishment icons. If, as some linguists maintain, "rap" is derived from the French *repartie* (retort) and can be used to describe both a sharp blow and a criminal charge, the most highly politicized segment of the hip-hop community had good reason to consider rhymed verbal protest legitimate endeavor.[191] Many would risk ostracism and censure by striking a musical blow against the prevailing business-as-usual mind-set.

Toughened and transformed by the regressive economic policies of the Reagan years, rap lyrics expressed their creators' profound discontent. Block parties and boom boxes became bully pulpits whenever they spoke out against influence peddling in Washington and corporate real estate acquisitions in Harlem, championed South African liberation, and condemned the Persian Gulf War.[192] Some performers berated black conservative Supreme Court justice Clarence Thomas as well as voters in Arizona who were slow to authorize celebration of the Martin Luther King holiday.[193] Others scrutinized the media, calling TV "the Drug of the Nation" while complaining about biased coverage.[194] Still others criticized the health care and welfare systems in the hope that their acid-etched songs would call attention to inadequate emergency medical services in the inner city and make complacent public officials aware that "food stamps and free cheese / Can't be the cure for a sick disease."[195]

Above all, rappers railed against the criminal justice system. Law enforcement officials who practiced racial profiling or behaved as if the Constitution had given every "punk motherfucker with a badge and a gun" the right to brutalize minorities were deemed anathema.[196] Urban police, said Big Daddy Kane, "can't understand to see a black man / Drivin' a car that costs twenty-five grand. / The first thing they say is where'd ya steal her / And then they assume that I'm a drug dealer."[197] Even worse were trigger-happy types who felt it was their sworn duty "to serve, protect, and break a nigga's neck"—or to "kill kids with warnin' shots."[198] Hip-hop tunesmiths put these and all other conscienceless cops on notice: "pigs" would be turned into "sausage" whenever they picked "The Wrong Nigga to Fuck Wit."[199]

As their protests echoed across clubland, politically conscious performers became active participants in the hip-hop community's effort to redefine problematic terms and concepts. Like Black Power–era liberationists, they slipped the yoke of standard English whenever possible. Those in the know understood that "dropping science" was educational. "Dropping a dime" was the act of a traitor. "Def" (sometimes pronounced "death") and "dope" were used in ways that made the negative seem positive. Typically, rappers sought to avoid being dissed, played, jacked, capped, or bum rushed—or to gain a reputation for being wack, loc, or punk. All agreed that it was far safer to ride in a "hooptie" (an older model car in need of repair) than to participate in a "hooptie ride" (a drive-by killing).[200] Most critically, they were convinced that to be considered a "Nigga" was a supreme honor. Removed from white control, the epithet acquired a variety of new potentially empowering meanings. In this revised urban argot, it described a condition rather than a skin color or stereotype. More than a synonym for "oppressed," the word now connoted group strength and revealed a collective identity shaped by both race and class consciousness. Suitable for use as a term of endearment, "N-I-G-G-A" stood for "Never Ignorant, Getting Goals Accomplished." In the postindustrial-age 'hood, rappers were proud to be "Niggaz 4 Life."[201]

They also were eager to engage in musical insurgency by providing fans with a series of radically revised civics lessons. Hip-hop acts that promoted leftist ideologies were especially fond of demonizing government officials. Joining cultural criticism with hardcore rage, they scrutinized the administrative record of George Bush ("best liar in the world"), Bill Clinton ("a used-car salesman . . . [with] a smooth con"), and George W. Bush ("that asshole")—concluding that "every President we ever had lied."[202] As evidence of their disapproval, the boldest performers suited up in camouflage fatigues and struck paramilitary poses, had publicity pictures taken while standing on Old Glory, and issued periodic threats to destroy those who "built this wicked system." Public Enemy, KRS-One, Dead Prez, and other self-proclaimed "young urban capitalist guerrillas" considered rap a "revolutionary tool for changing the structure of racist America." Fellow travelers were urged to "take it to the full length" by meeting on Capitol Hill and "get[ting] up on some real shit."[203]

In organizing to "Fight the Power," hip-hop activists drew inspiration from the revolutionary nationalist Black Panther Party—but also from Afrocentric educators, '60s cultural nationalist groups, and the Nation of Islam. Legendary champions of a people's revolution, the Panthers of memory continued to be youth-culture style setters long after the original flesh-and-blood cadres had grown middle-aged and paunchy. During the 1980s and '90s, Panther-related iconography was updated for use in hip-hop cover art and advertising copy. Music world admirers named their children after exiled Panther heroes, appointed "ministers of information" to their crews, and made revolutionary statements by participating in protest rallies or touring with abrasive postpunk acts like Rage Against the Machine and England's Gang of Four. While the influence of Panther defense minister Huey P. Newton's conceptualization of the class struggle was most apparent in the repertoire of Bay Area rappers Paris and the Coup's Boots and E-Roc, impassioned speeches from "back in the day" found their way into a variety of songs. Bold and compelling, both the Black Power–era samples and the contemporary music into which they were incorporated encouraged militancy. As suggested by the title of a compilation CD "inspired by the Black Panthers," the lumpen underclass would continue to urge oppressed blacks to "Pump Ya Fist" at capitalist oppressors until state-sponsored tyranny was defeated.[204]

When "nation-conscious" acts like Poor Righteous Teachers, Brand Nubian, and Lakim Shabazz took the stage, they were more likely to pay homage to precolonial African ancestors than to Marx or Mao. Proud Afrocentric practitioners of a "purified and holy hip-hopness," these groups were fond of approximating Egyptian nobility. The black leather crowns, beads, ankhs, and nose rings worn by the members of X-Clan signified that Africa, not Europe, contained the ancient world's most resplendent civilizations, its most learned and beautiful people. "You ask who's the original and I reply I am," boasted Lord Mustafa Hasan Ma'd of Movement Ex. "At 200 degrees in the shade it couldn't be a white man / Must know and understand that their skin has no melanin."[205] In this and other equally iconoclastic selections from the cultural nationalist songbook, thematic elements were taken from debates over the genetic coding of "Ice People" and "Sun People," from racial genocide theories, and from the teachings of the Five Percenters—a Nation of Islam offshoot whose followers believe that "the Black man is God, and that the opposite is the farthest thing from a God."[206] When enhanced by hip-hop backbeats and rhythm loops, this celebration of the race's glorious past fulfilled a born-again Afrocentrist's sacred mission to promote self-knowledge while maintaining continued vigilance against white conspiracies, that is, "The plans at hand / To destroy the Black Man."[207]

If the message rappers furrowed brows within the mainstream, true fans honored them as organic intellectuals—gifted grassroots individuals who possessed a profound, popularly accredited understanding of group history and who were well attuned to the requisites of oppositional politics. Unintimidated by sloganeering and sectarianism, youthful aficionados embraced politically conscious/nation-conscious performers and celebrated the visionary—frequently apocalyptic—messages forwarded in their songs.[208]

By way of comparison, gangsta rappers often appeared unsophisticated and thuggish. They also gave the unmistakable impression that what others thought about their appearance and demeanor was of little consequence. Less overtly "political" and far more fatalistic than message rap, the music of groups such as N.W.A., Geto Boys, Above the Law, and Compton's Most Wanted presented the hip-hop community with an ideological alternative. For those, like Public Enemy's Chuck D, who sought to "market nationalism" and to convince African American youth that "a gold brain is more important than a gold chain," even the gangsta's occasional message-oriented raps failed to impress. In 1997 he complained that they had transformed a genre overflowing with declarations of righteous discontent into a "fashion state-ment" featuring AK-47s and Uzis. As a result, trend-conscious teenagers were being led astray—drawn into self-destructive lifestyles by hard-core rhymes. If casual listeners failed to ascertain the difference, hip-hop veterans could distinguish positive from negative messages. Typically, the former were presented by socially conscious N-I-G-G-A-Z imbued with an uplift-oriented protest ethic. In many respects, they reflected the worldview of tra-ditional black social bandits. The latter, according to *Source* writer Clarence Mohammed, were the crudely expressed, socially regressive sentiments of "Non-Intelligent Gun-Grabbing Asshole[s]."[209]

The gangsta subgenre was populated by unsmiling crews of hip-hop hard cases as well as by an assortment of wannabes and poseurs. If a select few were facile enough to fuse the gangsta persona with black Muslim eschatol-ogy or make an occasional issue-oriented foray into radical politics, many others were single-minded in cultivating the image of street toughs. Un-moved by what N.W.A.'s Eazy-E termed "the whole positive black thing," these cynical show business hoodlums loved to shock—"to come out in everybody's face" by manifesting an antisocial attitude toward both the dom-inant society and fellow African Americans. According to cultural studies scholar Eithne Quinn, this behavior constituted a conscious rejection of the belief that "responsible" black artists were duty-bound to present the public with ennobling racial representations. As an irreverent rejoinder to middle-class presumptions of superiority, gangstas would assume the black man's burden, but it would be a "burden of irresponsibility." Abdicating community-sanctioned roles that would have permitted them to remain so-cial bandits in good standing, they dissed Pan-African nationalism, Afrocen-tric celebrations of the past—all "that Black Power shit"—and turned their attention to less idealistic agendas.[210]

A gangsta rapper's chief concerns resembled those of the urban criminal element. This is hardly surprising since many popular acts displayed a "bad black" street mentality that either was authentic or well rehearsed. However acquired, it was unlikely to be altered by the act of signing a recording con-tract. As record buyers developed an appetite for ghettocentric "drama," mar-keting considerations also entered into the equation. Reality was manipu-lated in the hope of increasing sales. The resulting commercially enhanced product was obsessive in its celebration of gangland allegiances and score settling. Rap performers adopted Godfatheresque stage names (Scarface,

Capone-N-Noreaga, Mobb Deep, Untouchables Goodfellas, Three 6 Mafia), modeled the latest in mafioso chic, and subjected rivals to obscene verbal assaults. Existing tensions in troubled inner-city neighborhoods were heightened whenever a new song debuted that contained a "shout out" to a specific gang or dissed the competition by making a clear distinction between "ghetto niggas and phony niggas."[211]

Among the most disturbing gangsta odes were those that provided graphic accounts of black-on-black crime. In their quest to become what hip-hop bad boy Tupac Shakur once described as "the evillest, meanest, wacked-out nigga" this side of hell, gangsta rappers abandoned all subtlety.[212] Their homicidal rants made country music murder ballads such as "The Banks of the Ohio" ("I threw her in to drown, / I watched her as she floated down") and Johnny Cash's "Folsom Prison Blues" ("I shot a man in Reno / Just to watch him die") seem like nursery rhymes.[213] "Here's a little somethin' 'bout a nigga like me / Never shoulda been let out the penitentiary," began a typically defiant track on N.W.A.'s *Straight Outta Compton*. "Taking a life or two / That's what the hell I do / You don't like how I'm living / Well, fuck you!" Subsequent songs on this and similar CDs were elaborations on a profoundly violent theme. Reflecting rage, alienation, and the "gotta-get-mine" perspective of the streets, they described how reputations were enhanced by shooting up funerals, setting off car bombs, and killing "your mother, your sister, your daughter, your wife"—even the "blind, crippled, or crazy"—in cold blood.[214] After getting high by freebasing cocaine or smoking sherm (marijuana cigarettes laced with PCP or formaldehyde), a self-proclaimed "son of Mephisto" was capable of almost anything. This included "pimpin' hos," "passin' crack" to grade schoolers, stealing social security checks from the elderly, and "stab[bing] my own moms in the back for a stack." Cross the line, the merciless gangstas warned, and "your ass is mine."[215]

Although only a small segment of the hip-hop community gained notoriety by singing about how good "it feels . . . to be paid / Regardless of how many victims get slayed," a far larger number of performers felt the scorn of those who believed that any rap act was a potential threat to the nation's moral fiber.[216] To such critics, gangstas and the most seditious of their nation-conscious musical brethren were only the worst of a very bad lot—the proverbial bad apples that spoiled the bushel. In part, this negative assessment can be traced to the contemporary youth culture's commitment to "keeping it real." A perceived need to gain street credibility—even if by proxy—moved both hip-hop artists and their core audience to become self-consciously aware of "authenticity." To meet the demand for music indigenous to the rootsiest, rhyme-ready sector of the black underclass, record company publicity departments worked overtime to provide consumers with a dose of carefully scripted urban reality. As the formula hardened into convention, stereotyping and tar brushing were inevitable.

On the other hand, for some rappers, acting like a thug really wasn't acting. It was second nature. As noted by Crenshaw High/Crip alum Tracy Marrow, aka Ice-T, "Once you grow up in the inner city, it's always gonna be in you. It's not like you suddenly leave and wake up the next day acting square."[217] Throughout the era, performers working in a variety of hip-hop styles ran afoul of the law. Alleged infractions ran the gamut from attempted murder (Slick Rick), rape (Mystikal), and assault (Ghostface Killah) to misdemeanor marijuana possession (Snoop Dogg), animal cruelty (DMX), and shoplifting (Ol' Dirty Bastard). Appropriately, among those who faced charges in connection with shooting deaths were rappers Corey Miller and McKinley Phipps—better known as C-Murder and Mac the Camouflage Assassin. If prosecutors had been even half as successful as they were in similar cases involving less well-connected members of the black underclass, hip-hop theme suites could have been built in prisons on each coast.

Predictably, this extensive record of indefensible behavior generated a chorus of "I-told-you-so's" from solid middle-class citizens. But if a collective mea culpa seemed to be in order, it was not immediately forthcoming. Performers defended both themselves and their songs by adopting the role of streetwise participant-observer. Many maintained that they simply were "telling it like it was, not like it should be"—relating the "actual, stone-cold facts" of ghetto life. Their musical compositions were rapumentary narratives of events experienced or witnessed firsthand. Typically, the most circumspect performers stopped short of self-incrimination. "Nobody did half of that shit they talkin' about," claimed Kool G Rap, whose catalog contains songs with titles such as "No More Mister Nice Guy," "Mafioso," and "Hitman's Diary." "You make shit like this 'cause that's what go on around you. I ain't doin' it, but I know people that kill mufuckas." As Ice-T explained, speaking on behalf of many nonrappers as well, "I'm singing in the first person as a character who is fed up with police brutality. I ain't never killed no cop. I felt like it a lot of times. But I never did it."[218]

For those familiar with gangland, such claims rang true. Hip-hop acts were deemed "authentic" if they kept close to the streets. But they also could be seen as musical method actors who spent their time soaking up atmosphere for use in the creation of popular art. Outsiders struggled with these concepts. Having no appropriate frame of reference, they missed important interpretive nuances. Relatively few gained an appreciation for the more ironic elements of ghetto "shit talkin'." As result, many took the songs literally. For such individuals, a CD like the LOX's *We Are the Streets* with its X-rated skits and rage-fueled rhymes about "Felony Niggas" was far too graphic to be fictionalized. It seemed a prime example of what Guru and DJ Premier of Gang Starr called a "Soliloquy of Chaos"—the audio verité celebration of some imminent societal disorder.[219]

Failing to understand that rap lyrics likely would become less objectionable only after significant improvements were made in the life expectations of inner-city residents, critics of the music devoted an inordinate amount of time to vilifying hip-hop messengers. Relatively little reformist energy was expended on analyzing hip-hop messages. Rappers were portrayed as "doggerel chanters" whose "knuckle-dragging sub-pidgin" verse ranged from "the perverse to the mercifully unintelligible." Their glorification of violence and promotion of deviant sexual behavior was said to be "tearing cherished mores and standards . . . into shreds." As these "charismatic celebrator[s] of scum" conspired to debase their young listeners' "budding concepts of good sex, good relationships and good times," even holiday songs and fairy tales were vulgarized. Indeed, the rawness of album cuts like 2 Live Crew's "Dirty Nursery Rhymes" and "Merry Muthafuckin' Xmas" by Eazy-E suggested that rap should be considered a moral contagion. "It is difficult to convey just how debased rap is," critics concluded. "The obscenity of thought and word is staggering."[220]

Within certain circles, including influential segments of the black public sphere, the threat posed by hip-hop culture was real—albeit greatly enhanced by misunderstanding and exaggeration. The impression that rappers were "dark messengers delivering grim bulletins of hopelessness and doom" came from press accounts of violent episodes that occurred at a scattering of concert venues, but also from widely circulated rumors about rap's incendiary nature.[221] For example, Tone-Lōc's best-selling "Wild Thing" was linked both to promiscuous sexual activity and to "wilding"—a late-century urban phenomenon in which roaming bands of black toughs made a sport out of committing random acts of robbery and assault.[222] In "Black Korea," music morphed into manifesto as a deadly serious Ice Cube demanded that Asian store owners in the inner city "pay respect to the black fist" or see their businesses burned "right down to a crisp." Other cold-blooded compositions like "AmeriKKKa's Most Wanted" and "My Summer Vacation" seemed to foreshadow a massive "nigger invasion" of the hinterland. Worst-case scenarios proliferated as stone-faced rappers with names like Havoc, Fiend, Kurupt, and Bad Azz boasted that they were about to go "on the warpath." "When I'm finished," they growled, "It's gonna be a bloodbath."[223]

As the profane epidemic spread to foreign lands and moved white performers like Vanilla Ice, Remedy, Eminem, and Bubba Sparxxx to try their hand at articulating street wisdom, specific gender-based concerns surfaced. Critics accused the rappers of teaching that aggression and dominance were the hallmarks of masculine identity; that black women were potential emasculators who had to be controlled through language (objectified as "bitches," "skeezers," or "hos") and sadistic sex. Too Short, Sir Mix-a-Lot, JT Money, and similar acts that adopted the playa-hustla-pimp persona were obvious targets. But mack-daddy boasting was widespread.[224] Violent, misogynistic images of female subordination appeared frequently on album covers and in promotional ads and music videos. Unlike the sensitive soul men of an earlier era, aspiring rap patriarchs had no use for romance—or even for erotic foreplay. Otis Redding's deep soul entreaty to "Try a Little Tenderness" now was considered passé—to be replaced by hypersexual assertions of masculinist desire and derision. "Hos," said 2 Live Crew's Luther Campbell, were "the garbage cans of this universe," neither demanding nor receiving respect. And there was a bit of ho "in all women either on the surface or buried on some level inside." As noted in the storyline of a song popularized by Slick Rick, the best advice one could give a friend entering a new relationship was to "Treat Her Like a Prostitute."[225]

Instead of emotional expressiveness and longing, rap lyrics reflected male narrators' profound fear of romantic vulnerability, manipulation, or rejection. Through a series of preemptive musical strikes, they sought to buttress bruised male egos; to guard against the negation of manhood that was said to occur whenever underclass men were forced to compete with upwardly mobile black women. Typically, such verbal warfare was a take-no-prisoners affair. Tactical weapons included exploitative sex, the stigmatizing of female adversaries as gold diggers and ball busters, celebration of male potency, and a propagandistic disparagement of homosexuality. Purposely insensitive and downright nasty, sex raps were a testosterone-fueled gang bang in which "Blac Vagina Findas" made it clear to all that "Bitches Ain't Shit."[226]

Songs about date rape, the deflowering of virgins, and having "rough and painful" sex with some "little whore" generated both disgust and fear.[227] To the critics of hip-hop culture, these over-the-top odes to bestiality and bondage were evidence of a spiritual malaise at least as serious as drug addiction. The antiwoman sentiment generated by misogynistic rap lyrics was said to weaken communal bonds by promoting dysfunctional gender relationships. By conceptualizing male freedom as sexual release and domination, moral standards were eroded. Transgressive sexual behavior was encouraged. Ancient myths about black hypersexuality and promiscuity were given new life. It was believed that in treating the verbal abuse and victimization of African American women as gangland rites of passage, rappers desensitized listeners to patriarchal brutality. According to religious studies professor and cultural critic Michael Eric Dyson, hip-hop-inspired visions of "the black phallus out of control" caused black men to be viewed as "sexual villains."[228]

Some male performers tried to distance themselves from charges that their music was a "soundtrack for sociopaths" by speaking out against sexism. "I have a 6-year-old son," noted Darryl McDaniel of the pioneering trio Run-DMC. "I don't want him thinking that drinking champagne and slapping bitches is what he has to do." Chicago MC Lonnie Rashied Lynn, aka Common, agreed, adding, "The endless strip-club videos and the sexist views toward women aren't where hip-hop should be. Our women are the queens of the universe."[229] Others became defensive, claiming that "libber bulldykes and girls with balls" misunderstood both their intentions and their lyrics: they were sexual not sexist. Words that some considered demeaning to women actually were either gender neutral or employed as terms of "endearment." In any case, said the preening macho men, female fans didn't seem to be offended. If they were, noted Luther Campbell, they wouldn't be "tugging on my shorts . . . encourag[ing] you to do strange shit."[230]

Although no single point of view dominated debate over these claims, certain of the female performers' responses raised eyebrows and gave their critics fits. It seemed that for every rap-feminist who expressed hurt or outrage by providing a homegirl-to-homegirl critique of their male counterparts' lack of "life-affirming goals," there was a politically incorrect sista intent on bumrushing the stage and acting thuggish. Instead of taking musical deportment lessons from Queen Latifah and Salt 'n Pepa—countering disrespectful language and behavior by referring to men as "tramps" and women as "royalty"—these acts adopted key elements of the gangsta persona as their own.[231]

Embellishing rather than overturning racial stereotypes, hardcore aggregations such as BWP (Bytches With Problems) and H.W.A. (Hoez With Attitude) mocked the sexual prowess of "two-minute brother[s]" but kept the music focused on steamy action between the sheets. Unlike the risqué rhymes popularized by early blues queens, hip-hop album cuts with titles like "Az Much Ass Azz U Want" and "Fuck Dem Other Hoes" made little use of dou-

ble entendre. Leaving nothing to the imagination, the rude girls of rap demanded immediate oral gratification. "My neck, my back / Lick my pussy
and my crack"; "Open up my legs / Put your head in between 'em / Till I bust
like lead from a heater," ordered self-styled "baddest bitches" Khia and Trina.
In such situations, a gentleman caller's failure to perform could be hazardous—causing him to receive "2 to da Head" and necessitating a call to
"1-800-Body-Bags." Peppered with profane outbursts and celebratory accounts of black-on-black violence, the "thug misses'" X-rated narratives set a
new standard for female autonomy and sexual assertiveness. But in assuming the role of an insatiable bitch-diva and threatening to "pimp slap you and
take your strap from you" if they were disrespected, hip-hop B-girls obscured
potential liberationist messages. Even when set to the catchiest urban dance
rhythms, their homicidal revenge fantasies caused many to perceive black female rappers as distaff side villains.[232]

Whether offering graphic assertions of a woman's right to sexual fulfillment or serving as the miniskirted arm candy of MTV bad boys, hip-hop se-
ductresses were well aware that many found their behavior just as appalling
as that of male gangstas. This negative opinion varied over time and was influenced by a variety of factors, but a *Newsweek* poll published in the fall of
2000 showed that even fans of the music felt that undue emphasis was being
placed on booty and bling-bling. Sixty-three percent of those who listened at
least occasionally to rap said it had a bad attitude toward women. Almost two-
thirds believed it was too violent. Substantial majorities felt the genre had become too materialistic and contained too much sexual content.[233] Indeed, for
those most deeply troubled by the musicians' excesses, the logo used by New
York rap quartet Onyx (the group's name ending in a blood-drenched X
perched atop an angry, unsmiling "happy face") seemed an appropriate symbol of disapproval.

Organized efforts to censure offending acts generated the passions of an
evangelical crusade. At its peak during the years 1992 through 1996, this
spirited antirap campaign pitted politically conservative defenders of "family
values" against advocates of unfettered pop cultural expression. For a time,
those who held that coerced self-censorship constituted "intellectual prior restraint" and was to art "what lynching is to justice" seemed to be swimming
against the tide. Negative fallout from protests over Ice-T's inflammatory
speed-metal song "Cop Killer," as well as from several rounds of high-profile
hearings initiated by leaders of the Congressional Black Caucus, moved
record company executives to compromise their commitment to First
Amendment guarantees. This heightened public pressure led to a series of

restrictive actions against "pornographic smut."[234] It was every civil libertarian's nightmare. Controversial songs were re-recorded or suppressed. Video footage was edited. Albums containing objectionable lyrics either were given a "Parental Advisory" warning sticker or denied distribution. In some locales, a ban was placed on rap concerts. In others, promoters faced unreasonably high insurance requirements—or cancellation of shows when police refused to provide customary security services. Demonstrations were held at retail outlets and undercover "sting" operations targeted merchants who supplied fans with "obscene" audiocassettes. Ultimately, it became difficult to decide which was more "chilling" to free speech: the spectacle of Harlem minister Calvin Butts perched atop a steamroller, threatening to crush boxes of rap recordings donated by congregants, or the fact that Sacramento rapper Shawn "C-Bo" Thomas was returned to jail after corrections officials determined that his most recent album, *Til My Casket Drops,* promoted criminal behavior, thereby violating the terms of his parole.[235]

Hoping to counter claims that rap music "comes straight from hell and smells like smoke," the hip-hop community developed its own disinformation campaign. "Morality policemen," it was said, were a pathetic lot. These New Age "Salem witch-hunt[ers]" tended to be "people with tiny, frightened minds who look out at the world through a combination of religious fervor, self-delusion, hypocrisy, suspicion, paranoia, and sheer ignorance." Unwilling to admit that "Life is X rated; it's not rated R," some repressed their natural sexual urges. As a result, they became bitter and accusatory. Others adopted a double standard, condemning the rappers while "doing all the crazy shit" behind closed doors. In either case, the outcome was the same: unmerited persecution and the abridgement of constitutional guarantees. It was believed that a far better course of action would be for critics to heed the "public service announcement" on D12's *Devil's Night* album. Here, in an opening skit, crew member Kuniva offered sound advice for the faint of heart: "If you get offended by words like 'bitch,' 'ho,' 'sissy,' 'faggot,' 'homo,' 'lesbian,' 'fudge packer,' 'clit eater'—all that shit like that—then you should turn this shit off right now."[236]

Although agreeing with Ice-T that "We ain't the problems, we ain't the villains / It's the suckers deprivin' the truth from our children / . . . Yo, you gotta be high to believe / That you gonna change the world by a sticker on a record sleeve," other performers sought to alter negative opinion by taking a less confrontational stance.[237] Worthy causes were embraced with gusto. Rappers condemned domestic violence, drug abuse, and black-on-black crime while endorsing safe sex, AIDS awareness, and a national gang truce.

Hip-hop volunteers recorded promotional announcements for Big Brother/ Big Sister and the United Negro College Fund; for Stay in School and Rock/ Rap the Vote campaigns. Sean Combs, Queen Latifah, and the members of the Wu-Tang Clan, among others, established charitable foundations to support community-based youth services and to fund college scholarships. Many other well-known acts addressed the problems facing their core audience by helping shape the agendas of various unity conferences and national rap "summits." According to these stars, "keepin' it real" meant taking responsibility—"Increasing the peace. Spreading the music. Elevating and educating." It had absolutely nothing to do with "carrying a gun or smoking blunts."[238]

Perhaps not. But throughout the early years of the new century, hip-hop's toughest critics continued to believe that the music constituted a negative social force and a clear moral danger. Its swelling popularity made performers whom Ice-T had described as "self-made monster[s] of the city streets / Remotely controlled by hard hip-hop beats" back in 1987 seem more of a threat than ever. Because even their smallest nonconforming acts were spotlighted in the media, offending rappers found it difficult to shake the "bad black" image. Some made matters worse by toying with the public—claiming to represent "the dark side." As a result, declarations that a particularly violent, vulgar rhyme was no more than a cautionary tale or musical cartoon often were dismissed as self-serving rhetoric. The genre's explicit lyrical content made rap far more problematic than other modes of "street reporting." Its ability to conjure up pure deviltry was displayed openly on countless community center dance floors as couples ground hips, "juking" and "freaking" the night away. For many, rap's "slang poetry" remained hazardous to one's spiritual health.[239]

* * *

Joined by a commitment to egregious incivility, hip-hop hedonists, black mobsters and gangbangers, and prison inmates seemed the perfect prototypical villains. To borrow a popular new millennial metaphor, this unholy band of brothers—and sistas—could be said to constitute a domestic "axis of evil." Their profane street ethic caused whites to dread the arrival of what one classic album cut celebrated as "The Day the Niggaz Took Over." All manner of gangland residents had reason to ponder the meaning of another track on which a disembodied voice reanimated ancient fears by declaring: "I'm blacker than the shadow / In the darkest alley . . . Boo!"[240] Nevertheless, impressionistic, still-accumulating data suggests that the *actual* threat that these "bad blacks" pose to the body politic has been overstated. Inherited notions of racial villainy have served to confirm rumor as actuality, make exceptions the rule, and provide a rationale for clannishness, paranoia, and distrust. If these harmful representations have made actual gangland social problems worse by making them appear intractable, they also have spawned unjustified fears, generating interracial ill will in the process. Thus, while only a tiny segment of the nation's most vilified racial minority exhibit any of the nihilistic or pathological behaviors that are said to be characteristic of the black underclass, cultural stereotypes make such behaviors seem normative; their negative impact on future generations all but assured.

Conclusion

In the wake of the 1967 Newark and Detroit riots, president Lyndon Johnson established the National Advisory Commission on Civil Disorders. Headed by Illinois governor Otto Kerner, the eleven-person investigatory body included two African American members, NAACP executive director Roy Wilkins and Massachusetts senator Edward Brooke. Issued in March 1968, the commission's final report surprised many by indicting white racism, not the revolutionary ideology of black militants, as the underlying cause of civil unrest. To transform chaos into community, comprehensive open-housing legislation, an end to police brutality, and massive government aid to the nation's cities was recommended. According to the commissioners, time was short and the stakes were high. Racial polarization had to stop before America split into "two societies, one black, one white—separate and unequal." Feeling that this particular ship already had sailed, skeptics smirked. Those with a more optimistic outlook were galvanized by the officials' call for a "compassionate, massive, and sustained" effort to reconstruct inner-city neighborhoods. The truly committed took the commission's most difficult challenge to heart. "Every American," they believed, would need to adopt "new attitudes, new understanding, and, above all, new will" if existing racial and socioeconomic divisions were to be erased.[1]

Unfortunately, the Kerner Commission's hope that all Americans would adopt revised beliefs about race remains illusory. The seriousness of the situation is revealed in recent studies that show that many whites do not view blacks as particularly disadvantaged or in need of assistance to attain economic and social parity.[2] To be sure, progress has been made. But, as they say, the Devil's in the details. A racial divide continues to scar the new millennial landscape. An approximation of the chasm's breadth and depth is provided in the U.S. Labor Department's monthly unemployment tally. It can be seen in comparative epidemiological, infant mortality, and life-expectancy data compiled by Health and Human Services. But other measuring devices also are being utilized. In recent years, academicians have attempted to measure the gap by focusing on electoral politics, interracial marriages, vernacular English usage—even teen smoking habits and home-computer ownership.[3] Educational researchers note that white public school students are disproportionately represented in advanced placement and talented-and-gifted programs while their African American counterparts lead in suspensions and expulsions.[4] Network pollsters tell us that black and white television audiences seldom find common ground during prime time.[5] And, then, there is the ongoing debate over whether former football great O.J. Simpson should have been acquitted of murdering his wife, Nicole, and her friend Ronald Goldman. Surveys conducted before, during, and after the 1995 trial were consistent in showing that some 70 percent of African American respondents considered Simpson innocent. A comparable percentage of whites believed he was guilty as charged and had escaped imprisonment due to his wealth and fame.[6] Taken together, these various data sets support the belief that divergent group histories and experiences make it possible for black and white Americans to perceive reality in vastly different ways; to champion what seem to be diametrically opposed solutions to common problems; to misunderstand one another on a regular basis. Here, common sense dictates that we consider Simpson attorney Johnnie Cochran's approach to dealing with the nation's racial past: "Don't run and hide. Acknowledge the divide."[7]

As this study has shown, these societal fissures were present at the creation of the Republic and are both actual and perceptual. They reflect quantifiable disparities in wealth as well as differences in how members of each racial constituency view themselves and others. Public policies that seem benign or neutral may have far more ominous meanings for minority populations. The salience of specific discriminatory acts varies greatly as well. In the cultural arena, one group's heroes often have been the other's villains. Because European Americans greatly outnumber African Americans, their definitions have predominated. Typically, white opinion shapers' first priority has been to highlight the achievements of their own group. Occurring too often to be accidental, blacks have been used as foils and fall guys—typecast as either one-dimensional simpletons or dangerous subversives. In order to compensate, minority-group researchers and writers labored to uncover skeletons in white folks' ancestral closets. They also promoted their own heroes—some of whom were honored as social bandits but considered villains within the mainstream. Thus, over time, each of these archetypal figures has become highly representational. They have been endowed with the idealized characteristics of their creators. Both fictive and flesh-and-blood heroes and villains are viewed and interpreted in this light. As a result, policy-makers seeking to bridge the U.S. racial divide have been required to do more than level the playing field by improving ghetto schools, housing, and job opportunities. As if this wasn't sufficiently challenging, they have been forced to grapple with both racial stereotypes and well-oiled self-defense mechanisms. To a degree greater than many have realized, both the villainization of blacks and the valorization of black villains are to blame for our inability to alter the status quo in racial relationships.

The skin-color coding of villainy is an ancient practice. It takes a multitude of forms and serves both social and psychological purposes. As a result, it has been difficult to eradicate. Just as villainy of any sort gives definition to heroism, black evildoers help define honor and virtue for whites. They assist in establishing group standards for spiritual purity and physical beauty. Over time, both flesh-and-blood and reality-enhanced African American villains have been assigned the task of boosting European Americans' self-esteem. By making villains black and blacks villains, European Americans have elevated whiteness to a rarified status. As critical race theorists have noted, membership in this socially constructed racial group brings numerous perquisites. Skin-color privilege confers unearned advantage and authority. It makes one "normative," but at the same time dominant—an exemplar of aesthetic, intellectual, and moral refinement.[8] That whites would be hesitant to give up such an effective support network is understandable. That they have been so determined to forestall change is shameful and has resulted in great human tragedy.

By comparison, dark-complected individuals are oddities. They are considered "peculiar" or "bad" because they have failed to be white. As negative signifiers for European American civilization, villainous blacks provide a convenient behavioral yardstick for those who maintain that mainstream mores promote truth and justice. Transgressive in nature, the threat African American villains pose to these hallowed standards allows nonblacks to diverge from them. Their deviancy enables white people to feel righteous about doing wrong. In this fashion, hereditary bondage, social segregation, and spectacle lynching have been defended as requisites of eternal vigilance. Certainly, capitulation to the bestial dark-skinned hordes would be unconscionable—a prologue to forced equality, mongrelization, and racial decline. The threat posed by villainous blacks inflames the white heroic. Their defeat, even if only temporary, enhances the victor's egocentrism, solidifying white supremacy.

While ill-behaving blacks are capable of generating panic among the beneficiaries of skin-color privilege, fellow African Americans often have great affection for them. Oppression invariably creates unity of purpose among the oppressed, and fellow sufferers known as social bandits are among history's most effective champions of black solidarity. When guided by a coherent countermorality and grounded in subcultural folkways, the social bandit's rebelliousness is applauded. They are credited with acting bad for the greater good: smashing Tomish stereotypes and confuting assumptions of white supremacy. Individual bandits help law-abiding folk cope with institutional restrictions through vicarious wish fulfillment, but also by nurturing insurgent political impulses and taking risks. Some assist in formulating grassroots responses to racial injustice by drafting plans to even out disparities in the allocation of societal power. Others make a terrible fuss when confronted with presumptuous white people—inspiring efforts to beat the odds simply by rejecting pity and demanding to be treated with respect. Collectively, their proactive approach encourages hope that one day the prototypical societal underdog will "stick it to the Man" and become top dog. To quote and redirect sociologist E. Franklin Frazier's description of the positive psychological uplift provided during the 1920s by Marcus Garvey's black nationalist movement, properly socialized bandits give supporters exactly what they need, "the identification with something that makes them feel like somebody among white people who have said they were nobody."[9]

But black social bandits have been known to overplay their hand and overstay their welcome. When rage is no longer tempered with reason or antisocial behavior is misdirected, the consequences can be tragic. Vengeance against white oppressors may be joined with indiscriminate cruelty toward fellow blacks. The weak are viewed as prey or abandoned to their own devices. Unity crumbles. As concern for the collective welfare is displaced by self-aggrandizement, force and fatalism become the bandit's defining characteristics. Attempts to level the playing field benefit no one but themselves. Their characteristic hypermasculinity rages out of control, souring gender relationships and endangering the entire minority community. In worst-case scenarios, bandit misbehavior inspires fear, not admiration, among former admirers. Emulation is discouraged and the malefactors are treated as victims of cultural dislocation. Now a decided threat to group solidarity, they are considered race traitors, that is, "bad blacks," not "*baadd* blacks."

As villains frequently mimic the behavior of their moral betters in order to gain advantage, it is entirely possible that such individuals were ill intentioned from the outset. They never deserved community support. In the

African American worldview, true black villains resemble white enemies. The worst are said to possess the vices of both races and the virtues of neither. Often they are considered incorrigible, their villainy intractable. But their bad behavior cannot be attributed to racial inheritance. It is a personal moral failing—the result of avarice or desperation. Emotionally disconnected from their roots, they heedlessly undermine unity by promoting partisan causes and compromising activist agendas. Some lure ghetto youth into self-destructive behaviors while others forge alliances of convenience with reactionary power brokers. All test the limits of racial brotherhood by becoming racial embarrassments to some subset of the black population.

Throughout history, African Americans have identified white-on-black crime as the most pressing problem facing the race. In the black worldview, the racially oppressed are seen as more sinned against than sinning. The nation's inglorious record of enslaving, segregating, and dehumanizing people of color provides ample support for these beliefs. Certainly, historians who neglect to note the role of white villainy in shaping a black folk tradition of race consciousness and resistance tread on thin interpretive ice. Nevertheless, in recent years, the growth of a predatory urban underclass has complicated matters. As a result, those accustomed to attributing every central city social ailment to the machinations of white conspirators need to reevaluate previous assumptions. The scope and seriousness of black-on-black crime make it difficult for members of a criminally marginalized constituency to deny that people very much like themselves can be oppressors; that the threat that bad blacks pose to both personal security and group progress has increased markedly. Celebrating the social bandit's idiosyncratic code of honor and giving racial kinsmen benefit of the doubt in interracial disputes may still be warranted, but uncritical acceptance of bad behavior is not. Implausible excuses for aberrant acts stretch the bounds of credulity, distort reality, and give deviancy a tacit stamp of approval. Accurate reporting, clear thinking, and the willingness to ask hard questions without fear of self-incrimination will be needed if community leaders hope to solve problems caused both by the black villains in their midst and by mythic beliefs about racial villainy that continue to circulate within middle America.

One hundred years ago, in *The Souls of Black Folk,* W. E. B. Du Bois declared that "the problem of the twentieth century is the problem of the color-line." Sixty-five years later, the Kerner Commission issued its controversial challenge. Today, against sound advice and common sense, our "two societies, one black, one white," still employ the color line to allocate merit and to distinguish virtue from vice. On each side of the racial divide, there is a continual quest to locate group-based surrogates for individual sinners—to racially essentialize as many heroes and villains as possible. Frequently, the "double self" that Du Bois described as "two souls, two thoughts, two unreconciled strivings; two warring ideals in one dark body" is manifested in the iconic figure of the black villain/social bandit.[10] Both a social and a popular cultural construction, the villain/bandit remains one of our most recognizable moral signifiers. As in earlier years, these versatile color-coded rogues reflect as well as promote societal division.

To move beyond this point in our troubled racial history, we will need what the Kerner Commission rightly conceptualized as an unprecedented level of commitment to change. As true today as in the late 1960s or in Du Bois's day, both "new attitudes" and "new will" will be required of all. Only a joint initiative has a chance of succeeding where less well-coordinated efforts have failed. Thus, among the first challenges of the new millennium is to round up both real and imagined hoodlums and interrogate them thoroughly—without malice of forethought or romanticization. Until their role(s) in the nation's longest-running morality play is fully understood, half-truths masquerading as fact will shape public opinion and mislead policymakers. Past mistakes will be repeated and valuable human resources squandered.

Nonblacks hoping to participate in this fact-finding effort would be well advised to leave their egos at home, to listen carefully to the conversations of others, and, at all times, to think before speaking. They should investigate rapper Snoop Dogg's claim that "there's nothing so tripped out about black America that you can't trace back to the culture at large" and ponder Chuck D's observation that "people who have problems with rap usually have problems with black people."[11] Whenever possible, they should scrutinize mass-mediated images that simultaneously celebrate and condemn black males as inherently violent and sexually aggressive. By doing so, many likely will acquire a revised understanding of their relationship to dark-skinned hoodlums: contrary to longstanding belief, being black is not the same as being bad. Black villainy is not required for the flowering of white virtue.

In like manner, African Americans who manage to quell internecine bickering and either to postpone or abandon the search for white conspirators will be able to view familiar gangland vistas from a new vantage point. Hopefully, many will draw upon an untapped wellspring of willpower and enter into alliances with ideological opponents once dismissed as subjectivists, rejectionists, scoundrels, or hustlers. The most courageous will steel themselves against the inevitable cross-cultural faux pas and work in unison with whites to solve the problems of the urban underclass. Such individuals will realize that it is possible to distance oneself from unproductive values and lifestyles without abandoning racial kinsmen intellectually or spiritually. They may even come to understand that white America's obsession with black villainy frequently has caused their own group self-defense mechanisms to work overtime. As a result, political adversaries have been demonized and bad blacks miscast as social bandits—practices that confuse outsiders, encouraging them to overstate the prevalence of villainy within the subculture.

Only time will tell whether an informed, empathetic understanding of black villains and social bandits will lead to a noticeable improvement in the racial climate. Of course, villains and bandits are fully capable of sabotaging law-abiding folks' best efforts to calm intraracial disputes and expand multicultural initiatives. Even apparent victories can sour and become defeats. After being humbled or driven into exile by the forces of righteousness, the evil ones may return. And all we will hear before they strike is that dreaded "bump" in the night. Ironically, the villains' depredations also spur feelings of mutual self-interest that transcend class boundaries and racial divisions. Simply by being their own bad—or *baadd*—selves, hoodlums have the potential to unify ancient rivals in the common cause of societal reformation.

Notes

Chapter One

1. *Sleeping Beauty* (Walt Disney, 1959); *Flash Gordon Conquers the Universe* (Universal, 1940); Sir Thomas Malory, *Le Morte d'Arthur* (1485; New York: Modern Library, 1994).

2. *101 Dalmatians* (Walt Disney, 1961, 1996); *Pinocchio* (Walt Disney, 1940); *Perils of Nyoka* (Republic, 1942).

3. *The Texas Chain Saw Massacre* (Vortex, 1974).

4. Charles Dickens, *Oliver Twist* (1838; Oxford: Clarendon, 1966), 76.

5. Harriet Beecher Stowe, *Uncle Tom's Cabin* (1852; New York: Washington Square, 1966), 341.

6. Ian Fleming, *Goldfinger* (London: Jonathan Cape, 1959), 38.

7. *The French Connection* (20th Century Fox, 1971); *French Connection II* (20th Century Fox, 1975); Frederick Forsyth, *The Day of the Jackal* (New York: Viking, 1971); *Ben-Hur* (Metro-Goldwyn-Mayer, 1959).

8. *The Mysterious Dr. Fu Manchu* (Paramount, 1929); *On Her Majesty's Secret Service* (United Artists, 1969); *Moonraker* (United Artists, 1979); *Dr. No* (United Artists, 1962).

9. Stephen Knight, *Robin Hood: A Complete Study of the English Outlaw* (Cambridge: Blackwell, 1994); Baroness [Emmuska] Orczy, *The Scarlet Pimpernel* (London: Greening, 1905); Ken Kesey, *One Flew Over the Cuckoo's Nest* (New York: Viking, 1962); *The Cabinet of Dr. Caligari* (Decla, 1919); Stephen Sondheim and Hugh Wheeler, *Sweeney Todd: The Demon Barber of Fleet Street* (New York: Applause Theatre, 1991); *The Shadow* (Columbia, 1940).

10. *Dracula* (Universal, 1931); *The Silence of the Lambs* (Orion, 1990); *Popeye the Sailor* (1989; Burbank Video, 1992).

11. *Billy Jack* (Warner Brothers, 1971); *Deliverance* (Warner Brothers, 1972); Michael J. Friedman, *Batman & Robin* (New York: Warner, 1997).

12. *Goldfinger* (United Artists, 1964); *The Spy Who Loved Me* (United Artists, 1977); *Frankenstein* (Universal, 1931); *The Wizard of Oz* (Metro-Goldwyn-Mayer, 1939).

13. Gregory William Mank, *The Hollywood Hissables* (Metuchen, NJ: Scarecrow, 1989), 339–40. For a well-ordered categorization of villainous types, see Orrin E. Klapp, *Heroes, Villains, and Fools: The Changing American Character* (Englewood Cliffs, NJ: Prentice-Hall, 1962), 52–67. Specific theatrical and literary villains are treated in Janet Pate, *The Black Book of Villains* (London: David & Charles, 1975); John Mortimer, ed., *The Oxford Book of Villains* (New York: Oxford University Press, 1992); Jan Stacy and Ryder Syvertsen, *The Great*

Book of Movie Villains (Chicago: Contemporary, 1984); Ollie Johnston and Frank Thomas, *The Disney Villain* (New York: Hyperion, 1993); and William K. Everson, *The Bad Guys: A Pictorial History of the Movie Villain* (New York: Citadel, 1964).

14. On this point, see Jean Starobinski, *Blessings in Disguise, or, The Morality of Evil* (1989; Cambridge: Harvard University Press, 1993), 8–9.

15. *The Adventures of Robin Hood* (CBS, 1955–58). On social banditry, see Eric Hobsbawm, *Bandits* (New York: Delacorte, 1969).

16. On the social function of heroes, see Marshall W. Fishwick, *American Heroes: Myth and Reality* (Washington, DC: Public Affairs, 1954); Marshall Fishwick, *The Hero, American Style* (New York: David McKay, 1969); Dixon Wecter, *The Hero in America: A Chronicle of Hero-Worship* (New York: Charles Scribner's Sons, 1941); James D. Wilson, *The Romantic Heroic Ideal* (Baton Rouge: Louisiana State University Press, 1982); and Joseph Campbell, *The Hero with a Thousand Faces* (Princeton: Princeton University Press, 1968).

17. William Shakespeare, *The Tragedy of King Lear* (1623; New York: Washington Square, 1993), 1.2.128–32.

18. See, for example, Cesare Beccaria, *On Crimes and Punishments and Other Writings* (1764), ed. Richard Bellamy (Cambridge: Cambridge University Press, 1995); and Jeremy Bentham, *An Introduction to the Principles of Morals and Legislation* (1789), ed. J. H. Burns and H. L. A. Hart (London: University of London, 1970).

19. Clarence Ray Jeffery, "An Integrated Theory of Crime and Criminal Behavior," *Journal of Criminal Law, Criminology and Police Science* 49 (March–April 1959): 533–52; Sigmund Freud, *The Ego and the Id* (1923), trans. Joan Riviere (New York: W. W. Norton, 1962), 42; Albert Bandura and Richard H. Walters, *Adolescent Aggression: A Study of the Influence of Child-Training Practices and Family Interrelationships* (New York: Ronald, 1959), 35–44, 88–92; Ernst Papanek, "Some Factors in the Treatment of Juvenile Delinquency," *International Journal of Social Psychiatry* 7 (Summer 1961): 216–17; U.S. Department of Labor, Office of Policy Planning and Research, *The Negro Family: The Case for National Action* (Washington, DC: U.S. Government Printing Office, 1965), 29–48.

20. Giuseppe Verdi, *Otello* (1887; London: John Calder, 1981), 45.

21. Cesare Lombroso, *Criminal Man* (1876), ed. Gina Lombroso Ferrero (New York: G. P. Putnam's Sons, 1911), xv, 7–8, 16–18, 20, 101.

22. Ibid., 135. For a critique of recent "organic" models, see Stephen A. Diamond, *Anger, Madness, and the Daimonic: The Psychological Genesis of Violence, Evil, and Creativity* (Albany: State University of New York Press, 1996), 169–71.

23. Max G. Schlapp and Edward H. Smith, *The New Criminology: A Consideration of the Chemical Causation of Abnormal Behavior* (New York: Boni and Liveright, 1928), 88–102; J. I. Rodale, *Natural Health, Sugar and the Criminal Mind* (New York: Pyramid, 1968); Lawrence Taylor, *Born to Crime: The Genetic Causes of Criminal Behavior* (Westport, CT: Greenwood, 1984), 51, 58; Harold Persky, "Relation of Psychologic Measures of Aggression and Hostility to Testosterone Production in Man," *Psychosomatic Medicine* 33 (May–June 1971): 65–77; Ernest B. Hook, "Behavioral Implications of the Human XYY Genotype," *Science* (January 12, 1973): 139–50; Hans J. Eysenck and Gisli H. Gudjonsson, *The Causes and Cures of Criminality* (New York: Plenum, 1989), 41; Norman Cavior and L. Ramona Howard, "Facial Attractiveness and Juvenile Delinquency among Black and White Offenders," *Journal of Abnormal Child Psychology* 1 (April–June 1973): 202–13.

24. H. L. Philp, *Jung and the Problem of Evil* (London: Rockliff, 1958), 18. See also Georg Wilhelm Friedrich Hegel, *Lectures on the Philosophy of Religion* (1832), ed. E. B. Speirs (New York: Humanities, 1962), 1:276.

25. Augustine, *Concerning the City of God against the Pagans* (1467), trans. Henry Betten-son (New York: Penguin, 1984), 523.

26. Jeffrey Burton Russell, *The Prince of Darkness: Radical Evil and the Power of Good in History* (Ithaca: Cornell University Press, 1988), 4–5; Andrew Delbanco, *The Death of Satan: How Americans Have Lost the Sense of Evil* (New York: Farrar, Straus and Giroux, 1995), 24.

27. Charles Baudelaire, "The Generous Gamester" (1869), in *Twenty Prose Poems*, trans. Michael Hamburger (London: Jonathan Cape, 1968), 43.

28. See, for example, the illustrations collected in Genevieve Morgan and Tom Morgan, *The Devil: A Visual Guide to the Demonic, Evil, Scurrilous, and Bad* (San Francisco: Chronicle, 1996).

29. Montague Rhodes James, *The Apocryphal New Testament* (Oxford: Clarendon, 1960), 468.

30. *Dracula* (Universal 1931); George du Maurier, *Trilby* (1894; New York: Oxford University Press, 1995), 11; *Blackbeard the Pirate* (RKO, 1952); J. M. Barrie, *Peter Pan* (London: Hodder and Stoughton, 1928), 51; Jan Rogoziński, *Pirates! Brigands, Buccaneers, and Privateers in Fact, Fiction, and Legend* (New York: Facts On File, 1995), 174; Hans Turley, *Rum, Sodomy, and the Lash: Piracy, Sexuality, and Masculine Identity* (New York: New York University Press, 1999), 3–6.

31. Hennig Cohen and Tristram Potter Coffin, eds., *The Folklore of American Holidays* (Detroit: Gale Research, 1991), 72–73.

32. John Harvey, *Men in Black* (Chicago: University of Chicago Press, 1995), 13; Ad Reinhardt, "Black as Symbol and Concept" (1967), in *Art-as-Art: The Selected Writings of Ad Reinhardt*, ed. Barbara Rose (New York: Viking, 1975), 86; Linda Van Norden, *The Black Feet of the Peacock: The Color-Concept 'Black' from the Greeks through the Renaissance* (Lanham, MD: University Press of America, 1985), 1–10.

33. Harvey, *Men in Black*, 42–43, 50, 52; John Bartlett, *Familiar Quotations* (1855), ed. Justin Kaplan (Boston: Little, Brown, 1992), 779.

34. John 1:4–9; Plato, *Plato's Cosmology: The Timaeus*, ed. Francis Macdonald Cornford (London: Routledge & Kegan Paul, 1966), 152–53; William Shakespeare, *Love's Labour's Lost* (1598; Oxford: Clarendon, 1990), 4.3.251–52. On the extramission theory of vision in which animal spirit or rays of light are held to be emitted from the eyes, see David C. Lindberg, *Theories of Vision from Al-Kindi to Kepler* (Chicago: University of Chicago Press, 1976), 1–146; and Simon Kemp, *Medieval Psychology* (Westport, CT: Greenwood, 1990), 36–40. On negative connotations of the color black in various non-Western traditions, see Kenneth J. Gergen, "The Significance of Skin Color in Human Relations," in *Color and Race*, ed. John Hope Franklin (Boston: Houghton Mifflin, 1968), 119–20.

35. Homer, *The Iliad*, trans. Richmond Lattimore (Chicago: University of Chicago Press, 1976), 70, 455; Diodorus Siculus, *Diodorus of Sicily*, trans. C. H. Oldfather (Cambridge: Harvard University Press, 1967), 2:91–93; Heliodorus of Emesa, *Ethiopian Story*, trans. Walter Lamb (London: J. M. Dent & Sons, 1961), 235–43; Herodotus, *The History*, trans. David Grene (Chicago: University of Chicago Press, 1987), 191; Aeschylus, *Prometheus Bound*,

trans. James Scully and C. J. Herington (New York: Oxford University Press, 1975), 68–69; Frank M. Snowden Jr., *Blacks in Antiquity: Ethiopians in the Greco-Roman Experience* (Cambridge: Belknap Press of Harvard University Press, 1970), 148; Homer, *The Odyssey*, trans. Robert Fitzgerald (Garden City, NY: Anchor, 1963), 361.

36. Menander, *Menander: The Principal Fragments*, trans. Francis G. Allinson (London: William Heinemann, 1951), 481; Luxorius, "About Olympius, an Egyptian Hunter," in Morris Rosenblum, *Luxorius: A Latin Poet among the Vandals* (New York: Columbia University Press, 1961), 151; Asklepiades, "Didyme Epigram," in *The Greek Anthology and Other Ancient Greek Epigrams*, ed. Peter Jay (London: Allen Lane, 1973), 59; Ovid, "Sappho to Phaon," in *Heroides*, trans. Daryl Hine (New Haven: Yale University Press, 1991), 152; Virgil, *Eclogues*, trans. Barbara Hughes Fowler (Chapel Hill: University of North Carolina Press, 1997), 4, 30. See also H. C. Baldry, *The Unity of Mankind in Greek Thought* (Cambridge: Cambridge University Press, 1965).

37. On the slave systems of Greece and Rome, see Yvon Garlan, *Slavery in Ancient Greece* (Ithaca: Cornell University Press, 1988); and Keith Bradley, *Slavery and Society at Rome* (Cambridge: Cambridge University Press, 1994).

38. Plutarch, *Lives*, trans. Bernadotte Perrin (London: William Heinemann, 1970), 6:235; Aelius Spartianus, "Severus," in *Historia Augusta*, trans. David Magie (London: William Heinemann, 1967), 1:425; Eleanor Irwin, *Colour Terms in Greek Poetry* (Toronto: A. M. Hakkert, 1974), 151–87; Lloyd A. Thompson, *Romans and Blacks* (Norman: University of Oklahoma Press, 1989), 110–13; Horace, *Satires and Epistles*, trans. Smith Palmer Bovie (Chicago: University of Chicago Press, 1959), 55.

39. For a modern interpretation of Genesis 9, see Ephraim Isaac, "Genesis, Judaism, and the 'Sons of Ham,'" *Slavery & Abolition* 1 (May 1980): 3–17.

40. *Midrash Rabbah*, trans. H. Freedman and Maurice Simon (London: Soncino, 1961), 1:293; 4:219; *Babylonian Talmud*, trans. H. Freedman (London: Soncino, 1935), 2:745.

41. Abu Ja'far Muhammad b. Jarir al-Tabari, *The History of al-Tabari*, trans. Franz Rosenthal (Albany: State University of New York Press, 1989), 1:365, 368; Bernard Lewis, *Race and Slavery in the Middle East: An Historical Enquiry* (New York: Oxford University Press, 1990), 88.

42. *The Koran*, trans. J. M. Rodwell (London: J. M. Dent & Sons, 1957), sura 74, lines 26–29; Augustine, *City of God*, 651; Ambrose, "Commentaria in Epistolam B. Pauli Ad Philippenses," in *Patrologiae Curses Completus, Series Latina*, ed. J. P. Migne (Paris: Vrayet, 1845), 17:409; George Best, "A True Discourse of the Three Voyages of Discoverie . . . of Martin Frobisher" (1578), in *The Principal Navigations, Voyages, Traffiques & Discoveries of the English Nation*, ed. Richard Hakluyt (New York: E. P. Dutton, 1907), 5:182.

43. On these developments, see William McKee Evans, "From the Land of Canaan to the Land of Guinea: The Strange Odyssey of the 'Sons of Ham,'" *American Historical Review* 85 (February 1980): 15–43; and William D. Phillips Jr., *Slavery from Roman Times to the Early Transatlantic Trade* (Minneapolis: University of Minnesota Press, 1985).

44. Leonard Cassuto, *The Inhuman Race: The Racial Grotesque in American Literature and Culture* (New York: Columbia University Press, 1997), xiii–xv, 6–7, 16–17, 220.

45. See John Block Friedman, *The Monstrous Races in Medieval Art and Thought* (Cambridge: Harvard University Press, 1981); and Richard Bernheimer, *Wild Men in the Middle*

Ages: A Study in Art, Sentiment, and Demonology (Cambridge: Harvard University Press, 1952).

46. Friedman, *Monstrous Races*, 12, 19, 27, 55, 183, 190–96, 205; Árpád P. Orbán, "Anonymi Teutonici Commentum in Theodoli Eclogam," *Vivarium* 11 (May 1973): 6–7.

47. On Prester John of the "Three Indias," see Vsevolod Slessarev, *Prester John: The Letter and the Legend* (Minneapolis: University of Minnesota Press, 1959); and Ronald Sanders, *Lost Tribes and Promised Lands* (1978; New York: HarperCollins, 1992), 39–52.

48. Walter Wren, "The Voyage of M. George Fenner to Guinie, and the Islands of Cape Verde, in the Yeere of 1566," in Hakluyt, *Principal Navigations*, 4:143; Best, "Three Voyages," 181; Duarte Pacheco Pereira, *Esmeraldo de Situ Orbis* (ca. 1518), trans. George H. T. Kimble (London: Hakluyt Society, 1937), 2; "A Description and Historicall Declaration of the Golden Kingdome of Guinea" (1600), in *Hakluytus Posthumus or Purchas His Pilgrimes*, ed. Samuel Purchas (Glasgow: James MacLehose and Sons, 1905), 6:251.

49. John Hawkins, "The Third Troublesome Voyage . . . to the Parts of Guinea, and the West Indies, in the Yeeres 1567 and 1568," in Hakluyt, *Principal Navigations*, 7:54; Richard Eden, "The Second Voyage to Guinea . . . in the Yere 1554," in ibid., 4:57; Andrew Battell, *The Strange Adventures of Andrew Battell of Leigh, in Angola and the Adjoining Regions* (1625; London: Hakluyt Society, 1901), 18, 21, 32–34; Thomas Herbert, *Some Years Travels into Divers Parts of Africa and Asia the Great* (London: R. Everingham, 1677), 18.

50. Edward Topsell, *The History of Four-Footed Beasts and Serpents* (London: E. Cotes, 1658), 10; John Mocquet, *Travels and Voyages into Africa, Asia, and America, the East and West-Indies, Syria, Jerusalem, and the Holy-Land*, trans. Nathaniel Pullen (London: William Newton, Joseph Shelton, and William Chandler, 1696), 45; Herbert, *Some Years Travels*, 7, 10; William Strachey, *The Historie of Travell into Virginia Britania* (1612), ed. Louis B. Wright and Virginia Freund (London: Hakluyt Society, 1953), 54; Joannes Boemus, *The Manners, Lawes, and Customes of All Nations* (London: G. Eld, 1611), 49; Peter Heylyn, *Cosmographie* (London: Anne Seile, 1666), 985; William Bosman, *A New and Accurate Description of the Coast of Guinea* (1704; London: Frank Cass, 1967), 117.

51. *The Creation* (ca. 1388), in *The Towneley Plays*, ed. George England (London: Kegan Paul, Trench, Trubner, 1897), 5. On medieval drama, see Glynne Wickham, *The Medieval Theatre* (Cambridge: Cambridge University Press, 1987); and Robert A. Potter, *The English Morality Play: Origins, History, and Influence of a Dramatic Tradition* (London: Routledge & Kegan Paul, 1975).

52. Ben Jonson, *The Masque of Blackness* (1605), in *Ben Jonson: The Complete Masques*, ed. Stephen Orgel (New Haven: Yale University Press, 1969), 48, 56. On the masques, see Enid Welsford, *The Court Masque: A Study in the Relationship between Poetry and the Revels* (Cambridge: Cambridge University Press, 1927).

53. *La Chanson de Roland* (ca. 1150), trans. Howard S. Robertson (London: J. M. Dent & Sons, 1972), 57. On black portraiture in Elizabethan drama, see Anthony Gerard Barthelemy, *Black Face, Maligned Race: The Representation of Blacks in English Drama from Shakespeare to Southerne* (Baton Rouge: Louisiana State University Press, 1987); Eldred Jones, *Othello's Countrymen: The African in English Renaissance Drama* (London: Oxford University Press: 1965); and Elliot H. Tokson, *The Popular Image of the Black Man in English Drama, 1550–1688* (Boston: G. K. Hall, 1982).

54. George Peele, *The Battle of Alcazar* (1589), in *The Dramatic Works of George Peele*, ed. Frank S. Hook and John Yoklavich (New Haven: Yale University Press, 1961), 2:296, 337, 342.

55. William Shakespeare, *Titus Andronicus* (1594), ed. Jonathan Bate (London: Routledge, 1995), 2.3.6–7; 3.1.203–6; 4.2.25; 5.1.40, 45; 5.3.188–89.

56. Thomas Dekker, *Lust's Dominion* (1600), in *The Dramatic Works of Thomas Dekker*, ed. Fredson Bowers (Cambridge: Cambridge University Press, 1961), 4:149, 154, 155.

57. William Rowley, *All's Lost by Lust* (1622), in *William Rowley: His All's Lost by Lust and A Shoemaker, A Gentleman*, ed. Charles Wharton Stork (Philadelphia: John C. Winston, 1910); Aphra Behn, *Abdelazer, or, The Moor's Revenge* (London: J. Magnes and R. Bentley, 1677); Edward Ravenscroft, *Titus Andronicus, or, The Rape of Lavinia* (London: J. Hindmarsh, 1687). For portrayals of Moorish waiting-women whose treacherous, licentious demeanor complemented that of the male villains, see Zanthia in John Marston's *Wonder of Women, or, The Tragedie of Sophonisba* (London: William Sheares, 1633); Zanche in John Webster's *The White Devil* (London: Thomas Archer, 1612); and Abdella in John Fletcher, Nathan Field, and Philip Massinger, *The Knight of Malta* (1618), in *The Dramatic Works in the Beaumont and Fletcher Canon*, ed. Fredson Bowers and George Walton Williams (Cambridge: Cambridge University Press, 1992).

58. Rowley, *All's Lost*, 146.

Chapter Two

1. Arthur Barlowe, "First Voyage Made to the Coasts of America," in *The Principal Navigations, Voyages, Traffiques & Discoveries of the English Nation*, ed. Richard Hakluyt (1584; New York: E. P. Dutton, 1907), 6:122.

2. Mary Rowlandson, *The Sovereignty and Goodness of God, Together with the Faithfulness of His Promises Displayed* (1682), ed. Neal Salisbury (Boston: Bedford, 1997), 67.

3. William Penn, "Letter from William Penn to the Committee of the Free Society of Traders, 1683," in *Narratives of Early Pennsylvania, West New Jersey, and Delaware, 1630–1707*, ed. Albert Cook Myers (New York: Charles Scribner's Sons, 1912), 234; Cotton Mather, *Decennium Luctuosum* (1699), in *Narratives of the Indian Wars, 1675–1699*, ed. Charles H. Lincoln (New York: Charles Scribner's Sons, 1913), 208. Penn forwarded a commonplace notion that the Indians' complexion was "Black, but by design, as the Gypsie in England: They grease themselves with Bears-fat clarified, and using no defence against Sun or Weather, their skins must needs be swarthy." Penn, "Letter," 230.

4. "Virginias Verger," in *Hakluytus Posthumus or Purchas His Pilgrimes*, ed. Samuel Purchas (1625; Glasgow: James MacLehose and Sons, 1906), 19:231.

5. William Byrd, "History of the Dividing Line" (1728), in *The Writings of Colonel William Byrd of Westover in Virginia, Esqr.*, ed. John Spencer Bassett (New York: Doubleday, Page, 1901), 102; Edward Waterhouse, "A Declaration of the State of the Colonie and Affaires in Virginia" (1622), in *Records of the Virginia Company of London*, ed. Susan Myra Kingsbury (Washington, DC: U.S. Government Printing Office, 1933), 3:557.

6. For a representative sample of historiographical opinion on this issue, see Carl N. Degler, "Slavery and the Genesis of American Race Prejudice," *Comparative Studies in Soci-*

ety and History 2 (October 1959): 49–66; Winthrop D. Jordan, "Modern Tensions and the Origins of American Slavery," *Journal of Southern History* 28 (February 1962): 18–30; and George M. Fredrickson, "Toward a Social Interpretation of the Development of American Racism," in *Key Issues in the Afro-American Experience,* ed. Nathan I. Huggins, Martin Kilson, Daniel M. Fox (New York: Harcourt Brace Jovanovich, 1971), 1:240–54.

7. John Murdock, *The Beau Metamorphized; or, The Generous Maid* (Philadelphia: Joseph C. Charless, 1800), iv.

8. Timothy Dwight, *Travels in New-England and New-York* (London: W. Baynes and Son, 1823), 1:477.

9. Thomas Jefferson to Nathaniel Burwell, March 14, 1818, in *Basic Writings of Thomas Jefferson,* ed. Philip S. Foner (Garden City, NY: Halcyon House, 1950), 755.

10. "The Desperate Negroe," *Massachusetts Magazine* 5 (October 1793): 583–84; see also *The American in Algiers, or the Patriot of Seventy-Six in Captivity* (New York: J. Buel, 1797), 28, 30, 32; Thomas Branagan, *Avenia, or a Tragical Poem, on the Oppression of the Human Species; and Infringement on the Rights of Man* (1805; Philadelphia: J. Cline, 1810), 210–12; and William Cullen Bryant, "The African Chief" (1825), in *The Poetical Works of William Cullen Bryant,* ed. Parke Godwin (New York: D. Appleton, 1883), 1:141–43.

11. Harriet Beecher Stowe, *Uncle Tom's Cabin* (1852; New York: Washington Square, 1966), xix, 167.

12. Robert Munford, *The Candidates; or the Humours of a Virginia Election* (1798), ed. Jay B. Hubbell and Douglass Adair (Williamsburg: Institute of Early American History and Culture, 1948), 19.

13. A. B. Lindsley, *Love and Friendship; or, Yankee Notions* (New York: D. Longworth, 1809), 13.

14. "Dandy Jim O'Caroline," in Gumbo Chaff [Elias Howe], *The Ethiopian Glee Book* (Boston: Elias Howe, 1848), 7; L. V. H. Crosby, "Gal from the South" (1850), in Sam Dennison, *Scandalize My Name: Black Imagery in American Popular Music* (New York: Garland, 1982), 126.

15. "I'm Sailin' on de Old Canal," in Chaff, *Ethiopian Glee Book,* 40.

16. "In de Wild Rackoon Track," in ibid., 24–25; Cool White, "Lubly Fan Will You Cum Out To Night?" (1844), in *Series of Old American Songs Reproduced in Facsimile from Original or Early Editions in the Harris Collection of American Poetry and Plays, Brown University,* ed. S. Foster Damon (Providence: Brown University Library, 1936), 164.

17. "De Yaller Corn," in Chaff, *Ethiopian Glee Book,* 12; Crosby, "Gal from the South," 126.

18. Harriet Beecher Stowe, *The Christian Slave* (Boston: Phillips, Sampson, 1855), 40.

19. John P. Kennedy, *Swallow Barn, or A Sojourn in the Old Dominion* (Philadelphia: Carey & Lea, 1832), 2:3.

20. William Lloyd Garrison, "To Louis Kossuth," in *The Liberty Bell* (Boston: National Anti-Slavery Bazaar, 1853), 298; Timothy Dwight, "Greenfield Hill" (1794), in *The Major Poems of Timothy Dwight,* ed. William J. McTaggart and William K. Bottorff (Gainesville: Scholars' Facsimiles & Reprints, 1969), 404; M. Roland Markham, *Alcar, the Captive Creole: A Story of the South, in Verse* (Homer, NY: Joseph R. Dixon, 1857), 19; "I May Not Be a Poet" and "Appeal to America," in William Denton, *Poems for Reformers* (Dayton, OH: William and

Elizabeth M. F. Denton, 1856), 8, 52; John Greenleaf Whittier, "The Farewell of a Virginia Slave Mother to Her Daughters Sold into Southern Bondage" (1838), in *The Poetical Works of John Greenleaf Whittier* (Boston: Houghton, Mifflin, 1892), 3:56.

21. Stowe, *Uncle Tom's Cabin*, 67.

22. Benjamin Rush, *An Address to the Inhabitants of the British Settlements, on the Slavery of the Negroes in America* (Philadelphia: John Dunlap, 1773), 2.

23. Dwight, "Greenfield Hill," 403, 531.

24. Stowe, *Uncle Tom's Cabin*, 274.

25. W. J. Grayson, *The Hireling and the Slave* (Charleston: John Russell, 1855), 31, 46.

26. Ibid., 27, 46; Robert Criswell, *"Uncle Tom's Cabin" Contrasted with Buckingham Hall* (New York: D. Fanshaw, 1852), 57.

27. L.B.C., "Reflections on the Slavery of the Negroes, Addressed to the Conscience of Every American Citizen," *Rural Magazine: or, Vermont Repository* 2 (July 1796): 360.

28. Kennedy, *Swallow Barn*, 2:240, 250.

29. Richard Hildreth, *The White Slave; or, Memoirs of a Fugitive* (Boston: Tappan and Whittemore, 1852), 173–82, 189–205.

30. Madison Tensas [Henry Clay Lewis], *Odd Leaves from the Life of a Louisiana "Swamp Doctor"* (Philadelphia: T. B. Peterson, 1843), 192.

31. Harriet Beecher Stowe, *Dred; A Tale of the Great Dismal Swamp* (Boston: Phillips, Sampson, 1856), 1:241, 244, 257; 2:6–7, 291.

32. Ibid., 2:215.

33. Robert Montgomery Bird, *Sheppard Lee* (New York: Harper & Brothers, 1836), 2:194, 195, 198, 203, 207, 209.

34. William Lloyd Garrison, "Universal Emancipation," *Liberator*, January 1, 1831.

35. William Alexander Caruthers, *The Knights of the Golden Horse-Shoe* (1845; Chapel Hill: University of North Carolina Press, 1970), 200–203; Bird, *Sheppard Lee*, 2:210.

36. William Gilmore Simms, *The Yemassee: A Romance of Carolina* (1853; New York: Twayne, 1964), 414; Mary Langdon [Mary Hayden Pike], *Ida May; A Story of Things Actual and Possible* (Boston: Phillips, Sampson, 1854), 40, 44.

37. Stowe, *Dred*, 2:274.

38. Langdon, *Ida May*, 49.

39. Edgar Allan Poe, *The Narrative of Arthur Gordon Pym of Nantucket* (1838; New York: Penguin, 1982), 201, 204.

40. Ibid., 215, 231, 233.

41. Ibid., 236. On the antebellum racial landscape as seen in Poe's writings, see *Romancing the Shadow: Poe and Race*, ed. J. Gerald Kennedy and Liliane Weissberg (New York: Oxford University Press, 2001).

42. William Goodell, *The American Slave Code in Theory and Practice* (New York: American and Foreign Anti-Slavery Society, 1853), 17.

43. George M. Stroud, *A Sketch of the Laws Relating to Slavery in the Several States of the United States of America* (Philadelphia: By the author, 1856), v.

44. Thomas R. R. Cobb, *An Inquiry into the Law of Negro Slavery in the United States of America* (Philadelphia: T. & J. W. Johnson, 1858), 40.

45. Roger Brooke Taney, "Opinion of the Court in Dred Scott, Plaintiff in Error v. John

F. A. Sandford" (1857), in *Dred Scott v. Sandford,* ed. Paul Finkelman (Boston: Bedford, 1997), 61.

46. Betty Wood, *Slavery in Colonial Georgia, 1730–1775* (Athens: University of Georgia Press, 1984), 123.

47. "An Act for settling some doubts and differences of opinion, in relation to the benefit of Clergy . . . and to disable certain Persons, therein mentioned, to be Witnesses" (1732), in *The Statutes at Large; Being a Collection of All the Laws of Virginia,* ed. William Waller Henig (Richmond: Franklin, 1820), 4:327.

48. Philip J. Schwarz, *Twice Condemned: Slaves and the Criminal Laws of Virginia, 1705–1865* (Baton Rouge: Louisiana State University Press, 1988), 79.

49. Alan Watson, *Slave Law in the Americas* (Athens: University of Georgia Press, 1989), 70.

50. "An Act for the better Ordering and Governing Negroes and other Slaves in this Province" (1755), in *Colonial Records of the State of Georgia,* ed. Allen D. Candler (Atlanta: Charles P. Byrd, 1910), 18:130.

51. Schwarz, *Twice Condemned,* ix.

52. Daniel Meaders, *Dead or Alive: Fugitive Slaves and White Indentured Servants before 1830* (New York: Garland, 1993), 63.

53. Marvin L. Michael Kay and Lorin Lee Cary, *Slavery in North Carolina, 1748–1775* (Chapel Hill: University of North Carolina Press, 1995), 71, 75–76.

54. Michael Stephen Hindus, *Prison and Plantation: Crime, Justice, and Authority in Massachusetts and South Carolina, 1767–1878* (Chapel Hill: University of North Carolina Press, 1980), 131–33.

55. "An Act for amending the act entitled An act directing the trial of slaves committing capital crimes . . ." (1765), in Henig, *Laws of Virginia,* 8:139; "An Act to reduce into one, the several acts concerning slaves, free negroes, and mulattoes" (1792), in *The Statutes at Large of Virginia,* ed. Samuel Shepherd (Richmond: Samuel Shepherd, 1835), 1:125; Stroud, *Laws Relating to Slavery,* 77–80.

56. Bertram Wyatt-Brown, *Southern Honor: Ethics and Behavior in the Old South* (New York: Oxford University Press, 1982); Bertram Wyatt-Brown, *Honor and Violence in the Old South* (New York: Oxford University Press, 1986); Kenneth S. Greenberg, *Masters and Statesmen: The Political Culture of American Slavery* (Baltimore: Johns Hopkins University Press, 1985); Kenneth S. Greenberg, *Honor & Slavery* (Princeton: Princeton University Press, 1996).

57. John Stainback Wilson, "The Peculiarities and Diseases of Negroes" (1860), in *Advice among Masters: The Ideal in Slave Management in the Old South,* ed. James O. Breeden (Westport, CT: Greenwood, 1980), 112.

58. Robert Collins, "Essay on the Management of Slaves," *Southern Cultivator* 12 (July 1854): 206; Wilson, "Peculiarities," 243.

59. H, "Remarks on Overseers, and the Proper Treatment of Slaves," *Farmers' Register* 5 (September 1837): 302.

60. Southron, "The Policy of the Southern Planter," *American Cotton Planter and Soil of the South* 1 (October 1857): 295.

61. Strait Edge, "Plantation Regulations," *Soil of the South* 1 (February 1851): 21.

62. A Planter, "Notions on the Management of Negroes, &c." *Farmers' Register* 4 (January 1837): 574.

63. H.C., "On the Management of Negroes. Addressed to the Farmers and Overseers of Virginia," *Farmers' Register* 1 (February 1834): 565.

64. Wilson, "Peculiarities," 264; A Minister of the Gospel, "'Tattler' on the Management of Negroes," *Southern Cultivator* 9 (June 1851): 86.

65. Harris Smith Evans, "Rules for the Government of the Negroes, Plantation, &c. at the Float Swamp, Wilcox County, South-Alabama," *Southern Agriculturist* 5 (May 1832): 231, 234; Collins, "Management of Slaves," 205; Strait Edge, "Plantation Regulations," *Soil of the South* 1 (May 1851): 68; H.C., "On the Management of Negroes," *Southern Agriculturist* 7 (July 1834): 370.

66. George Fitzhugh, *Slavery Justified, by a Southerner* (1850), in *Slavery Defended: The Views of the Old South*, ed. Eric L. McKitrick (Englewood Cliffs, NJ: Prentice-Hall, 1963), 44; James Henry Hammond to Thomas Clarkson, January 28, 1845, in *The Ideology of Slavery: Proslavery Thought in the Antebellum South, 1830–1860*, ed. Drew Gilpin Faust (Baton Rouge: Louisiana State University Press, 1981), 192; John C. Calhoun, "Speech on the Reception of Abolition Petitions" (1837), in *The Works of John C. Calhoun*, ed. Richard K. Crallé (New York: D. Appleton, 1860), 2:630.

67. Thomas R. Dew, "Abolition of Negro Slavery," *American Quarterly Review* 12 (September 1832): 228, 233, 235, 237.

68. Henry Home [Lord Kames], *Sketches of the History of Man* (Edinburgh: W. Creech, 1778), 1:82–84.

69. On the Great Chain continuum, see Arthur O. Lovejoy, *The Great Chain of Being: A Study of the History of an Idea* (Cambridge: Harvard University Press, 1936).

70. Thomas Jefferson, *Notes on the State of Virginia* (1787), ed. William Peden (Chapel Hill: University of North Carolina Press, 1955), 143.

71. J. C. Nott and George R. Gliddon, *Types of Mankind* (Philadelphia: Lippincott, Grambo, 1854), 79, 185, 189, 405.

72. J. H. Van Evrie, *Negroes and Negro "Slavery": The First an Inferior Race: The Latter Its Normal Condition* (New York: Van Evrie, Horton, 1861), 277.

73. Josiah C. Nott, *Two Lectures on the Natural History of the Caucasian and Negro Races* (1844), in Faust, *Ideology of Slavery*, 224.

74. Peter A. Browne to Samuel George Morton, ca. January 1851, in *Proceedings of the Academy of Natural Sciences of Philadelphia* 5 (February 1851): 145–46; P. A. Browne, "A Microscopic Examination and Description of Some of the Piles of the Head of Albinos," *Proceedings of the American Association for the Advancement of Science* 3 (1850): 108–14.

75. Samuel A. Cartwright, "Diseases and Peculiarities of the Negro," in *The Industrial Resources, Statistics, Etc. of the United States*, ed. J. D. B. DeBow (New York: D. Appleton, 1854), 2:315, 317, 327.

76. Samuel George Morton, "Observations on the Size of the Brain in Various Races and Families of Man," *Proceedings of the Academy of Natural Sciences of Philadelphia* 4 (September 1849): 222–23; Nott, *Natural History*, 231; George R. Gliddon to Samuel George Morton, January 9, 1848, quoted in William Stanton, *The Leopard's Spots: Scientific Attitudes toward Race in America, 1815–59* (Chicago: University of Chicago Press, 1960), 100.

77. Samuel A. Cartwright, "Natural History of the Prognathous Species of Mankind," in

Cotton Is King, and Pro-Slavery Arguments, ed. E. N. Elliott (Augusta, GA: Pritchard, Abbott & Loomis, 1860), 714.

78. Samuel George Morton, "Origin of the Human Species," in Nott and Gliddon, *Types of Mankind*, 305, 318; Cartwright, "Peculiarities," 318.

79. James Cowles Prichard, *The Natural History of Man* (London: Hippolyte Bailliere, 1848), 26.

80. Thomas F. Gossett, *Race: The History of an Idea in America* (1963; New York: Schocken, 1970), 82.

81. Carolus Linnaeus, *Systema Naturae* (1789), trans. Walter Scheidt, in *This Is Race*, ed. Earl W. Count (New York: Henry Schuman, 1950), 356–57.

82. Winthrop D. Jordan, *White over Black: American Attitudes toward the Negro, 1550–1812* (Chapel Hill: University of North Carolina Press, 1968), 221, 227.

83. Johann Friedrich Blumenbach, *On the Natural Variety of Mankind* (1795), in *The Anthropological Treatises of Johann Friedrich Blumenbach*, ed. and trans. Thomas Bendyshe (London: Longman, Green, Longman, Roberts, & Green, 1865), 196–200; Prichard, *Natural History*, 107; Samuel Stanhope Smith, *An Essay on the Causes of the Variety of Complexion and Figure in the Human Species* (1810; Cambridge: Belknap Press of Harvard University Press, 1965), 12.

84. James Cowles Prichard, *Researches into the Physical History of Man* (London: John and Arthur Arch, 1813), 235–36; Smith, *Variety*, 37–38, 61.

85. John Bachman, *The Doctrine of the Unity of the Human Race—Examined on the Principles of Science* (Charleston: C. Canning, 1850); J. L. Cabell, *The Testimony of Modern Science to the Unity of Mankind* (New York: R. Carter & Brothers, 1859); Lester D. Stephens, *Science, Race, and Religion in the American South: John Bachman and the Charleston Circle of Naturalists, 1815–1895* (Chapel Hill: University of North Carolina Press, 2000), 165–94.

86. Smith, *Variety*, 119, 125.

87. Blumenbach, *Natural Variety*, 265–66, 269.

88. Prichard, *Natural History*, 140; Smith, *Variety*, 37, 72–73, 153.

89. Blumenbach, *Natural Variety*, 269.

90. Eugene D. Genovese, *Roll, Jordan, Roll: The World the Slaves Made* (New York: Pantheon, 1974), 599.

91. William W. Rex to Daniel C. E. Brady, March 15, 1861, quoted in Robert S. Starobin, *Industrial Slavery in the Old South* (New York: Oxford University Press, 1970), 79.

92. Frederick Law Olmsted, *The Cotton Kingdom: A Traveller's Observations on Cotton and Slavery in the American Slave States* (1861), ed. Arthur M. Schlesinger (New York: Modern Library, 1969), 94.

93. Ibid., 78.

94. Charles C. Jones, *The Religious Instruction of the Negroes in the United States* (Savannah: Thomas Purse, 1842), 135.

95. *The American Slave: A Composite Autobiography. South Carolina Narratives*, ed. George P. Rawick (Westport, CT: Greenwood, 1972), 2: part 2, 110.

96. Henry Bibb, *Narrative of the Life and Adventures of Henry Bibb, An American Slave*, in *Puttin' On Ole Massa* (1849), ed. Gilbert Osofsky (New York: Harper & Row, 1969), 125; Frederick Douglass, *Life and Times of Frederick Douglass* (1892; New York: Collier, 1962), 105.

97. Alex Lichtenstein, "'That Disposition to Theft, with Which They Have Been

Branded': Moral Economy, Slave Management, and the Law," *Journal of Social History* 21 (Spring 1988): 421.

98. Frederick Law Olmsted, *A Journey in the Back Country* (1860; New York: Schocken, 1970), 79.

99. Larry Gara, *The Liberty Line: The Legend of the Underground Railroad* (Lexington: University of Kentucky Press, 1961), 38; John Hope Franklin and Loren Schweninger, *Runaway Slaves: Rebels on the Plantation* (New York: Oxford University Press, 1999), 282.

100. *Pennsylvania Gazette*, April 29, 1762, in *Blacks Who Stole Themselves: Advertisements for Runaways in the Pennsylvania Gazette, 1728–1790*, ed. Billy G. Smith and Richard Wojtowicz (Philadelphia: University of Pennsylvania Press, 1989), 54.

101. On the gentry's use of runaway notices to confirm prevailing hierarchies, see Jonathan Prude, "To Look upon the 'Lower Sort': Runaway Ads and the Appearance of Unfree Laborers in America, 1750–1800," *Journal of American History* 78 (June 1991): 134.

102. *Georgia Gazette*, September 6, 1764, in *Runaway Slave Advertisements: A Documentary History from the 1730s to 1790*, ed. Lathan A. Windley (Westport, CT: Greenwood, 1983), 4:8; *Virginia Gazette*, January 30, 1752, February 13, 1752, in Windley, *Runaway Slave Advertisements*, 1:25; *Pennsylvania Gazette*, May 14, 1783, in Smith and Wojtowicz, *Blacks Who Stole Themselves*, 145.

103. *Georgia Gazette*, July 14, 1763, in Windley, *Runaway Slave Advertisements*, 4:2; François Jean Chastellux, *Travels in North-America, in the Years 1780, 1781, and 1782* (London: G. G. J. and J. Robinson, 1787), 2:196; *South-Carolina Gazette*, April 27, 1734. On the slaveholders' attribution of "good" and "bad" character traits to various West African peoples, see Daniel C. Littlefield, *Rice and Slaves: Ethnicity and the Slave Trade in Colonial South Carolina* (Baton Rouge: Louisiana State University Press, 1981), 8–32; Darold D. Wax, "Preferences for Slaves in Colonial America," *Journal of Negro History* 58 (October 1973): 371–401.

104. Cartwright, "Peculiarities," 322–25.

105. *Virginia Gazette*, September 7, 1769.

106. Meaders, *Dead or Alive*, 16. At least one southern newspaper made the unholy connection visual by illustrating an ad for a runaway named John with a blockprint of a trident-bearing demon hovering over a dutiful field hand. Presumably, the slave's head was being filled with "unnatural" thoughts of freedom. See *Virginia Gazette and General Advertiser*, January 27, 1796.

107. *Maryland Gazette*, April 4, 1754, in Windley, *Runaway Slave Advertisements*, 2:19; Daniel E. Meaders, "South Carolina Fugitives as Viewed through Local Colonial Newspapers with Emphasis on Runaway Notices, 1732–1801," *Journal of Negro History* 60 (April 1975): 313; Jefferson, *Notes on the State of Virginia*, 138; *Pennsylvania Gazette*, June 8, 1749; April 29, 1762; April 27, 1774; April 12, 1775; January 26, 1785, in Smith and Wojtowicz, *Blacks Who Stole Themselves*, 31, 54, 118, 121, 150.

108. *South-Carolina Gazette*, June 28, 1735.

109. Richard A. Lewis et al. to Thomas Bragg, August 25, 1856, quoted in Herbert Aptheker, *American Negro Slave Revolts* (1943; New York: International, 1968), 346; Herbert Aptheker, "Maroons within the Present Limits of the United States," *Journal of Negro History* 24 (April 1939): 171, 176; *Georgia Gazette*, June 24, 1767, in Windley, *Runaway Slave Advertisements*, 4:23; Jane Landers, *Black Society in Spanish Florida* (Urbana: University of Illinois Press, 1999), 29–60.

110. On white efforts to thwart joint African American–Native American initiatives, see William S. Willis, "Divide and Rule: Red, White, and Black in the Southeast," *Journal of Negro History* 48 (July 1963): 157–76. On black-Seminole relations, see Kenneth W. Porter, *The Black Seminoles: History of a Freedom-Seeking People*, ed. Alcione M. Amos and Thomas P. Senter (Gainesville: University Press of Florida, 1996); Kevin Mulroy, *Freedom on the Border: The Seminole Maroons in Florida, the Indian Territory, Coahuila, and Texas* (Lubbock: Texas Tech University Press, 1993); and John D. Milligan, "Slave Rebelliousness and the Florida Maroon," *Prologue* 6 (Spring 1974): 4–18.

111. Thomas Paine, *Rights of Man, Common Sense, and Other Political Writings* (1776), ed. Mark Philp (New York: Oxford University Press, 1995), 34–35; Peter H. Wood, "'Taking Care of Business' in Revolutionary South Carolina: Republicanism and the Slave Society," in *The Southern Experience in the American Revolution*, ed. Jeffrey J. Crow and Larry E. Tise (Chapel Hill: University of North Carolina Press, 1978), 281; Jeffrey J. Crow, "Slave Rebelliousness and Social Conflict in North Carolina, 1775 to 1802," *William and Mary Quarterly* 37 (January 1980): 89. Recent studies have estimated that as many as 100,000 slaves may have left their owners during the war years. See Sylvia R. Frey, *Water from the Rock: Black Resistance in a Revolutionary Age* (Princeton: Princeton University Press, 1991), 211.

112. *The Journal of Peter Gordon, 1732–1735*, ed. E. Merton Coulter (1733; Athens: University of Georgia Press, 1963), 57; Freddie L. Parker, *Running for Freedom: Slave Runaways in North Carolina, 1775–1840* (New York: Garland, 1993), 45; Richard C. Wade, *Slavery in the Cities: The South 1820–1860* (New York: Oxford University Press, 1964), 86. For statistics on black overrepresentation in urban prisons, penitentiaries, jails, and workhouses, see Leonard P. Curry, *The Free Black in Urban America, 1800–1850: The Shadow of the Dream* (Chicago: University of Chicago Press, 1981), 112–19.

113. Jonathan Katz, *Resistance at Christiana* (New York: Thomas Y. Crowell, 1974), 86, 156; Thomas P. Slaughter, *Bloody Dawn: The Christiana Riot and Racial Violence in the Antebellum North* (New York: Oxford University Press, 1991), 63; William Still, *The Underground Rail Road* (Philadelphia: Porter & Coates, 1872), 368. For other accounts of fugitive slaves' spirited resistance to recapture, see Norrece T. Jones Jr., *Born a Child of Freedom, Yet a Slave: Mechanisms of Control and Strategies of Resistance in Antebellum South Carolina* (Hanover, NH: Wesleyan University Press/University Press of New England, 1990), 171–74.

114. For a comparative, hemispheric perspective on slave insurrections, see Eugene D. Genovese, *From Rebellion to Revolution: Afro-American Slave Revolts in the Making of the Modern World* (Baton Rouge: Louisiana State University Press, 1979), 1–50; and Michael Mullin, *Africa in America: Slave Acculturation and Resistance in the American South and the British Caribbean, 1736–1831* (Urbana: University of Illinois Press, 1992).

115. Thomas Branagan, *The Penitential Tyrant* (Philadelphia: By the author, 1805), 1.

116. Charles William Janson, *The Stranger in America, 1793–1806* (1807; New York: Press of the Pioneers, 1935), 366.

117. "Evils of Slavery," *Liberator*, January 28, 1832.

118. "Extract of a Letter from Surinam," *Georgia Gazette*, July 7, 1763; James Sidbury, "Saint Domingue in Virginia: Ideology, Local Meanings, and Resistance to Slavery, 1790–1800," *Journal of Southern History* 63 (August 1997): 539; Alfred N. Hunt, *Haiti's Influence on Antebellum America: Slumbering Volcano in the Caribbean* (Baton Rouge: Louisiana State University Press, 1988), 107–46.

119. Whitemarsh B. Seabrook, *A Concise View of the Critical Situation, and Future Prospects of the Slave-holding States, in Relation to Their Coloured Population* (Charleston: A. E. Miller, 1825), 13.

120. "Extract of Two Letters from South Carolina," *Boston Weekly News-Letter,* October 15–22, 1730.

121. William D. Piersen, *Black Yankees: The Development of an Afro-American Subculture in Eighteenth-Century New England* (Amherst: University of Massachusetts Press, 1988), 83–84; Lorenzo Johnston Greene, *The Negro in Colonial New England* (1942; New York: Atheneum, 1969), 153; "Petition in Regard to a Slave, 1773," in *Virginia Historical Magazine* 18 (January 1910), 395; Edmund Kirke [James Roberts Gilmore], *Among the Pines: or, South in Secession-Time* (New York: J. R. Gilmore, 1862), 90.

122. Allan Kulikoff, *Tobacco and Slaves: The Development of Southern Cultures in the Chesapeake, 1680–1800* (Chapel Hill: University of North Carolina Press, 1986), 330; Old Virginia, "To the Editors of the Enquirer" (1831), in *The Southampton Slave Revolt of 1831: A Compilation of Source Material,* ed. Henry Irving Tragle (Amherst: University of Massachusetts Press, 1971), 144–45; Ezekial Butler to Ben Thomas, September 21, 1831, in Wade, *Slavery in the Cities,* 228.

123. In his pioneering *American Negro Slave Revolts,* Herbert Aptheker claimed to have found records of approximately 250 domestic revolts and conspiracies involving a minimum of ten disaffected bondsmen per incident. Other historians have treated most types of black conspiratorial activity as "resistance" and applied more exacting definitional standards to the term "revolt." According to these revised calculations, there were "at least nine" and "probably not more than a dozen" actual revolts. Aptheker, *Slave Revolts,* 162; John W. Blassingame, *The Slave Community: Plantation Life in the Antebellum South* (New York: Oxford University Press, 1972), 125; Jordan, *White over Black,* 113.

124. *Boston News-Letter,* April 7–14, 1712; Aptheker, *Slave Revolts,* 172; Graham Russell Hodges, *Root & Branch: African Americans in New York & East Jersey, 1613–1863* (Chapel Hill: University of North Carolina Press, 1999), 63–68.

125. William Stephens, *A Journal of the Proceedings in Georgia Beginning October 20, 1737* (1739), in *Colonial Records of the State of Georgia,* ed. Allen D. Candler (Atlanta: Franklin Printing and Publishing, 1906), 4:412; *Report of the Committee Appointed to Enquire into the Causes of the Disappointment of Success in the Late Expedition against St. Augustine,* in *Colonial Records of South Carolina. Journal of the Commons House of Assembly, May 18, 1741–July 10, 1742,* ed. J. H. Easterby (Columbia: Historical Commission of South Carolina, 1953), 83; Darold D. Wax, "'The Great Risque We Run': The Aftermath of Slave Rebellion at Stono, South Carolina, 1739–1745," *Journal of Negro History* 67 (Summer 1982): 141–42; *South-Carolina Gazette,* March 14, 1743; "Negro School-house at Charles-town," *South-Carolina Gazette,* April 2, 1744.

126. Lionel H. Kennedy and Thomas Parker, *An Official Report of the Trials of Sundry Negroes, Charged with an Attempt to Raise an Insurrection in the State of South Carolina* (Charleston: James R. Schenck, 1822), 42, 76, 78, 137; *Designs against Charleston: The Trial Record of the Denmark Vesey Slave Conspiracy of 1822,* ed. Edward A. Pearson (Chapel Hill: University of North Carolina Press, 1999), 196.

127. Martha Proctor Richardson to James P. Screven, July 6, 1822, in *Denmark Vesey: The*

Slave Conspiracy of 1822, ed. Robert S. Starobin (Englewood Cliffs, NJ: Prentice-Hall, 1970), 83; John Lofton, *Denmark Vesey's Revolt: The Slave Plot that Lit a Fuse to Fort Sumter* (1964; Kent, OH: Kent State University Press, 1983), 179; Kennedy and Parker, *Trials of Sundry Negroes,* 11, 136, 161; Anna Hayes Johnson to Elizabeth Haywood, July 18, 1822, in Starobin, *Slave Conspiracy,* 73.

128. Douglas R. Egerton, *Gabriel's Rebellion: The Virginia Slave Conspiracies of 1800 and 1802* (Chapel Hill: University of North Carolina Press, 1993), 53; Gerald W. Mullin, *Flight and Rebellion: Slave Resistance in Eighteenth-Century Virginia* (New York: Oxford University Press, 1972), 144, 148–49, 152.

129. Timothy Dwight, "Triumph of Democracy," *New-England Palladium,* January 6, 1801.

130. John Hampden Pleasants, "Southampton Affair" (1831), in *Nat Turner,* ed. Eric Foner (Englewood Cliffs, NJ: Prentice-Hall, 1971), 21; John Floyd, "Governor Floyd's Message to the Legislature, December 6, 1831," in ibid., 102.

131. William C. Parker to John Floyd, September 14, 1831, in Tragle, *Southampton Slave Revolt,* 420; *The Confessions of Nat Turner, The Leader of the Late Insurrection in Southampton, Va. As Fully and Voluntarily Made to Thomas R. Gray* (1831), in *The Confessions of Nat Turner and Related Documents,* ed. Kenneth S. Greenberg (Boston: Bedford, 1996), 40–41, 45–48, 54–55.

132. Charles Edward Morris, "Panic and Reprisal: Reaction in North Carolina to the Nat Turner Insurrection, 1831," *North Carolina Historical Review* 62 (January 1985): 29–52; Wade, *Slavery in the Cities,* 228; John Hampden Pleasants, "Extract of a Letter from the Senior Editor" (1831), in Tragle, *Southampton Slave Revolt,* 51.

133. "Southampton Insurrection" (1831), in Foner, *Nat Turner,* 27.

134. Peter H. Wood, "Nat Turner: The Unknown Slave as Visionary Leader," in *Black Leaders of the Nineteenth Century,* ed. Leon Litwack and August Meier (Urbana: University of Illinois Press, 1988), 22–23.

135. *Confessions of Nat Turner,* 42.

136. Caroline Lee Hentz, *The Planter's Northern Bride* (1854; Chapel Hill: University of North Carolina Press, 1970), 16; Mrs. Sidney F. Bateman, *Self* (1856), in *Representative Plays by American Dramatists,* ed. Montrose J. Moses (New York: E. P. Dutton, 1925), 2:745.

137. Henry Clay Preuss, *Fashions and Follies of Washington Life* (Washington, DC: By the author, 1857), 16; J. Thornton Randolph [Charles Jacobs Peterson], *The Cabin and Parlor; or, Slaves and Masters* (Philadelphia: T. B. Peterson, 1852), 23; Stowe, *Christian Slave,* 66.

138. Washington Irving, *Salmagundi: or, The Whim-Whams and Opinions of Launcelot Langstaff, Esq. and Others* (1807; London: T. Davison, 1824), 280.

139. "Epitaph on a Negro," *Philadelphia Minerva,* August 5, 1797.

140. Ronald Takaki, "The Black Child-Savage in Ante-Bellum America," in *The Great Fear: Race in the Mind of America,* ed. Gary B. Nash and Richard Weiss (New York: Holt, Rinehart and Winston, 1970), 39.

141. Ronald T. Takaki, *Iron Cages: Race and Culture in Nineteenth-Century America* (New York: Alfred A. Knopf, 1979), 109–28.

142. Jordan, *White over Black,* 97.

143. Daniel Horsmanden, *The New-York Conspiracy, or a History of the Negro Plot* (1810), ed. Thomas J. Davis (Boston: Beacon, 1971), 106–7.

Chapter Three

1. Martin Robison Delany, *The Condition, Elevation, Emigration, and Destiny of the Colored People of the United States* (Philadelphia: By the author, 1852), 10, 209.

2. James Theodore Holly, *A Vindication of the Capacity of the Negro Race for Self-Government, and Civilized Progress . . .* , in *Black Separation and the Caribbean, 1860*, ed. Howard H. Bell (Ann Arbor: University of Michigan Press, 1970), 23; "The Black Beauty," *Freedom's Journal*, June 8, 1827, 52; Joseph C. Holly, "The Noble Aim," in *Freedom's Offering, A Collection of Poems* (Rochester: Charles H. McDonnell, 1853), 35; Frank J. Webb, *The Garies and Their Friends* (London: G. Routledge, 1857), 4, 9.

3. Hosea Easton, *A Treatise on the Intellectual Character, and Civil and Political Condition of the Colored People of the United States . . .* (Boston: Isaac Knapp, 1837), 12, 18.

4. James W. C. Pennington, *A Text Book of the Origin and History, &c. &c. of the Colored People* (Hartford, CT: L. Skinner, 1841), 48, 50; William Cooper Nell, *The Colored Patriots of the American Revolution* (Boston: Robert F. Wallcut, 1855), 73–75, 265–70.

5. William Wells Brown, *The Black Man: His Antecedents, His Genius, and His Achievements* (New York: Thomas Hamilton, 1863), 49.

6. Frances Ellen Watkins, "Tennessee Hero," in *Poems on Miscellaneous Subjects* (Philadelphia: Merrihew & Thompson, 1857), 33–34; "The Fugitive," in Holly, *Freedom's Offering*, 19–20; "The Fugitives," in *Star of Emancipation* (Boston: Friends of the Massachusetts Female Emancipation Society, 1841), 37.

7. Henry Highland Garnet, *An Address to the Slaves of the United States of America* (1848; New York: Arno Press and the New York Times, 1969), 95–96; James M. Whitfield, "To Cinque" (1853), in *Early Black American Poets*, ed. William H. Robinson Jr. (Dubuque: William C. Brown, 1969), 49.

8. Frederick Douglass, "The Heroic Slave" (1853), in *Violence in the Black Imagination*, ed. Ronald T. Takaki (New York: Capricorn, 1972), 40, 64, 75–77.

9. Martin R. Delany, *Blake; or, The Huts of America* (1859; Boston: Beacon, 1970), 51, 67, 76; Webb, *Garies*, 267; Elymas Payson Rogers, "On the Fugitive Slave Law" (1855), in Robinson, *Early Black American Poets*, 62.

10. "An Act for the Better Ordering and Governing Negroes and Other Slaves in This Province" (1755), in *Colonial Records of the State of Georgia*, ed. Allen D. Candler (Atlanta: Charles P. Byrd, 1910), 18:131–32.

11. Plowden C. J. Weston, "Rules on the Rice Estate of P. C. Weston" (1856), in *Plantation and Frontier Documents, 1649–1863*, ed. Ulrich B. Phillips (Cleveland: Arthur H. Clark, 1909), 1:122. On the content and character of the antebellum slave narratives, see William L. Andrews, *To Tell a Free Story: The First Century of Afro-American Autobiography, 1760–1865* (Urbana: University of Illinois Press, 1986); and Frances Smith Foster, *Witnessing Slavery: The Development of Ante-Bellum Slave Narratives* (Westport, CT: Greenwood, 1979). On the evolution of slaveholders' attitudes toward draconian punishments, see Willie Lee Rose, "The Domestication of Domestic Slavery," in *Slavery and Freedom*, ed. William W. Freehling (New York: Oxford University Press, 1982), 18–36.

12. James Henry Hammond to Thomas Clarkson, January 28, 1845, in *The Ideology of Slavery: Proslavery Thought in the Antebellum South, 1830–1860*, ed. Drew Gilpin Faust (Baton Rouge: Louisiana State University Press, 1981), 188; Thomas R. Dew, "Abolition of Negro Slavery," *American Quarterly Review* 12 (September 1832): 250.

13. Solomon Northup, *Twelve Years a Slave: Narrative of Solomon Northup* (1853), in *Puttin' on Ole Massa*, ed. Gilbert Osofsky (New York: Harper & Row, 1969), 363.

14. Ibid., 288.

15. Richard C. Wade, *Slavery in the Cities: The South 1820–1860* (New York: Oxford University Press, 1964), 182, 188.

16. Kenneth Scott, "The Slave Insurrection in New York in 1712," *New-York Historical Society Quarterly* 45 (January 1961): 57, 66–67.

17. Eugene D. Genovese, *From Rebellion to Revolution: Afro-American Slave Revolts in the Making of the Modern World* (Baton Rouge: Louisiana State University Press, 1979), 107.

18. Robert S. Starobin, "Denmark Vesey's Slave Conspiracy of 1822: A Study in Rebellion and Repression," in *American Slavery: The Question of Resistance*, ed. John H. Bracey Jr., August Meier, and Elliott Rudwick (Belmont, CA: Wadsworth, 1971), 147–48; Edwin C. Holland, *A Refutation of the Calumnies Circulated against the Southern & Western States, Respecting the Institution and Existence of Slavery among Them* (Charleston: A. E. Miller, 1822), 86.

19. John Hampden Pleasants to *Richmond Whig*, August 27, 1831, in *Nat Turner*, ed. Eric Foner (Englewood Cliffs, NJ: Prentice-Hall, 1971), 16; William Sidney Drewry, *The Southampton Insurrection* (Washington, DC: Neale, 1900), 102; Peter H. Wood, "Nat Turner: The Unknown Slave as Visionary Leader," in *Black Leaders of the Nineteenth Century*, ed. Leon Litwack and August Meier (Urbana: University of Illinois Press, 1988), 31–33; Harriet A. Jacobs, *Incidents in the Life of a Slave Girl* (1861; Cambridge: Harvard University Press, 1987), 64.

20. Mia Bay, *The White Image in the Black Mind: African-American Ideas about White People, 1830–1925* (New York: Oxford University Press, 2000), 5–7, 162, 165.

21. David Walker, *Walker's Appeal in Four Articles* (1829; New York: Arno Press and the New York Times, 1969), 35–36, 71–73. On the Africans' belief in white cannibalism, see William D. Piersen, "White Cannibals, Black Martyrs: Fear, Depression, and Religious Faith as Causes of Suicide among New Slaves," *Journal of Negro History* 62 (April 1977): 147–59; Alan Rice, "'Who's Eating Whom': The Discourse of Cannibalism in the Literature of the Black Atlantic from Equiano's Travels to Toni Morrison's *Beloved*," *Research in African Literatures* 29 (Winter 1998): 106–21.

22. Henry Highland Garnet, "The Past and Present Condition and the Destiny of the Colored Race, Troy, 1848," in Earl Ofari, *"Let Your Motto Be Resistance": The Life and Thought of Henry Highland Garnet* (Boston: Beacon, 1972), 166; Easton, *Treatise*, 19; Brown, *Black Man*, 34.

23. William Wells Brown, *Clotel; or, The President's Daughter: A Narrative of Slave Life in the United States* (1853; New York: Collier, 1970), 69–74; Delany, *Blake*, 26; Henry Bibb, *Narrative of the Life and Adventures of Henry Bibb, an American Slave* (1849), in Osofsky, *Ole Massa*, 118–19; William Wells Brown, *The Escape; or, A Leap for Freedom* (1858; New York: Prologue, 1969), 15, 19, 23.

24. Delany, *Blake*, 16, 18, 20, 41.

25. Ibid., 17, 20–21, 38, 43, 83, 101.

26. Ibid., 16.

27. Frederick Douglass, *My Bondage and My Freedom* (1855; Urbana: University of Illinois Press, 1987), 60–61.

28. On the universality of the social bandit tradition, see Eric Hobsbawm, *Bandits* (New York: Delacorte, 1969).

29. On the geographic distribution and size of the black masters' holdings, see Michael P. Johnson and James L. Roark, "Strategies of Survival: Free Negro Families and the Problem of Slavery," in *In Joy and in Sorrow: Women, Family, and Marriage in the Victorian South, 1830–1900,* ed. Carol Bleser (New York: Oxford University Press, 1991), 95–98; and Loren Schweninger, *Black Property Owners in the South, 1790–1915* (Urbana: University of Illinois Press, 1990), 104–5, 111.

30. David O. Whitten, *Andrew Durnford: A Black Sugar Planter in Antebellum Louisiana* (Natchitoches, LA: Northwestern State University Press, 1981), 34, 64, 121. On the fraternal and protective aspects of black slave ownership, see Philip J. Schwarz, "Emancipators, Protectors, and Anomalies: Free Black Slaveowners in Virginia," *Virginia Magazine of History and Biography* 95 (July 1987): 317–38.

31. Delany, *Blake,* 116.

32. Edwin Adams Davis and William Ransom Hogan, *The Barber of Natchez* (Baton Rouge: Louisiana State University Press, 1954), 57; *William Johnson's Natchez: The Antebellum Diary of a Free Negro,* ed. William Ransom Hogan and Edwin Adams Davis (Baton Rouge: Louisiana State University Press, 1951), 259, 764. On Charleston's African American benevolent societies, see Robert L. Harris Jr., "Charleston's Free Afro-American Elite: The Brown Fellowship Society and the Humane Brotherhood," *South Carolina Historical Magazine* 82 (October 1981): 289–310; and Michael P. Johnson and James L. Roark, "'A Middle Ground': Free Mulattoes and the Friendly Moralist Society of Antebellum Charleston," *Southern Studies* 21 (Fall 1982): 246–65.

33. *The American Slave: A Composite Autobiography. Alabama and Indiana Narratives,* ed. George P. Rawick (Westport, CT: Greenwood, 1972), 6:135.

34. Larry Koger, *Black Slaveowners: Free Black Slave Masters in South Carolina, 1790–1860* (Jefferson, NC: McFarland, 1985), 113–18.

35. Michael P. Johnson and James L. Roark, *Black Masters: A Free Family of Color in the Old South* (New York: W. W. Norton, 1984), 306–7; Gary B. Mills, *The Forgotten People: Cane River's Creoles of Color* (Baton Rouge: Louisiana State University Press, 1977), 230.

36. Koger, *Black Slaveowners,* 87; Hogan and Davis, *William Johnson's Natchez,* 224.

37. Rawick, *American Slave. Texas Narratives,* 5: part 4, 156.

38. Frederick Law Olmsted, *The Cotton Kingdom: A Traveller's Observations on Cotton and Slavery in the American Slave States,* ed. Arthur M. Schlesinger (1861; New York: Modern Library, 1969), 262.

39. On the duties and rewards of the driver post, see James M. Clifton, "The Rice Driver: His Role in Slave Management," *South Carolina Historical Magazine* 82 (October 1981): 331–53. For examples of drivers who served as helpmeets to their fellow bondsmen, see William L. Van Deburg, *The Slave Drivers: Black Agricultural Labor Supervisors in the Antebellum South* (1979; New York: Oxford University Press, 1988), 51–58, 86–87.

40. See Eugene D. Genovese, *Roll, Jordan, Roll: The World the Slaves Made* (New York: Pantheon, 1974), 365–88; Randall M. Miller, "The Man in the Middle: The Black Slave Driver," *American Heritage* 30 (October/November 1979): 40–49.

41. Robert Collins, "Essay on the Management of Slaves," *Southern Cultivator* 12 (July

1854): 206; J. G. Clinkscales, *On the Old Plantation: Reminiscences of his Childhood* (Spartanburg, SC: Band & White, 1916), 7.

42. Rawick, *American Slave. Texas Narratives*, 5: part 3, 76; Frances Anne Kemble, *Journal of a Residence on a Georgian Plantation in 1838–1839* (1863; New York: Alfred A. Knopf, 1961), 270; Rawick, *American Slave. North Carolina Narratives*, 14: part 1, 14; Rawick, *American Slave. Alabama and Indiana Narratives*, 6:52, 66.

43. Rawick, *American Slave. Texas Narratives*, 4: part 2, 164; part 1, 205; Rawick, *American Slave. Alabama and Indiana Narratives*, 6:416; Lyle Saxon, Edward Dreyer, and Robert Tallant, *Gumbo Ya-Ya: A Collection of Louisiana Folk Tales* (Boston: Houghton Mifflin, 1945), 240; Lewis Clarke and Milton Clarke, *Narrative of the Sufferings of Lewis and Milton Clarke . . .* (Boston: Bela Marsh, 1846), 27.

44. Rawick, *American Slave. South Carolina Narratives*, 2: part 2, 49.

45. Rawick, *American Slave. Texas Narratives*, 4: part 2, 43; Moses Grandy, *Narrative of the Life of Moses Grandy, Late a Slave in the United States of America* (Boston: Oliver Johnson, 1844), 17.

46. Clarke and Clarke, *Narrative*, 122; Rawick, *American Slave. North Carolina Narratives*, 14: part 1, 14; Rawick, *American Slave. South Carolina Narratives*, 3: part 3, 49; Rawick, *American Slave. Georgia Narratives*, 12: part 2, 51; M. F. Jamison, *Autobiography and Work of Bishop M. F. Jamison, D.D.* (Nashville: M. E. Church, South, 1912), 25–27; William Grimes, *Life of William Grimes, the Runaway Slave, Brought Down to the Present Time* (1855), in *Five Black Lives*, ed. Arna Bontemps (Middletown, CT: Wesleyan University Press, 1971), 65–67, 70; Rawick, *American Slave. Alabama and Indiana Narratives*, 6:66.

47. "Hail, Mary," in *Slave Songs of the United States*, ed. William Francis Allen, Charles Pickard Ware, and Lucy McKim Garrison (New York: A. Simpson, 1867), 45.

48. Orland Kay Armstrong, *Old Massa's People: The Old Slaves Tell Their Story* (Indianapolis: Bobbs-Merrill, 1931), 218; A. Franklin Pugh Diary, May 28, 1853 entry, Pugh Family Papers, Barker Texas History Center, University of Texas, Austin; Robert Nesbit to Robert F. W. Allston, December 26, 1837, in *The South Carolina Rice Plantation as Revealed in the Papers of Robert F. W. Allston*, ed. J. H. Easterby (Chicago: University of Chicago Press, 1945), 76; Leslie Howard Owens, *This Species of Property: Slave Life and Culture in the Old South* (New York: Oxford University Press, 1976), 122–23.

49. Clarke and Clarke, *Narrative*, 119.

50. Rawick, *American Slave. South Carolina Narratives*, 2: part 1, 15.

51. Genovese, *Roll, Jordan, Roll*, 606–8, 631; Genovese, *Rebellion to Revolution*, 77–78.

52. Jacob Stroyer, *My Life in the South* (Salem, MA: Newcomb & Gauss, 1898), 58–59.

53. James Oliver Horton, *Free People of Color: Inside the African American Community* (Washington, DC: Smithsonian Institution Press, 1993), 64–65.

54. Austin Steward, *Twenty-two Years a Slave, and Forty Years a Freeman* (1857; Reading, MA: Addison-Wesley, 1969), 21–22; H. C. Bruce, *The New Man: Twenty-nine Years a Slave, Twenty-nine Years a Free Man* (York, PA: P. Anstadt & Sons, 1895), iv. On collaborationists' fear of retaliation by conjurers, see William D. Piersen, *Black Yankees: The Development of an Afro-American Subculture in Eighteenth-Century New England* (Amherst: University of Massachusetts Press, 1988), 83; Michael A. Gomez, *Exchanging Our Country Marks: The Transformation of African Identities in the Colonial and Antebellum South* (Chapel Hill: University of North Carolina Press, 1998), 2.

55. Northup, *Twelve Years a Slave*, 362–63; Herbert Aptheker, *American Negro Slave Revolts* (1943; New York: International, 1968), 257–58; Douglas R. Egerton, *Gabriel's Rebellion: The Virginia Slave Conspiracies of 1800 and 1802* (Chapel Hill: University of North Carolina Press, 1993), 139–40, 148–49, 173–74.

56. Delany, *Blake*, 28.

57. Rawick, *American Slave. Arkansas Narratives*, 8: part 1, 36.

58. George W. Williams, *History of the Negro Race in America from 1619 to 1880* (New York: G. P. Putnam's Sons, 1883), 1:115, 296, 323; 2:36.

59. Charles W. Chesnutt, *The Colonel's Dream* (New York: Doubleday, Page, 1905), 193; Frances E. W. Harper, *Iola Leroy, or Shadows Uplifted* (1892; New York: Oxford University Press, 1988), 216; Calvin C. Hernton, "Jitterbugging in the Streets," in *Black Fire*, ed. LeRoi Jones and Larry Neal (New York: William Morrow, 1968), 207.

60. Modern historical treatments of these developments include Eric Foner, *Reconstruction: America's Unfinished Revolution, 1863–1877* (New York: Harper & Row, 1988); William Cohen, *At Freedom's Edge: Black Mobility and the Southern White Quest for Racial Control, 1861–1915* (Baton Rouge: Louisiana State University Press, 1991); George C. Rable, *But There Was No Peace: The Role of Violence in the Politics of Reconstruction* (Athens: University of Georgia Press, 1984); Allen W. Trelease, *White Terror: The Ku Klux Klan Conspiracy and Southern Reconstruction* (New York: Harper & Row, 1971); William Gillette, *Retreat from Reconstruction, 1869–1879* (Baton Rouge: Louisiana State University Press, 1979); and Leon F. Litwack, *Trouble in Mind: Black Southerners in the Age of Jim Crow* (New York: Alfred A. Knopf, 1998).

61. Albert C. Smith, "'Southern Violence' Reconsidered: Arson as Protest in Black-Belt Georgia, 1865–1910," *Journal of Southern History* 51 (November 1985): 527.

62. See, for example, James Allen, *Without Sanctuary: Lynching Photography in America* (Santa Fe: Twin Palms, 2000); David Margolick, *Strange Fruit: Billie Holiday, Café Society, and an Early Cry for Civil Rights* (Philadelphia: Running Press, 2000); Sandra Gunning, *Race, Rape, and Lynching: The Red Record of American Literature, 1890–1912* (New York: Oxford University Press, 1996); Jerry H. Bryant, *Victims and Heroes: Racial Violence in the African American Novel* (Amherst: University of Massachusetts Press, 1997); and Judith L. Stephens, "Anti-Lynch Plays by African American Women: Race, Gender, and Social Protest in American Drama," *African American Review* 26 (Summer 1992): 329–39.

63. Walter White, *Rope & Faggot: A Biography of Judge Lynch* (New York: Alfred A. Knopf, 1929), 17; James Weldon Johnson, *Along This Way* (1933; New York: Viking, 1969), 318, 361.

64. Frederick Douglass, *The Lesson of the Hour* (1894), in *The Life and Writings of Frederick Douglass*, ed. Philip S. Foner (New York: International, 1955), 4:492.

65. W. Fitzhugh Brundage, *Lynching in the New South: Georgia and Virginia, 1880–1930* (Urbana: University of Illinois Press, 1993), 8; Herbert Shapiro, *White Violence and Black Response: From Reconstruction to Montgomery* (Amherst: University of Massachusetts Press, 1988), 31, 477; Stewart E. Tolnay and E. M. Beck, *A Festival of Violence: An Analysis of Southern Lynchings, 1882–1930* (Urbana: University of Illinois Press, 1995), 4, 33, 36.

66. White, *Rope & Faggot*, viii; W. E. B. Du Bois, "Murder," *Crisis* 32 (July 1926): 112; W. E. B. Du Bois, "Mob Tactics," *Crisis* 34 (August 1927): 204.

67. Douglass, *Lesson*, 491; Ida B. Wells-Barnett, *Mob Rule in New Orleans* (1900), in *On Lynchings* (New York: Arno Press and the New York Times, 1969), 48; White, *Rope & Faggot*,

3–5, 152, 168; Wells-Barnett, *A Red Record* (1895), in *On Lynchings*, 98; Wells-Barnett, *Southern Horrors* (1892), in *On Lynchings*, 1.

68. Trudier Harris, *Exorcising Blackness: Historical and Literary Lynching and Burning Rituals* (Bloomington: Indiana University Press, 1984), 195.

69. Clayton Adams [Charles Henry Holmes], *Ethiopia: The Land of Promise* (New York: Cosmopolitan, 1917), 5, 78; Sutton E. Griggs, *The Hindered Hand: or, The Reign of the Repressionist* (Nashville: Orion, 1905), 299.

70. James Weldon Johnson, *The Autobiography of an Ex-Colored Man* (1912; New York: Penguin, 1990), 136; Walter F. White, *The Fire in the Flint* (New York: Alfred A. Knopf, 1924), 205, 226; Adams, *Ethiopia*, 124; Richard Wright, *Uncle Tom's Children* (1938; New York: Harper & Row, 1965), 48; J. McHenry Jones, *Hearts of Gold* (1896; College Park, MD: McGrath, 1969), 226–27.

71. Jean Toomer, *Cane* (1923; New York: Harper & Row, 1969), 171–72.

72. Jones, *Hearts of Gold*, 224–25, 227; SANDA [Walter H. Stowers and William H. Anderson], *Appointed: An American Novel* (Detroit: Detroit Law Printing, 1894), 352–53; Angelina Weld Grimké, *Rachel* (1916), in *Strange Fruit: Plays on Lynching by American Women*, ed. Kathy A. Perkins and Judith L. Stephens (Bloomington: Indiana University Press, 1998), 40; Regina M. Anderson Andrews, *Climbing Jacob's Ladder: A Tragedy of Negro Life* (1931), in ibid., 131; May Miller, *Nails and Thorns* (1933), in ibid., 180.

73. W. E. Burghardt Du Bois, *Darkwater: Voices from within the Veil* (New York: Harcourt, Brace and Howe, 1920), 25; Pauline E. Hopkins, *Contending Forces: A Romance Illustrative of Negro Life North and South* (1900; New York: Oxford University Press, 1988), 256; Langston Hughes, *Not without Laughter* (1930; New York: Collier, 1969), 72; Jones, *Hearts of Gold*, 222; SANDA, *Appointed*, 327; Langston Hughes, *The Ways of White Folks* (New York: Alfred A Knopf, 1934), 46; George W. Lee, *River George* (New York: Macaulay, 1937), 112.

74. Chesnutt, *Colonel's Dream*, 194.

75. Griggs, *Hindered Hand*, 136.

76. Harper, *Iola Leroy*, 217.

77. Toomer, *Cane*, 179; Waters Edward Turpin, *These Low Grounds* (New York: Harper & Brothers, 1937), 332; Harper, *Iola Leroy*, 218, 259; SANDA, *Appointed*, 355; Johnson, *Autobiography*, 138.

78. SANDA, *Appointed*, 349, 358; Adams, *Ethiopia*, 77; Turpin, *Low Grounds*, 334–35.

79. Claude McKay, "The Lynching," in *Harlem Shadows* (New York: Harcourt Brace, 1922), 51; Grimké, *Rachel*, 41; Harper, *Iola Leroy*, 255, 260; Robert L. Waring, *As We See It* (1910; College Park, MD: McGrath, 1969), 124.

80. Chesnutt, *Colonel's Dream*, 164, 283; Sarah Lee Brown Fleming, *Hope's Highway* (New York: Neale, 1918), 43; Waring, *As We See It*, 108; Hughes, *Not without Laughter*, 70, 73, 75.

81. W. E. B. Du Bois, "The Song of the Smoke," *Horizon* 1 (February 1907), 5.

82. Harper, *Iola Leroy*, 173.

83. W. E. Burghardt Du Bois, *The Gift of Black Folk: The Negroes in the Making of America* (1924; New York: Washington Square, 1970), 158, 178; W. E. Burghardt Du Bois, *Dusk of Dawn: An Essay toward an Autobiography of a Race Concept* (1940; New York: Schocken, 1968), 147–48, 150–51; W. E. Burghardt Du Bois, *The Souls of Black Folk* (1903; Boston: Bedford, 1997), 43.

84. W. E. Burghardt Du Bois, "Criteria of Negro Art," *Crisis* 32 (October 1926): 292; W. E. Burghardt Du Bois, *The World and Africa: An Inquiry into the Part which Africa Has Played in World History* (1947; New York: International, 1965), 23–24; W. E. B. Du Bois, "Jefferson Davis as a Representative of Civilization" (1890), in *Writings*, ed. Nathan I. Huggins (New York: Library of America, 1986), 811–13.

85. W. E. B. Du Bois, "The Shadow of Years," *Crisis* 15 (February 1918): 160; Du Bois, *Dusk of Dawn*, 153; W. E. B. Du Bois, "The Conservation of Races" (1897), in *Writings*, 822; Du Bois, *Souls of Black Folk*, 39.

86. W. E. B. Du Bois, *Dark Princess* (1928; Jackson: University Press of Mississippi, 1995), 78.

87. Elijah Muhammad, *Message to the Blackman in America* (Chicago: Muhammad's Temple No. 2, 1965), 223; Elijah Muhammad, "What Do the Muslims Want?" (1962), in *Black Nationalism in America*, ed. John H. Bracey Jr., August Meier, and Elliott Rudwick (Indianapolis: Bobbs-Merrill, 1970), 404; Morroe Berger, "The Black Muslims," *Horizon* 6 (Winter 1964): 58; E. U. Essien-Udom, *Black Nationalism: A Search for an Identity in America* (Chicago: University of Chicago Press, 1962), 130, 263.

88. Muhammad, *Message*, 53, 304; C. Eric Lincoln, *The Black Muslims in America* (Boston: Beacon, 1961), 73, 77; Claude Andrew Clegg III, *An Original Man: The Life and Times of Elijah Muhammad* (New York: St. Martin's, 1997), 64–67.

89. Essien-Udom, *Black Nationalism*, 140; Muhammad, *Message*, 64, 104–6; Elijah Muhammad, *The Fall of America* (Chicago: Muhammad's Temple of Islam No. 2, 1973), 28, 89.

90. Muhammad, *Fall of America*, 90.

91. Elijah Muhammad, *How to Eat to Live, Book One* (Atlanta: Messenger Elijah Muhammad Propagation Society, 1967), 9, 61; Elijah Muhammad, *How to Eat to Live, Book No. 2* (Atlanta: Messenger Elijah Muhammad Propagation Society, 1972), 7, 10, 15, 17, 65, 78, 82, 96, 115, 133, 142.

92. Muhammad, *How to Eat to Live, Book One*, 107–8, 114–15; Muhammad, *How to Eat to Live, Book No. 2*, 15, 59, 86, 147, 189–90.

93. N. Xavier Arnold, *The Genocide Files* (Marlow Heights, MD: Tana Lake, 1997), 69, 114–23; Michael Bradley, *The Iceman Inheritance: Prehistoric Sources of Western Man's Racism, Sexism and Aggression* (1978; New York: Kayode, 1991), 26–28.

94. Frances Cress Welsing interview, in *First Word: Black Scholars, Thinkers, Warriors*, ed. Kwaku Person-Lynn (New York: Harlem River, 1996), 81–82; Frances Cress Welsing, *The Isis (Yssis) Papers* (Chicago: Third World, 1991), ii–v, 4–5, 9–10, 33; Bernard R. Ortiz de Montellano, "Melanin, Afrocentricity, and Pseudoscience," *Yearbook of Physical Anthropology* 36 (1993): 37–54; "Skin Deep 101," *Time*, February 14, 1994, 16.

95. Quoted in Brian Hecht, "Dr. Uncool J," *New Republic*, March 2, 1992, 11–12.

96. Tony Brown, *Empower the People: A 7-Step Plan to Overthrow the Conspiracy That Is Stealing Your Money and Freedom* (New York: William Morrow, 1998), xv, 13.

97. Leonard Jeffries Jr. interview, in Person-Lynn, *First Word*, 242; Historical Research Department, Nation of Islam, *The Secret Relationship between Blacks and Jews* (Chicago: Nation of Islam, 1991), 1: vii, 17, 89–91, 121–22.

98. Louis Farrakhan, *The Announcement: A Final Warning to the U.S. Government* (Chicago: Final Call, 1989), 10; Tony Brown, *Black Lies, White Lies: The Truth according to*

Tony Brown (New York: William Morrow, 1995), 119; James Traub, "The Hearts and Minds of City College," *New Yorker,* June 7, 1993, 45–46.

99. Del Jones, *Black Holocaust: Global Genocide* (Philadelphia: Hikeka, 1992), 14, 28; Brown, *Black Lies,* 94.

100. Shapiro, *White Violence,* 421; William L. Patterson, ed., *We Charge Genocide: The Historic Petition to the United Nations for Relief from a Crime of the United States Government against the Negro People* (1951; New York: International, 1970), 3, 6, 8, 10, 12, 15, 19.

101. Malcolm X, *Malcolm X Speaks,* ed. George Breitman (1965; New York: Grove, 1966), 165; C. T. Vivian, *Black Power and the American Myth* (Philadelphia: Fortress, 1970), 132; Nathan Wright, "Black Power vs. Black Genocide," *Black Scholar* 1 (December 1969): 50–51.

102. Black Panther Party, "Call for Revolutionary People's Constitutional Convention, September 7, 1970, Philadelphia, PA," in *The Black Panthers Speak,* ed. Philip S. Foner (Philadelphia: J. B. Lippincott, 1970), 267–68; Huey P. Newton, *To Die for the People* (New York: Vintage, 1972), 14; Bobby Seale, *Seize the Time: The Story of the Black Panther Party and Huey P. Newton* (New York: Random House, 1970), 305–6; Stokely Carmichael, *Stokely Speaks: Black Power Back to Pan-Africanism* (New York: Vintage, 1971), 112, 117, 218.

103. Newton, *To Die,* 15–16, 20; *Eldridge Cleaver: Post-Prison Writings and Speeches,* ed. Robert Scheer (1968; New York: Random House, 1969), 175; Black Panther Party, "Call," 271.

104. Joseph A. Walker, *Ododo* (1968), in *Black Drama Anthology,* ed. Woodie King and Ron Milner (New York: New American Library, 1971), 383; Ted Joans, "The White Ban," in *Black Pow-Wow* (New York: Hill and Wang, 1969), 67.

105. Floyd McKissick, "Diary of a Black Man." in *Three-Fifths of a Man* (New York: Macmillan, 1969), 160–63.

106. Ben Caldwell, *Top Secret, or A Few Million after B.C., Drama Review* 12 (Summer 1968): 47–50.

107. John A. Williams, *The Man Who Cried I Am* (Boston: Little, Brown, 1967), 371–76; Mari Evans, "The Third Stop in Caraway Park," *Black World* 22 (March 1975): 54–62; Julia Wright Hervé, "The Forget-for-Peace-Program," *Black World* 22 (May 1973): 57–64; Raymond Washington, "Moon Bound," in *New Black Voices,* ed. Abraham Chapman (New York: New American Library, 1972), 389–90.

108. LeRoi Jones, "The Black Man Is Making New Gods," in *Black Magic: Collected Poetry, 1961–1967* (Indianapolis: Bobbs-Merrill, 1969), 206; Joseph Bevans Bush, "Nitty-gritty," in *We Speak as Liberators: Young Black Poets,* ed. Orde Coombs (New York: Dodd, Mead, 1970), 5; Julian Moreau [J. Denis Jackson], *The Black Commandos* (Atlanta: Cultural Institute Press, 1967), 185.

109. Michael Billig, "Anti-Semitic Themes and the British Far Left: Some Social-Psychological Observations on Indirect Aspects of the Conspiracy Tradition," in *Changing Conceptions of Conspiracy,* ed. Carl F. Graumann and Serge Moscovici (New York: Springer-Verlag, 1987), 132.

110. Jones, *Black Holocaust,* 8.

111. On the night doctor tradition in the South, see Gladys-Marie Fry, *Night Riders in Black Folk History* (Knoxville: University of Tennessee Press, 1975), 170–211.

112. James H. Jones, *Bad Blood: The Tuskegee Syphilis Experiment* (New York: Free Press, 1981), 216–17.

113. Jones, *Black Holocaust*, 92–101.

114. Robert G. Weisbord, *Genocide? Birth Control and the Black American* (Westport, CT: Greenwood, 1975), 82–84, 130–32; Angela Y. Davis, *Women, Race & Class* (1981; New York: Vintage, 1983), 202–21; Dorothy Roberts, *Killing the Black Body: Race, Reproduction, and the Meaning of Liberty* (New York: Pantheon, 1997), 89–103.

115. Cathy J. Cohen, *The Boundaries of Blackness: AIDS and the Breakdown of Black Politics* (Chicago: University of Chicago Press, 1999), 21–23, 25–26.

116. Marimba Ani [Dona Richards], *Yurugu: An African-centered Critique of European Cultural Thought and Behavior* (Trenton: Africa World, 1994), 437–44; Patricia A. Turner, *I Heard It through the Grapevine: Rumor in African-American Culture* (Berkeley: University of California Press, 1993), 151–63; Karen Grigsby Bates, "Is It Genocide?" *Essence* 21 (September 1990): 78; Daniel Pipes, *Conspiracy: How the Paranoid Style Flourishes and Where It Comes From* (New York: Free Press, 1997), 3; Boyd E. Graves, *State Origin: The Evidence of the Laboratory Birth of AIDS*, http://sun-city.net/stateorigin/home.html (accessed January 24, 2003).

117. Brown, *Black Lies*, 176; David France, "Challenging the Conventional Stance on AIDS," *New York Times*, December 22, 1998; Clarence Page, "Deathly Silence," *New Republic*, December 2, 1991, 17; Mattias Gardell, *In the Name of Elijah Muhammad: Louis Farrakhan and the Nation of Islam* (Durham, NC: Duke University Press, 1996), 327.

118. Ishmael Reed, *The Terrible Twos* (New York: St. Martin's/Marek, 1982), 53–58.

119. David France, "Groups Debate Role of Milk in Building a Better Pyramid," *New York Times*, June 29, 1999.

120. Turner, *Through the Grapevine*, 82–83, 101, 139, 171, 227; Gary Alan Fine and Patricia A. Turner, *Whispers on the Color Line: Rumor and Race in America* (Berkeley: University of California Press, 2001), 84–97.

121. Gregory L. Vistica and Vern E. Smith, "Was the CIA Involved in the Crack Epidemic?" *Newsweek*, September 30, 1996, 72.

122. Quoted in Gardell, *In the Name of Elijah Muhammad*, 301.

123. Clarence Page, "Congress Should Probe CIA on Alleged Link to Drugs, Gangs," *Capital Times* (Madison, WI), September 30, 1996.

124. Gary Webb, *Dark Alliance: The CIA, the Contras, and the Crack Cocaine Explosion* (New York: Seven Stories, 1998), 438.

125. Ishmael Reed, "The Word on the Vine: Ghetto Paranoia about a Drug Conspiracy May Have a Basis in Fact," *Washington Post*, September 15, 1996.

126. Jawanza Kunjufu, *Countering the Conspiracy to Destroy Black Boys* (Chicago: Afro-Am Publishing, 1984), vii–ix; Mark P. Fancher, *Genocide with a Smile: The Campaign to Destroy Africans Born in America* (Ann Arbor, MI: JurisAfricana, 1997), 1, 65–82.

127. Robert D. Bullard, *Dumping in Dixie: Race, Class, and Environmental Quality* (Boulder, CO: Westview, 1994), 26–36; Charles Lee, "Beyond Toxic Wastes and Race," in *Confronting Environmental Racism: Voices from the Grassroots*, ed. Robert D. Bullard (Boston: South End, 1993), 41–52.

128. Karl Evanzz, *The Judas Factor: The Plot to Kill Malcolm X* (New York: Thunder's Mouth, 1992); Mark Lane and Dick Gregory, *Code Name "Zorro": The Murder of Martin Luther King, Jr.* (Englewood Cliffs, NJ: Prentice-Hall, 1977).

129. Paul Ruffins, "The Tuskegee Experiment's Long Shadow," *Black Issues in Higher Education*, October 29, 1998, 26; Jones, *Black Holocaust*, 59.

130. Chris Albertson, *Bessie* (1972; New York: Stein and Day, 1985), 215–26; Spencie Love, *One Blood: The Death and Resurrection of Charles R. Drew* (Chapel Hill: University of North Carolina Press, 1996), 32, 47–48, 261–62.

131. Jones, *Black Holocaust*, 58–69.

132. Jonathan Vankin and John Whalen, *The Seventy Greatest Conspiracies of All Time: History's Biggest Mysteries, Coverups, and Cabals* (New York: Citadel, 1998), 392–98.

133. Paul Shepard, "Census Race ID Shift: Less Representation?" *Capital Times* (Madison, WI), February 19–20, 2000; Jill Nelson, "Mixed Thoughts on Census Race Question," *USA Today*, February 18, 2000.

134. William Still, *The Underground Rail Road* (Philadelphia: Porter & Coates, 1872), 51, 103, 202, 206.

135. Pauline Elizabeth Hopkins, *Peculiar Sam; or, The Underground Railroad* (1879), in *The Roots of African American Drama: An Anthology of Early Plays, 1858–1938*, ed. Leo Hamalian and James V. Hatch (Detroit: Wayne State University Press, 1991), 118.

136. On the animal trickster tales, see John W. Roberts, *From Trickster to Badman: The Black Folk Hero in Slavery and Freedom* (Philadelphia: University of Pennsylvania Press, 1989), 17–48; and Lawrence W. Levine, *Black Culture and Black Consciousness: Afro-American Folk Thought from Slavery to Freedom* (New York: Oxford University Press, 1977), 102–21. On the West African tales, see Robert D. Pelton, *The Trickster in West Africa: A Study of Mythic Irony and Sacred Delight* (Berkeley: University of California Press, 1980).

137. Paul Laurence Dunbar, "We Wear the Mask," in *The Complete Poems of Paul Laurence Dunbar* (New York: Dodd, Mead, 1913), 71.

138. Ralph Ellison, *Shadow and Act* (New York: Random House, 1964), 55.

139. Bruce Jackson, *"Get Your Ass in the Water and Swim Like Me": Narrative Poetry from Black Oral Tradition* (Cambridge: Harvard University Press, 1974), 191–95.

140. Daryl Cumber Dance, *Shuckin' and Jivin': Folklore from Contemporary Black Americans* (Bloomington: Indiana University Press, 1978), 229–32; Mlanjeni Nduma, "The Legend of Dolemite," in *Talk that Talk: An Anthology of African-American Storytelling*, ed. Linda Goss and Marian E. Barnes (New York: Simon and Schuster/Touchstone, 1989), 451–55.

141. Jackson, *Narrative Poetry*, 168; Oscar Brown Jr., "Signifyin' Monkey," in Goss and Barnes, *Talk that Talk*, 457.

142. Frank Richard Prassel, *The Great American Outlaw: A Legacy of Fact and Fiction* (Norman: University of Oklahoma Press, 1993), 110, 114–15, 164–66, 326–29.

143. William Loren Katz, *The Black West* (Seattle: Open Hand, 1987), 155; Arthur T. Burton, *Black, Red and Deadly: Black and Indian Gunfighters of the Indian Territory, 1870–1907* (Austin: Eakin, 1991), 40–61, 77–79.

144. Billy Jaynes Chandler, "Harmon Murray: Black Desperado in Late Nineteenth-Century Florida," *Florida Historical Quarterly* 73 (October 1994): 193–97.

145. Burton, *Black, Red and Deadly*, 113; Philip Durham and Everett L. Jones, *The Negro Cowboys* (1965; Lincoln: University of Nebraska Press, 1983), 179–88.

146. Katz, *Black West*, 320.

147. Levine, *Black Culture*, 407–20.

148. For exposition of the Stagolee legend, see Cecil Brown, *Stagolee Shot Billy* (Cambridge: Harvard University Press, 2003); Roger D. Abrahams, *Deep Down in the Jungle: Negro Narrative Folklore from the Streets of Philadelphia* (Chicago: Aldine, 1970), 75–79, 129–42; and Julius Lester, *Black Folklore* (New York: Richard W. Baron, 1969), 113–35. For Railroad Bill's exploits, see Paul Oliver, "Railroad Bill," *Jazz and Blues* 1 (May 1971): 12–14; and Norm Cohen, *Long Steel Rail: The Railroad in American Folksong* (Urbana: University of Illinois Press, 1981), 122–28. On Devil Winston, see Mary Wheeler, *Steamboatin' Days: Folk Songs of the River Packet Era* (Baton Rouge: Louisiana State University Press, 1944), 106–9.

149. William Labov, Paul Cohen, Clarence Robins, and John Lewis, "Toasts," in *Mother Wit from the Laughing Barrel: Readings in the Interpretation of Afro-American Folklore*, ed. Alan Dundes (Englewood Cliffs, NJ: Prentice-Hall, 1973), 345; "Brother Bill," in *American Negro Folktales*, ed. Richard M. Dorson (Greenwich, CT: Fawcett, 1967), 356.

150. Dennis Wepman, Ronald B. Newman, and Murray B. Binderman, *The Life: The Lore and Folk Poetry of the Black Hustler* (Philadelphia: University of Pennsylvania Press, 1976), 36.

151. Jackson, *Narrative Poetry*, 207.

152. Olympics, "Big Boy Pete" (Arvee 595, 1960); Wepman, Newman, and Binderman, *Life*, 61–71.

153. Wepman, Newman, and Binderman, *Life*, 96, 155, 159, 162; Abrahams, *Deep Down*, 163.

154. Thomas Kochman, *Black and White Styles in Conflict* (Chicago: University of Chicago Press, 1981), 29–30; Geneva Smitherman, *Talkin and Testifyin: The Language of Black America* (Boston: Houghton Mifflin, 1977), 79–85; Edith A. Folb, *Runnin' Down Some Lines: The Language and Culture of Black Teenagers* (Cambridge: Harvard University Press, 1980), 90–91.

155. *Intruder in the Dust* (Metro-Goldwyn-Mayer, 1949); *No Way Out* (20th Century Fox, 1950). Casts, credits, and plot summaries for many of the films may be found in James Robert Parish and George H. Hill, *Black Action Films* (Jefferson, NC: McFarland, 1989). For entertaining, somewhat more impressionistic treatments of the genre, see Darius James, *That's Blaxploitation!* (New York: St. Martins, 1995); and Gerald Martinez, Diana Martinez, and Andres Chavez, *What It Is . . . What It Was!: The Black Film Explosion of the '70s in Words and Pictures* (New York: Hyperion, 1998).

156. Melvin Van Peebles quoted in James Murray, *To Find an Image: Black Films from Uncle Tom to Super Fly* (Indianapolis: Bobbs-Merrill, 1973), 165.

157. *A Fistful of Dollars* (Metro-Goldwyn-Mayer, 1964); *Dirty Harry* (Warner Brothers, 1971); *Death Wish* (Paramount, 1974).

158. For Peters's early contributions to the development of black male portraiture, see *Carmen Jones* (20th Century Fox, 1954), *Porgy and Bess* (Columbia, 1959), *To Kill a Mockingbird* (Universal-International, 1962), and *The Pawnbroker* (Landau-Unger, 1965); for Kotto's, see *Nothing but a Man* (Du Art, 1964); and *The Liberation of L. B. Jones* (Columbia, 1970); for Brown's, see *The Dirty Dozen* (Metro-Goldwyn-Mayer, 1967), *Dark of the Sun* (Metro-Goldwyn-Mayer, 1968), and *100 Rifles* (20th Century Fox, 1969).

159. Pauline Kael, "Notes on Black Movies," *New Yorker,* December 2, 1972, 162–63; Doris Black, "Hollywood's New King of Ego," *Sepia* 22 (August 1973): 42.

160. Melvin Van Peebles, *The Making of "Sweet Sweetback's Baadasssss Song"* (New York:

Lancer, 1972), 13; "Sweet Song of Success," *Newsweek*, June 21, 1971, 89. Such cinematic depictions of violence as a cleansing and empowering force leading to black self-actualization
owed a great deal to psychiatrist Frantz Fanon's *The Wretched of the Earth* (New York: Grove,
1968).

161. *The Black Godfather* (Cinemation, 1974).

162. *Trick Baby* (Universal, 1973).

163. *The Mack* (Cinerama, 1973); *Black Caesar* (American International, 1973).

164. *Black Caesar*.

165. *Cool Breeze* (Metro-Goldwyn-Mayer, 1972); *The Mack*.

166. *Slaughter* (American International, 1972).

167. *A Rage in Harlem* (Miramax, 1991); *Hoodlum* (United Artists, 1997); *I'm Gonna Git
You Sucka* (United Artists, 1988); *Original Gangstas* (Orion, 1996).

168. Donald Goines, *Whoreson: The Story of a Ghetto Pimp* (Los Angeles: Holloway
House, 1972); Donald Goines, *Daddy Cool* (Los Angeles: Holloway House, 1974); Donald
Goines, *Eldorado Red* (Los Angeles: Holloway House, 1974).

169. Nelson George, *Hip Hop America* (New York: Viking, 1998), 104–5.

170. Bruce, *New Man*, 99.

171. G. Langhorne Pryor, *Neither Bond nor Free* (New York: J. S. Ogilvie, 1902), 237–38.

172. Charles W. Chesnutt, *The House Behind the Cedars* (1900; New York: Collier, 1969),
189, 208, 222, 235, 256; Pryor, *Neither Bond nor Free*, 18, 69.

173. Willis Richardson, *The Flight of the Natives* (1927), in *Black Theater, U.S.A.: Forty-
Five Plays by Black Americans, 1847–1974*, ed. James V. Hatch and Ted Shine (New York: Free
Press, 1974), 383; Joseph S. Cotter Sr., *Caleb the Degenerate* (1901), in ibid., 70, 78–80.

174. *Body and Soul* (Republic, 1925); *The Black King* (Southland, 1932).

175. Tolnay and Beck, *Festival of Violence*, 93.

176. Brundage, *Lynching in the New South*, 30; E. M. Beck and Stewart E. Tolnay, "When
Race Didn't Matter: Black and White Mob Violence against Their Own Color," in *Under Sen-
tence of Death: Lynching in the South*, ed. W. Fitzhugh Brundage (Chapel Hill: University of
North Carolina Press, 1997), 140–42.

177. Du Bois, *Souls of Black Folk*, 45.

178. Willard B. Gatewood, *Aristocrats of Color: The Black Elite, 1880–1920* (Bloomington:
Indiana University Press, 1990), ix.

179. George S. Schuyler, "The Negro-Art Hokum," *Nation*, June 16, 1926, 662.

180. Langston Hughes, "The Negro Artist and the Racial Mountain," *Nation*, June 23,
1926, 692; Gatewood, *Aristocrats of Color*, 25; E. Franklin Frazier, *Black Bourgeoisie: The Rise
of a New Middle Class in the United States* (1957; New York: Collier, 1962), 110–11, 189–90;
Rudolph Fisher, *The Walls of Jericho* (New York: Alfred A. Knopf, 1928), 98–100.

181. Charles W. Chesnutt, "The Wife of His Youth" (1899), in *Conjure Tales and Stories of
the Color Line*, ed. William L. Andrews (New York: Penguin, 1992), 103; John Edward Bruce,
"Color Prejudice among Negroes" (1916), in *The Selected Writings of John Edward Bruce: Militant Black Journalist*, ed. Peter Gilbert (New York: Arno Press and the New York Times,
1971), 125–27.

182. Kathy Russell, Midge Wilson, and Ronald Hall, *The Color Complex: The Politics of
Skin Color among African Americans* (New York: Doubleday Anchor, 1993), 27.

183. Samuel Barrett, "A Plea for Unity," *Colored American Magazine* 7 (January 1904):

48–49; Wallace Thurman, *The Blacker the Berry . . .* (1929; New York: Collier, 1970), 4; Langston Hughes, "Professor" (1952), in *Something in Common and Other Stories* (New York: Hill and Wang, 1963), 143; Dorothy West, *The Living Is Easy* (Boston: Houghton Mifflin, 1948), 45.

184. Hughes, *Ways of White Folks*, 50, 52; West, *Living Is Easy*, 105.

185. Jessie Redmon Fauset, *Comedy: American Style* (1933; New York: G. K. Hall, 1995), 89, 205; Walter White, *Flight* (New York: Alfred A. Knopf, 1926), 53–54; Jessie Redmon Fauset, *There Is Confusion* (New York: Boni and Liveright, 1924), 198, 270.

186. Kelly Miller, "Washington's Policy," *Boston Evening Transcript*, September 18, 1903.

187. Du Bois, *Dusk of Dawn*, 75–76; Marcus Garvey, "The Negro's Greatest Enemy," *Current History* 18 (September 1923): 954, 957; Stephen R. Fox, *The Guardian of Boston: William Monroe Trotter* (New York: Atheneum, 1971), 174.

188. "Du Bois Fails as a Theorist," *Messenger* 2 (December 1919): 7; George Padmore, "Bankruptcy of Negro Leadership," *Negro Worker* 12 (December 1931): 4–5.

189. Booker T. Washington to Francis Jackson Garrison, May 17, 1905, in *Booker T. Washington Papers*, ed. Louis R. Harlan and Raymond W. Smock (Urbana: University of Illinois Press, 1979), 8:280; Du Bois, *Souls of Black Folk*, 64; Fox, *William Monroe Trotter*, 31.

190. Marcus Garvey, "'Home to Harlem,' Claude McKay's Damaging Book, Should Earn Wholesale Condemnation of Negroes," *Negro World*, September 29, 1928.

191. W. E. B. Du Bois, "The Drive," *Crisis* 22 (May 1921): 8; George S. Schuyler, "Views and Reviews," *Pittsburgh Courier*, July 23, 1927; W. E. B. Du Bois, "A Lunatic or a Traitor," *Crisis* 28 (May 1924): 9; Chandler Owen interview, August 20, 1920, in James Weinstein, ed., "Black Nationalism: The Early Debate," *Studies on the Left* 4 (Summer 1964): 55; "A Supreme Negro Jamaican Jackass," *Messenger* 5 (January 1923): 561.

192. Booker T. Washington, *Up from Slavery* (1901; New York: Oxford University Press, 1995), 129; Du Bois, *Dusk of Dawn*, 78; William Monroe Trotter, "Why Be Silent?" *Guardian*, December 20, 1902; Elliott M. Rudwick, "Booker T. Washington's Relations with the National Association for the Advancement of Colored People," *Journal of Negro Education* 29 (Spring 1960): 135, 144; Fox, *William Monroe Trotter*, 29, 36–37.

193. Marcus Garvey, "W. E. Burghardt Du Bois as a Hater of Dark People," *Negro World*, February 13, 1923; E. David Cronon, *Black Moses: The Story of Marcus Garvey and the Universal Negro Improvement Association* (1955; Madison: University of Wisconsin Press, 1972), 131; Elliott M. Rudwick, "Du Bois versus Garvey: Race Propagandists at War," *Journal of Negro Education* 28 (Fall 1959): 424; Booker T. Washington to Charles William Anderson, July 11, 1910, *Booker T. Washington Papers*, ed. Harlan and Smock, 10:355.

194. Fox, *William Monroe Trotter*, 40; Benjamin J. Davis, "The Negro People's Liberation Movement," *Political Affairs* 27 (September 1948): 888–89; Kevin K. Gaines, *Uplifting the Race: Black Leadership, Politics, and Culture in the Twentieth Century* (Chapel Hill: University of North Carolina Press, 1996), 246–60.

195. *The End of White World Supremacy: Four Speeches by Malcolm X*, ed. Benjamin Karim (1963; New York: Seaver, 1971), 134–35; Stokely Carmichael, "Toward Black Liberation," *Massachusetts Review* 7 (Autumn 1966): 646, 649; Grace Boggs and James Boggs, "The City Is the Black Man's Land," *Monthly Review* 17 (April 1966): 41; Nathan Hare, *The Black Anglo-Saxons* (New York: Marzani & Munsell, 1965), 21, 29.

196. Stokely Carmichael and Charles V. Hamilton, *Black Power: The Politics of Liberation*

in America (New York: Random House, 1967), 40–41, 53–55; Eldridge Cleaver, "The Land Question," *Ramparts* 6 (May 1968): 51; Charles V. Hamilton, "The Nationalist vs. the Integrationist," *New York Times Magazine,* October 1, 1972, 46; Robert S. Browne, "The Case for Two Americas—One Black, One White," *New York Times Magazine,* August 11, 1968, 51, 56; Addison Gayle Jr., "Existential Politics," *Liberator* 9 (January 1969): 5.

197. James H. Meredith, "Big Changes Are Coming," *Saturday Evening Post,* August 13, 1966, 26; Ossie Sykes, "The Dream World of Rev. King: A Critical Analysis, Part 2," *Liberator* 5 (March 1965): 12; John Oliver Killens, *Black Man's Burden* (New York: Trident, 1965), 108, 112; Julius Lester, *Look Out, Whitey! Black Power's Gon' Get Your Mama!* (New York: Grove, 1969), 105; Carmichael, *Stokely Speaks,* 56; Addison Gayle Jr., "Nat Turner vs. Black Nationalists," *Liberator* 8 (February 1968), 6.

198. LeRoi Jones, *Home: Social Essays* (New York: William Morrow, 1966), 138–41; Malcolm X, *Malcolm X Speaks,* 134; John O. Killens, James Wechsler, and Lorraine Hansberry, "The Black Revolution and the White Backlash" (1964), in *Black Protest,* ed. Joanne Grant (Greenwich, CT: Fawcett, 1974), 443; Lester, *Look Out, Whitey!,* 98; "A Visit From the FBI" (1964), in *Malcolm X: The Man and His Times,* ed. John Henrik Clarke (New York: Collier, 1969), 201; Louis E. Lomax, *To Kill a Black Man* (Los Angeles: Holloway House, 1968), 79.

199. Ed Bullins, *Clara's Ole Man, Drama Review* 12 (Summer 1968): 161; Ed Bullins, *The Electronic Nigger* (1968), in *Five Plays by Ed Bullins* (Indianapolis: Bobbs-Merrill, 1969), 220–21; Herbert Stokes, *The Man Who Trusted the Devil Twice,* in *New Plays from the Black Theatre,* ed. Ed Bullins (New York: Bantam, 1969), 121; John Oliver Killens, *The Cotillion; or One Good Bull Is Half the Herd* (New York: Trident, 1971), 138, 152–53; LeRoi Jones, *Great Goodness of Life: A Coon Show* (1966), in *Four Black Revolutionary Plays* (Indianapolis: Bobbs-Merrill, 1969), 62.

200. Ed Bullins, *Death List* (1970), in *Four Dynamite Plays* (New York: William Morrow, 1972), 35; John A. Williams, *Sons of Darkness, Sons of Light* (New York: Pocket, 1970), 8, 202.

201. Bullins, *Death List,* 35; Henry Van Dyke, *Dead Piano* (New York: Farrar, Straus & Giroux, 1971), 73; Jimmy Garrett, *And We Own the Night, Drama Review* 12 (Summer 1968): 68–69; Nikki Giovanni, "Concerning One Responsible Negro with Too Much Power," in *Black Feeling, Black Talk-Black Judgement* (New York: William Morrow, 1970), 52–53; Ted Joans, "How Do You Want Yours?" in Joans, *Black Pow-Wow,* 7.

202. Bullins, *Death List,* 34; Blyden Jackson, *Operation Burning Candle* (New York: Pyramid, 1974), 25.

203. Whitney M. Young Jr., "Separatism? We ARE Separated—and That's the Cause of All Our Woes," *Ebony* 25 (August 1970), 94; "The Black Neo-Segregationists," *Crisis* 74 (November 1967): 439–40; Kenneth B. Clark, "Thoughts on Black Power," *Dissent* 15 (March–April 1968): 192; Bayard Rustin, "The Failure of Black Separatism," *Harper's Magazine* 240 (January 1970): 34.

204. Bayard Rustin, "'Black Power' and Coalition Politics," *Commentary* 42 (September 1966): 35–36; Martin Luther King Jr., *Where Do We Go from Here: Chaos or Community?* (New York: Harper & Row, 1967), 46, 54–59, 61–63.

205. Joseph R. Washington Jr., "Black Nationalism: Potentially Anti-Folk and Anti-Intellectual," *Black World* 22 (July 1973): 32–39; Charles T. Davis, "The American Scholar, the Black Arts, and/or Black Power" (1969), in *Black is the Color of the Cosmos: Essays on Afro-American Literature and Culture, 1942–1981,* ed. Henry Louis Gates Jr. (New York: Gar-

land, 1982), 29–46; Saunders Redding, "The Black Arts Movement in Negro Poetry," *American Scholar* 42 (Spring 1973): 330–35; "When State Magicians Fail: An Interview with Ishmael Reed," *Journal of Black Poetry* 1 (Summer–Fall 1969): 73–75; Sherley Anne Williams, *Give Birth to Brightness: A Thematic Study in Neo-Black Literature* (New York: Dial, 1972), 240.

206. Jo Ann E. Gardner and Charles W. Thomas, "Different Strokes for Different Folks," *Psychology Today* 4 (September 1970): 49; Frances Beale, "Double Jeopardy: To Be Black and Female," in *The Black Woman: An Anthology,* ed. Tony Cade (New York: New American Library, 1970), 92–94; Linda La Rue, "The Black Movement and Women's Liberation," *Black Scholar* 1 (May 1970): 36–42; Gwendolyn Evans, "The Panthers' Elaine Brown, Does She Say What She Means, Does She Mean What She Says?" *Ms.* 4 (March 1976): 106; Michele Wallace, "A Black Feminist's Search for Sisterhood" (1975), in *All the Women Are White, All the Blacks Are Men, But Some of Us Are Brave: Black Women's Studies,* ed. Gloria T. Hull, Patricia Bell Scott, and Barbara Smith (New York: Feminist Press, 1982), 6–7.

207. Assata Shakur, *Assata: An Autobiography* (Westport, CT: Lawrence Hill, 1987), 230.

208. Nathan Hare, "What Happened to the Black Movement," *Black World* 25 (January 1976): 20, 30–32; *The Autobiography of LeRoi Jones/Amiri Baraka* (New York: Freundlich, 1984), 323, 326; Ron Karenga, "Overturning Ourselves: From Mystification to Meaningful Struggle," *Black Scholar* 4 (October 1972): 7, 12–13.

209. William H. Hastie, "The Black Mystique Pitfall," *Crisis* 78 (October 1971): 243–47; Walt Thompson, "What's Left of the Black Left?" *Ramparts* 10 (June 1972): 46–53.

210. On these sociocultural changes, see Rowland Evans and Robert Novak, *The Reagan Revolution* (New York: E. P. Dutton, 1981); Richard Reeves, *The Reagan Detour* (New York: Simon & Schuster, 1985); Kevin P. Phillips, *The Politics of Rich and Poor: Wealth and the American Electorate in the Reagan Aftermath* (New York: Random House, 1990); Haynes Johnson, *Sleepwalking through History: American in the Reagan Years* (New York: W. W. Norton, 1991); James Combs, *The Reagan Range: The Nostalgic Myth in American Politics* (Bowling Green, OH: Bowling Green State University Popular Press, 1993); Dan T. Carter, *From George Wallace to Newt Gingrich: Race in the Conservative Counterrevolution, 1963–1994* (Baton Rouge: Louisiana State University Press, 1996), 55–86.

211. Shelby Steele, *The Content of Our Character: A New Vision of Race in America* (1990; New York: HarperCollins, 1991), 19–20, 116; Ken Hamblin, *Pick a Better Country: An Unassuming Colored Guy Speaks His Mind about America* (New York: Simon & Schuster, 1996), 186, 234; Brad Stetson, "'The Sage of South Central': An Interview with Larry Elder," in *Black and Right: The Bold New Voice of Black Conservatives in America,* ed. Stan Faryna, Brad Stetson, and Joseph G. Conti (Westport, CT: Praeger, 1997), 161.

212. Sylvester Monroe, "Nothing Is Ever Simply Black and White," *Time,* August 12, 1991, 6; George Hesselberg, "Civil Rights Chief Speaks His Mind," *Wisconsin State Journal,* October 10, 1985.

213. Stetson, "Interview with Larry Elder," 158; Clarence Thomas, *Why Black Americans Should Look to Conservative Policies* (Washington, DC: Heritage Foundation, 1987), 1.

214. Angela D. Dillard, *Guess Who's Coming to Dinner Now? Multicultural Conservatism in America* (New York: New York University Press, 2001), 99–136; Steele, *Content of Our Character,* 167–72; Stetson, "Interview with Larry Elder," 159.

215. Peter McGrath and Diane Weathers, "Breaking the Code," *Newsweek*, October 21, 1985, 87; quoted in Jacob V. Lamar Jr., "Redefining the American Dilemma," *Time*, November 11, 1985, 36.

216. Hamblin, *Pick a Better Country*, 103–7; Stanley Crouch, *The All-American Skin Game, or, The Decoy of Race* (New York: Pantheon, 1995), 32, 253; Stanley Crouch, *Notes of a Hanging Judge: Essays and Reviews, 1979–1989* (New York: Oxford University Press, 1990), 204, 242; Stanley Crouch, *Always in Pursuit: Fresh American Perspectives, 1995–1997* (New York: Pantheon, 1998), 250.

217. Steele, *Content of Our Character*, 174; Hamblin, *Pick a Better Country*, 52, 114, 179, 195, 200.

218. Hamblin, *Pick a Better Country*, 124, 177.

219. Crouch, *Hanging Judge*, 3.

220. "Baraka vs. Steele," *Mother Jones* 16 (May–June 1991): 11.

221. James Jennings, "The 'New' Black Neo-Conservativism: A Critique," *Trotter Institute Review* 1 (Fall 1987): 16–17; Elwood Watson, "Guess What Came to American Politics?—Contemporary Black Conservatism," *Journal of Black Studies* 29 (September 1998): 78, 82; Adolph Reed Jr., "The Descent of Black Conservatism," *Progressive* 61 (October 1997): 18, 20; Preston H. Smith, "'Self-Help,' Black Conservatives, and the Reemergence of Black Privatism," in *Without Justice for All: The New Liberalism and Our Retreat from Racial Equality*, ed. Adolph Reed Jr. (Boulder, CO: Westview, 1999), 258–59; Glenn C. Loury, "A Call to Arms for Black Conservatives," in *A Conservative Agenda for Black Americans*, ed. Joseph Perkins (Washington, DC: Heritage Foundation, 1990), 18; Michael Klein, *The Man Behind the Sound Bite: The Real Story of the Rev. Al Sharpton* (New York: Castillo International, 1991), 186.

222. Thomas Sowell, *Civil Rights: Rhetoric or Reality?* (New York: William Morrow, 1984), 123; Joseph G. Conti, "An Interview with Ezola Foster," in Faryna, Stetson, and Conti, *Black and Right*, 154; Hamblin, *Pick a Better Country*, 200; Shelby Steele, *A Dream Deferred: The Second Betrayal of Black Freedom in America* (New York: HarperCollins, 1998), 4; Thomas, *Conservative Policies*, 5, 7.

223. Klein, *Al Sharpton*, 210; Watson, "Black Conservatism," 79.

Chapter Four

1. On Jemima's 1989 makeover, see M. M. Manring, *Slave in a Box: The Strange Career of Aunt Jemima* (Charlottesville: University Press of Virginia, 1998), 172–80. For images of the militant Jemima, see Betye Saar, *The Liberation of Aunt Jemima*, 1972; Betye Saar, *Workers and Warriors: The Return of Aunt Jemima* series, 1998.

2. Sonia Sanchez, *We a BaddDDD People* (Detroit: Broadside, 1970).

3. Thomas Dixon Jr., *The Traitor: A Story of the Fall of the Invisible Empire* (New York: Grosset & Dunlap, 1907), 316; Thomas Dixon Jr., *The Clansman: An Historical Romance of the Ku Klux Klan* (New York: Grosset & Dunlap, 1905), 248–49, 274, 293; Thomas Nelson Page, *Red Rock: A Chronicle of Reconstruction* (New York: Charles Scribner's Sons, 1898), 291; Thomas Dixon Jr., *The Leopard's Spots: A Romance of the White Man's Burden—1865–1900* (1902; New York: Doubleday, Page, 1903), 98, 200.

4. Hinton Rowan Helper, *Nojoque: A Question for a Continent* (New York: George W. Carleton, 1867), 15, 79, 211; William Benjamin Smith, *The Color Line: A Brief in Behalf of the Unborn* (New York: McClure, Phillips, 1905), 9, 175, 189; Thomas Nelson Page, *The Negro: The Southerner's Problem* (New York: Charles Scribner's Sons, 1904), 292; Frederick L. Hoffman, "Race Traits and Tendencies of the American Negro," *Publications of the American Economic Association* 11 (August 1896): 66.

5. Ariel [Buckner H. Payne], *The Negro: What Is His Ethnological Status?* . . . (Cincinnati: n.p., 1867), 45; Charles Carroll, *"The Negro a Beast" or "In the Image of God"* . . . (St. Louis: American Book and Bible House, 1900), 38, 166, 219; Charles Carroll, *The Tempter of Eve; or, The Criminality of Man's Social, Political, and Religious Equality with the Negro, and the Amalgamation to which These Crimes Inevitably Lead* (St. Louis: Adamic Publishing, 1902), 405–6; A. Hoyle Lester, *The Pre-Adamite, or Who Tempted Eve?* . . . (Philadelphia: J. B. Lippincott, 1875), 25–26; Prospero, *Caliban: A Sequel to "Ariel"* (New York: n.p., 1868), 21; Mason Stokes, "Someone's in the Garden with Eve: Race, Religion, and the American Fall," *American Quarterly* 50 (December 1998): 718–44.

6. Raymond A. Browne and Henry Clay Smith, "The Mormon Coon" (New York: Sol Bloom, 1905).

7. *Old Zip Coon* (1874), in *This Grotesque Essence: Plays from the American Minstrel Stage*, ed. Gary D. Engle (Baton Rouge: Louisiana State University Press, 1978), 52.

8. Rayford W. Logan, *The Betrayal of the Negro: From Rutherford B. Hayes to Woodrow Wilson* (New York: Collier, 1965), 218–41.

9. Helper, *Nojoque*, 69, 82.

10. Bertram Wilbur Doyle, *The Etiquette of Race Relations in the South: A Study in Social Control* (Chicago: University of Chicago Press, 1937), 118, 142–48, 153; Neil R. McMillen, *Dark Journey: Black Mississippians in the Age of Jim Crow* (Urbana: University of Illinois Press, 1989), 23–28.

11. For a survey of spontaneous collective violence from the colonial era to the late twentieth century, see Paul A. Gilje, *Rioting in America* (Bloomington: Indiana University Press, 1996).

12. Roberta Senechal, *The Sociogenesis of a Race Riot: Springfield, Illinois, in 1908* (Urbana: University of Illinois Press, 1990), 42.

13. Arthur I. Waskow, *From Race Riot to Sit-In, 1919 and the 1960s: A Study in the Connections between Conflict and Violence* (1966; Garden City, NY: Doubleday Anchor, 1967), 58, 184; Elliott Rudwick, *Race Riot at East St. Louis, July 2, 1917* (1964; New York: Atheneum, 1972), 24, 27–28, 48, 54; William M. Tuttle Jr., *Race Riot: Chicago in the Red Summer of 1919* (1970; New York: Atheneum, 1974), 117, 171, 185; Vincent P. Franklin, "The Philadelphia Race Riot of 1918," *Pennsylvania Magazine of History and Biography* 99 (July 1975): 338, 349.

14. Scott Ellsworth, *Death in a Promised Land: The Tulsa Race Riot of 1921* (1982; Baton Rouge: Louisiana State University Press, 1992), 45–47, 63–66; Oklahoma Commission to Study the Tulsa Race Riot of 1921, *Tulsa Race Riot* (Oklahoma City: The Commission, 2001), 13, 57–58; Alfred L. Brophy, *Reconstructing the Dreamland: The Tulsa Riot of 1921: Race, Reparations, and Reconciliation* (New York: Oxford University Press, 2002), 24–62.

15. John Dittmer, *Black Georgia in the Progressive Era, 1900–1920* (1977; Urbana: University of Illinois Press, 1980), 124–30; Mark Bauerlein, *Negrophobia: A Race Riot in Atlanta, 1906* (San Francisco: Encounter, 2001), 136–41; Charles Crowe, "Racial Violence and Social

Reform—Origins of the Atlanta Riot of 1906," *Journal of Negro History* 53 (July 1968): 249, 253.

16. William Ivy Hair, *Carnival of Fury: Robert Charles and the New Orleans Race Riot of 1900* (Baton Rouge: Louisiana State University Press, 1976), 140; "Negro Grabs Girl as She Steps Out on Back Porch," *Atlanta Sunday News,* September 23, 1906; Rudwick, *Race Riot,* 71; Lawrence J. Friedman, *The White Savage: Racial Fantasies in the Postbellum South* (Englewood Cliffs, NJ: Prentice-Hall, 1970), 122–24; Leon F. Litwack, *Trouble in Mind: Black Southerners in the Age of Jim Crow* (New York: Alfred A. Knopf, 1998), 301–2.

17. McMillen, *Dark Journey,* 235; Martha Hodes, *White Women, Black Men: Illicit Sex in the Nineteenth-Century South* (New Haven: Yale University Press, 1997), 178–79; Angela Y. Davis, *Women, Race & Class* (1981; New York: Vintage, 1983), 187.

18. Orlando Patterson, *Rituals of Blood: Consequences of Slavery in Two American Centuries* (Washington, DC: Civitas/Counterpoint, 1998), 175; Lothrop Stoddard, *The Rising Tide of Color against White World-Supremacy* (1920; New York: Charles Scribner's Sons, 1927), 8, 303; Howard W. Odum, *Race and Rumors of Race: Challenge to American Crisis* (Chapel Hill: University of North Carolina Press, 1943), 100, 111, 134–35.

19. Governor's Commission on the Los Angeles Riots, *Violence in the City—An End or a Beginning?* (Los Angeles: State of California, 1965), 23–24; David O. Sears and John B. McConahay, *The Politics of Violence: The New Urban Blacks and the Watts Riot* (Boston: Houghton, Mifflin, 1973), 9, 13.

20. Gerald Horne, *Fire This Time: The Watts Uprising and the 1960s* (1995; New York: Da Capo, 1997), 91, 103, 137; Sears and McConahay, *Watts Riot,* 150; Joe Domanick, "Police Power," in *Inside the L.A. Riots,* ed., Don Hazen (New York: Institute for Alternative Journalism, 1992), 23.

21. Nathan E. Cohen, "The Context of the Curfew Area," in *The Los Angeles Riots: A Socio-Psychological Study,* ed. Nathan Cohen (New York: Praeger, 1970), 42–47; Governor's Commission, *Violence in the City,* 3.

22. "Trigger of Hate," *Time,* August 20, 1965, 16; Jerry Cohen and William S. Murphy, *Burn, Baby, Burn!: The Los Angeles Race Riot, August, 1965* (New York: E. P. Dutton, 1966), 87, 123; Spencer Crump, *Black Riot in Los Angeles: The Story of the Watts Tragedy* (Los Angeles: Trans-Anglo, 1966), 46; Horne, *Fire This Time,* 39, 68–69.

23. Robert Conot, *Rivers of Blood, Years of Darkness* (New York: Bantam, 1967), 218; Horne, *Fire This Time,* 67, 80; Terry Ann Knopf, *Rumors, Race, and Riots* (New Brunswick, NJ: Transaction, 1975), 214.

24. Conot, *Rivers of Blood,* 370; Horne, *Fire This Time,* 125.

25. Conot, *Rivers of Blood,* 325.

26. Crump, *Black Riot,* 29; Daryl F. Gates and Diane K. Shah, *Chief: My Life in the LAPD* (New York: Bantam, 1992), 91, 92, 100, 103.

27. David O. Sears and T. M. Tomlinson, "Riot Ideology in Los Angeles: A Study of Negro Attitudes," *Social Science Quarterly* 49 (December 1968): 487–94; Richard T. Morris and Vincent Jeffries, "The White Reaction Study," in Cohen, *Los Angeles Riots,* 487–88.

28. Thomas J. Foley, "Racial Unrest Laid to Negro Family Failure," *Los Angeles Times,* August 14, 1965; Kenneth O'Reilly, "The FBI and the Politics of the Riots, 1964–1968," *Journal of American History* 75 (June 1988): 99.

29. Helen Webber, *Summer Mockery* (Milwaukee: Aestas, 1986).

30. John Spiegel, "Hostility, Aggression and Violence," in *Racial Violence in the United States*, ed. Allen D. Grimshaw (Chicago: Aldine, 1969), 335–37; Daniel P. Moynihan, *The Negro Family: The Case for National Action* (Washington, DC: U.S. Government Printing Office, 1965), 29–30; Abram Kardiner and Lionel Ovesey, *The Mark of Oppression: Explorations in the Personality of the American Negro* (1951; Cleveland: World, 1969), 387; Kenneth B. Clark, *Dark Ghetto: Dilemmas of Social Power* (1965; New York: Harper & Row, 1967), 81–110; Lillian R. Boehme, *Carte Blanche for Chaos* (New Rochelle, NY: Arlington House, 1970), 6, 95, 154, 212–14.

31. Staff of the *Los Angeles Times*, *Understanding the Riots: Los Angeles Before and After the Rodney King Case* (Los Angeles: Los Angeles Times, 1992), 98.

32. Jerome H. Skolnick and James J. Fyfe, *Above the Law: Police and the Excessive Use of Force* (New York: Free Press, 1993), 3.

33. Lee A. Daniels, "Some Identified as Jurors Aren't in Accord on TV," *New York Times*, May 1, 1992; Bob Cohn and David A. Kaplan, "How the Defense Dissected the Tape," *Newsweek*, May 11, 1992, 37; Hiroshi Fukurai, Richard Krooth, and Edgar W. Butler, "The Rodney King Beating Verdicts," in *The Los Angeles Riots: Lessons for the Urban Future*, ed. Mark Baldassare (Boulder, CO: Westview, 1994), 86–87.

34. Lou Cannon, *Official Negligence: How Rodney King and the Riots Changed Los Angeles and the LAPD* (New York: Times/Random House, 1997), 25–37; Stacey C. Koon and Robert Deitz, *Presumed Guilty: The Tragedy of the Rodney King Affair* (Washington, DC: Regnery Gateway, 1992), 20–46.

35. Koon and Deitz, *Presumed Guilty*, 21, 31; Cannon, *Official Negligence*, 31.

36. Patricia J. Williams, "The Rules of the Game," in *Reading Rodney King, Reading Urban Uprising*, ed. Robert Gooding-Williams (New York: Routledge, 1993), 53; Robert Gooding-Williams, "Look, a Negro!" in Gooding-Williams, *Rodney King*, 166.

37. Alphonso Pinkney, "Rodney King and Dred Scott," in *Why L.A. Happened: Implications of the '92 Los Angeles Rebellion*, ed. Haki R. Madhubuti (Chicago: Third World, 1993), 43; Thomas L. Dumm, "The New Enclosures: Racism in the Normalized Community," in Gooding-Williams, *Rodney King*, 180.

38. Cannon, *Official Negligence*, 281; Mike Davis, "In L.A., Burning All Illusions," *Nation*, June 1, 1992, 745.

39. Jesse Jackson, "Safe on Broken Pieces," in *Dreams on Fire/Embers of Hope: From the Pulpits of Los Angeles After the Riots*, ed. Ignacio Castuera (St. Louis: Chalice, 1992), 44.

40. David Whitman, "The Untold Story of the L.A. Riot," *U.S. News & World Report*, May 31, 1993, 50, 52.

41. Cannon, *Official Negligence*, 318–20, 330.

42. Whitman, "Untold Story," 57.

43. Carol Tice, "Helicopter Journalism," in Hazen, *L.A. Riots*, 121.

44. Cannon, *Official Negligence*, 296.

45. Mark Schubb, "Race, Lies & Videotape: The L.A. Upheaval and the Media," *Extra!* 5 (July–August 1992): 8–11; Erna Smith, *Transmitting Race: The Los Angeles Riot in Television News* (Cambridge: Harvard University, 1994), 1–15; Charles E. Simmons, "The Los Angeles Rebellion: Class, Race and Misinformation," in Madhubuti, *Why L.A. Happened*, 149–50.

46. H. Khalif Khalifah, ed., *Rodney King and the L.A. Rebellion: A 1992 Black Rebellion in the United States*, (Hampton, VA: U.B. & U.S. Communications Systems, 1992), 1; Yusuf Jah and Shah'Keyah Jah, *Uprising: Crips and Bloods Tell the Story of America's Youth in the Crossfire* (New York: Scribner, 1995), 218.

47. Gates and Shah, *Chief*, 314.

48. Margot Harry, *"Attention, MOVE! This Is America!"* (Chicago: Banner, 1987), 10; Kenneth O'Reilly, *"Racial Matters": The FBI's Secret File on Black America, 1960–1972* (New York: Free Press, 1989), 273–74; Todd Gitlin, *The Sixties: Years of Hope, Days of Rage* (New York: Bantam, 1993), 349.

49. John Edgar Wideman, *Two Cities* (New York: Houghton, Mifflin, 1998), 97–98.

50. John H. McWhorter, *Losing the Race: Self-Sabotage in Black America* (New York: Free Press, 2000), 61–70; James Kirkpatrick Davis, *Spying on America: The FBI's Domestic Counterintelligence Program* (New York: Praeger, 1992), 108–11; Ward Churchill and Jim Vander Wall, *The COINTELPRO Papers: Documents from the FBI's Secret Wars against Domestic Dissent* (Boston: South End, 1990), 116–17, 120–21, 130–35, 152–53; O'Reilly, *"Racial Matters,"* 300–309, 319–20.

51. Katheryn K. Russell, *The Color of Crime: Racial Hoaxes, White Fear, Black Protectionism, Police Harassment, and Other Macroaggressions* (New York: New York University Press, 1998), 157–73.

52. Eric W. Hickey, *Serial Murderers and Their Victims* (Belmont, CA: Wadsworth, 1997), 103.

53. Quoted in Anastasia Toufexis, "Dances with Werewolves," *Time*, April 4, 1994, 64–66.

54. Hickey, *Serial Murderers*, 103, 136; James Alan Fox and Jack Levin, *Overkill: Mass Murder and Serial Killing Exposed* (New York: Plenum, 1994), 16.

55. Peter Hernon, *A Terrible Thunder: The Story of the New Orleans Sniper* (Garden City, NY: Doubleday, 1978), 101–2, 112–14, 255–56; Elliott Leyton, *Compulsive Killers: The Story of Modern Multiple Murder* (New York: Washington Mews/New York University Press, 1986), 189–221; "The Battle of New Orleans," *Newsweek*, January 22, 1973, 26–27.

56. Clark Howard, *Zebra* (1979; New York: Berkley, 1980), 14, 25–26, 228, 371, 385; "Nothing Personal," *Newsweek*, February 11, 1974, 26; Jack Levin and James Alan Fox, *Mass Murder: America's Growing Menace* (New York: Plenum, 1985), 85–87.

57. Quoted in Howard, *Zebra*, 230–31.

58. David Lohr, "Alton Coleman & Debra Brown," http://www.angelfire.com/zine2/serialarchive/coleman.html (accessed February 26, 2002); Jason Lapeyre, "The Serial Killer the Cops Ignored: The Henry Louis Wallace Murders," http://crimemagazine.com/henrylouiswallacemurders.htm (accessed February 26, 2002); David Johnston and Don Van Natta Jr., "In the Sights of the Sniper: 23 Fearful Days in October," *New York Times*, October 27, 2002.

59. Bernard Headley, *The Atlanta Youth Murders and the Politics of Race* (Carbondale: Southern Illinois University Press, 1998), 1–5, 136–40, 145.

60. Joseph C. Fisher, *Killer among Us: Public Reactions to Serial Murder* (Westport, CT: Praeger, 1997), 156–61; James Baldwin, *The Evidence of Things Not Seen* (New York: Holt, Rinehart and Winston, 1985), 10–16.

61. Toni Cade Bambara, *Those Bones Are Not My Child* (New York: Pantheon, 1999), 3–21; Patricia A. Turner, *I Heard It through the Grapevine: Rumor in African-American Culture* (Berkeley: University of California Press, 1993), 2, 81.

62. Andrew Hacker, *Two Nations: Black and White, Separate, Hostile, Unequal* (1992; New York: Ballantine, 1993), 181–83.

63. Randall Kennedy, *Race, Crime, and the Law* (New York: Pantheon, 1997), 19–20.

64. Russell, *Color of Crime*, 111, 114; David Cole, *No Equal Justice: Race and Class in the American Criminal Justice System* (New York: New Press, 1999), 42; William Julius Wilson, *When Work Disappears: The World of the New Urban Poor* (New York: Alfred A. Knopf, 1996), 61.

65. Ken Auletta, *The Underclass* (1982; New York: Vintage, 1983), xv–xvi, 43–44; Douglas G. Glasgow, *The Black Underclass: Poverty, Unemployment, and Entrapment of Ghetto Youth* (1980; New York: Vintage, 1981), 7–8.

66. Leon Dash, *Rosa Lee: A Mother and Her Family in Urban America* (New York: Basic Books, 1996), 4, 33, 41, 73, 176, 199.

67. Fox Butterfield, *All God's Children: The Bosket Family and the American Tradition of Violence* (New York: Alfred A. Knopf, 1995), xiv, 86, 92, 99, 101, 148.

68. Ibid., xi–xii, 149, 176, 186.

69. Ibid., 275–77, 316.

70. Mark S. Fleisher, *Beggars and Thieves: Lives of Urban Street Criminals* (Madison: University of Wisconsin Press, 1995), 4.

71. Jah and Jah, *Uprising*, 217; William Shakespeare, *The Merry Wives of Windsor* (1623), ed. H. J. Oliver (London: Methuen, 1971), 4.2.98.

72. Martín Sánchez Jankowski, *Islands in the Street: Gangs and American Urban Society* (Berkeley: University of California Press, 1991), 1–3; Herbert Asbury, *The Gangs of New York: An Informal History of the Underworld* (Garden City, NY: Garden City Publishing, 1928), 21, 239–40; David E. Ruth, *Inventing the Public Enemy: The Gangster in American Culture, 1918–1934* (Chicago: University of Chicago Press, 1996), 1–9.

73. James M. O'Kane, *The Crooked Ladder: Gangsters, Ethnicity, and the American Dream* (New Brunswick, NJ: Transaction, 1992), 169–72; *Dressed to Kill* (William Fox, 1928); *The Racketeer* (Pathe, 1929); *All through the Night* (Warner Brothers, 1941).

74. Ruth, *Inventing the Public Enemy*, 5, 87; *Sinner's Holiday* (Warner Brothers, 1930); *The Unholy Three* (Metro-Goldwyn-Mayer, 1925; *The Doorway to Hell* (Warner Brothers, 1930).

75. John Springhall, *Youth, Popular Culture and Moral Panics: Penny Gaffs to Gangsta-Rap, 1830–1996* (New York: St. Martin's, 1998), 113.

76. Eugene Rosow, *Born to Lose: The Gangster Film in America* (New York: Oxford University Press, 1978), 179; John McCarty, *Hollywood Gangland: The Movies' Love Affair with the Mob* (New York: St. Martin's, 1993), 5; Marilyn Yaquinto, *Pump 'Em Full of Lead: A Look at Gangsters on Film* (New York; Twayne, 1998), xii; Jonathan Munby, *Public Enemies, Public Heroes: Screening the Gangster from Little Caesar to Touch of Evil* (Chicago: University of Chicago Press, 1999), 24; Nicole Rafter, *Shots in the Mirror: Crime Films and Society* (New York: Oxford University Press, 2000), 141–64.

77. Daniel J. Leab, "A Pale Black Imitation: All-Colored Films, 1930–60," *Journal of Popular Film* 4, no.1 (1975): 57–76; Thomas Cripps, *Slow Fade to Black: The Negro in American Film, 1900–1942* (New York: Oxford University Press, 1977), 170–202, 309–48.

78. John Kisch and Edward Mapp, *A Separate Cinema: Fifty Years of Black-Cast Posters* (New York: Noonday/Farrar, Straus & Giroux, 1992), 22, 140.

79. Cripps, *Slow Fade to Black*, 199.

80. William L. Van Deburg, *Black Camelot: African-American Culture Heroes in Their Times, 1960–1980* (Chicago: University of Chicago Press, 1997), 127–96.

81. *Slaughter's Big Rip-Off* (American International, 1973).

82. Ed Guerrero, *Framing Blackness: The African American Image in Film* (Philadelphia: Temple University Press, 1993), 113–37; *The Godfather* (Paramount, 1972); *Dirty Harry* (Warner Brothers, 1971); *Rocky* (United Artists, 1976); *48 Hours* (Paramount, 1982); *Soul Man* (New World, 1986); *The Toy* (Columbia, 1982).

83. S. Craig Watkins, *Representing: Hip Hop Culture and the Production of Black Cinema* (Chicago: University of Chicago Press, 1998), 169–76, 187–95; Roger Ebert, "Black New Wave Movies," *Capital Times* (Madison, WI), June 10, 1991; Roger Ebert, "Brilliant 'Boyz N the Hood' Combines Substance, Style," *Chicago Sun-Times*, July 12, 1991; *A Rage in Harlem* (Miramax, 1991); *Do the Right Thing* (Universal, 1989); *Jungle Fever* (Universal, 1991).

84. *Streetwise* (Black Film Distributors, 1998); *Tear It Down* (Two Left Shoes, 1997); *Menace II Society* (New Line Cinema, 1993).

85. *Belly* (Artisan Entertainment, 1998); *Blood Brothers* (Power, 1993); *Corrupt* (Sterling, 1999); *Streetwise*.

86. *New Jack City* (Warner Brothers, 1991).

87. *Boyz N the Hood* (Columbia, 1991).

88. *Menace II Society*.

89. *Trespass* (Universal, 1992).

90. *In Too Deep* (Dimension, 1999); *Belly*.

91. *Streetwise; Belly; A Rage in Harlem; Clockers* (Universal, 1995); *Above the Rim* (New Line Cinema, 1994).

92. *South Central* (Warner Brothers, 1992); *Fresh* (Miramax, 1994); *Clockers*.

93. Brand Nubian, "Word Is Bond," *Everything Is Everything* (Elektra 61682, 1994).

94. *Hoodlum* (United Artists, 1997); *Dead Presidents* (Hollywood, 1995); *Hot Boyz* (Artisan Entertainment, 1999); *Straight Out of Brooklyn* (Samuel Goldwyn, 1991).

95. *New Jack City*.

96. Armond White, *The Resistance: Ten Years of Pop Culture that Shook the World* (Woodstock, NY: Overlook, 1995), 205–8, 347–51; Steven A. Holmes, "You Talking to Me? The Tough Black Man," *New York Times*, June 4, 1995; David Everitt, "The 'Gangstas' Chronicles," *Entertainment Weekly*, May 10, 1996, 46; Paul Scott, "Hollywood and the Pimping of Black Death," *Challenger*, July 5, 2001, 1, 7.

97. Rob Nelson, "Sir Duke," *City Pages*, September 3, 1997, http://citypages.com/databank/18/874/article1578.asp (accessed June 24, 2002); Jacquie Jones, "From Jump Street," *Black Film Review* 6, no. 4 (1992): 12.

98. Steven D. Kendall, *New Jack Cinema: Hollywood's African American Filmmakers* (Silver Spring, MD: J. L. Denser, 1994), 99; *Juice* (Paramount, 1992); *Boyz N the Hood; Menace II Society*.

99. *New Jack City; Blood Brothers; Tales from the Hood* (Savoy, 1995); *Caught Up* (Live Entertainment, 1998).

100. Yaquinto, *Gangsters on Film*, 200; Karen Grigsby Bates, "'They've Gotta Have Us': Hollywood's Black Directors," *New York Times Magazine*, July 14, 1991, 40.

101. Bernard Weinraub, "Black Film Makers Are Looking Beyond Ghetto Violence," *New York Times*, September 11, 1995; Alan Light, "Not Just One of the Boyz," *Rolling Stone*, September 5, 1991, 73.

102. *Don't Be a Menace to South Central While Drinking Your Juice in the Hood* (Miramax, 1996).

103. *Squeeze* (Miramax, 1996); *Sugar Hill* (20th Century Fox, 1994); *Original Gangstas* (Orion, 1996).

104. Mark S. Fleisher, *Dead End Kids: Gang Girls and the Boys They Know* (Madison: University of Wisconsin Press, 1998), 6.

105. Rufus Schatzberg, *Black Organized Crime in Harlem, 1920–1930* (New York: Garland, 1993), 103–4, 110–11, 113; O'Kane, *Crooked Ladder*, 134.

106. Gwendolyn Brooks, "The Blackstone Rangers" (1968), in *Blacks* (Chicago: Third World, 1994), 446.

107. Tom Morganthau, "The Drug Gangs," *Newsweek*, March 28, 1988, 20–27; Craig Reinarman and Harry G. Levine, "The Crack Attack: Politics and Media in the Crack Scare," in *Crack in America: Demon Drugs and Social Justice*, ed. Craig Reinarman and Harry G. Levine (Berkeley: University of California Press, 1997), 21, 24.

108. Carl S. Taylor, *Dangerous Society* (East Lansing: Michigan State University Press, 1990), 103.

109. Lee P. Brown, "Crime in the Black Community," in *The State of Black America 1988*, ed. Janet Dewart (New York: National Urban League, 1988), 101–2; Rufus Schatzberg and Robert J. Kelly, *African-American Organized Crime: A Social History* (1996; New Brunswick, NJ: Rutgers University Press, 1997), 5–6.

110. Elijah Anderson, *Code of the Street: Decency, Violence, and the Moral Life of the Inner City* (New York: W. W. Norton, 1999), 77, 93, 112; Jah and Jah, *Uprising*, 73.

111. Léon Bing, *Do or Die* (New York: HarperCollins, 1991), 198.

112. Ibid., 21; Anderson, *Code of the Street*, 33.

113. Taylor, *Dangerous Society*, 47; Jankowski, *Islands in the Street*, 40, 43, 53.

114. Jankowski, *Islands in the Street*, 45; John M. Hagedorn, *People and Folks: Gangs, Crime and the Underclass in a Rustbelt City* (Chicago: Lake View, 1988), 131.

115. *Colors* (Orion, 1988); Bing, *Do or Die*, 205.

116. William B. Sanders, *Gangbangs and Drive-Bys: Grounded Culture and Juvenile Gang Violence* (New York: Aldine De Gruyter, 1994), 73.

117. Scott H. Decker and Barrik Van Winkle, *Life in the Gang: Family, Friends, and Violence* (Cambridge: Cambridge University Press, 1996), 63.

118. Jah and Jah, *Uprising*, 23.

119. Gini Sikes, *8 Ball Chicks: A Year in the Violent World of Girl Gangsters* (New York: Anchor/Doubleday, 1997), 181–84; Anne Campbell, *The Girls in the Gang* (Cambridge, MA: Basil Blackwell, 1991), 27, 245.

120. Decker and Van Winkle, *Life in the Gang*, 69–71; Bing, *Do or Die*, 243; Sanyika Shakur, *Monster: The Autobiography of an L.A. Gang Member* (New York: Atlantic Monthly, 1993), 6–12, 71–72, 233.

121. Shakur, *Monster*, 12; Decker and Van Winkle, *Life in the Gang*, 63; Bing, *Do or Die*, 21, 257.

122. Malcolm W. Klein, *The American Street Gang: Its Nature, Prevalence, and Control* (New York: Oxford University Press, 1995), 5, 234; Decker and Van Winkle, *Life in the Gang*, 120.

123. William Kleinknecht, *The New Ethnic Mobs: The Changing Face of Organized Crime in America* (New York: Free Press, 1996), 10–11, 215–17, 227; Susan A. Phillips, *Wallbangin': Graffiti and Gangs in L.A.* (Chicago: University of Chicago Press, 1999), 21, 259.

124. Taylor, *Dangerous Society*, 56–57; Decker and Van Winkle, *Life in the Gang*, 183; Bing, *Do or Die*, 43; Lewis Yablonski, *Gangsters: Fifty Years of Madness, Drugs, and Death on the Streets of America* (New York: New York University Press, 1997), 19.

125. Jimmie L. Reeves and Richard Campbell, *Cracked Coverage: Television News, the Anti-Cocaine Crusade, and the Reagan Legacy* (Durham: Duke University Press, 1994), 130–31, 162–63; Hagedorn, *People and Folks*, 156–57; Jankowski, *Islands in the Street*, 292.

126. Shakur, *Monster*, 70; Hagedorn, *People and Folks*, 140.

127. Quoted in Klein, *American Street Gang*, 120.

128. Quoted in Bing, *Do or Die*, 145–46.

129. Cornel West, "Nihilism in Black America: A Danger that Corrodes from Within," *Dissent* 38 (Spring 1991): 223–24.

130. Jones, "From Jump Street," 12; Ken Hamblin, *Pick a Better Country: An Unassuming Colored Guy Speaks His Mind about America* (New York: Simon & Schuster, 1996), 88.

131. Quoted in Reeves and Campbell, *Cracked Coverage*, 142.

132. Shakur, *Monster*, 164, 208; Hagedorn, *People and Folks*, 162.

133. David J. Rothman, *The Discovery of the Asylum: Social Order and Disorder in the New Republic* (Boston: Little, Brown, 1971), 59, 71, 85, 103; Paul W. Keve, *Prisons and the American Conscience: A History of U.S. Federal Corrections* (Carbondale: Southern Illinois University Press, 1991), 39.

134. Blake McKelvey, *American Prisons: A History of Good Intentions* (Montclair, NJ: Patterson Smith, 1977), 261.

135. David J. Rothman, *Conscience and Convenience: The Asylum and Its Alternatives in Progressive America* (Boston: Little, Brown, 1980), 44, 83, 89–90, 179.

136. Matthew Silberman, *A World of Violence: Corrections in America* (Belmont, CA: Wadsworth, 1995), 42–43, 118; David Garland, *Punishment and Modern Society: A Study in Social Theory* (Chicago: University of Chicago Press, 1990), 6, 8.

137. Francis T. Cullen and Karen E. Gilbert, *Reaffirming Rehabilitation* (Cincinnati: Anderson, 1982), xxviii–xxix; Francis A. Allen, *The Decline of the Rehabilitative Ideal: Penal Policy and Social Purpose* (New Haven: Yale University Press, 1981), 30–31.

138. Norval Morris, "The Contemporary Prison: 1965–Present," in *The Oxford History of the Prison: The Practice of Punishment in Western Society*, ed. Norval Morris and David J. Rothman (New York: Oxford University Press, 1995), 236; Dan Baum, "Invisible Nation," *Rolling Stone*, December 7, 2000, 44–45; Cole, *No Equal Justice*, 4; Troy Duster, "Pattern, Purpose, and Race in the Drug War: The Crisis of Credibility in Criminal Justice," in Reinarman and Levine, *Crack in America*, 263; Jerome G. Miller, *Search and Destroy: African-American Males in the Criminal Justice System* (Cambridge: Cambridge University Press, 1996), 5–8.

139. Angela Davis, "Racialized Punishment and Prison Abolition," in *The Angela Y. Davis Reader*, ed. Joy James (Oxford: Blackwell, 1998), 105.

140. Eileen Poe-Yamagata and Michael A. Jones, *And Justice for Some: Differential Treatment of Minority Youth in the Justice System* (Washington, DC: Building Blocks for Youth, 2000), 1–5; Lincoln Quillian and Devah Pager, "Black Neighbors, Higher Crime? The Role of Racial Stereotypes in Evaluations of Neighborhood Crime," *American Journal of Sociology* 107 (November 2001): 717–67; David A. Vise, "Disparities Found in U.S. Death Penalty Prosecutions," *Washington Post*, September 13, 2000.

141. Russell, *Color of Crime*, 31.

142. Franklin E. Zimring and Gordon Hawkins, *Incapacitation: Penal Confinement and the Restraint of Crime* (New York: Oxford University Press, 1995), 15–16; Michael Tonry, *Malign Neglect: Race, Crime, and Punishment in America* (New York: Oxford University Press, 1995), 19; Reid H. Montgomery Jr. and Gordon A. Crews, *A History of Correctional Violence: An Examination of Reported Causes of Riots and Disturbances* (Lanham, MD: American Correctional Association, 1998), xiii; Peter Selvin, "Life after Prison: Lack of Services Has High Price," *Washington Post*, April 24, 2000.

143. Donald R. Kinder and Lynn M. Sanders, *Divided by Color: Racial Politics and Democratic Ideals* (Chicago: University of Chicago Press, 1996), 233–36; David C. Anderson, *Crime and the Politics of Hysteria: How the Willie Horton Story Changed American Justice* (New York: Times/Random House, 1995), 215–16; Tali Mendelberg, *The Race Card: Campaign Strategy, Implicit Messages, and the Norm of Equality* (Princeton: Princeton University Press, 2001), 134–68.

144. "The Power of Huddie's Music," in *American Negro Folklore*, ed. J. Mason Brewer (Chicago: Quadrangle, 1968), 43; Lead Belly, "Birmingham Jail" (1948), *Lead Belly's Last Sessions* (Smithsonian/Folkways 40068, 1995); Prisonaires, "A Prisoner's Prayer" (1953), *Just Walkin' in the Rain* (Bear Family 15523, 1990); Robert Pete Williams, "Pardon Denied Again" (1959), *I'm as Blue as a Man Can Be* (Arhoolie 394, 1994); Robert Pete Williams, "Free Again" (1960), (Prestige/Bluesville 1026, 1992); Big Joe Williams, "Greystone Blues" (1960), *Shake Your Boogie* (Arhoolie 315, 1990); Lightnin' Hopkins, "Prison Blues Come Down on Me" (1959), *Country Blues* (Tradition 1003, 1996).

145. "Lead Belly: Bad Nigger Makes Good Minstrel," *Life*, April 19, 1937, 39; Benjamin Filene, "'Our Singing Country': John and Alan Lomax, Leadbelly, and the Construction of an American Past," *American Quarterly* 43 (December 1991): 611; Lead Belly, "Thirty Days in the Work House" (1935), *The Essential Lead Belly* (Classic Blues 200003, 2001); Lead Belly, "Down in the Valley to Pray" (1940), *Let It Shine on Me* (Rounder 1046, 1991).

146. Nathan C. Heard, *House of Slammers* (New York: Macmillan, 1983), 95–97, 102–3, 130–33, 136, 195; Chester Himes, *Cast the First Stone* (1952; New York: Signet/New American Library, 1972), 108.

147. Lloyd L. Brown, *Iron City* (1951; Boston: Northeastern University Press, 1994), 31.

148. Heard, *House of Slammers*, 21, 191; Donald Goines, *White Man's Justice, Black Man's Grief* (Los Angeles: Holloway House, 1973), 86.

149. Daryl Cumber Dance, *Long Gone: The Mecklenburg Six and the Theme of Escape in Black Folklore* (Knoxville: University of Tennessee Press, 1987), 155–60.

150. *Brubaker* (20th Century Fox, 1980); *Against the Wall* (HBO, 1994); *Penitentiary III* (Cannon International, 1987); *The Hurricane* (Universal, 1999); *The Green Mile* (Warner

Brothers, 1999); *First Time Felon* (HBO NYC, 1997); *American History X* (New Line Cinema, 1998); *Slam* (Trimark, 1998).

151. John Bunyan, *Grace Abounding to the Chief of Sinners . . .* (London: George Larkin, 1666); Henry David Thoreau, *Civil Disobedience and Other Essays* (1849; New York: Dover, 1993); Martin Luther King Jr., *Why We Can't Wait* (1963; New York: Signet / New American Library, 2000), 64–84.

152. H. Bruce Franklin, *The Victim as Criminal and Artist: Literature from the American Prison* (New York: Oxford University Press, 1978), 130.

153. Roberta Ann Johnson, "The Prison Birth of Black Power," *Journal of Black Studies* 5 (June 1975): 395–414.

154. "The Folsom Prisoners Manifesto of Demands and Anti-Oppression Platform," in *If They Come in the Morning: Voices of Resistance*, ed. Angela Y. Davis (New York: Third Press, 1971), 63; Huey P. Newton, *Revolutionary Suicide* (New York: Ballantine, 1974), 291; James Carr, *Bad: An Autobiography* (New York: Herman Graf Associates, 1975), 205.

155. John Clutchette, "On Prison Reform," in Davis, *Voices of Resistance*, 137–38; George Jackson, *Soledad Brother: The Prison Letters of George Jackson* (New York: Bantam, 1970), 21, 24; Eldridge Cleaver, *Soul on Ice* (New York: Dell, 1968), 134; George L. Jackson, *Blood in My Eye* (New York: Random House, 1972), 107.

156. Donald Bogle, "Black and Proud Behind Bars," in *The Black Revolution: An Ebony Special Issue* (Chicago: Johnson Publishing, 1970), 55–62.

157. James A. Lang, "For My Ex-Wife"; Sayif, "revolution is"; Juno Bakali Tshombe, "Psychological Warfare at Norfolk Prison Camp," in Norfolk Prison Brothers, *Who Took the Weight?: Black Voices from Norfolk Prison* (Boston: Little, Brown, 1972), 59, 85, 92–93; Ericka Huggins, "for connie, a rollingstone," in Davis, *Voices of Resistance*, 103; Etheridge Knight, "For Malcolm: A Year After," in *For Malcolm: Poems on the Life and the Death of Malcolm X*, ed. Dudley Randall and Margaret G. Burroughs (Detroit: Broadside, 1969), 43; Etheridge Knight, "The Day the Young Blacks Came," in *Black Voices from Prison*, ed. Etheridge Knight (New York: Pathfinder, 1970), 165.

158. Rubin "Hurricane" Carter, *The Sixteenth Round: From Number 1 Contender to #45472* (New York: Viking, 1974), 165, 309.

159. Mutulu Shakur et al., "Primer to Counterinsurgency and Low Intensity Warfare" (1988), in *Black Prison Movements USA*, ed. Network of Black Organizers (Trenton, NJ: Africa World, 1995), 72–74.

160. Jerome Washington, *Iron House: Stories from the Yard* (Fort Bragg, CA: QED, 1994), vii–viii, 158; Mumia Abu-Jamal, *Death Blossoms: Reflections from a Prisoner of Conscience* (Farmington, PA: Plough, 1997), 149.

161. Mansfield B. Frazier, *From Behind the Wall: Commentary on Crime, Punishment, Race, and the Underclass by a Prison Inmate* (New York: Paragon House, 1995), xiii–xiv, 13, 37; Dhoruba Bin Wahad, "The Cutting Edge of Prison Technology," in *Still Black, Still Strong: Survivors of the U.S. War against Black Revolutionaries*, ed. Jim Fletcher, Tanaquil Jones, and Sylvère Lotringer (New York: Semiotext(e), 1993), 96; Mumia Abu-Jamal, *Live from Death Row* (Reading, MA: Addison-Wesley, 1995), 9–12; *Welcome to Hell: Letters & Writings from Death Row*, ed. Jan Arriens (1991; Boston: Northeastern University Press, 1997), 55, 88, 186; John Edgar Wideman, *Brothers and Keepers* (1984; New York: Penguin, 1985), 243; Abu-Jamal, *Death Blossoms*, 1; Howard Zehr, ed., *Doing Life: Reflections of Men and Women Serving*

Life Sentences (Intercourse, PA: Good, 1996), 25; Arthur Hamilton Jr. and William Banks, *Father Behind Bars* (Waco, TX: WRS, 1993), 71.

162. Ra'uf Abdullah et al., *Hidden Thoughts of Black Men in Prison* (Norristown, PA: G. Lliffe Enterprises, 1991), 6.

163. Arriens, *Welcome to Hell*, 39.

164. Montgomery and Crews, *History of Correctional Violence*, 33, 35, 39, 61; Robert Adams, *Prison Riots in Britain and the USA* (New York: St. Martin's, 1992), 83, 100–103.

165. Abdullah Ibraheem, "The Black People's Prison Survival Guide," http://www .thetalkingdrum.com/prisonguide.htm (accessed October 29, 2003).

166. Zehr, *Doing Life*, 10; Nathan McCall, *Makes Me Wanna Holler: A Young Black Man in America* (New York: Random House, 1994), 158–59, 169, 210.

167. Arriens, *Welcome to Hell*, 218–19; Carl Upchurch, *Convicted in the Womb: One Man's Journey from Prisoner to Peacemaker* (New York: Bantam, 1996), 93; Zehr, *Doing Life*, 18.

168. Mshairi Shujaa Maganga Alkebular, "Jive Chillin," in Abdullah et al., *Hidden Thoughts*, 37; Arriens, *Welcome to Hell*, pp. 88, 232; Frazier, *From Behind the Wall*, 236; Abu-Jamal, *Death Blossoms*, 59–60; McCall, *Makes Me Wanna Holler*, 215.

169. Shirley Dicks, *Death Row: Interviews with Inmates, Their Families and Opponents of Capital Punishment* (Jefferson, NC: McFarland, 1990), 67; Albert Race Sample, *Racehoss: Big Emma's Boy* (Austin, TX: Eakin, 1984), 264; Zehr, *Doing Life*, 34; "Prisoners Help Sight-Impaired by Translating Books into Braille," http://www.villagelife.org/news/archives/9–22–97_prison-braille.html (accessed October 28, 2003); Reese Ehrlich, "Inmates Refurbish Old Computers for a New Future," *Christian Science Monitor*, June 3, 1998, 12; "Society Dropouts Return to Troubled Neighborhoods to Help Youth," http://www.prisonactivist .org/pipermail/prisonact-list/1998-July/002067.html (accessed October 28, 2003).

170. Richard Wormser, *Lifers': Learn the Truth at the Expense of Our Sorrow* (Englewood Cliffs, NJ: Julian Messner, 1991), 67–72; *Scared Straight* (Animagination, 1978).

171. Hamilton and Banks, *Father Behind Bars*, 102; Stanley "Tookie" Williams and Barbara Cottman Becnel, *Life in Prison* (New York: Morrow, 1998); "Tookie's Corner," www .tookie.com (accessed August 8, 2002).

172. For commentary on music as a cultural mechanism for expressing emancipatory political perspectives, see Ray Pratt, *Rhythm and Resistance: Explorations in the Political Uses of Popular Music* (New York: Praeger, 1990); Reebee Garofalo, ed., *Rockin' the Boat: Mass Music and Mass Movements* (Boston: South End, 1992); Brian Ward, *Just My Soul Responding: Rhythm and Blues, Black Consciousness, and Race Relations* (Berkeley: University of California Press, 1998); and Craig Werner, *A Change Is Gonna Come: Music, Race & the Soul of America* (New York: Plume, 1999).

173. Maude Cuney-Hare, *Negro Musicians and Their Music* (Washington, DC: Associated Publishers, 1936), 156; Lawrence W. Levine, "Jazz and American Culture," in *The Unpredictable Past: Explorations in American Cultural History* (1989; New York: Oxford University Press, 1993), 179–80; Kathy J. Ogren, *The Jazz Revolution: Twenties America and the Meaning of Jazz* (New York: Oxford University Press, 1989), 115.

174. For a sampling of views on the nature and extent of the sacred/secular dichotomy in black music, see James H. Cone, *The Spirituals and the Blues: An Interpretation* (New York: Seabury, 1972); Paul Garon, *Blues & the Poetic Spirit* (London: Eddison, 1975); Michael W.

Harris, *The Rise of Gospel Blues: The Music of Thomas Andrew Dorsey in the Urban Church* (New York: Oxford University Press, 1992); and Jon Michael Spencer, *Blues and Evil* (Knoxville: University of Tennessee Press, 1993).

175. On Johnson, see Barry Lee Peterson and Bill McCulloch, *Robert Johnson: Lost and Found* (Urbana: University of Illinois Press, 2003); and Peter Guralnick, *Searching for Robert Johnson* (New York: E. P. Dutton, 1989). For fictionalized versions of the Delta crossroads legend, see Alan Greenberg, *Love in Vain: The Life and Legend of Robert Johnson* (Garden City, NY: Doubleday, 1983); *Crossroads* (Columbia, 1986); Walter Mosley, *RL's Dream* (New York: W. W. Norton, 1995); Ace Atkins, *Crossroad Blues* (New York: St. Martin's, 1998); Greg Kihn, *Mojo Hand* (New York: Tom Doherety Associates, 1999); and David Dalton, *Been Here and Gone: A Memoir of the Blues* (New York: William Morrow, 2000).

176. Muddy Waters, "I'm Your Hoochie Coochie Man" (Chess 1560, 1954); David Evans, *Tommy Johnson* (London: Studio Vista, 1971), 22–23; D. Thomas Moon, "'Memphis' Charlie Musselwhite: Remembering Big Joe Williams," *Blues Revue* (March/April 1995): 44–45; Mance Lipscomb, *I Say Me for a Parable: The Oral Autobiography of Mance Lipscomb, Texas Bluesman* (New York: W. W. Norton, 1993), 230–34; Samuel Charters, *Sweet as the Showers of Rain* (New York: Oak, 1977), 143–49; Bob Zeuschner, review of *Casey Bill: The Hawaiian Guitar Wizard, 1935–1938* by Casey Bill Weldon, *Blues Revue* (December/January 1996): 97–98.

177. Margey Peters, "Satan and Adam," *Living Blues* 27 (September/October 1996): 19–20; Adam Gussow, *Mister Satan's Apprentice: A Blues Memoir* (New York: Pantheon, 1998), 181, 273.

178. Robert Johnson, "Stones in My Passway" (Vocalion 3723, 1937); Muddy Waters, "I'm Ready" (Chess 1579, 1954); "Little Son" Jackson, "Evil Blues" (Gold Star 663, 1949); Koko Taylor, "Wang Dang Doodle" (Checker 1135, 1966).

179. Langston Hughes, "Jazzonia," in *The Weary Blues* (New York: Alfred A. Knopf, 1926), 25.

180. Alan Young, *Woke Me Up This Morning: Black Gospel Singers and the Gospel Life* (Jackson: University Press of Mississippi, 1997), 233.

181. Cynthia Rose, *Living in America: The Soul Saga of James Brown* (London: Serpent's Tail, 1990), 9.

182. On the musicians, see Craig Werner, *Higher Ground: Stevie Wonder, Aretha Franklin, Curtis Mayfield and the Rise and Fall of American Soul* (New York: Crown, 2004), 29–40, 66–89, 118–25, 139–47, 153–63, 205–10, 219–23, 266–72; David Ritz, *Divided Soul: The Life of Marvin Gaye* (New York: McGraw-Hill, 1985); and Timothy White, *Catch a Fire: The Life of Bob Marley* (New York: Henry Holt, 1989). For a sampling of their socially conscious music, see Curtis Mayfield & the Impressions, *The Anthology, 1961–1977* (MCA 10664, 1992); Marvin Gaye, *What's Going On* (1971; Motown 530883, 1998); Bob Marley & the Wailers, *Burnin'* (1973; Island/Tuff Gong 548894, 2001).

183. Russell A. Potter, *Spectacular Vernaculars: Hip-Hop and the Politics of Postmodernism* (Albany: State University of New York Press, 1995), 8–9.

184. Nelson George, *Hip Hop America* (New York: Viking, 1998), xi.

185. Sugarhill Gang, "Rapper's Delight" (Sugar Hill 542, 1979); Grandmaster Flash & the Furious Five, "The Message" (Sugar Hill 584, 1982); Run-DMC, "Walk This Way" (Profile 5112, 1986); Salt 'n Pepa, "Push It" (Next Plateau 315, 1987).

186. Emil Wilbekin, "Great Aspirations: Hip Hop and Fashion Dress for Excess and

Success," in *The Vibe History of Hip Hop*, ed. Alan Light (New York: Three Rivers, 1999), 277–83; Sacha Jenkins et al., *ego trip's Book of Rap Lists* (New York: St. Martin's Griffin, 1999), 111. On the commodification of various urban leisure-time activities, see Robin D. G. Kelley, *Yo' Mama's Disfunktional!: Fighting the Culture Wars in Urban America* (Boston: Beacon, 1997), 43–77.

187. Tanya Kersey-Henley, "Hip Hop Cinema: Hip Hop Artists Makin' Silver Screen Moves," *Black Talent News* 8 (January 2002): 9–11, 19; Tom Samiljan, "Games that Rock: Kiss, Public Enemy and Wu-Tang Clan Get into Gaming," *Rolling Stone*, October 14, 1999, 129–30.

188. Hip-hop-oriented magazines, past and present, include *ego trip, The Source, Rap Pages, Blaze, XXL, URB, Vibe, Black Beat, Murder Dog,* and *Right On!* Revolutionary Comics of San Diego included titles featuring rap acts Public Enemy and 2 Live Crew (April 1991), Ice-T (November 1991), and N.W.A. and Ice Cube (December 1991) in its early '90s Rock 'N' Roll Comics series. Elsewhere, rap representation in comic books has run the gamut from juvenile humor with "positive" messages (*Kid 'N Play*, Marvel, 1991) to "adults only" (*2 Live Crew*, Eros, 1991). On hip-hop pulp fiction, see Martin Arnold, "Coming Soon: Paperbacks that Sound Like Hip-Hop," *New York Times*, September 21, 2000.

189. Greg Tate, "What Is Hip-hop?" in *Rap on Rap: Straight-Up Talk on Hip-Hop Culture*, ed. Adam Sexton (1993; New York: Delta, 1995), 19–20.

190. Survey responses from the 1993–94 National Black Politics Study reveal a more than 40 percentage point gap in the approval for rap voiced by African Americans eighteen to twenty-nine years of age as opposed to those thirty and older. As a result, radio programmers who once could count on a fairly cohesive black audience now must consider the "rap gap" when selecting songs for airplay. Michael C. Dawson, "'Dis Beat Disrupts': Rap, Ideology, and Black Political Attitudes," in *The Cultural Territories of Race: Black and White Boundaries*, ed. Michèle Lamont (Chicago: University of Chicago Press, 1999), 327–28; John Leland and Allison Samuels, "The New Generation Gap," *Newsweek*, March 17, 1997, 52–57.

191. William Safire, "The Rap on Hip-Hop," *New York Times Magazine*, November 8, 1992, 618.

192. Laquan, "Imprison the President," *Notes of a Native Son* (4th & Broadway 444029, 1990); Public Enemy, "Night of the Living Baseheads," *It Takes a Nation of Millions to Hold Us Back* (Def Jam 44303, 1988); Stetsasonic, "A.F.R.I.C.A.," *On Fire* (Tommy Boy 1012, 1986); Geto Boys, "Fuck a War," *We Can't Be Stopped* (Rap-A-Lot/Priority 57161, 1991).

193. Boogie Down Productions, "Build and Destroy," *Sex and Violence* (Jive 41470, 1992); Public Enemy, "By the Time I Get to Arizona," *Apocalypse 91 . . . The Enemy Strikes Black* (Def Jam 47374, 1991).

194. Disposable Heroes of Hiphoprisy, "Television, the Drug of the Nation," *Hypocrisy Is the Greatest Luxury* (4th & Broadway 444043, 1992); Public Enemy, "Don't Believe the Hype," *It Takes a Nation of Millions to Hold Us Back*.

195. Public Enemy, "911 Is a Joke," *Fear of a Black Planet* (Def Jam 45413, 1990); Ice Cube, "Alive on Arrival," *Death Certificate* (Priority 57155, 1991); Paris, "The Devil Made Me Do It," *The Devil Made Me Do It* (Tommy Boy 1030, 1990).

196. LL Cool J, "Illegal Search," *Mama Said Knock You Out* (Def Jam 46888, 1990); N.W.A., "Fuck Tha Police," *Straight Outta Compton* (Ruthless/Priority 57102, 1988).

197. Big Daddy Kane, "Another Victory," *It's a Big Daddy Thing* (Cold Chillin' 25941, 1989).

198. Ice Cube, "Endangered Species (Tales from the Darkside)," *AmeriKKKa's Most Wanted* (Priority 57120, 1990); Ice-T, "Squeeze the Trigger," *Rhyme Pays* (Sire 25602, 1987).

199. Cypress Hill, "Pigs," *Cypress Hill* (Ruff House 47889, 1991); Ice Cube, "The Wrong Nigga to Fuck Wit," *Death Certificate*.

200. Rap lexicons include Fab 5 Freddy, *Fresh Fly Flavor: Words and Phrases of the Hip-Hop Generation* (Stamford, CT: Longmeadow, 1992); Alonzo Westbrook, *Hip Hoptionary: The Dictionary of Hip-Hop Terminology* (New York: Broadway, 2002); and *The Rap Dictionary*, http://www.rapdict.org.

201. 2 Pac, "Words of Wisdom," *2Pacalypse Now* (Interscope 91767, 1991); N.W.A., "Niggaz 4 Life," *Efil4zaggin* (Ruthless/Priority 57126, 1991).

202. Ice-T and Heidi Siegmund, *The Ice Opinion* (New York: St. Martin's, 1994), 158–59; Public Enemy, "Son of a Bush," *Revolverlution* (Slam Jamz/Koch 8388, 2002); KRS-One, "Ah-Yeah," *KRS-One* (Jive 41570, 1995).

203. Sister Souljah, "The Hate that Hate Produced," *360 Degrees of Power* (Epic 48713, 1992); Ice-T and Siegmund, *Ice Opinion*, 187; Alan Light, "Wisdom from the Street," *Rolling Stone*, May 30, 1991, 42; Dead Prez, "Assassination," *Let's Get Free* (Loud 1867, 2000).

204. Public Enemy, "Fight the Power," *Fear of a Black Planet*; Paris, "Panther Power," *The Devil Made Me Do It*; The Coup, "Fat Cats, Bigga Fish," "Pimps," "Takin' These," *Genocide & Juice* (Wild Pitch 29273, 1994); Various Artists, *Pump Ya Fist: Hip-Hop Inspired by the Black Panthers* (Avatar 124048, 1995).

205. Poor Righteous Teachers, "Rock Dis Funky Joint," *Holy Intellect* (Profile 1289, 1990); Movement Ex, "I Deal with Mathematics," *Movement Ex* (Columbia 46894, 1990).

206. On the Five Percent Nation, see Yusuf Nuruddin, "The Five Percenters: A Teenage Nation of Gods and Earths," in *Muslim Communities in North America*, ed. Yvonne Yazbeck Haddah and Jane Idleman Smith (Albany: State University of New York Press, 1994), 109–31; and Wise Intelligent and Culture Freedom interview, in *Nation Conscious Rap: The Hip Hop Vision*, ed. Joseph D. Eure and James G. Spady (Brooklyn: PC International, 1991), 59–76.

207. Prince Akeem, "Flush the Government," *Coming Down Like Babylon* (RCA 34900, 1991).

208. Jeffrey Louis Decker, "The State of Rap: Time and Place in Hip Hop Nationalism," in *Microphone Fiends: Youth Music and Youth Culture*, ed. Andrew Ross and Tricia Rose (New York: Routledge, 1994), 101–2; Ernest Allen Jr., "Making the Strong Survive: The Contours and Contradictions of Message Rap," in *Droppin' Science: Critical Essays on Rap Music and Hip Hop Culture*, ed. William Eric Perkins (Philadelphia: Temple University Press, 1996), 159–91.

209. Chuck D and Yusuf Jah, *Fight the Power: Rap, Race, and Reality* (New York: Delacorte, 1997), 250, 254, 257; Ronin Ro, *Have Gun Will Travel: The Spectacular Rise and Violent Fall of Death Row Records* (New York: Doubleday, 1998), 144.

210. Alan Light, "Beating Up the Charts," *Rolling Stone*, August 8, 1991, 66; Eithne Quinn, "'It's a Doggy-Dogg World': Black Cultural Politics, Gangsta Rap and the 'Post-Soul Man,'" in *Gender in the Civil Rights Movement*, ed. Peter J. Ling and Sharon Monteith (New York: Garland, 1999), 207; Robin D. G. Kelley, *Race Rebels: Culture, Politics, and the Black Working Class* (New York: Free Press, 1994), 212.

211. MC Shan, "The Bridge," "Kill that Noise," *Down by Law* (Cold Chillin' 25676, 1987); Boogie Down Productions, "South Bronx," "The Bridge Is Over," *Criminal Minded* (B Boy 4787, 1987); Ro, *Death Row Records*, 255.

212. Quoted in Armond White, *Rebel for the Hell of It: The Life of Tupac Shakur* (London: Quartet, 1997), 106.

213. Ruby Vass, "The Banks of the Ohio," *Southern Journey, Volume 2: Ballads and Break-downs* (Rounder 1702, 1997); Johnny Cash, "Folsom Prison Blues" (Sun 232, 1956).

214. N.W.A., "Gangsta Gangsta," *Straight Outta Compton;* Dr. Dre, "The Day the Niggaz Took Over," *The Chronic* (Death Row 57128, 1992); The Genius, "Life of a Drug Dealer," *Words from the Genius* (Cold Chillin' 26475, 1990); DMX, "The Professional," . . . *And Then There Was X* (Def Jam 546933, 1999); C.P.O., "Ballad of a Menace," *To Hell and Black* (Capitol 94522, 1990); Geto Boys, "Mind of a Lunatic," *Geto Boys* (Rap-A-Lot/Def American 24306, 1990).

215. Jayo Felony, "Sherm Stick," *Take a Ride* (JMJ 124038, 1995); C.P.O., "Ballad of a Menace"; Method Man, "I Get My Thang in Action," *Tical* (Def Jam 523839, 1994); Geto Boys, "Mind of a Lunatic."

216. The Genius, "Life of a Drug Dealer."

217. Ice-T and Siegmund, *Ice Opinion*, 20–21.

218. Snoop Dogg and Davin Seay, *Tha Doggfather: The Times, Trials, and Hardcore Truths of Snoop Dogg* (New York: William Morrow, 1999), 173; S. H. Fernando Jr., *The New Beats: Exploring the Music, Culture, and Attitudes of Hip-Hop* (New York: Anchor, 1994), 88–89; "Rapper Ice-T Defends Song against Spreading Boycott," *New York Times*, June 19, 1992.

219. Ice-T and Siegmund, *Ice Opinion*, 94–95; LOX, "Felony Niggas," *We Are the Streets* (Interscope 490599, 2000); Gang Starr, "Soliloquy of Chaos," *Daily Operation* (Chrysalis 21910, 1992).

220. Stanley Crouch, *The All-American Skin Game, or, The Decoy of Race* (New York: Pantheon, 1995), 30; Robert H. Bork, *Slouching towards Gomorrah: Modern Liberalism and American Decline* (New York: Regan/HarperCollins, 1996), 124; Minouche Kandel, "Racist Censorship and Sexist Rap," *Reconstruction* 1, no. 2 (1990): 23–24; Stanley Crouch, *Always in Pursuit: Fresh American Perspectives, 1995–1997* (New York: Pantheon, 1998), 24; 2 Live Crew, "Dirty Nursery Rhymes," *As Nasty as They Wanna Be* (Luke 107, 1989); Eazy-E, "Merry Muthafuckin' Xmas," *5150: Home 4 tha Sick* (Priority 53815, 1992).

221. Nathan McCall, *What's Going On: Personal Essays* (New York: Random House, 1997), 48.

222. Tone-Lōc, "Wild Thing," *Lōc-ed after Dark* (Delicious Vinyl 101033, 1989); Houston A. Baker Jr., *Black Studies, Rap, and the Academy* (Chicago: University of Chicago Press, 1993), 44–52.

223. Ice Cube, "Black Korea," "My Summer Vacation," *Death Certificate;* Ice Cube, "AmeriKKKa's Most Wanted," *AmeriKKKa's Most Wanted;* N.W.A., "Fuck tha Police."

224. Anthony B. Pinn, "'Gettin' Grown': Notes on Gangsta Rap Music and Notions of Manhood," *Journal of African American Men* 1 (Spring 1996): 28; Eithne Quinn, "'Who's the Mack?': The Performativity and Politics of the Pimp Figure in Gangsta Rap," *Journal of American Studies* 34 (April 2000): 115–36.

225. Otis Redding, "Try a Little Tenderness" (Volt 141, 1966); Luther Campbell and John R. Miller, *As Nasty as They Wanna Be: The Uncensored Story of Luther Campbell of the 2 Live*

Crew (Fort Lee, NJ: Barricade, 1992), 185–86, 191; Slick Rick, "Treat Her Like a Prostitute," *The Great Adventures of Slick Rick* (Def Jam 40513, 1988).

226. Tricia Rose, *Black Noise: Rap Music and Black Culture in Contemporary America* (Hanover, NH: Wesleyan University Press, 1994), 171–73; Onyx, "Blac Vagina Finda," *Bacdafucup* (JMJ/RAL 53302, 1993); Dr. Dre, "Bitches Ain't Shit," *The Chronic*.

227. Too Short, "Little Girls," *Born to Mack* (Jive 1100, 1988); 2 Live Crew, "Me So Horny," "The Fuck Shop," *As Nasty as They Wanna Be*.

228. Sonja Peterson-Lewis, "A Feminist Analysis of the Defense of Obscene Rap Lyrics," *Black Sacred Music* 5 (Spring 1991): 78–79; Michael Eric Dyson, "Rap Culture, the Church, and American Society," *Black Sacred Music* 6 (Spring 1992): 271; Michael Eric Dyson, "Rights and Responsibilities: 2 Live Crew and Rap's Moral Vision," *Black Sacred Music* 6 (Spring 1992): 276.

229. Clarence Lusane, "Rap, Race, and Politics," *Race & Class* 35 (July–September 1993): 42; Quoted in Allison Samuels, N'Gai Croal, and David Gates, "Battle for the Soul of Hip-Hop," *Newsweek*, October 9, 2000, 61.

230. Campbell and Miller, *Nasty*, 187, 233; Ronin Ro, *Gangsta: Merchandising the Rhymes of Violence* (New York: St. Martin's, 1996), 80; Fernando, *New Beats*, 142; Ice-T and Siegmund, *Ice Opinion*, 105.

231. Sister Souljah, *No Disrespect* (New York: Times/Random House, 1994), 357; Queen Latifah and Karen Hunter, *Ladies First: Revelations of a Strong Woman* (New York: William Morrow, 1999), 2; Robin Roberts, *Ladies First: Women in Music Videos* (Jackson: University Press of Mississippi, 1996), 138–62; Deborah Gregory, "Rapping Back," *Essence* 22 (August 1991): 61–62, 119–20; Salt 'n Pepa, "Tramp," *Hot, Cool & Vicious* (Next Plateau 828363, 1986).

232. BWP, "Two Minute Brother," *The Bytches* (RAL 47068, 1991); H.W.A., "Az Much Ass Azz U Want," *Az Much Ass Azz U Want* (Ruthless 5506, 1994); Khia, "Fuck Dem Other Hoes," "My Neck, My Back," *Thug Misses* (Artemis 751132, 2002); Trina, "69 Ways," *Da Baddest Bitch* (Atlantic 83335, 2000); Boss, "2 to da Head," "1-800-Body-Bags," *Born Gangstaz* (Chaos 52903, 1992); Brian Cross, *It's Not about a Salary . . . : Rap, Race and Resistance in Los Angeles* (New York: Verso, 1993), 304.

233. Samuels, Croal, and Gates, "Soul of Hip-Hop," 59–60.

234. Henry Louis Gates Jr., "2 Live Crew, Decoded," *New York Times*, June 19, 1990; Body Count, "Cop Killer," *Body Count* (Sire 45124, 1992); Barry Shank, "Fears of the White Unconscious: Music, Race, and Identification in the Censorship of 'Cop Killer,'" *Radical History Review* 66 (Fall 1996): 124–45; George Lipsitz, "The Hip Hop Hearings: Censorship, Social Memory, and Intergenerational Tensions among African Americans," in *Generations of Youth: Youth Cultures and History in Twentieth-Century America*, ed. Joe Austin and Michael Nevin Willard (New York: New York University Press, 1988). 395–411.

235. Betty Houchin Winfield, "Because of the Children: Decades of Attempted Controls of Rock 'n' Rap Music," in *Bleep!: Censoring Rock and Rap Music*, ed. Betty Houchin Winfield and Sandra Davidson (Westport, CT: Greenwood, 1999), 10–18; Stan Soocher, *They Fought the Law: Rock Music Goes to Court* (New York: Schirmer, 1999), 129–52; Clifford J. Levy, "Harlem Protest of Rap Lyrics Draws Debate and Steamroller," *New York Times*, June 6, 1993; Jonathan Lesser, "Sticks and Stones . . . : C-Bo's Lyrics Land Him in Jail," *Vibe* 6 (June/July 1998): 66.

236. Jeffrey Ressner, "On the Road with Rap's Outlaw Posse," *Rolling Stone*, August 9, 1990, 73; Campbell and Miller, *Nasty*, 72; Luther Campbell, "Today They're Trying to Censor Rap, Tomorrow . . . ," *Los Angeles Times*, November 5, 1990; Ice-T and Siegmund, *Ice Opinion*, 91; D12, "Another Public Service Announcement," *Devil's Night* (Shady/Interscope 490897, 2001).

237. Ice-T, "Freedom of Speech," *The Iceberg/Freedom of Speech . . . Just Watch What You Say* (Sire 26028, 1989).

238. Poetess, "Love Hurts," *Simply Poetry* (Interscope 92168, 1992); Professor X, "Close the Crackhouse," *Puss 'N Boots (The Struggle Continues . . .)* (Polygram 519360, 1993); Boogie Down Productions, "Stop the Violence," "Jimmy," *By All Means Necessary* (Jive 1097, 1988); Gregory D, "Down w/ HIV," *The Real Deal* (RCA 66078, 1992); Stephan Talty, "Represent," *Vibe* 8 (November 2000): 130–34; Yvonne Bynoe, "Hip Hop Summit on Social Responsibility," http://www.urbanthinktank.org/hiphopsummit.cfm (accessed September 18, 2001); "The Hip-Hop Summit: Taking Back Responsibility," http://www.rap.about. com/library/blsummitpressrelease.htm (accessed November 12, 2002); Snoop Dogg and Seay, *Doggfather*, 1; LL Cool J and Karen Hunter, *I Make My Own Rules* (New York: St. Martin's, 1997), 110.

239. Ice-T, "6 'N the Morning," *Rhyme Pays; Straight from the Streets* (Up Front, 1999); Jennifer Brown, "Suburban Schools Cracking Down on 'Dirty Dancing,'" *Detroit Free Press*, May 2, 2001.

240. Dr. Dre, "The Day the Niggaz Took Over"; X-Clan, "Funkin' Lesson," *To the East, Blackwards* (4th & Broadway 444019, 1990).

Conclusion

1. *Report of the National Advisory Commission on Civil Disorders* (Washington, DC: U.S. Government Printing Office, 1968), 1.

2. Richard Morin, "Misperceptions Cloud Whites' View of Blacks," *Washington Post*, July 11, 2001; Kevin Sack and Janet Elder, "Poll Finds Optimistic Outlook but Enduring Racial Division," *New York Times*, July 11, 2000; Leonard Steinhorn and Barbara Diggs-Brown, *By the Color of Our Skin: The Illusion of Integration and the Reality of Race* (New York: Dutton, 1999), 143–57.

3. Jeremy D. Mayer, *Running on Race: Racial Politics in Presidential Campaigns, 1960–2000* (New York: Random House, 2002), 273–90; Rachel F. Moran, *Interracial Intimacy: The Regulation of Race and Romance* (Chicago: University of Chicago Press, 2001), 101–25; John R. Rickford, *African American Vernacular English: Features, Evolution, Educational Implications* (Malden, MA: Blackwell, 1999), 252–80; Philip J. Hilts, "Black Teen-Agers Are Turning Away from Smoking, but Whites Puff On," *New York Times*, April 19, 1995; Katie Hafner, "A Credibility Gap in the Digital Divide," *New York Times*, March 5, 2000.

4. Tamar Lewin, "Study Finds Racial Bias in Public Schools," *New York Times*, March 1, 2000.

5. Donna Petrozzello, "Black-White Ratings Gap Is Widening," *New York Daily News*, April 16, 2002.

6. Darnell M. Hunt, *O.J. Simpson Facts and Fictions: News Rituals in the Construction of Reality* (Cambridge: Cambridge University Press, 1999), 19–21.

7. "Cochran: Admit the Split," *Capital Times* (Madison, WI), January 26, 1996.

8. Michael Omi and Howard Winant, *Racial Formation in the United States: From the 1960s to the 1980s* (New York: Routledge & Kegan Paul, 1986), 57–69; Richard Dyer, *White* (New York: Routledge, 1997), 1–2, 9, 58; George Lipsitz, *The Possessive Investment in Whiteness: How White People Profit from Identity Politics* (Philadelphia: Temple University Press, 1998), 1–23; David R. Roediger, *The Wages of Whiteness: Race and the Making of the American Working Class* (London: Verso, 1991), 19–36.

9. E. Franklin Frazier, "The Garvey Movement," *Opportunity* 4 (November 1926): 347.

10. W. E. Burghardt Du Bois, *The Souls of Black Folk* (1903; Boston: Bedford, 1997), 38–39, 45.

11. Snoop Dogg and Davin Seay, *Tha Doggfather: The Times, Trials, and Hardcore Truths of Snoop Dogg* (New York: William Morrow, 1999), 19; Michael Small, *Break It Down: The Inside Story from the New Leaders of Rap* (New York: Citadel, 1992), 15.

Index